Volume 3

by
Sang-Eun Lee

HAMBURG // LONDON // LOS ANGELES // TOKYO

IN THE LAST

LOVE OR MONEY

YENNI'S SCHEME SEEMS TO BE WORKING OUT PERFECTLY! SHE MANAGES TO CONVINCE JAE-HEE AND HIS FAMILY TO MOVE IN, BUT SHE DIDN'T EXPECT THAT IN-YOUNG WOULD STAY IN KOREA AND INVITE HIMSELF OVER-- PERMANENTLY! IN-YOUNG WANTS TO INTERFERE WITH YENNI'S MASTER PLAN...OR DOES HE? HAS HE SUDDENLY FALLEN HEAD OVER HEELS FOR YENNI? NOT IF JAE-HEE HAS A SAY IN THESE MATTERS OF LOVE AND MONEY!

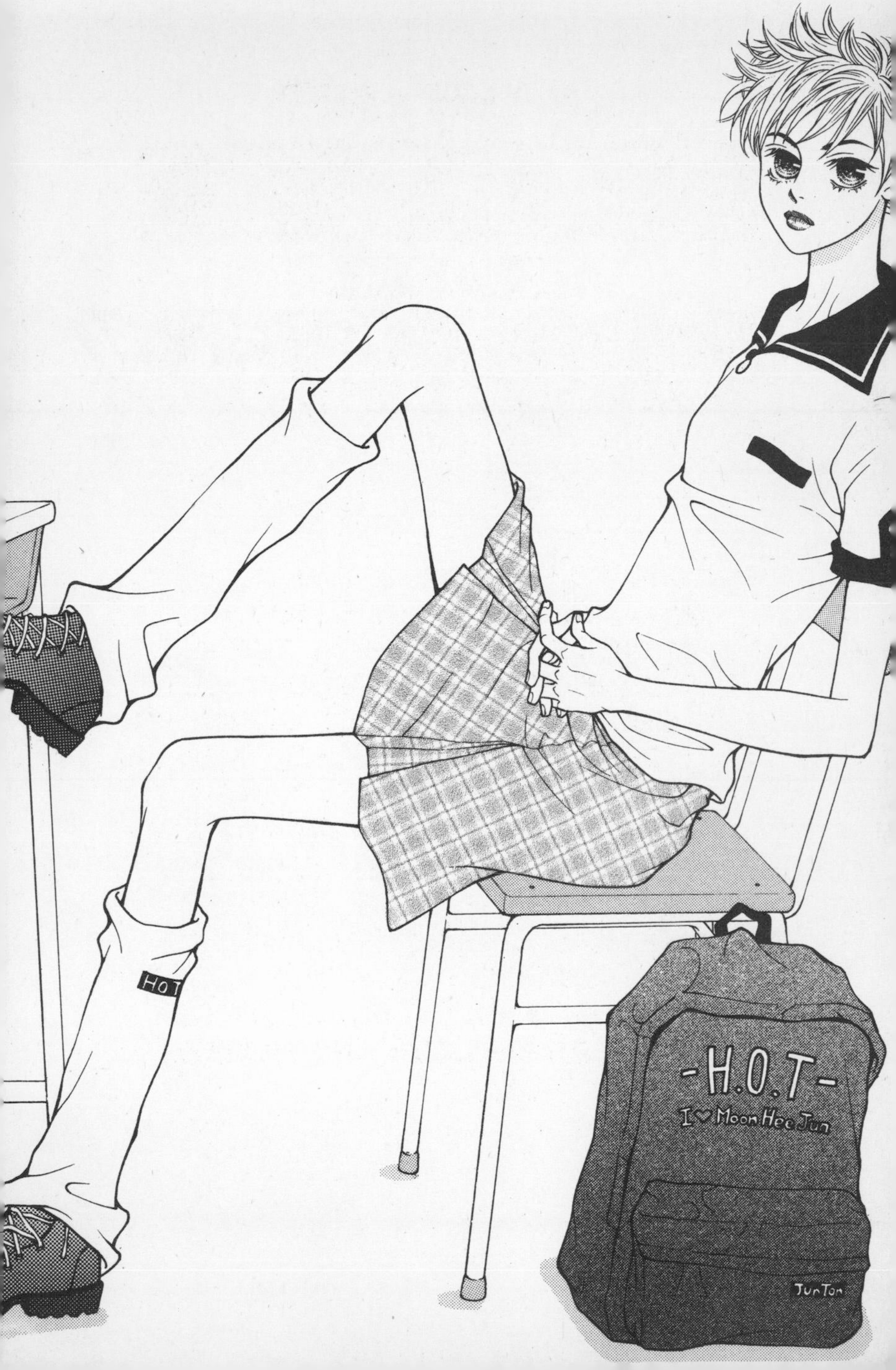
HOT
-H.O.T-
I ♡ Moon Hee Jun
JunTon

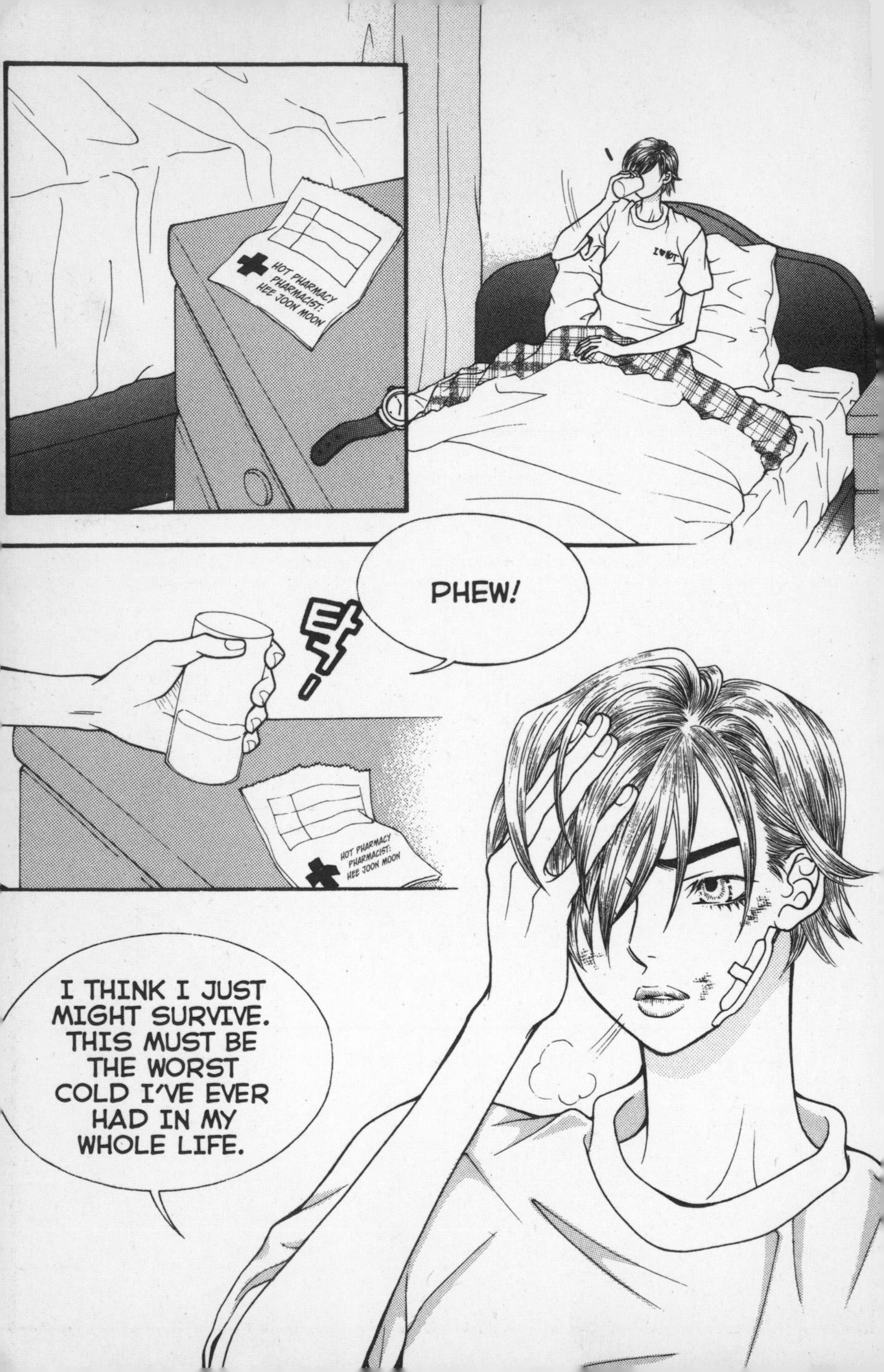
HOT PHARMACY
PHARMACIST: HEE JOON MOON
PHEW!
탁!
HOT PHARMACY
PHARMACIST: HEE JOON MOON
I THINK I JUST MIGHT SURVIVE. THIS MUST BE THE WORST COLD I'VE EVER HAD IN MY WHOLE LIFE.

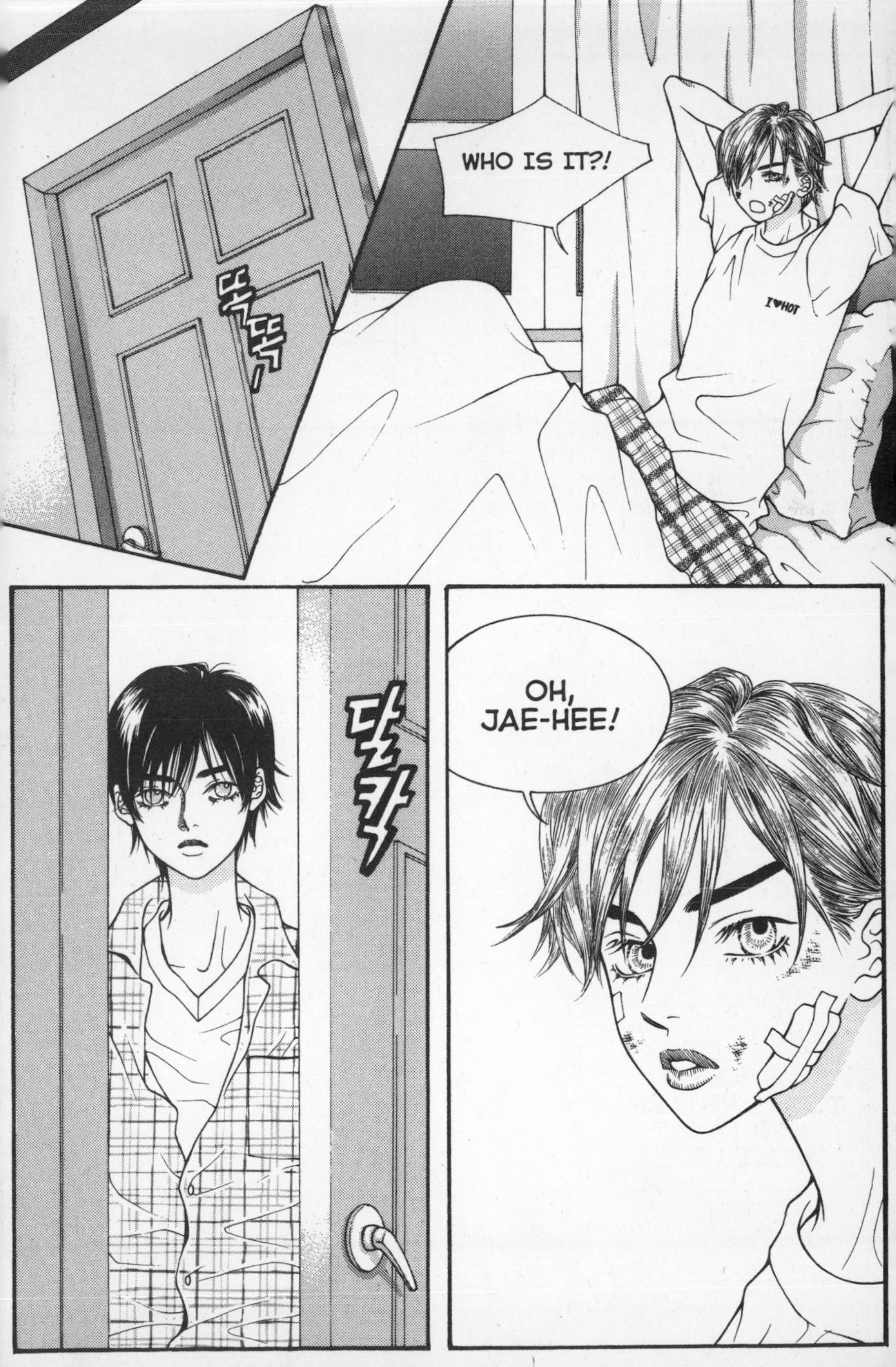
똑똑
WHO IS IT?!
달칵
OH, JAE-HEE!

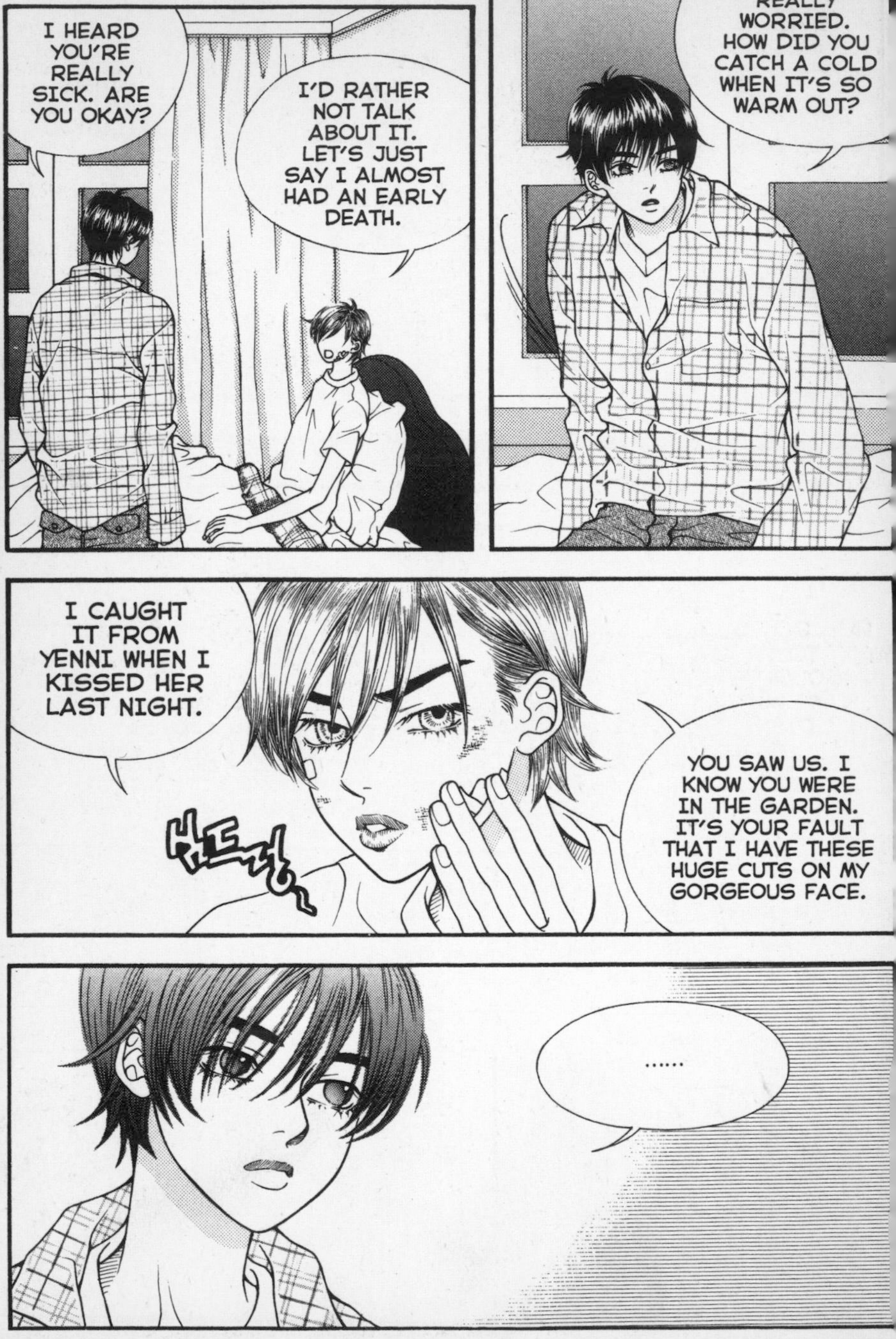
I HEARD YOU'RE REALLY SICK. ARE YOU OKAY?
I'D RATHER NOT TALK ABOUT IT. LET'S JUST SAY I ALMOST HAD AN EARLY DEATH.
MY MOTHER'S REALLY WORRIED. HOW DID YOU CATCH A COLD WHEN IT'S SO WARM OUT?
I CAUGHT IT FROM YENNI WHEN I KISSED HER LAST NIGHT.
YOU SAW US. I KNOW YOU WERE IN THE GARDEN. IT'S YOUR FAULT THAT I HAVE THESE HUGE CUTS ON MY GORGEOUS FACE.
......

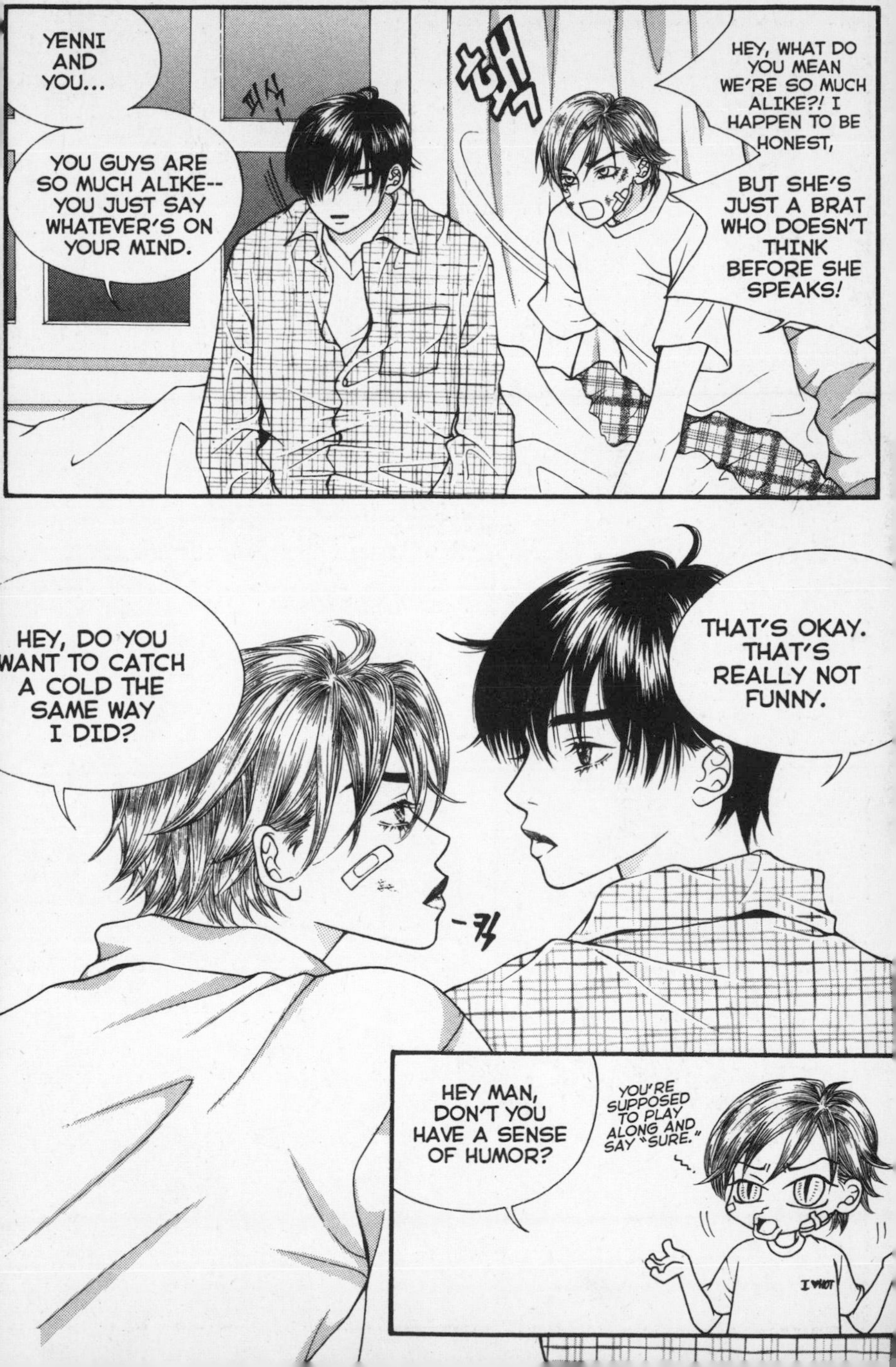
YENNI AND YOU...
YOU GUYS ARE SO MUCH ALIKE-- YOU JUST SAY WHATEVER'S ON YOUR MIND.
홱
HEY, WHAT DO YOU MEAN WE'RE SO MUCH ALIKE?! I HAPPEN TO BE HONEST,
BUT SHE'S JUST A BRAT WHO DOESN'T THINK BEFORE SHE SPEAKS!
HEY, DO YOU WANT TO CATCH A COLD THE SAME WAY I DID?
THAT'S OKAY. THAT'S REALLY NOT FUNNY.
HEY MAN, DON'T YOU HAVE A SENSE OF HUMOR?
YOU'RE SUPPOSED TO PLAY ALONG AND SAY "SURE."

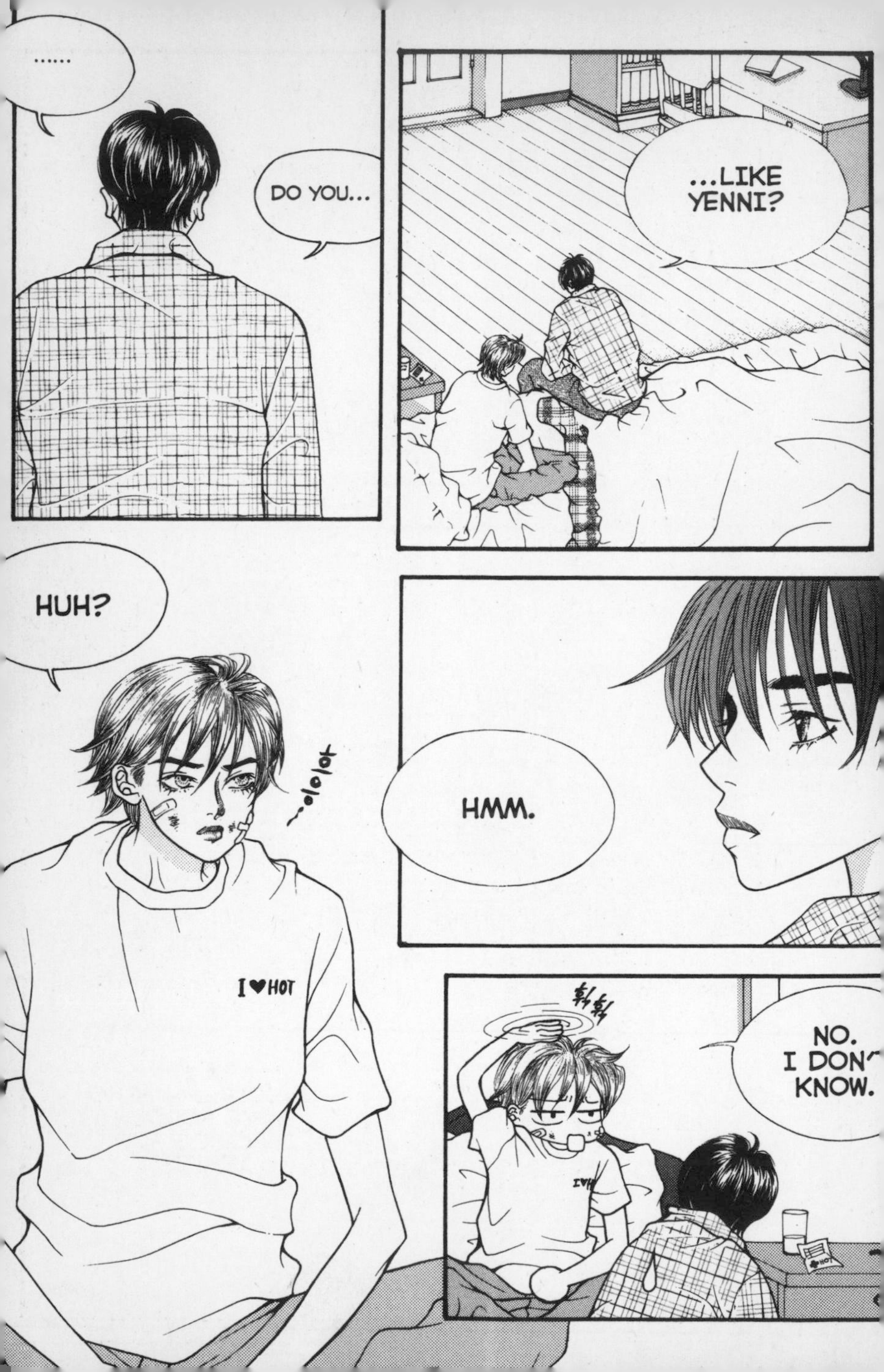
......
DO YOU...
...LIKE YENNI?
HUH?
HMM.
휙휙
NO. I DON'T KNOW.

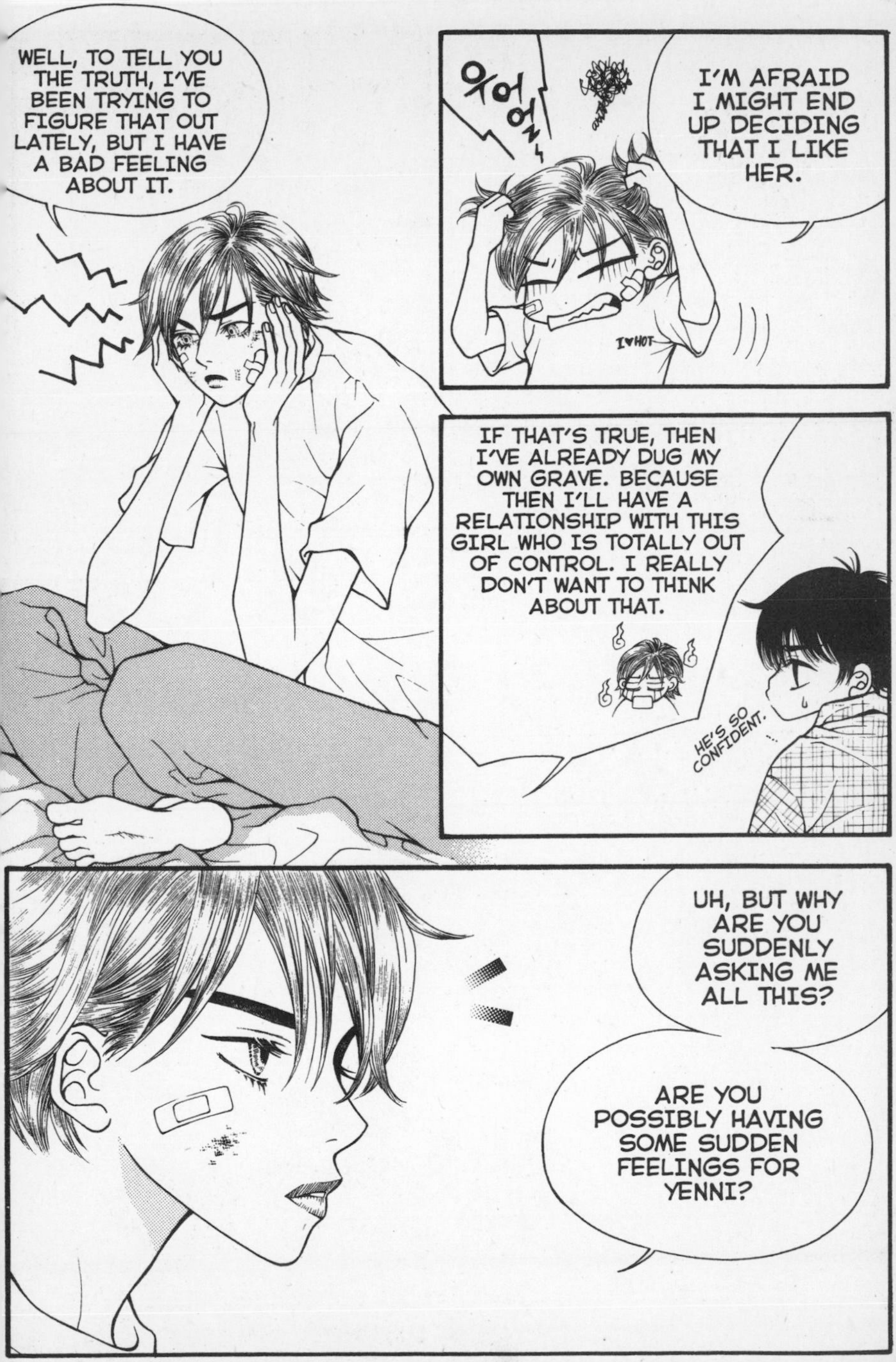
WELL, TO TELL YOU THE TRUTH, I'VE BEEN TRYING TO FIGURE THAT OUT LATELY, BUT I HAVE A BAD FEELING ABOUT IT.
우어얼
I'M AFRAID I MIGHT END UP DECIDING THAT I LIKE HER.
I♥HOT
IF THAT'S TRUE, THEN I'VE ALREADY DUG MY OWN GRAVE. BECAUSE THEN I'LL HAVE A RELATIONSHIP WITH THIS GIRL WHO IS TOTALLY OUT OF CONTROL. I REALLY DON'T WANT TO THINK ABOUT THAT.
HE'S SO CONFIDENT.
UH, BUT WHY ARE YOU SUDDENLY ASKING ME ALL THIS?
ARE YOU POSSIBLY HAVING SOME SUDDEN FEELINGS FOR YENNI?

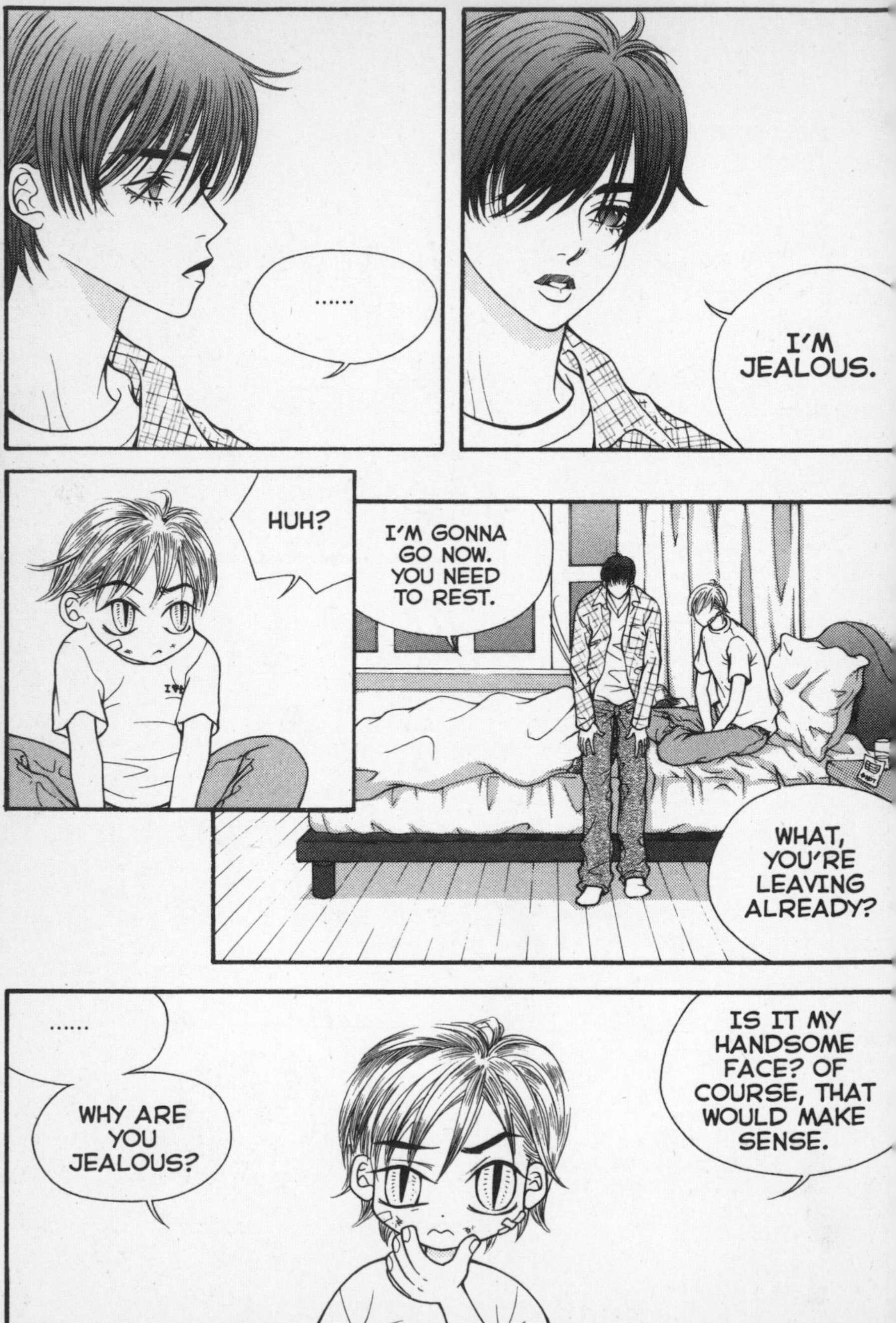
......
I'M JEALOUS.
HUH?
I'M GONNA GO NOW. YOU NEED TO REST.
WHAT, YOU'RE LEAVING ALREADY?
......
WHY ARE YOU JEALOUS?
IS IT MY HANDSOME FACE? OF COURSE, THAT WOULD MAKE SENSE.

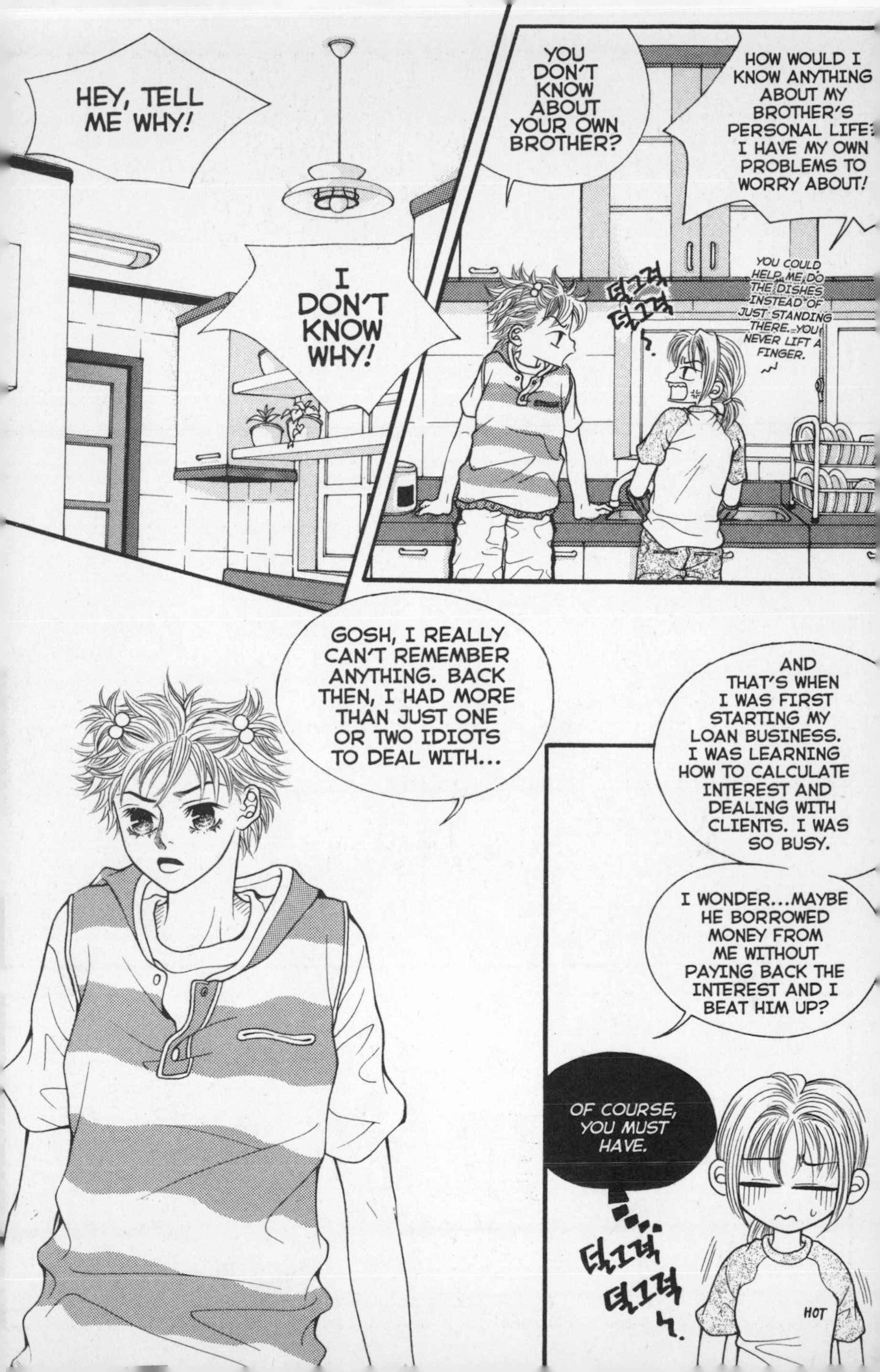
HEY, TELL ME WHY!
I DON'T KNOW WHY!
YOU DON'T KNOW ABOUT YOUR OWN BROTHER?
HOW WOULD I KNOW ANYTHING ABOUT MY BROTHER'S PERSONAL LIFE? I HAVE MY OWN PROBLEMS TO WORRY ABOUT!
덜그럭 덜그럭
YOU COULD HELP ME DO THE DISHES INSTEAD OF JUST STANDING THERE. YOU NEVER LIFT A FINGER.
GOSH, I REALLY CAN'T REMEMBER ANYTHING. BACK THEN, I HAD MORE THAN JUST ONE OR TWO IDIOTS TO DEAL WITH...
AND THAT'S WHEN I WAS FIRST STARTING MY LOAN BUSINESS. I WAS LEARNING HOW TO CALCULATE INTEREST AND DEALING WITH CLIENTS. I WAS SO BUSY.
I WONDER...MAYBE HE BORROWED MONEY FROM ME WITHOUT PAYING BACK THE INTEREST AND I BEAT HIM UP?
OF COURSE, YOU MUST HAVE.
덜그럭 덜그럭
HOT

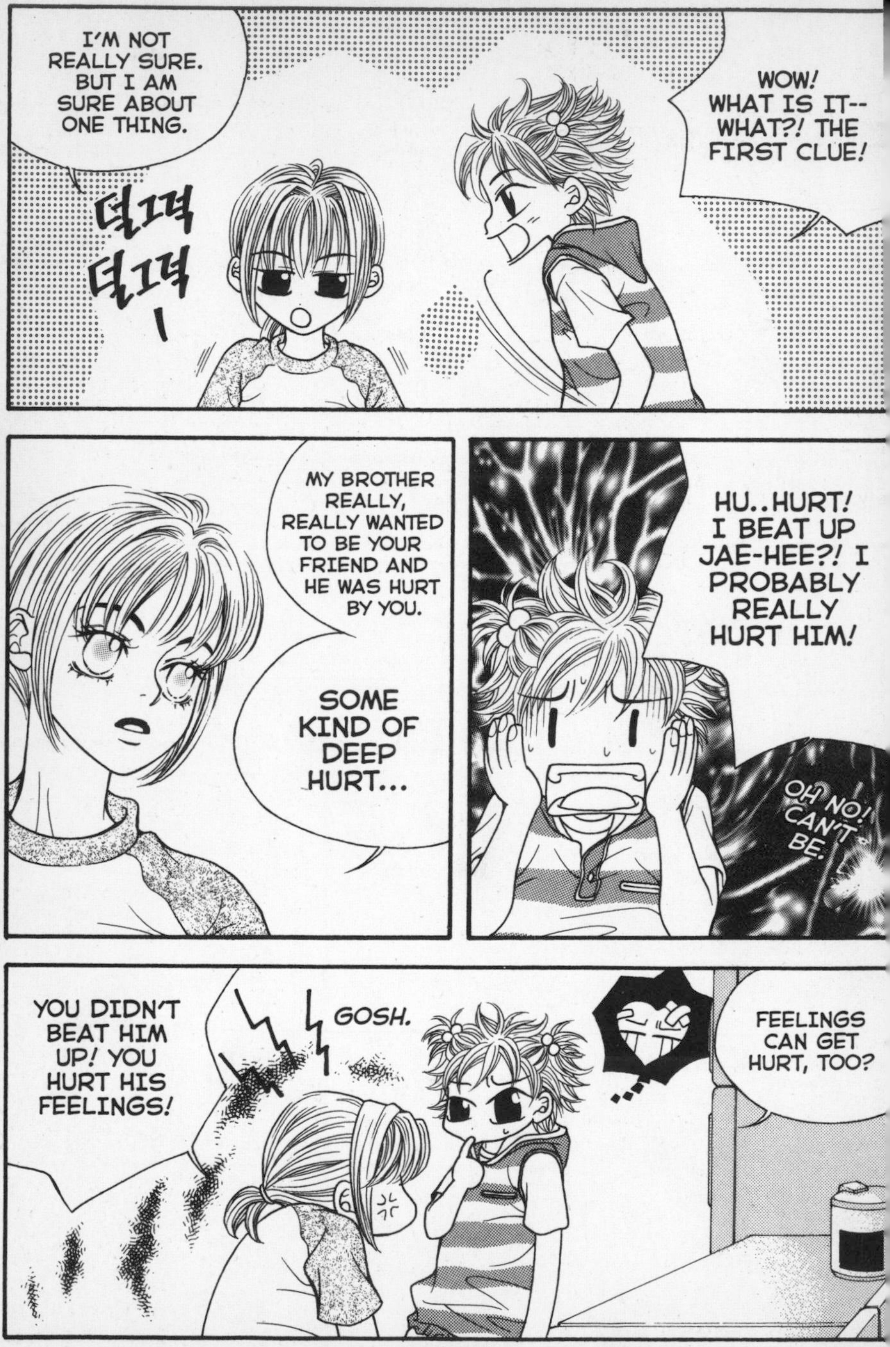
I'M NOT REALLY SURE. BUT I AM SURE ABOUT ONE THING.
덜그럭 덜그럭
WOW! WHAT IS IT-- WHAT?! THE FIRST CLUE!
MY BROTHER REALLY, REALLY WANTED TO BE YOUR FRIEND AND HE WAS HURT BY YOU.
SOME KIND OF DEEP HURT...
HU..HURT! I BEAT UP JAE-HEE?! I PROBABLY REALLY HURT HIM!
OH NO! CAN'T BE.
YOU DIDN'T BEAT HIM UP! YOU HURT HIS FEELINGS!
GOSH.
FEELINGS CAN GET HURT, TOO?

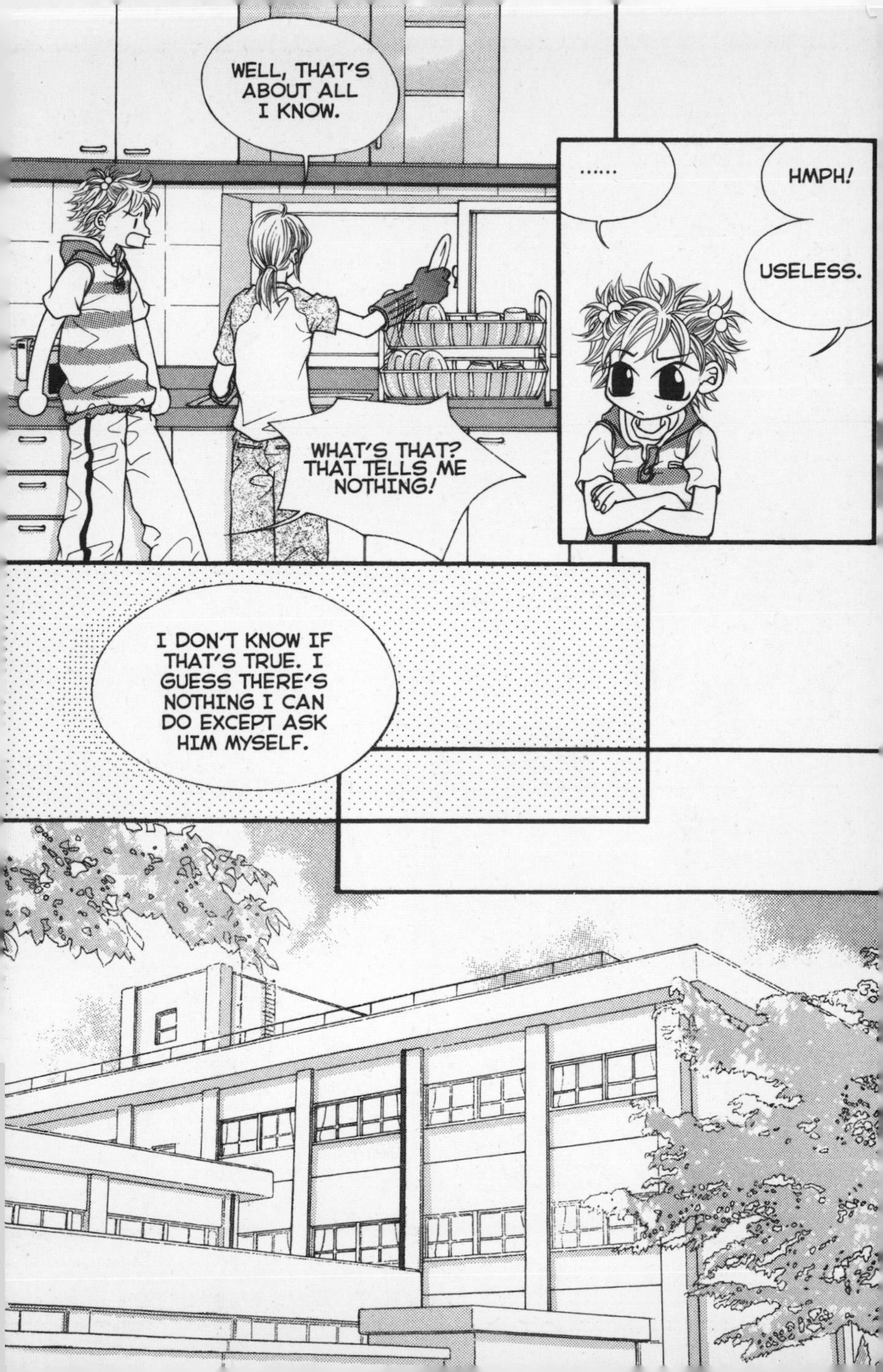
WELL, THAT'S ABOUT ALL I KNOW.
WHAT'S THAT? THAT TELLS ME NOTHING!
......
HMPH!
USELESS.
I DON'T KNOW IF THAT'S TRUE. I GUESS THERE'S NOTHING I CAN DO EXCEPT ASK HIM MYSELF.

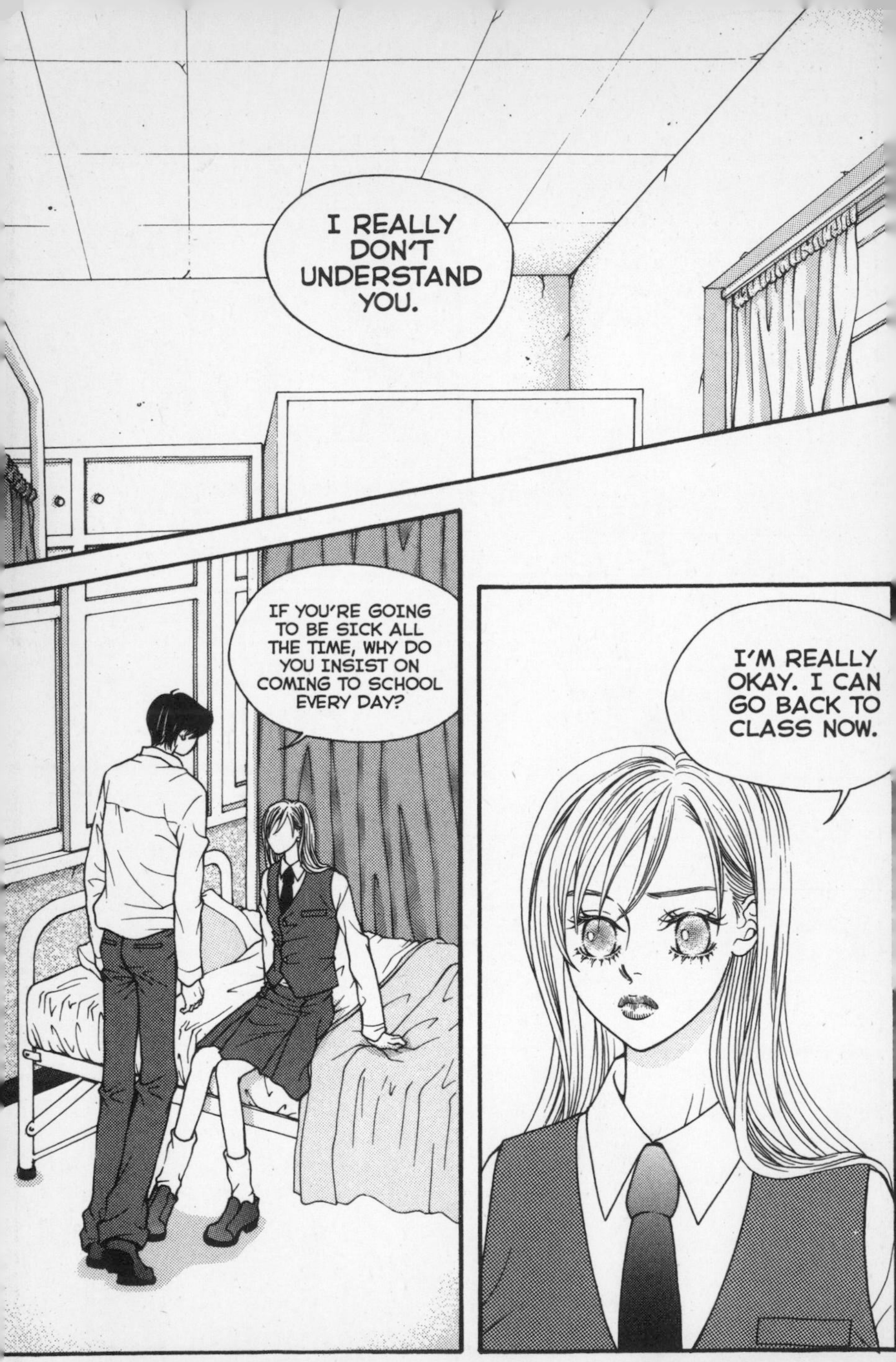
I REALLY DON'T UNDERSTAND YOU.
IF YOU'RE GOING TO BE SICK ALL THE TIME, WHY DO YOU INSIST ON COMING TO SCHOOL EVERY DAY?
I'M REALLY OKAY. I CAN GO BACK TO CLASS NOW.

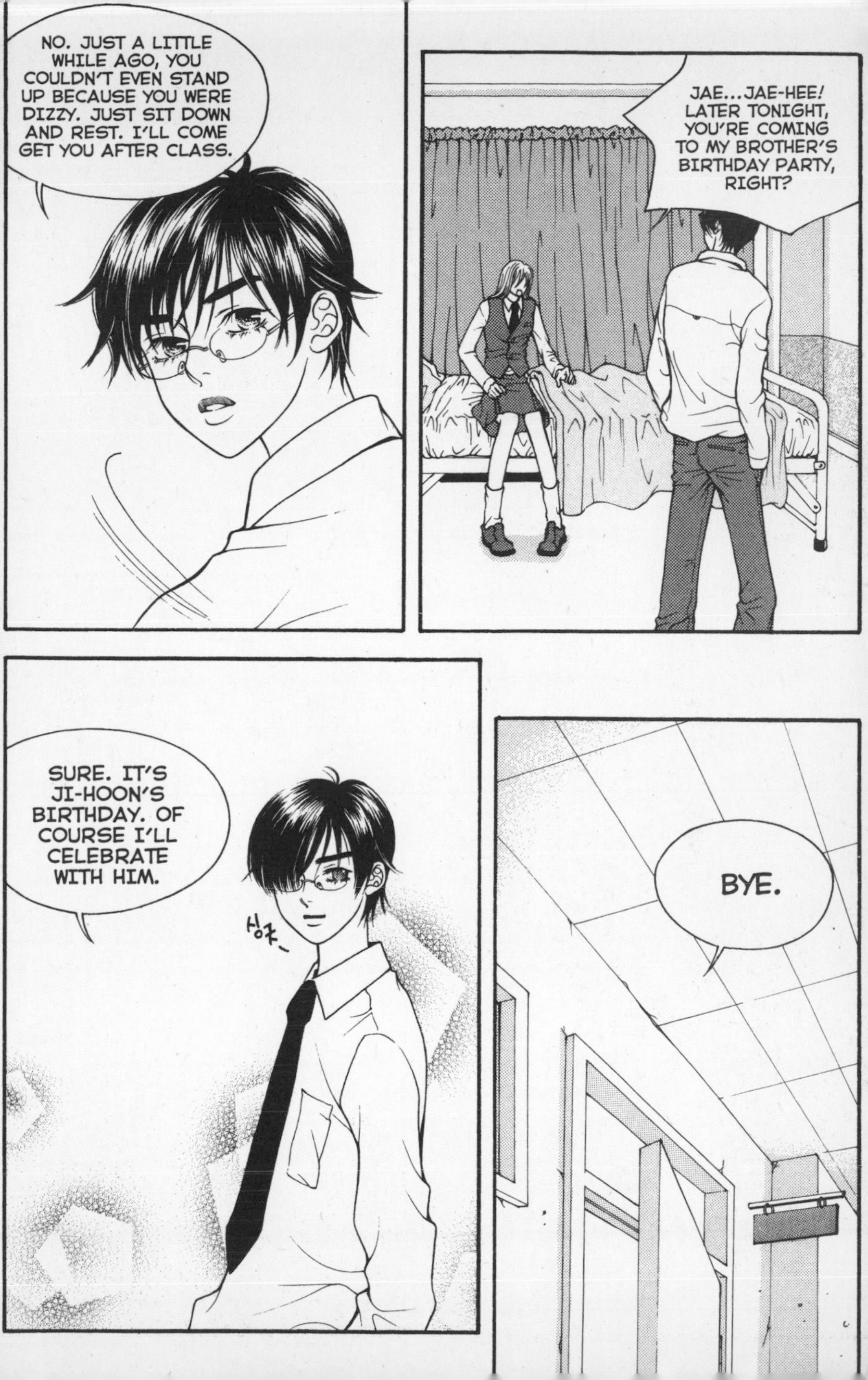

NO. JUST A LITTLE WHILE AGO, YOU COULDN'T EVEN STAND UP BECAUSE YOU WERE DIZZY. JUST SIT DOWN AND REST. I'LL COME GET YOU AFTER CLASS.
JAE...JAE-HEE! LATER TONIGHT, YOU'RE COMING TO MY BROTHER'S BIRTHDAY PARTY, RIGHT?
SURE. IT'S JI-HOON'S BIRTHDAY. OF COURSE I'LL CELEBRATE WITH HIM.
BYE.

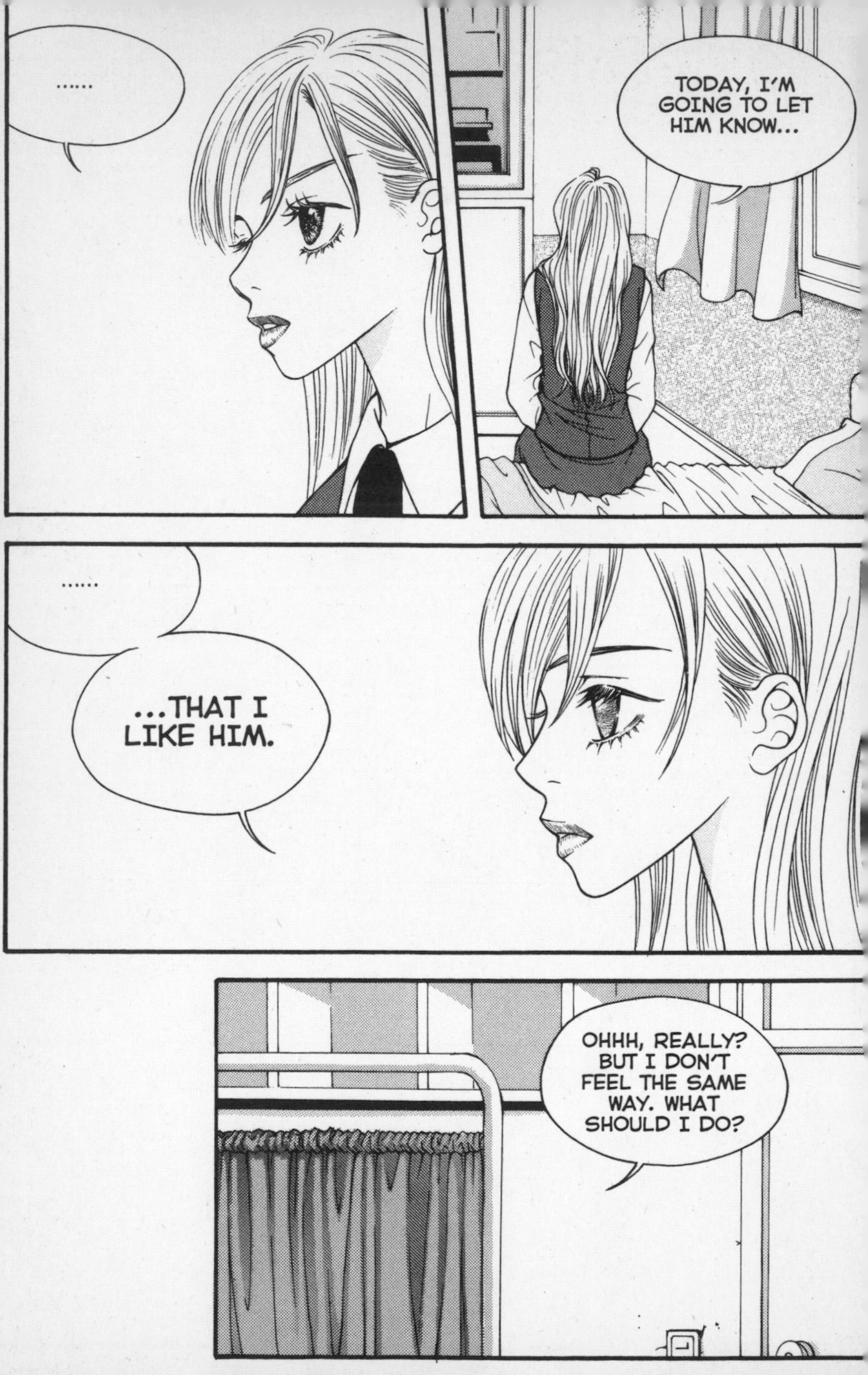
......
TODAY, I'M GOING TO LET HIM KNOW...
......
...THAT I LIKE HIM.
OHHH, REALLY? BUT I DON'T FEEL THE SAME WAY. WHAT SHOULD I DO?

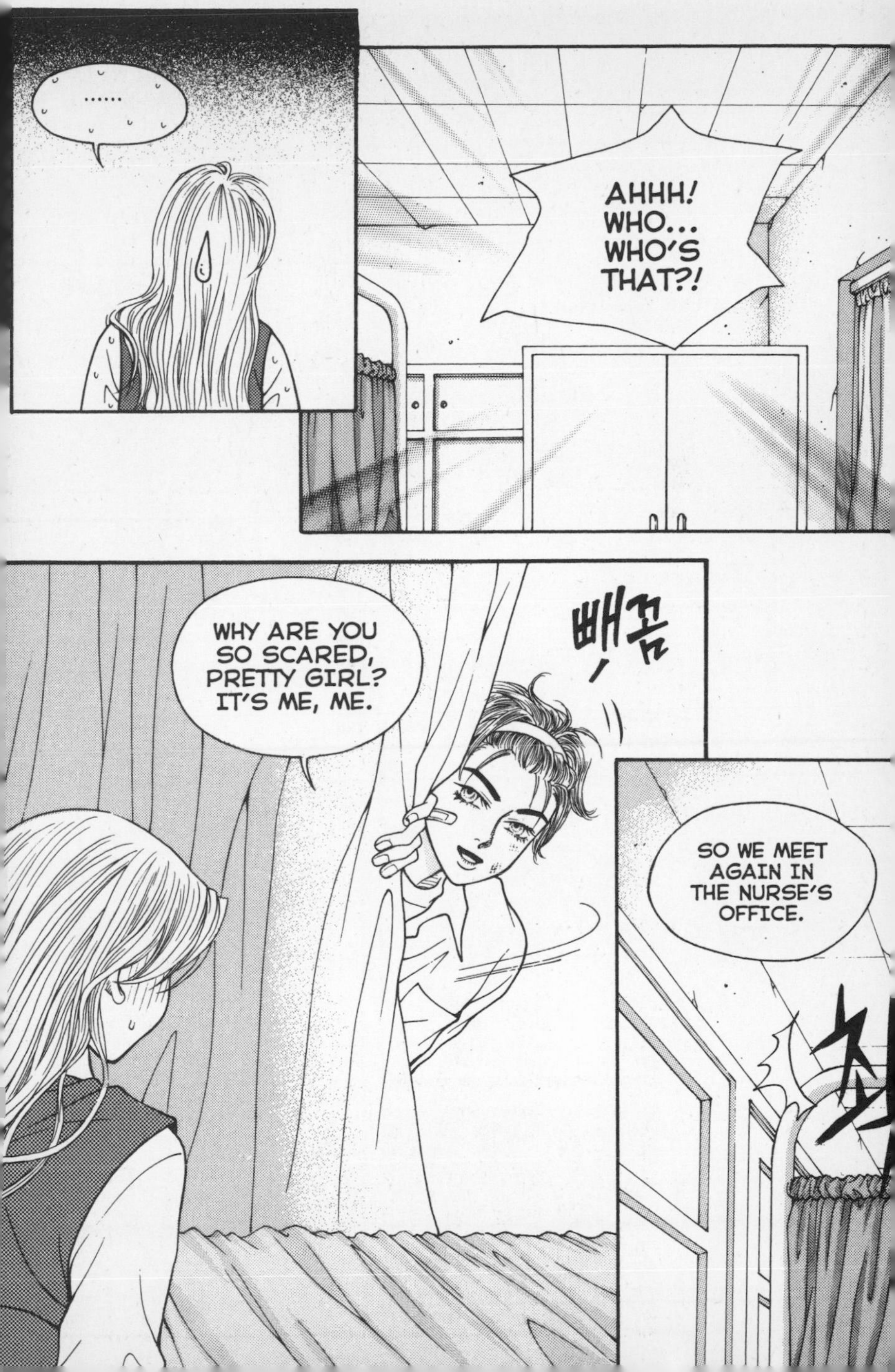
......
AHHH! WHO... WHO'S THAT?!
WHY ARE YOU SO SCARED, PRETTY GIRL? IT'S ME, ME.
빼꼼
SO WE MEET AGAIN IN THE NURSE'S OFFICE.

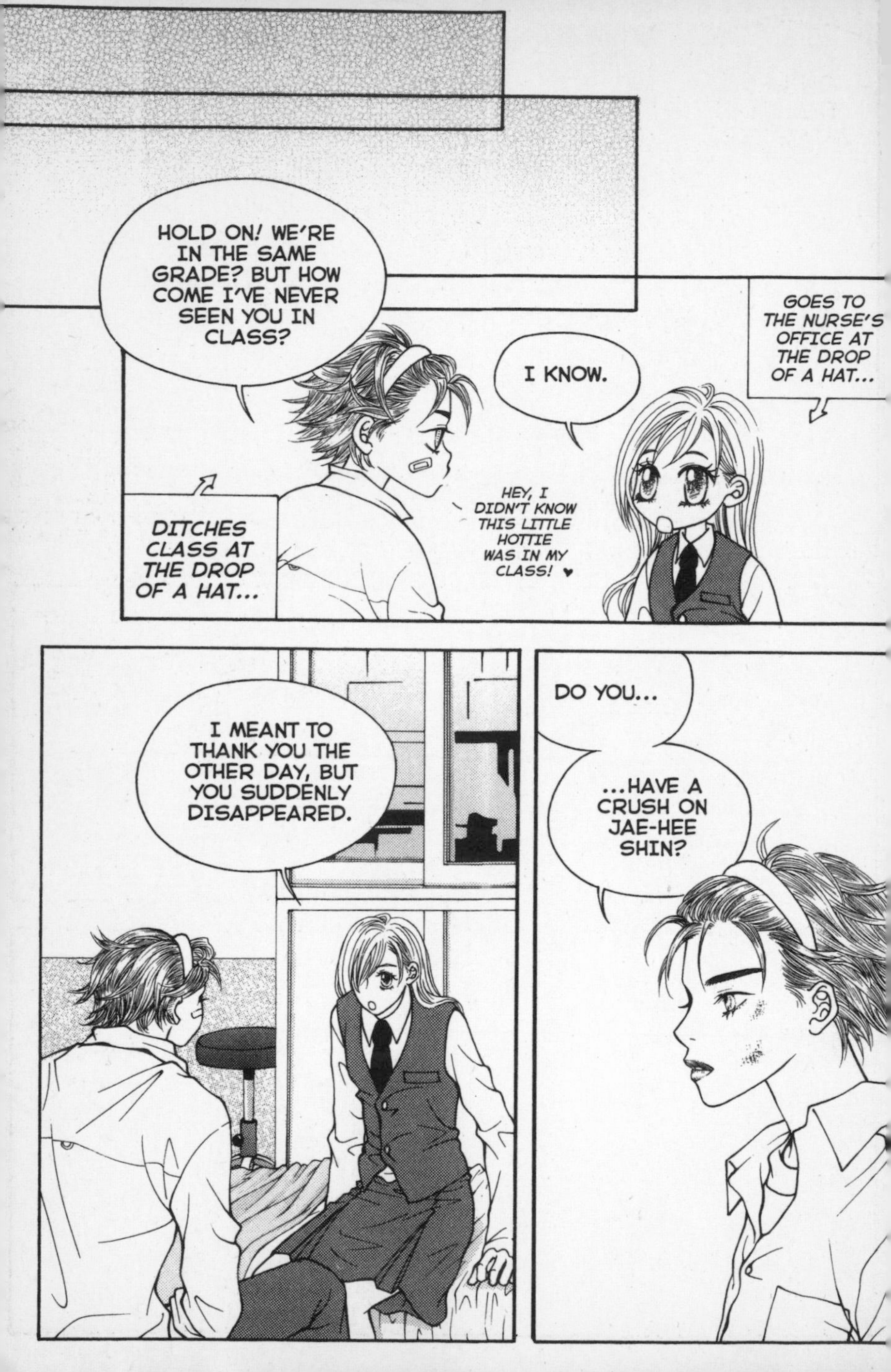
HOLD ON! WE'RE IN THE SAME GRADE? BUT HOW COME I'VE NEVER SEEN YOU IN CLASS?
DITCHES CLASS AT THE DROP OF A HAT...
HEY, I DIDN'T KNOW THIS LITTLE HOTTIE WAS IN MY CLASS! ♥
I KNOW.
GOES TO THE NURSE'S OFFICE AT THE DROP OF A HAT...
I MEANT TO THANK YOU THE OTHER DAY, BUT YOU SUDDENLY DISAPPEARED.
DO YOU...
...HAVE A CRUSH ON JAE-HEE SHIN?

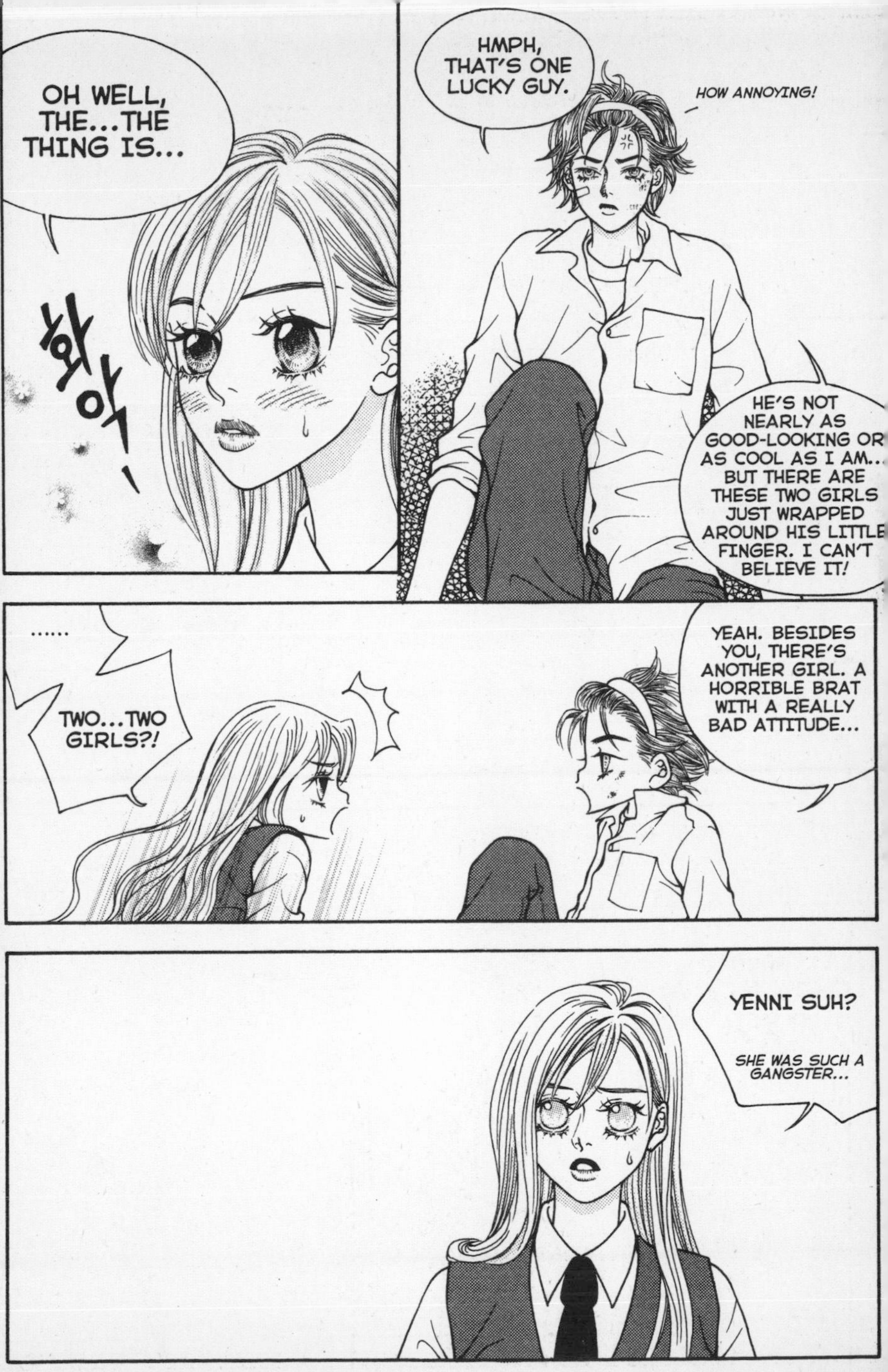
OH WELL, THE...THE THING IS...
확아
HMPH, THAT'S ONE LUCKY GUY.
HOW ANNOYING!
HE'S NOT NEARLY AS GOOD-LOOKING OR AS COOL AS I AM... BUT THERE ARE THESE TWO GIRLS JUST WRAPPED AROUND HIS LITTLE FINGER. I CAN'T BELIEVE IT!
......
TWO...TWO GIRLS?!
YEAH. BESIDES YOU, THERE'S ANOTHER GIRL. A HORRIBLE BRAT WITH A REALLY BAD ATTITUDE...
YENNI SUH?
SHE WAS SUCH A GANGSTER...

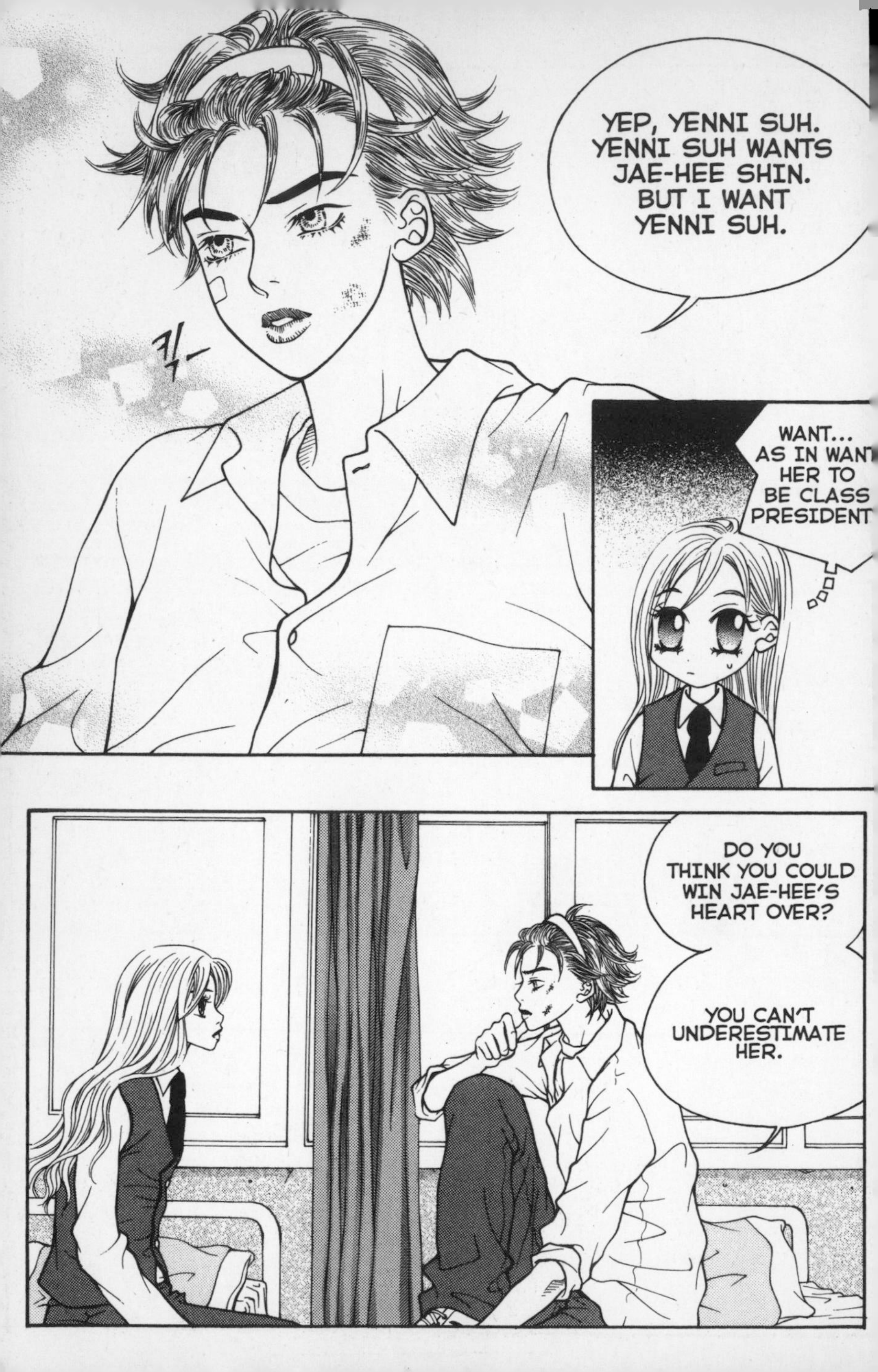

YEP, YENNI SUH. YENNI SUH WANTS JAE-HEE SHIN. BUT I WANT YENNI SUH.
WANT... AS IN WANT HER TO BE CLASS PRESIDENT
DO YOU THINK YOU COULD WIN JAE-HEE'S HEART OVER?
YOU CAN'T UNDERESTIMATE HER.

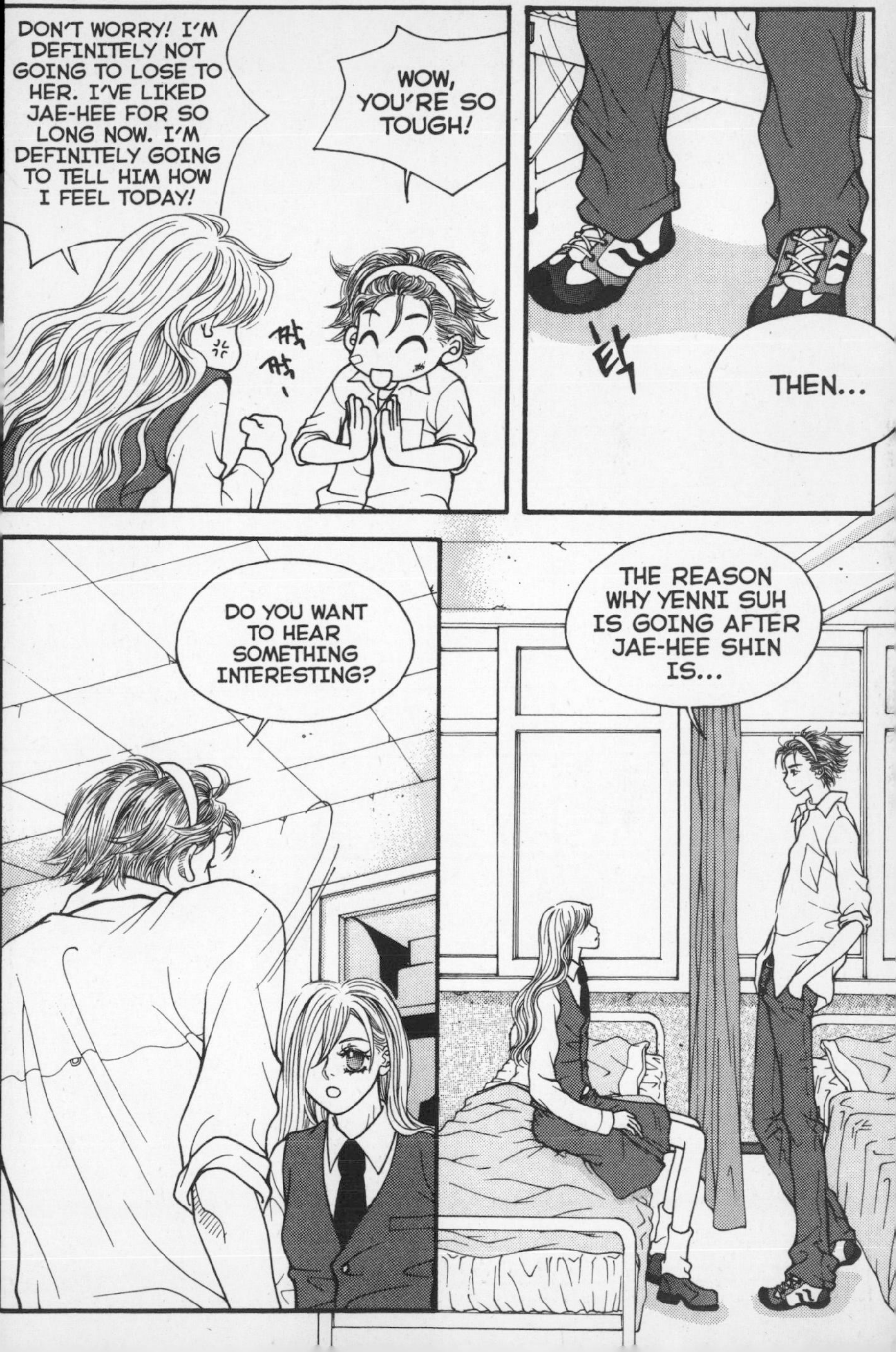
DON'T WORRY! I'M DEFINITELY NOT GOING TO LOSE TO HER. I'VE LIKED JAE-HEE FOR SO LONG NOW. I'M DEFINITELY GOING TO TELL HIM HOW I FEEL TODAY!
WOW, YOU'RE SO TOUGH!
탁
THEN...
DO YOU WANT TO HEAR SOMETHING INTERESTING?
THE REASON WHY YENNI SUH IS GOING AFTER JAE-HEE SHIN IS...

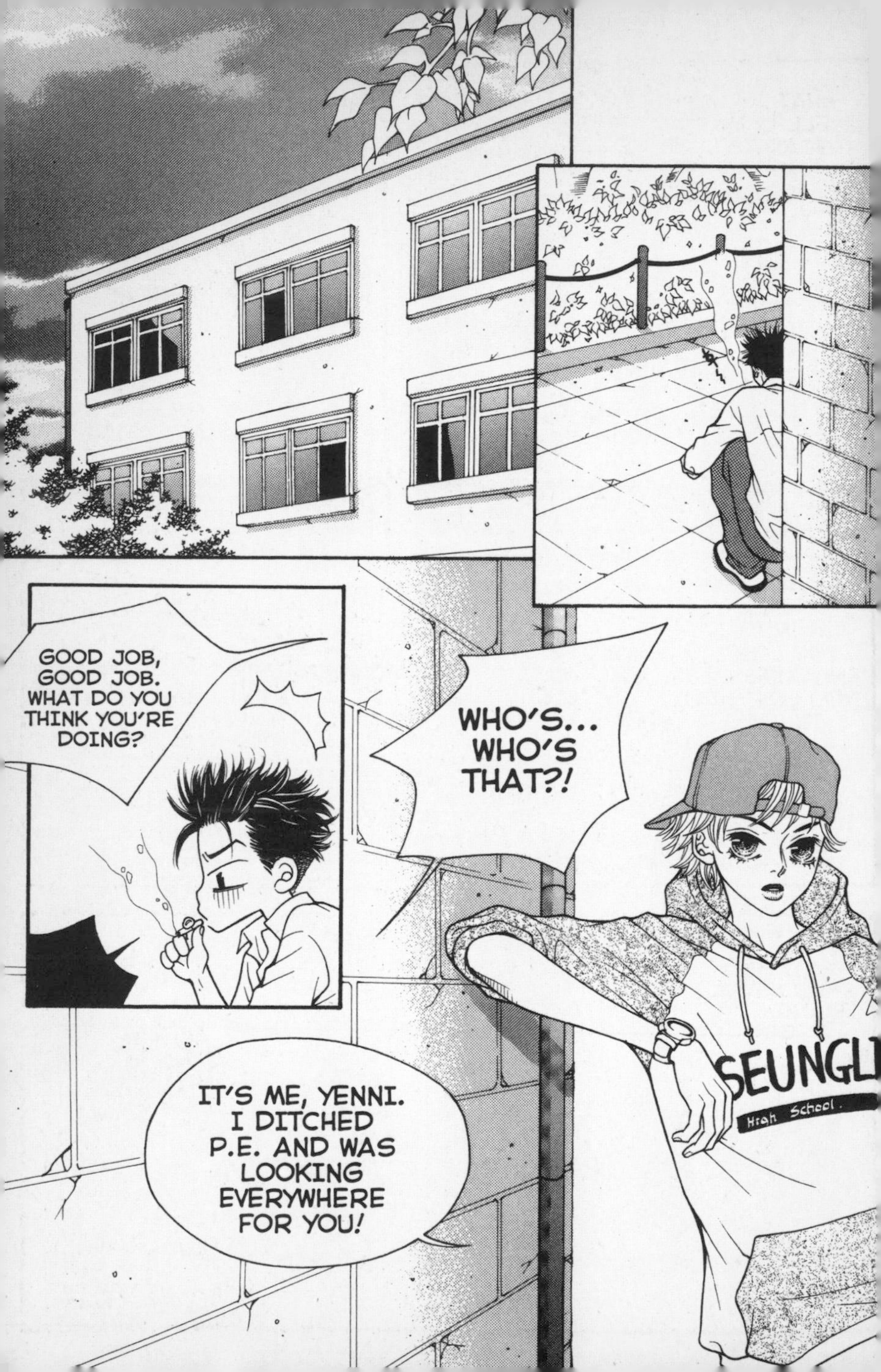
GOOD JOB, GOOD JOB. WHAT DO YOU THINK YOU'RE DOING?
WHO'S... WHO'S THAT?!
IT'S ME, YENNI. I DITCHED P.E. AND WAS LOOKING EVERYWHERE FOR YOU!
SEUNGLI
High School.

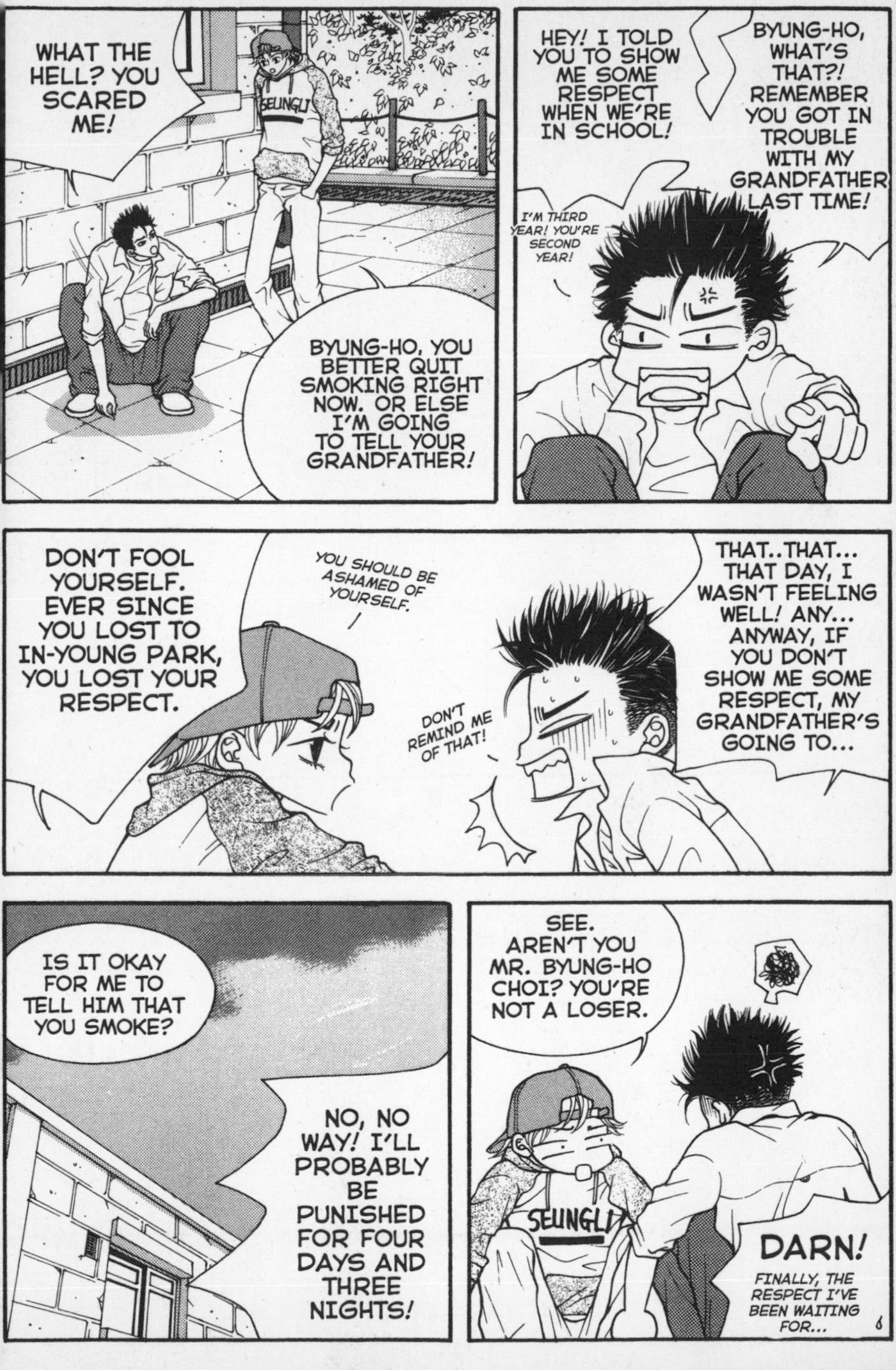
WHAT THE HELL? YOU SCARED ME!
SEUNGLI
BYUNG-HO, YOU BETTER QUIT SMOKING RIGHT NOW. OR ELSE I'M GOING TO TELL YOUR GRANDFATHER!
HEY! I TOLD YOU TO SHOW ME SOME RESPECT WHEN WE'RE IN SCHOOL!
I'M THIRD YEAR! YOU'RE SECOND YEAR!
BYUNG-HO, WHAT'S THAT?! REMEMBER YOU GOT IN TROUBLE WITH MY GRANDFATHER LAST TIME!
DON'T FOOL YOURSELF. EVER SINCE YOU LOST TO IN-YOUNG PARK, YOU LOST YOUR RESPECT.
YOU SHOULD BE ASHAMED OF YOURSELF.
DON'T REMIND ME OF THAT!
THAT..THAT... THAT DAY, I WASN'T FEELING WELL! ANY... ANYWAY, IF YOU DON'T SHOW ME SOME RESPECT, MY GRANDFATHER'S GOING TO...
IS IT OKAY FOR ME TO TELL HIM THAT YOU SMOKE?
NO, NO WAY! I'LL PROBABLY BE PUNISHED FOR FOUR DAYS AND THREE NIGHTS!
SEE. AREN'T YOU MR. BYUNG-HO CHOI? YOU'RE NOT A LOSER.
SEUNGLI
DARN!
FINALLY, THE RESPECT I'VE BEEN WAITING FOR...

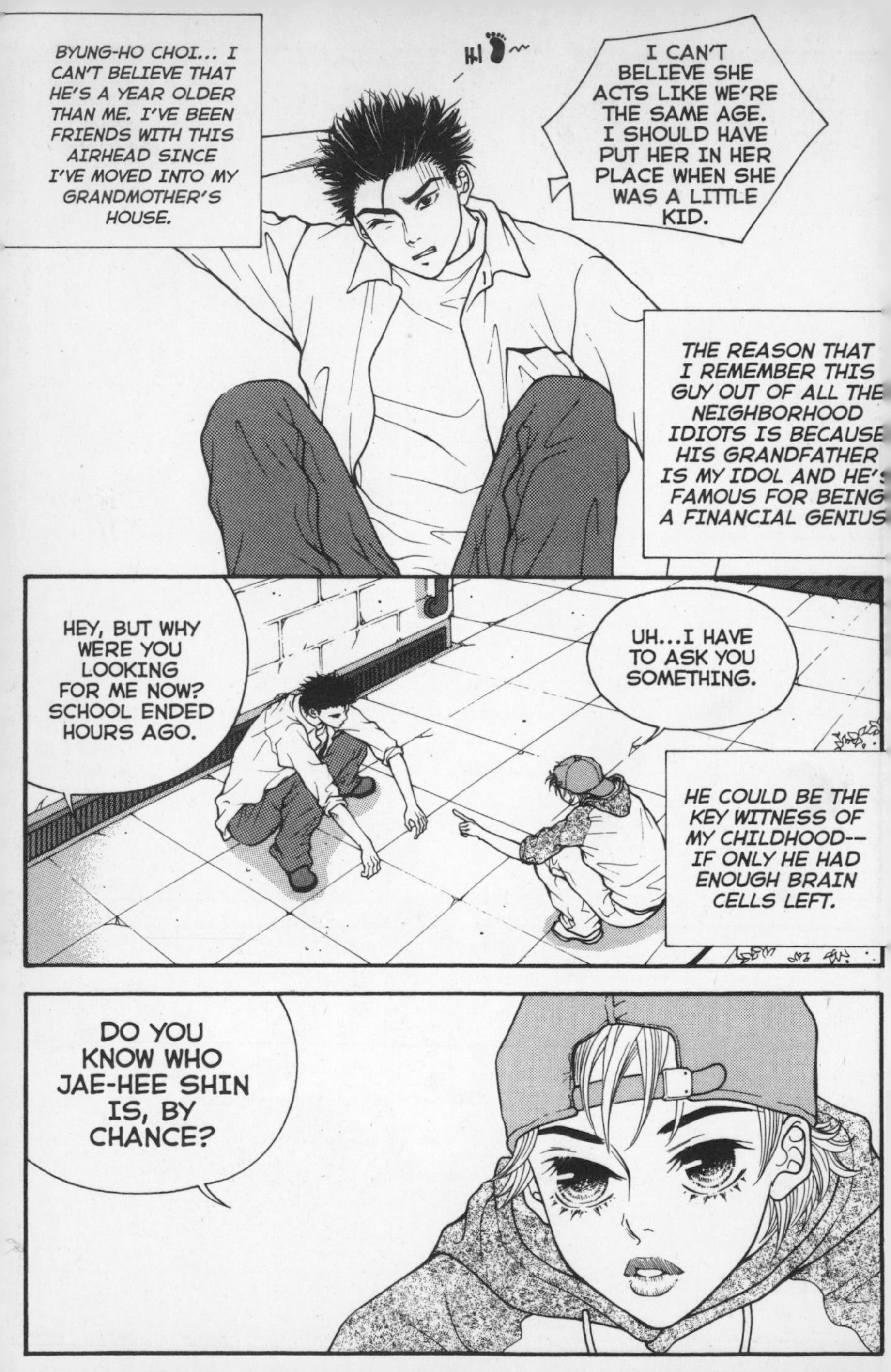
BYUNG-HO CHOI... I CAN'T BELIEVE THAT HE'S A YEAR OLDER THAN ME. I'VE BEEN FRIENDS WITH THIS AIRHEAD SINCE I'VE MOVED INTO MY GRANDMOTHER'S HOUSE.
I CAN'T BELIEVE SHE ACTS LIKE WE'RE THE SAME AGE. I SHOULD HAVE PUT HER IN HER PLACE WHEN SHE WAS A LITTLE KID.
THE REASON THAT I REMEMBER THIS GUY OUT OF ALL THE NEIGHBORHOOD IDIOTS IS BECAUSE HIS GRANDFATHER IS MY IDOL AND HE'S FAMOUS FOR BEING A FINANCIAL GENIUS
HEY, BUT WHY WERE YOU LOOKING FOR ME NOW? SCHOOL ENDED HOURS AGO.
UH...I HAVE TO ASK YOU SOMETHING.
HE COULD BE THE KEY WITNESS OF MY CHILDHOOD-- IF ONLY HE HAD ENOUGH BRAIN CELLS LEFT.
DO YOU KNOW WHO JAE-HEE SHIN IS, BY CHANCE?

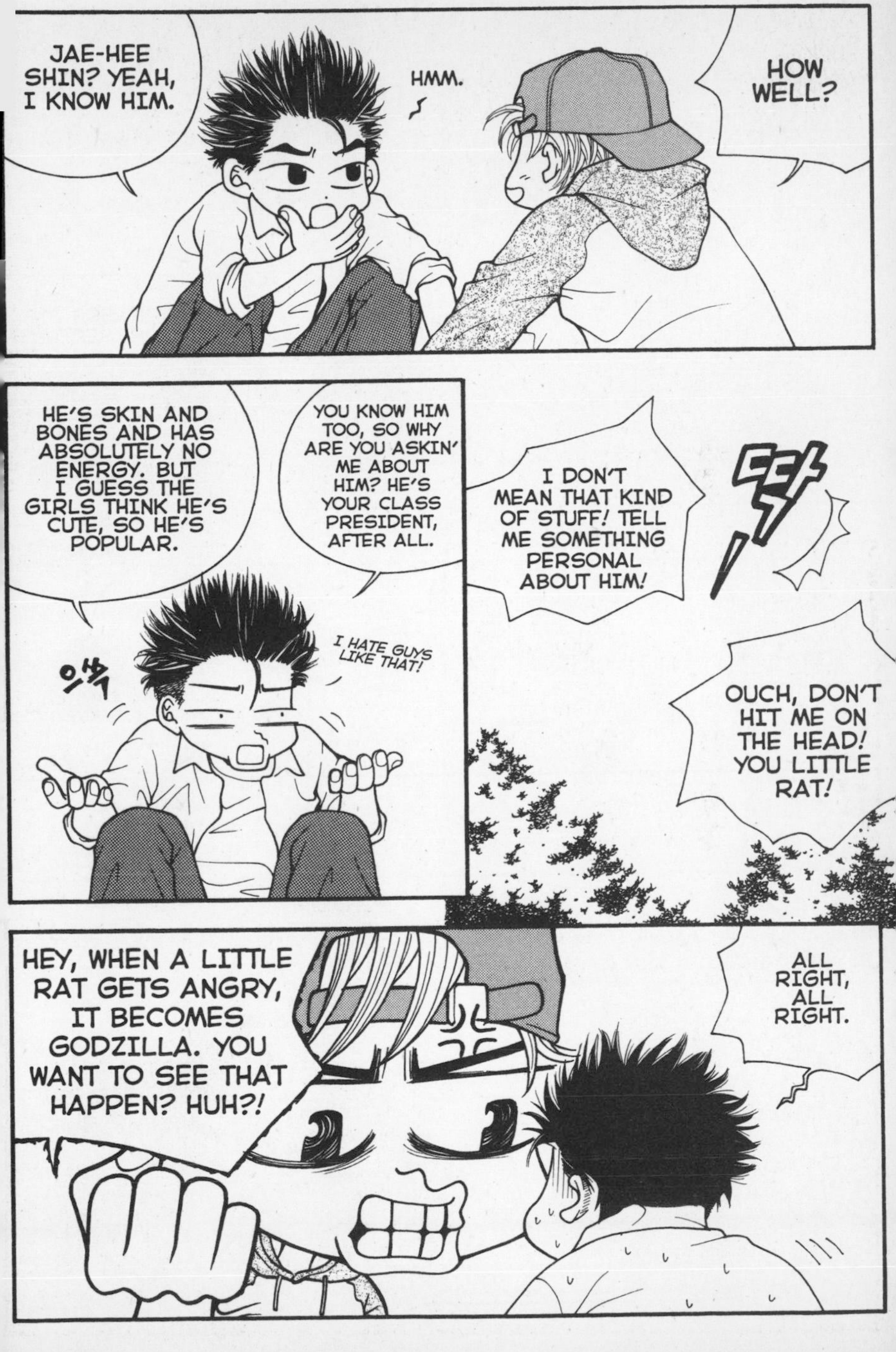
JAE-HEE SHIN? YEAH, I KNOW HIM.
HMM.
HOW WELL?
HE'S SKIN AND BONES AND HAS ABSOLUTELY NO ENERGY. BUT I GUESS THE GIRLS THINK HE'S CUTE, SO HE'S POPULAR.
YOU KNOW HIM TOO, SO WHY ARE YOU ASKIN' ME ABOUT HIM? HE'S YOUR CLASS PRESIDENT, AFTER ALL.
I HATE GUYS LIKE THAT!
I DON'T MEAN THAT KIND OF STUFF! TELL ME SOMETHING PERSONAL ABOUT HIM!
OUCH, DON'T HIT ME ON THE HEAD! YOU LITTLE RAT!
HEY, WHEN A LITTLE RAT GETS ANGRY, IT BECOMES GODZILLA. YOU WANT TO SEE THAT HAPPEN? HUH?!
ALL RIGHT, ALL RIGHT.

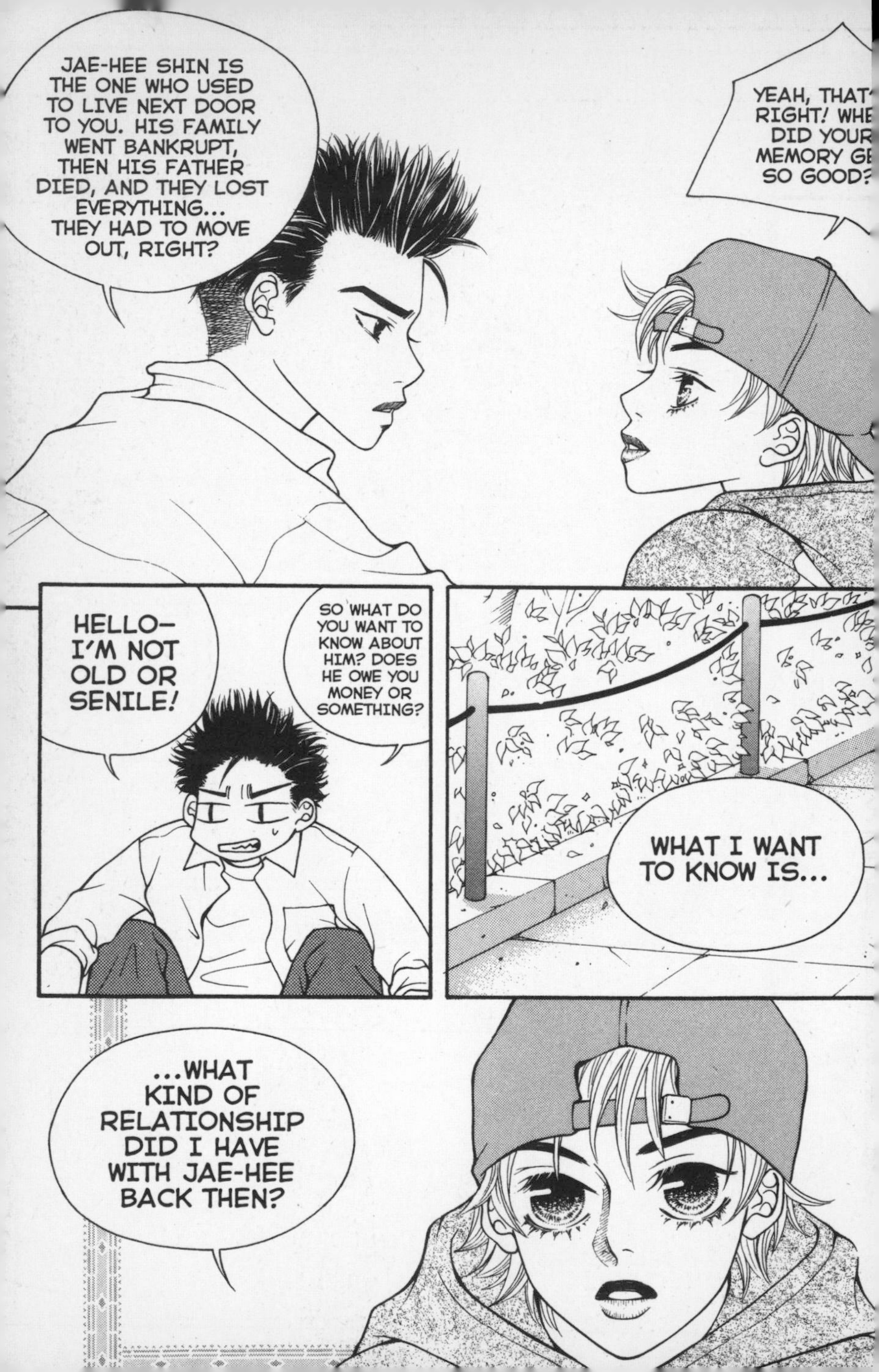
JAE-HEE SHIN IS THE ONE WHO USED TO LIVE NEXT DOOR TO YOU. HIS FAMILY WENT BANKRUPT, THEN HIS FATHER DIED, AND THEY LOST EVERYTHING... THEY HAD TO MOVE OUT, RIGHT?
YEAH, THAT' RIGHT! WHE DID YOUR MEMORY GE SO GOOD?
HELLO– I'M NOT OLD OR SENILE!
SO WHAT DO YOU WANT TO KNOW ABOUT HIM? DOES HE OWE YOU MONEY OR SOMETHING?
WHAT I WANT TO KNOW IS...
...WHAT KIND OF RELATIONSHIP DID I HAVE WITH JAE-HEE BACK THEN?

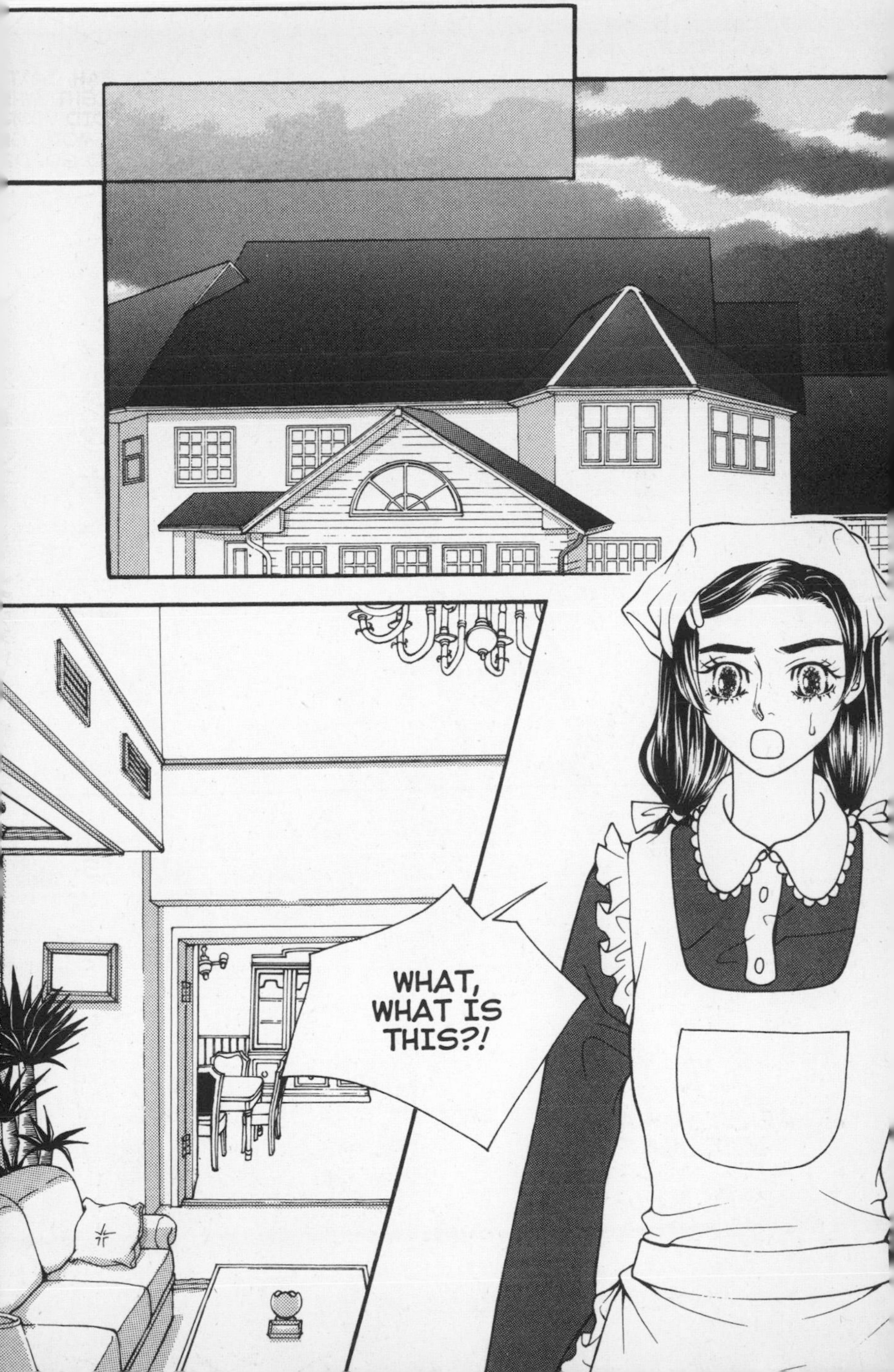
WHAT, WHAT IS THIS?!

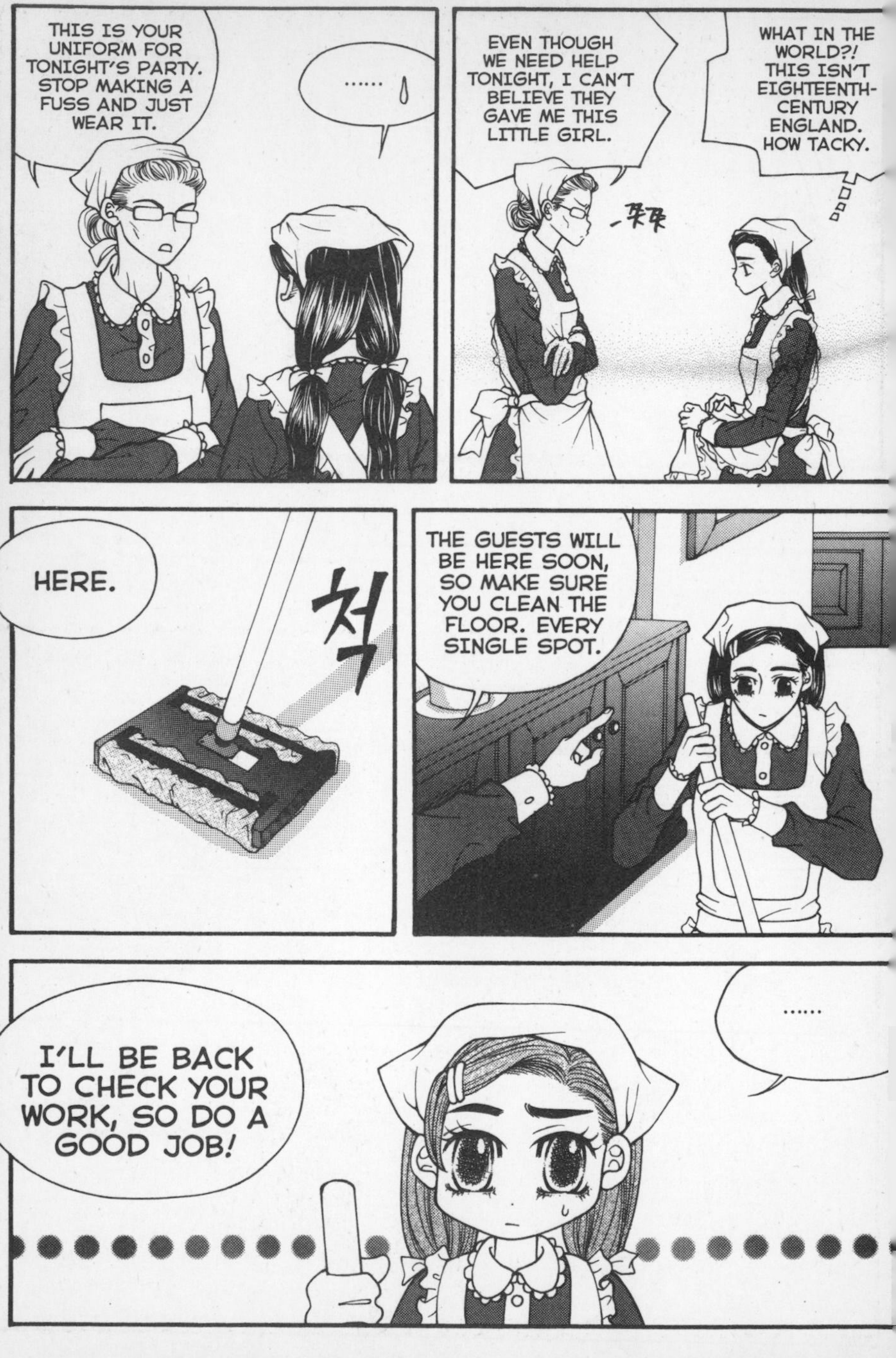
THIS IS YOUR UNIFORM FOR TONIGHT'S PARTY. STOP MAKING A FUSS AND JUST WEAR IT.
......
EVEN THOUGH WE NEED HELP TONIGHT, I CAN'T BELIEVE THEY GAVE ME THIS LITTLE GIRL.
WHAT IN THE WORLD?! THIS ISN'T EIGHTEENTH-CENTURY ENGLAND. HOW TACKY.
HERE.
척
THE GUESTS WILL BE HERE SOON, SO MAKE SURE YOU CLEAN THE FLOOR. EVERY SINGLE SPOT.
I'LL BE BACK TO CHECK YOUR WORK, SO DO A GOOD JOB!
......

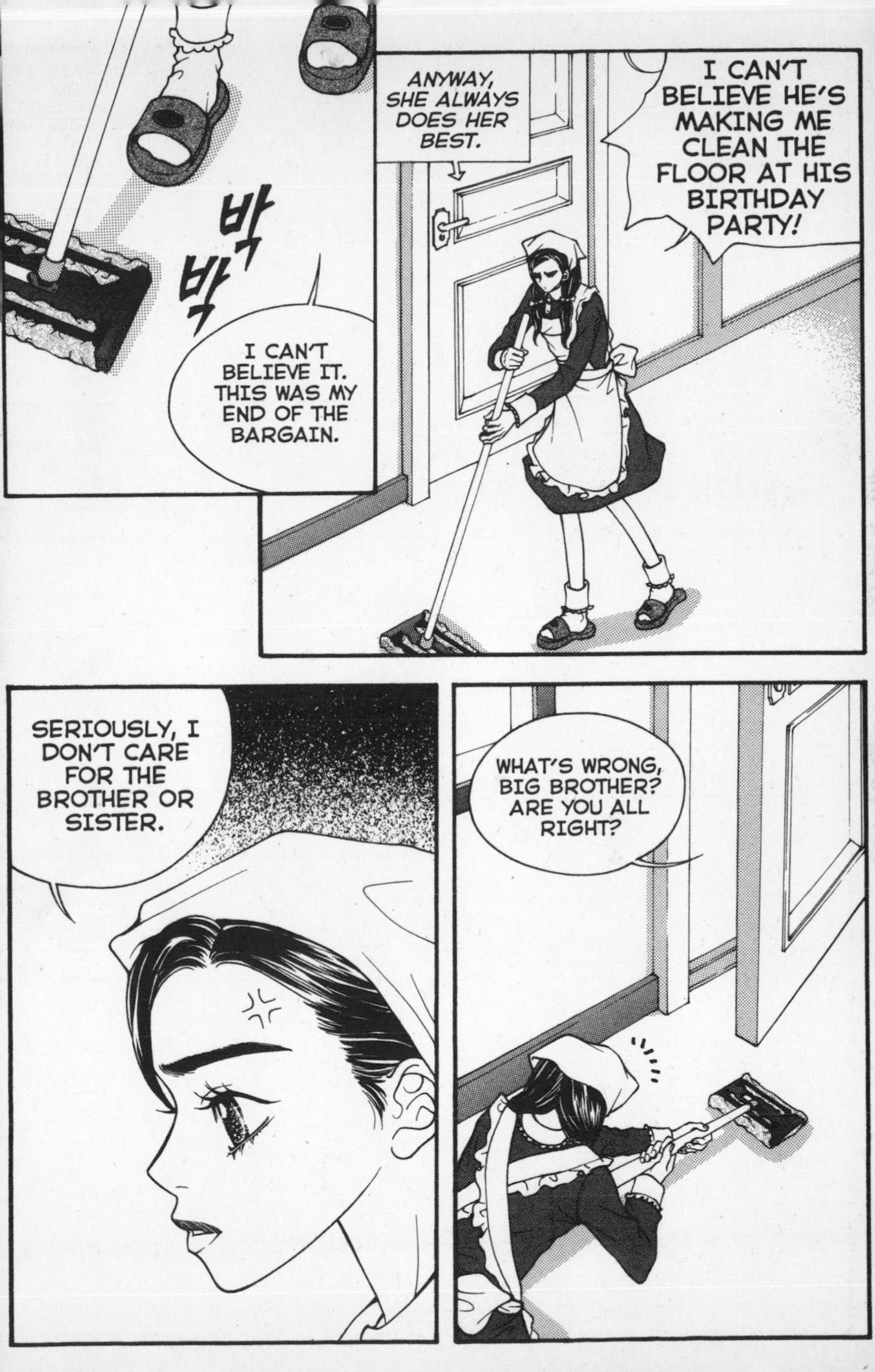
박 박
I CAN'T BELIEVE IT. THIS WAS MY END OF THE BARGAIN.
ANYWAY, SHE ALWAYS DOES HER BEST.
I CAN'T BELIEVE HE'S MAKING ME CLEAN THE FLOOR AT HIS BIRTHDAY PARTY!
SERIOUSLY, I DON'T CARE FOR THE BROTHER OR SISTER.
WHAT'S WRONG, BIG BROTHER? ARE YOU ALL RIGHT?

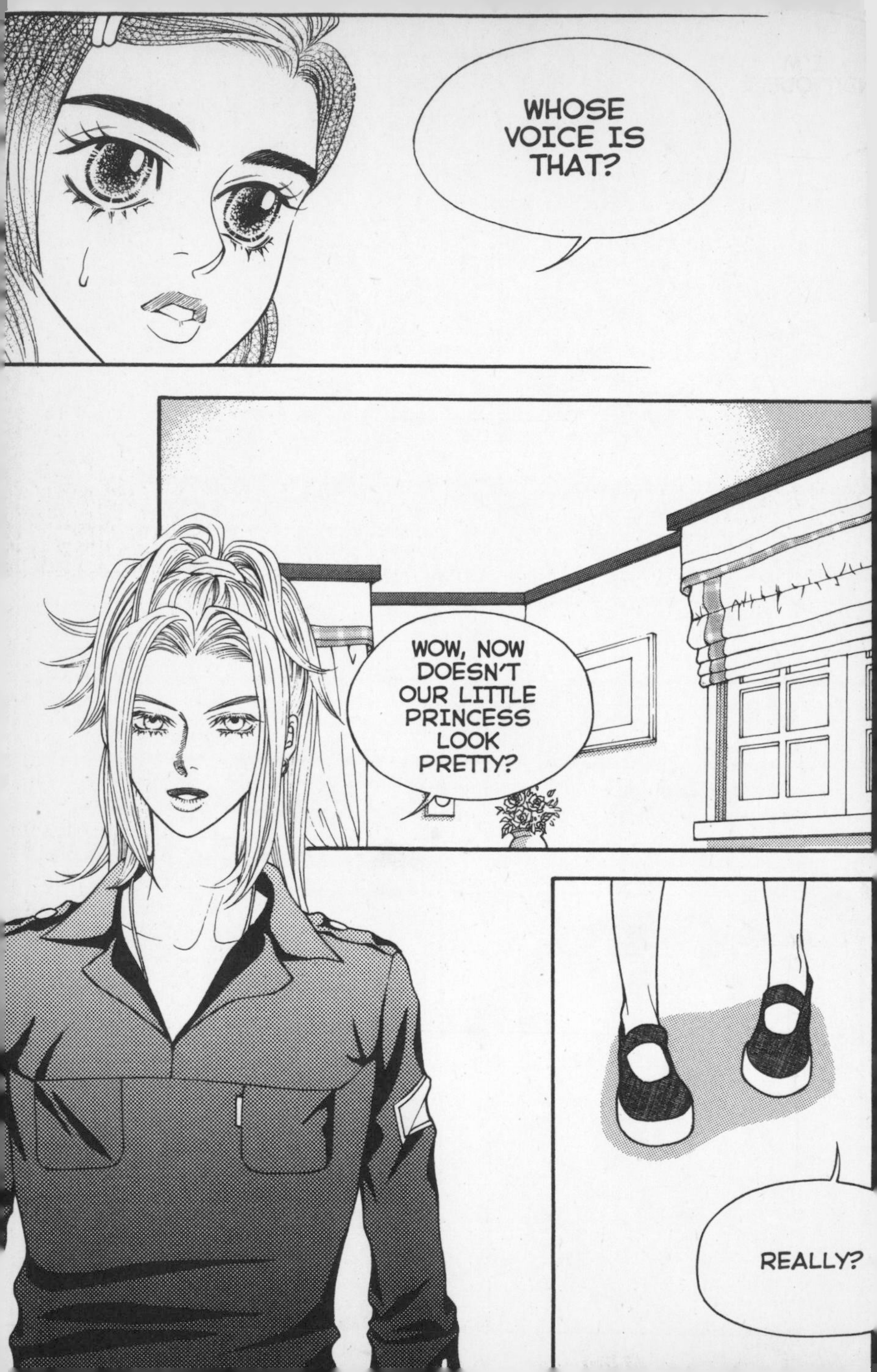
WHOSE VOICE IS THAT?
WOW, NOW DOESN'T OUR LITTLE PRINCESS LOOK PRETTY?
REALLY?

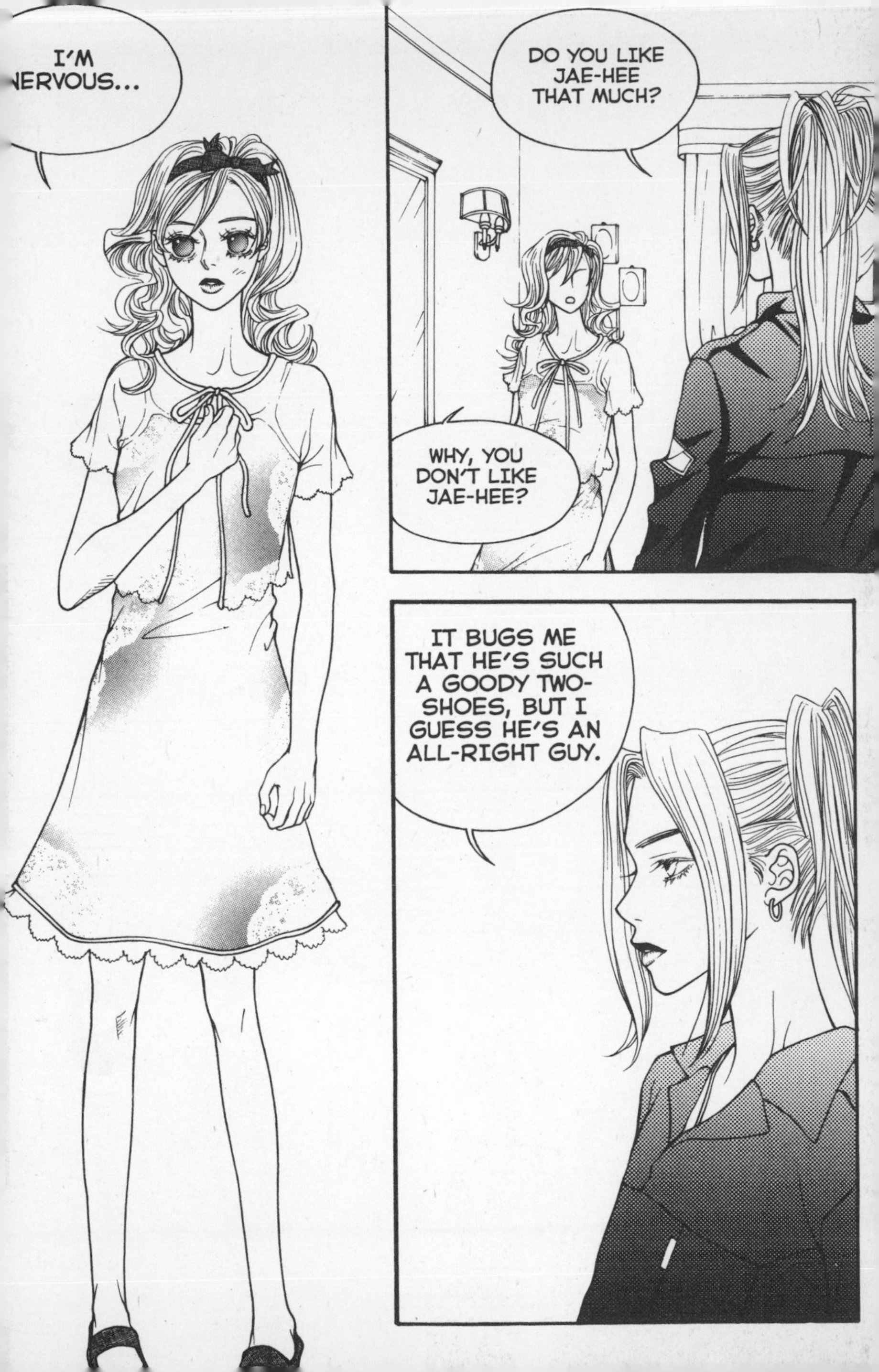
I'M NERVOUS...
DO YOU LIKE JAE-HEE THAT MUCH?
WHY, YOU DON'T LIKE JAE-HEE?
IT BUGS ME THAT HE'S SUCH A GOODY TWO-SHOES, BUT I GUESS HE'S AN ALL-RIGHT GUY.

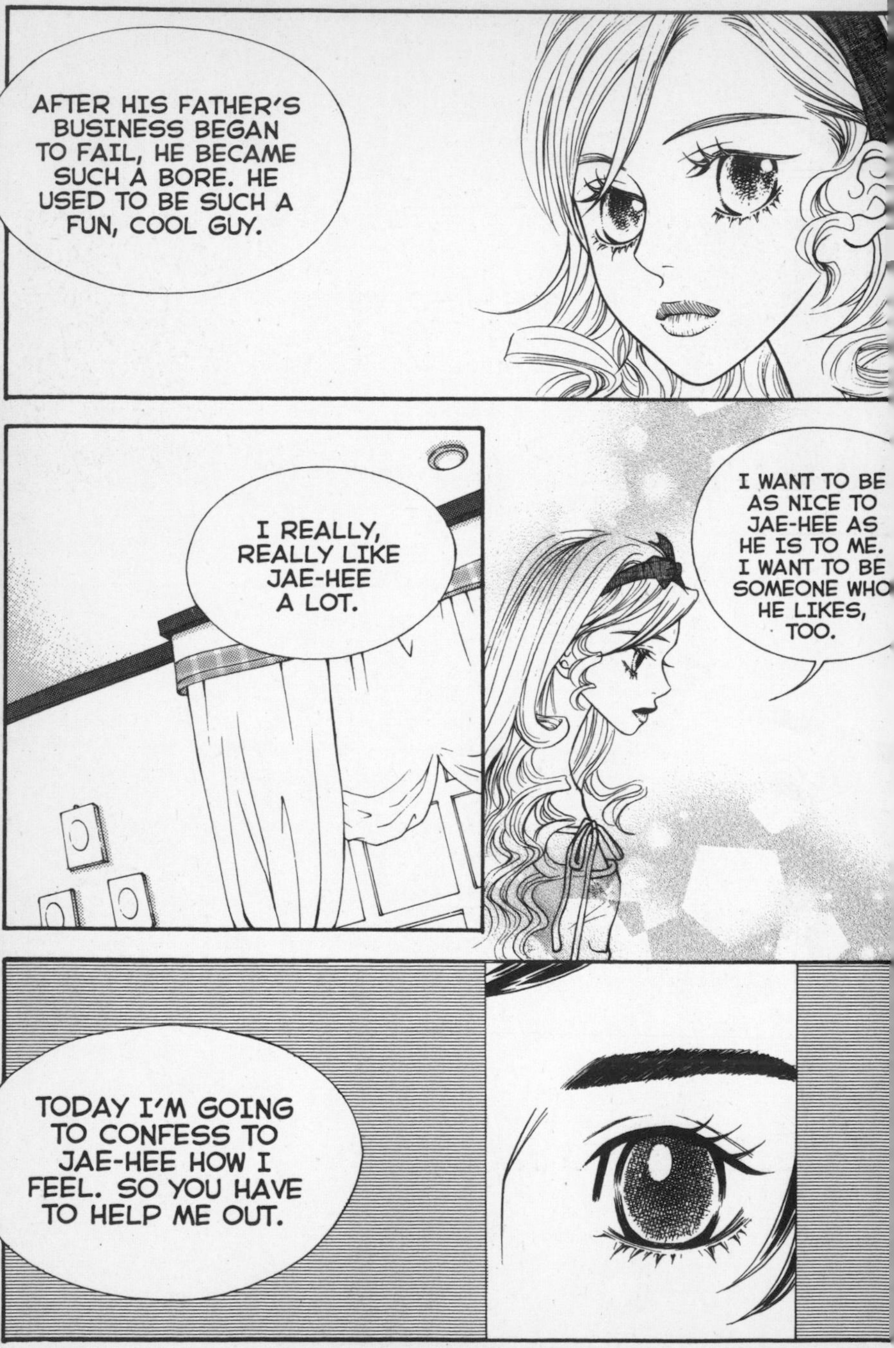
AFTER HIS FATHER'S BUSINESS BEGAN TO FAIL, HE BECAME SUCH A BORE. HE USED TO BE SUCH A FUN, COOL GUY.
I REALLY, REALLY LIKE JAE-HEE A LOT.
I WANT TO BE AS NICE TO JAE-HEE AS HE IS TO ME. I WANT TO BE SOMEONE WHO HE LIKES, TOO.
TODAY I'M GOING TO CONFESS TO JAE-HEE HOW I FEEL. SO YOU HAVE TO HELP ME OUT.

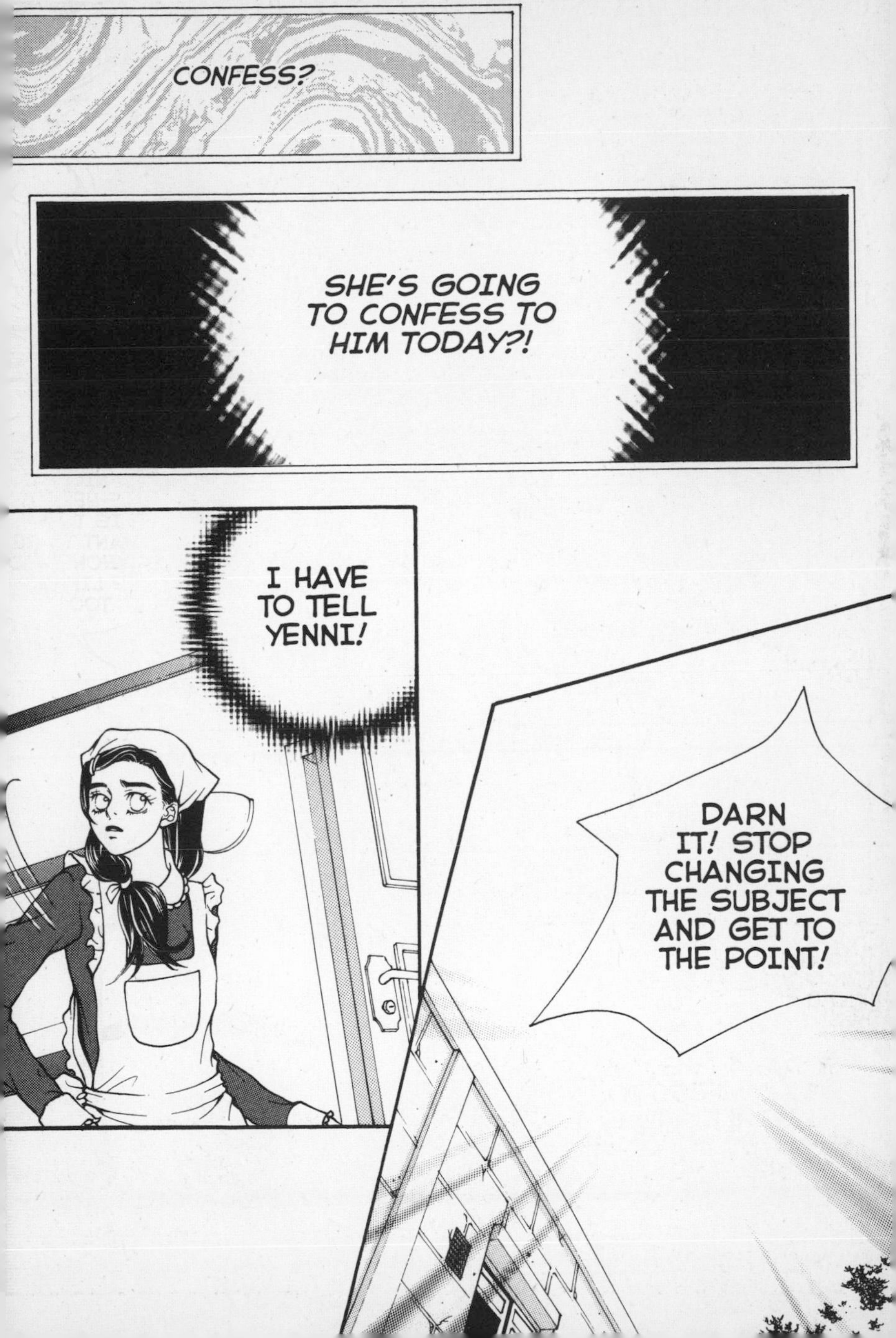
CONFESS?
SHE'S GOING TO CONFESS TO HIM TODAY?!
I HAVE TO TELL YENNI!
DARN IT! STOP CHANGING THE SUBJECT AND GET TO THE POINT!

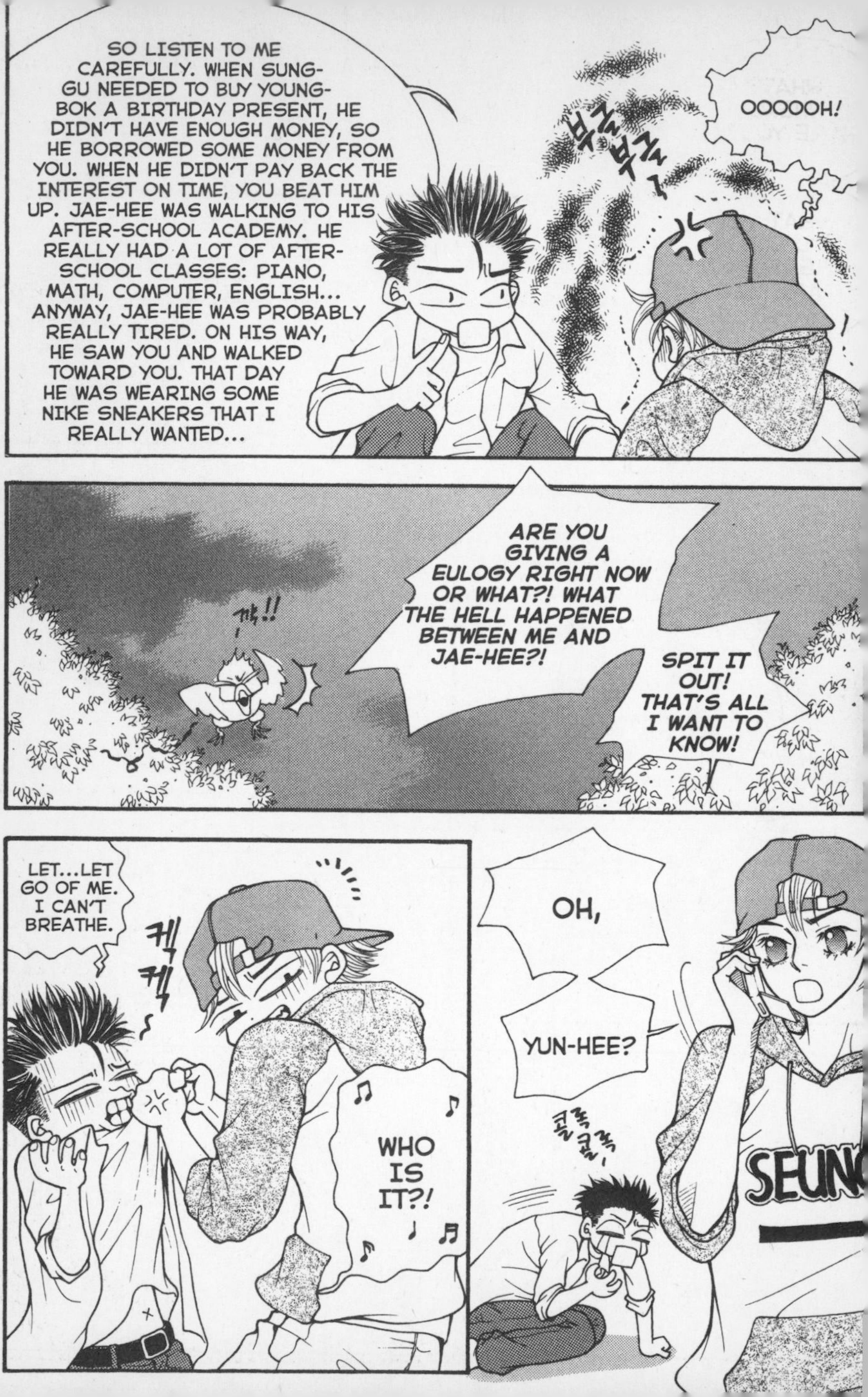
SO LISTEN TO ME CAREFULLY. WHEN SUNG-GU NEEDED TO BUY YOUNG-BOK A BIRTHDAY PRESENT, HE DIDN'T HAVE ENOUGH MONEY, SO HE BORROWED SOME MONEY FROM YOU. WHEN HE DIDN'T PAY BACK THE INTEREST ON TIME, YOU BEAT HIM UP. JAE-HEE WAS WALKING TO HIS AFTER-SCHOOL ACADEMY. HE REALLY HAD A LOT OF AFTER-SCHOOL CLASSES: PIANO, MATH, COMPUTER, ENGLISH... ANYWAY, JAE-HEE WAS PROBABLY REALLY TIRED. ON HIS WAY, HE SAW YOU AND WALKED TOWARD YOU. THAT DAY HE WAS WEARING SOME NIKE SNEAKERS THAT I REALLY WANTED...
부글부글
OOOOOH!
ARE YOU GIVING A EULOGY RIGHT NOW OR WHAT?! WHAT THE HELL HAPPENED BETWEEN ME AND JAE-HEE?!
SPIT IT OUT! THAT'S ALL I WANT TO KNOW!
LET...LET GO OF ME. I CAN'T BREATHE.
켁켁
WHO IS IT?!
OH,
YUN-HEE?

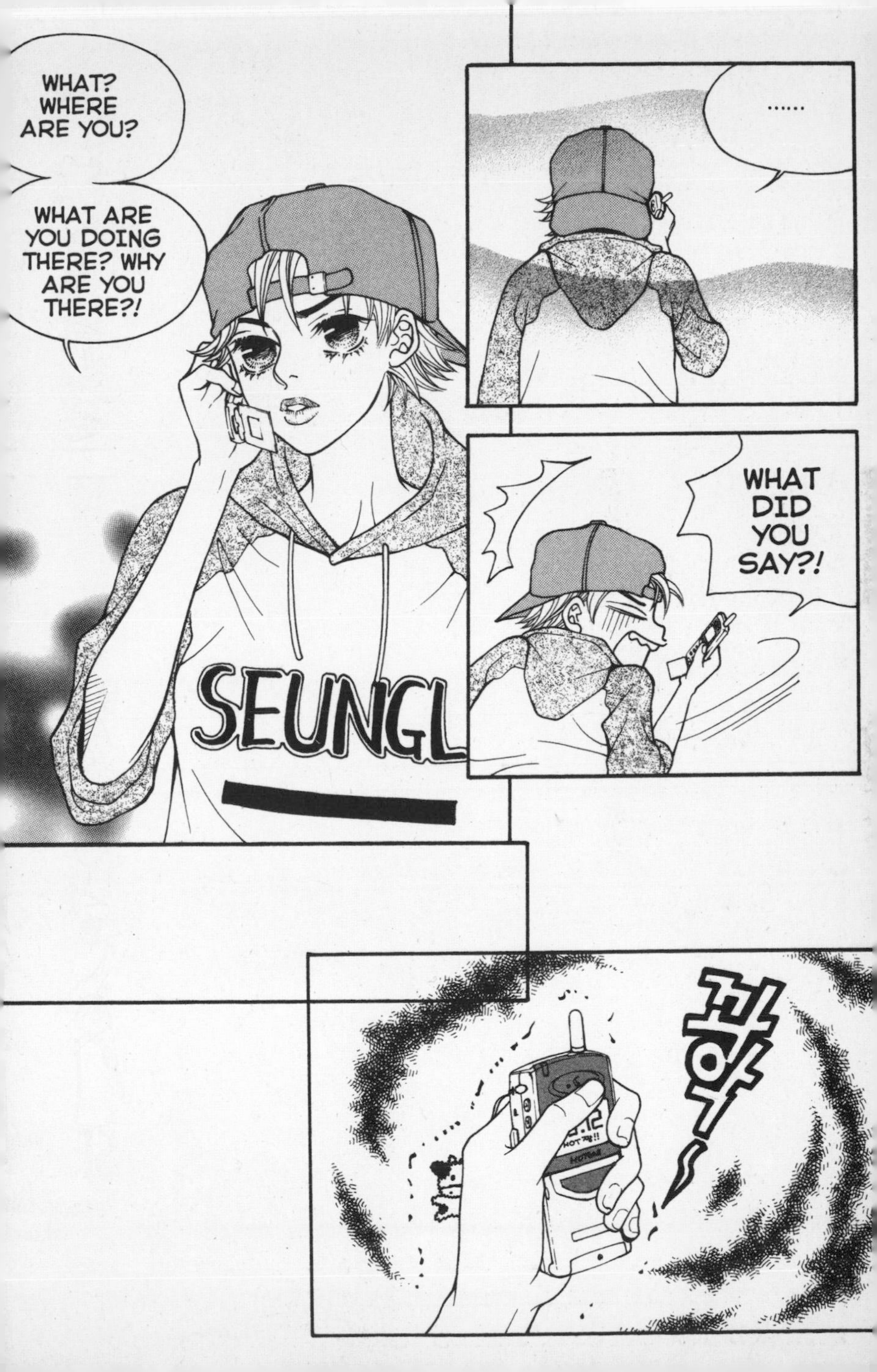
WHAT? WHERE ARE YOU?
WHAT ARE YOU DOING THERE? WHY ARE YOU THERE?!
......
WHAT DID YOU SAY?!
SEUNGL

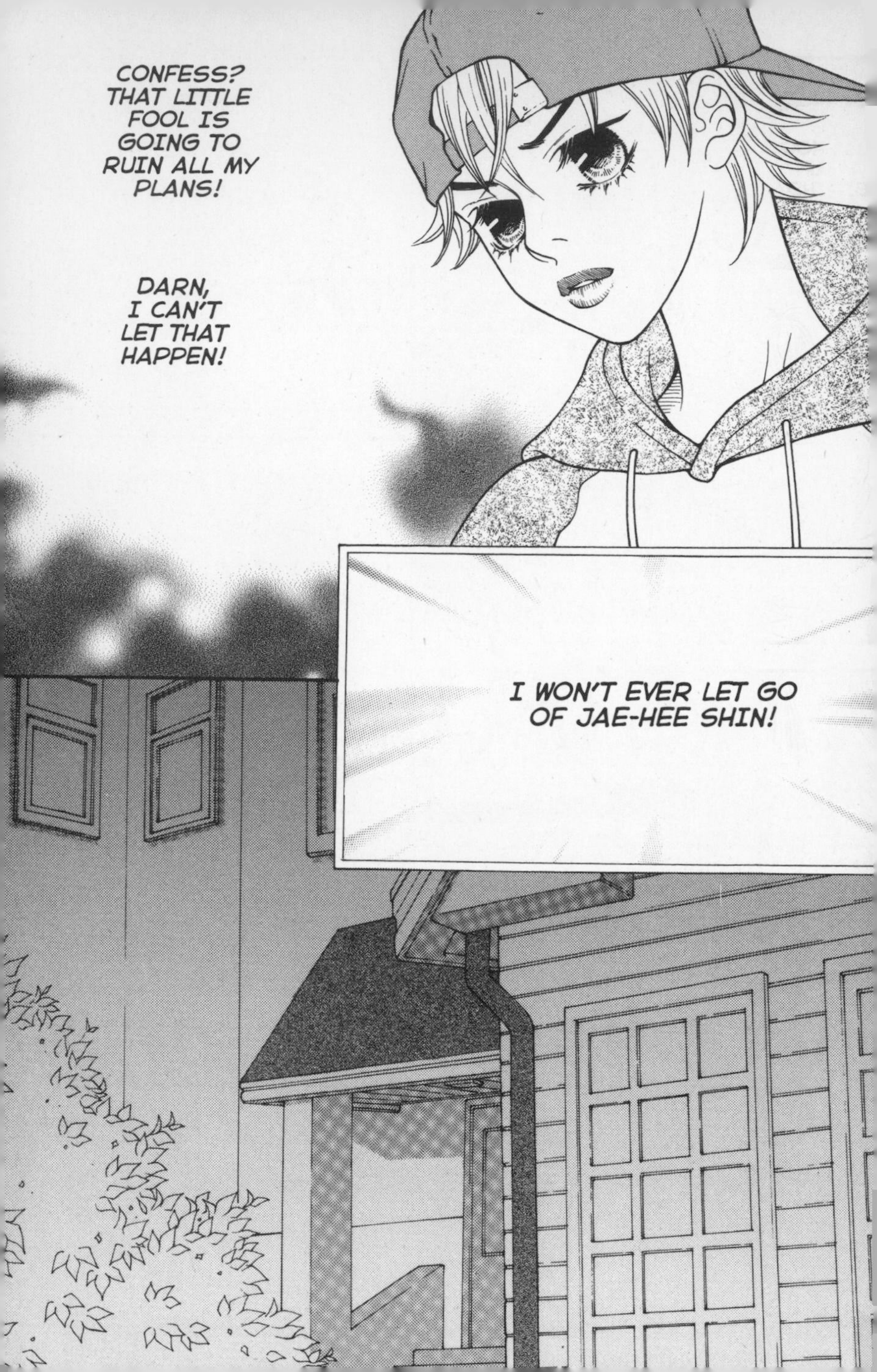
CONFESS? THAT LITTLE FOOL IS GOING TO RUIN ALL MY PLANS!
DARN, I CAN'T LET THAT HAPPEN!
I WON'T EVER LET GO OF JAE-HEE SHIN!

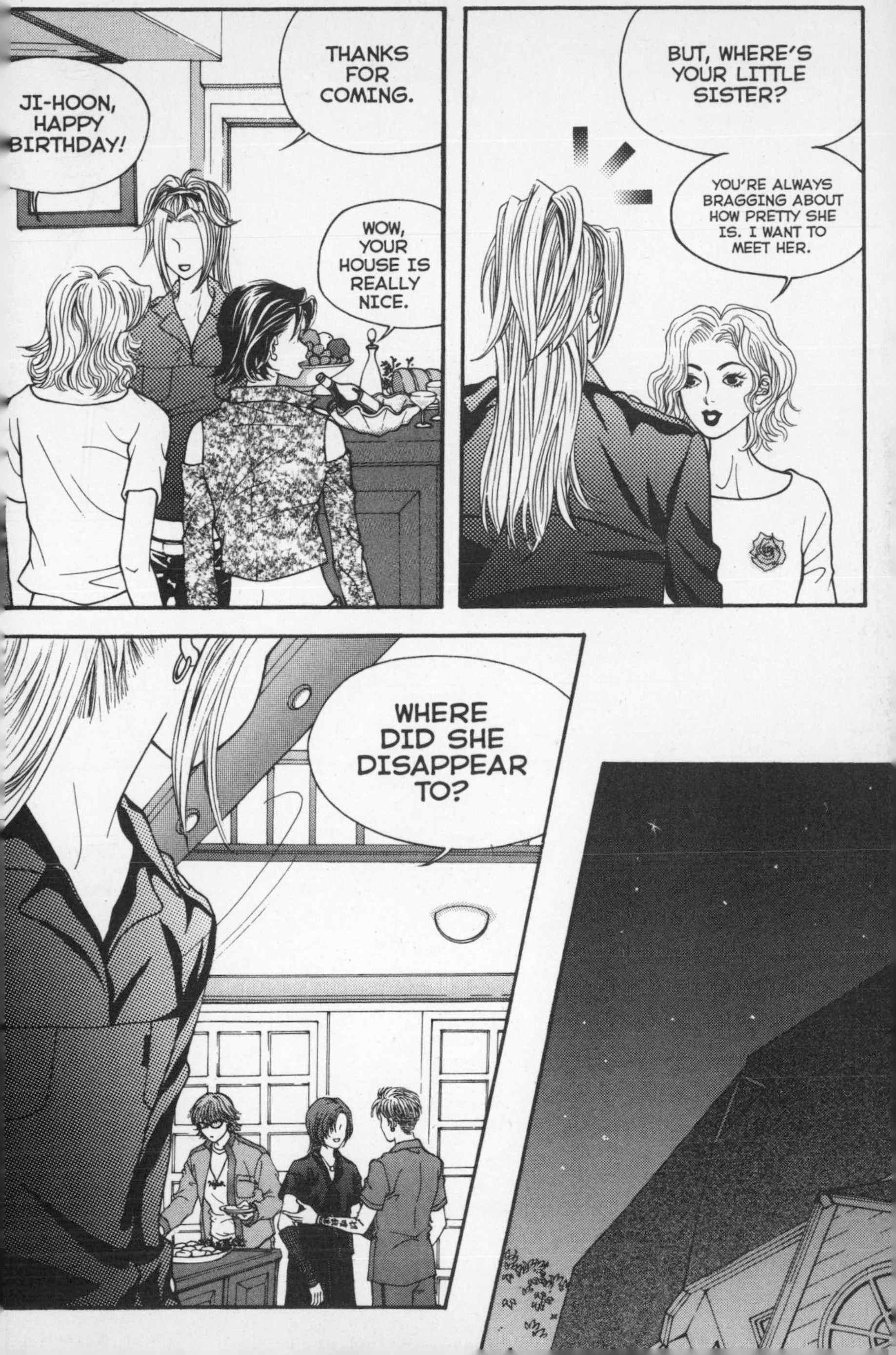

JI-HOON, HAPPY BIRTHDAY!
THANKS FOR COMING.
WOW, YOUR HOUSE IS REALLY NICE.
BUT, WHERE'S YOUR LITTLE SISTER?
YOU'RE ALWAYS BRAGGING ABOUT HOW PRETTY SHE IS. I WANT TO MEET HER.
WHERE DID SHE DISAPPEAR TO?

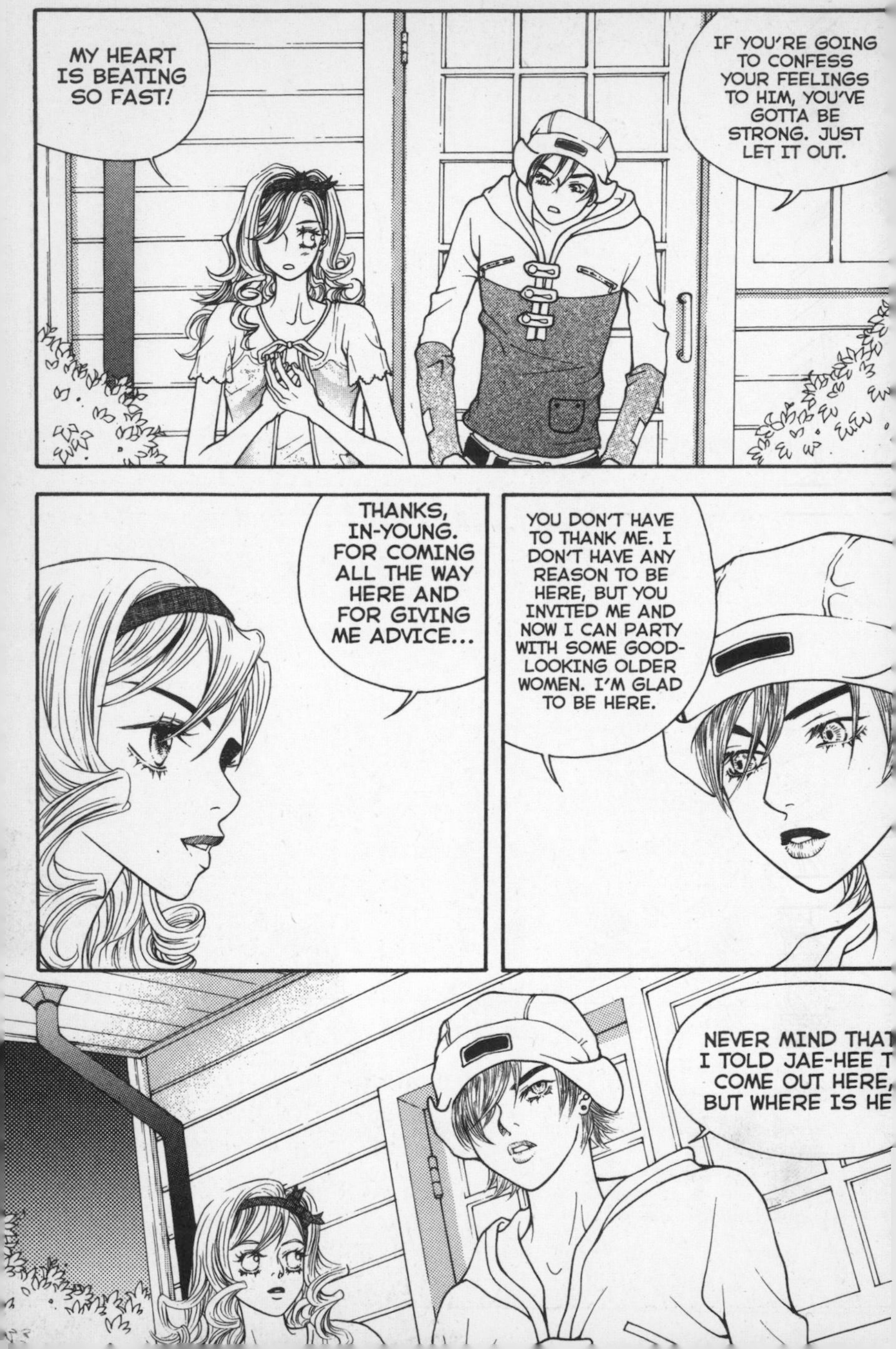
MY HEART IS BEATING SO FAST!
IF YOU'RE GOING TO CONFESS YOUR FEELINGS TO HIM, YOU'VE GOTTA BE STRONG. JUST LET IT OUT.
THANKS, IN-YOUNG. FOR COMING ALL THE WAY HERE AND FOR GIVING ME ADVICE...
YOU DON'T HAVE TO THANK ME. I DON'T HAVE ANY REASON TO BE HERE, BUT YOU INVITED ME AND NOW I CAN PARTY WITH SOME GOOD-LOOKING OLDER WOMEN. I'M GLAD TO BE HERE.
NEVER MIND THAT I TOLD JAE-HEE T COME OUT HERE, BUT WHERE IS HE

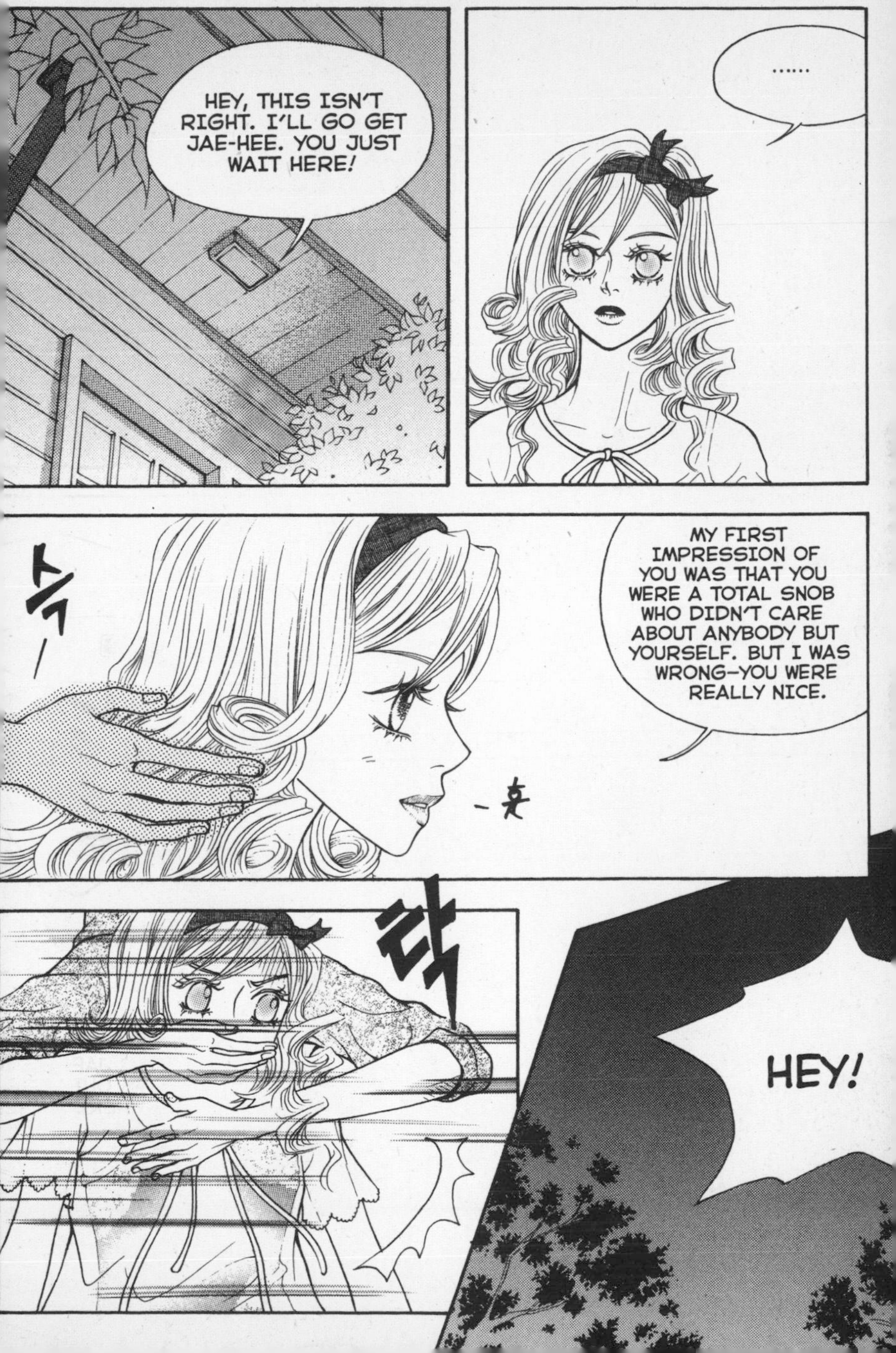
HEY, THIS ISN'T RIGHT. I'LL GO GET JAE-HEE. YOU JUST WAIT HERE!
......
MY FIRST IMPRESSION OF YOU WAS THAT YOU WERE A TOTAL SNOB WHO DIDN'T CARE ABOUT ANYBODY BUT YOURSELF. BUT I WAS WRONG–YOU WERE REALLY NICE.
탁
HEY!

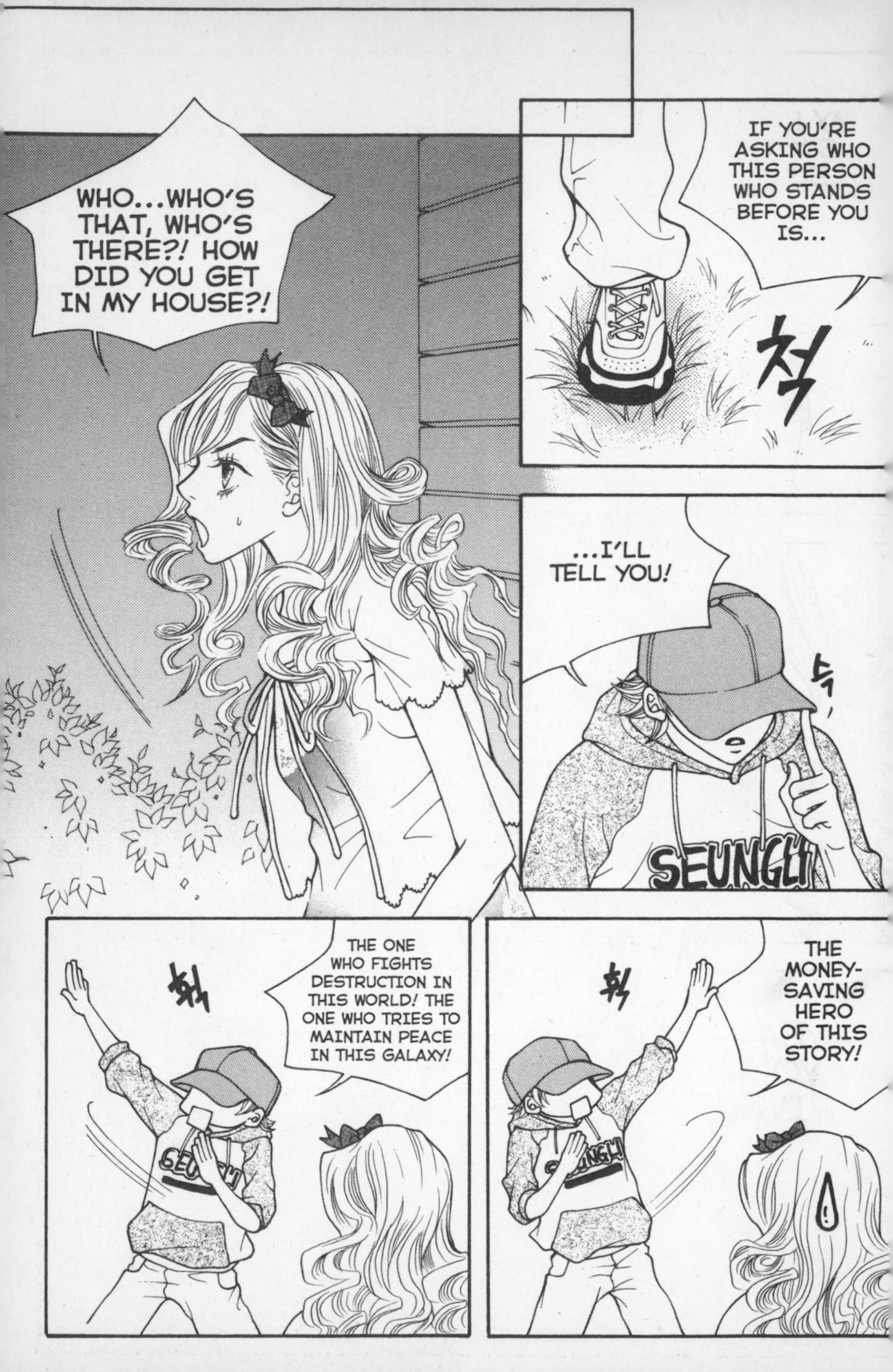
WHO...WHO'S THAT, WHO'S THERE?! HOW DID YOU GET IN MY HOUSE?!
IF YOU'RE ASKING WHO THIS PERSON WHO STANDS BEFORE YOU IS...
척
...I'LL TELL YOU!
SEUNGLI
휙
THE ONE WHO FIGHTS DESTRUCTION IN THIS WORLD! THE ONE WHO TRIES TO MAINTAIN PEACE IN THIS GALAXY!
휙
THE MONEY-SAVING HERO OF THIS STORY!

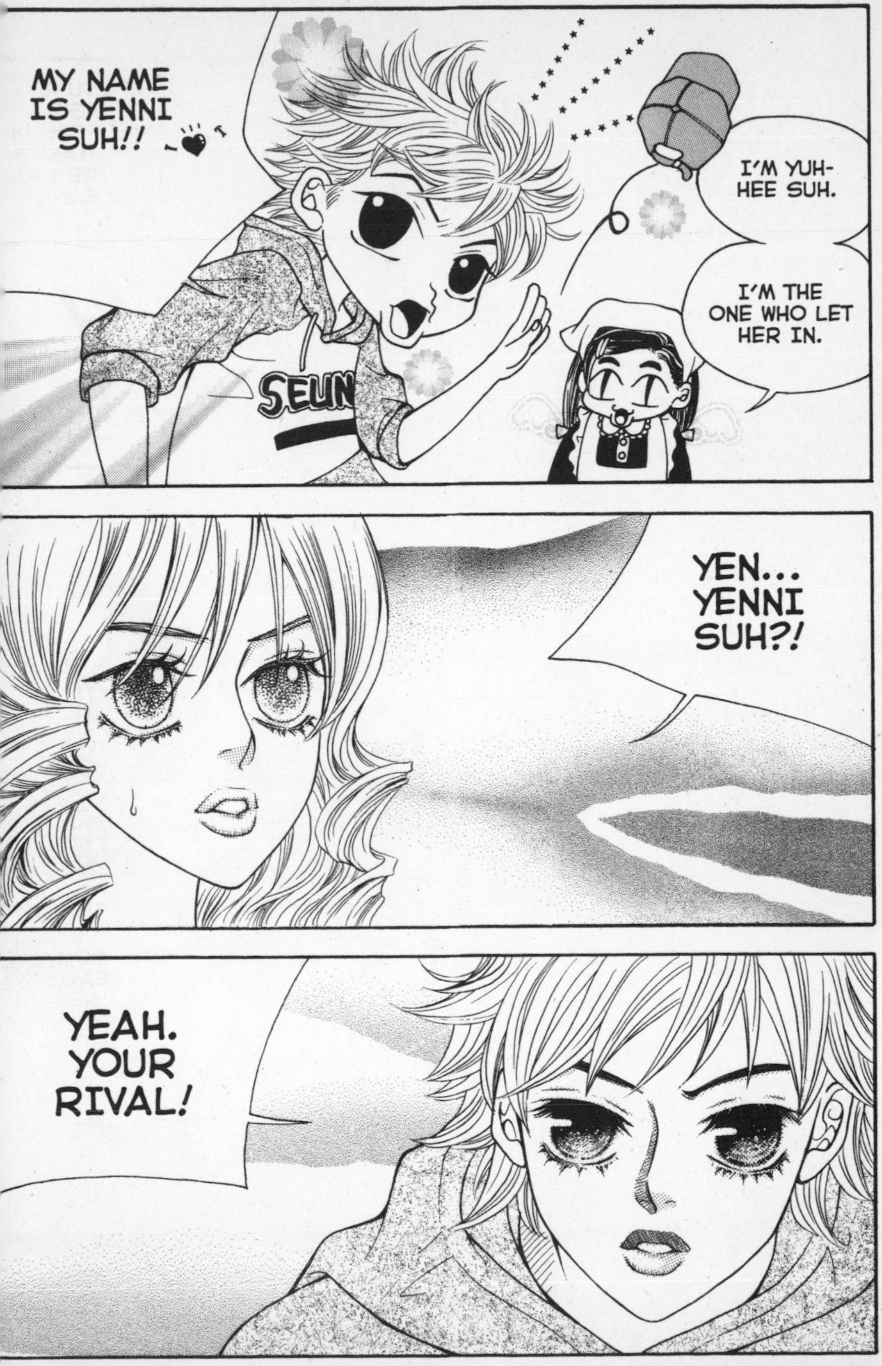
MY NAME IS YENNI SUH!!
I'M YUH-HEE SUH.
I'M THE ONE WHO LET HER IN.
SEUN
YEN... YENNI SUH?!
YEAH. YOUR RIVAL!

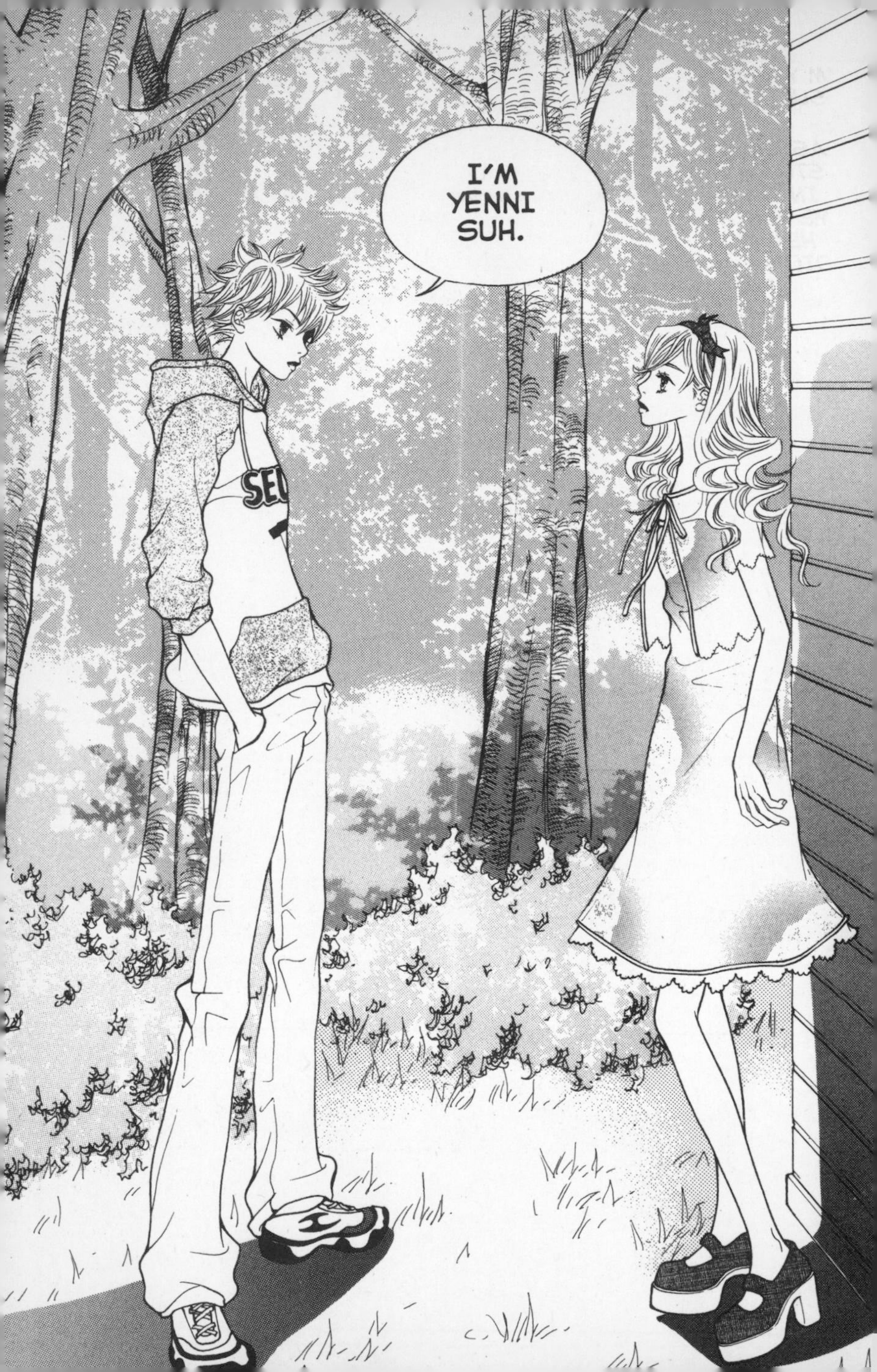
I'M YENNI SUH.
SEOUL

I'M YENNI SUH...

AS THAT GIRL STOOD THERE IN FRONT OF ME TELLING ME HER NAME, I DIDN'T KNOW...

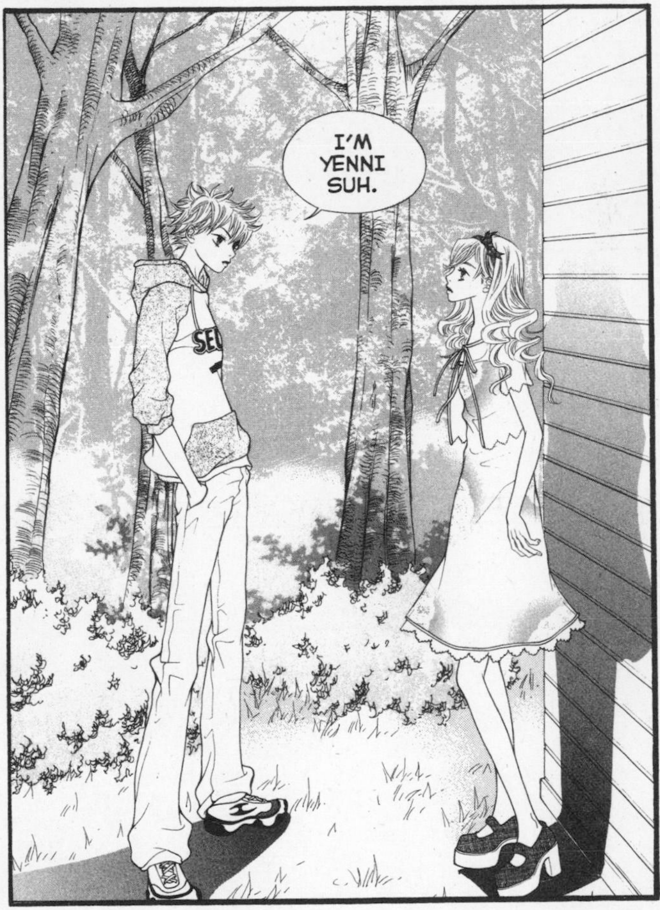
I'M YENNI SUH.

...THIS GIRL WOULD BECOME SUCH A SPECIAL PERSON TO ME.

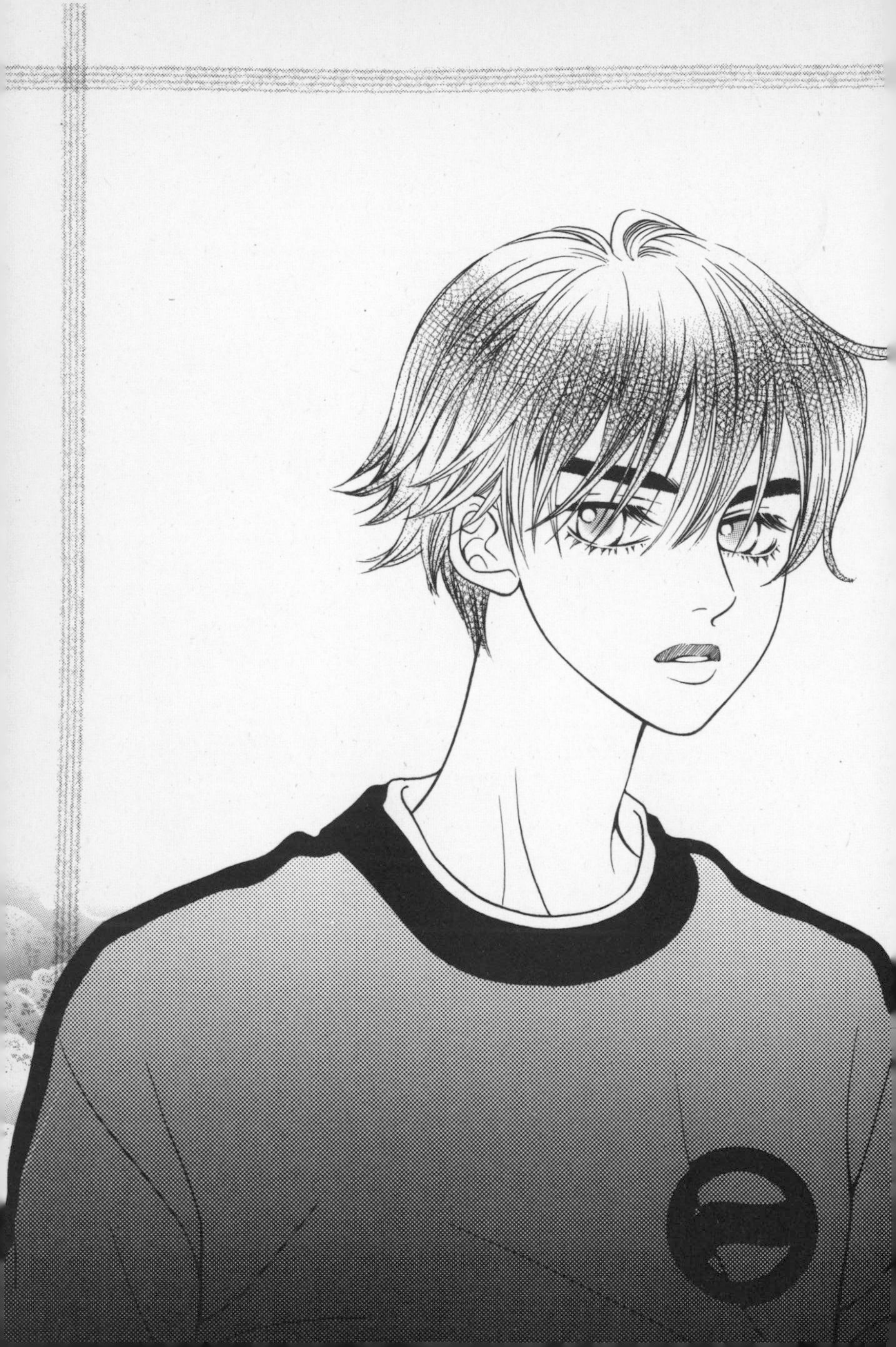

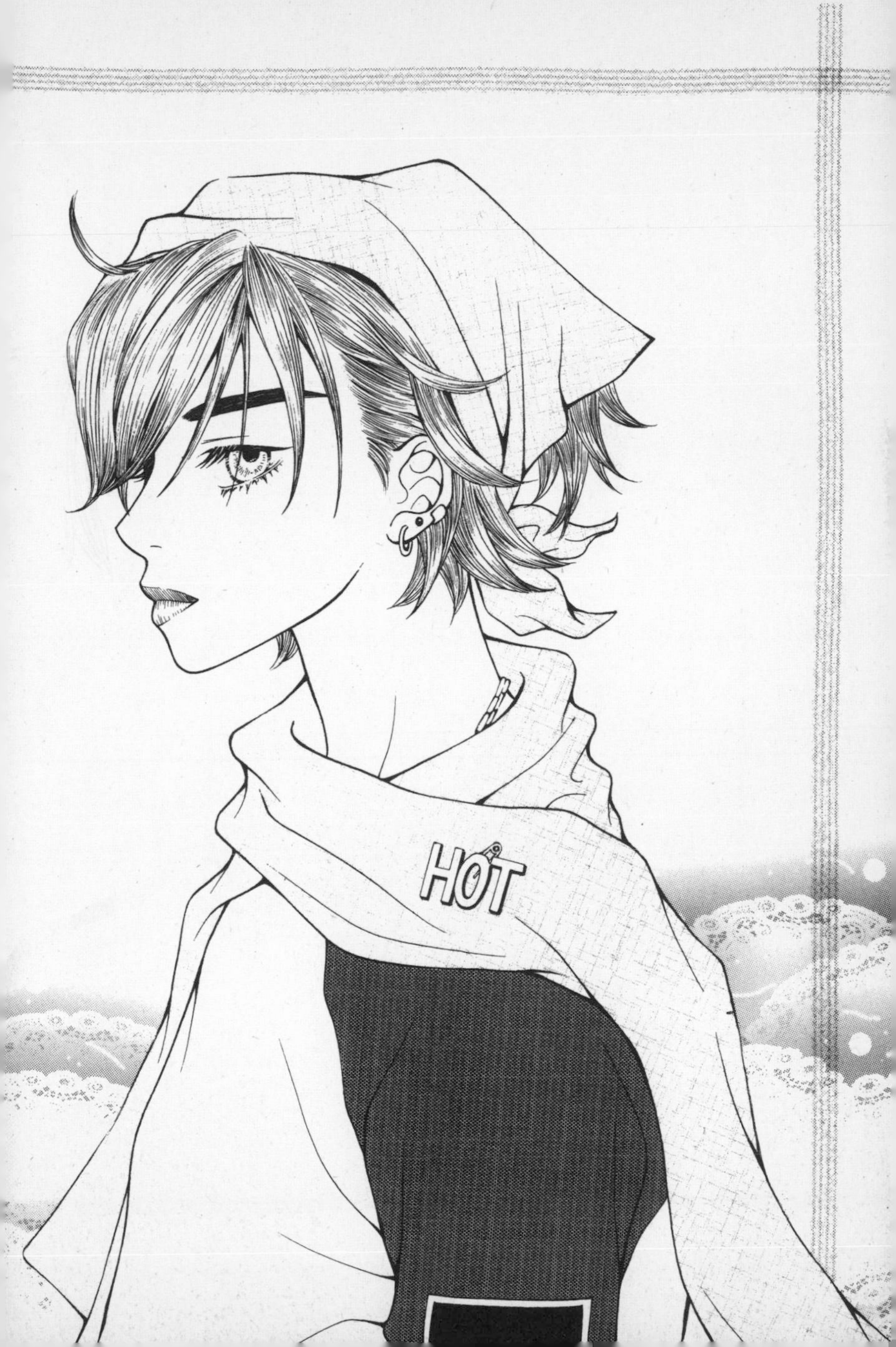
HOT

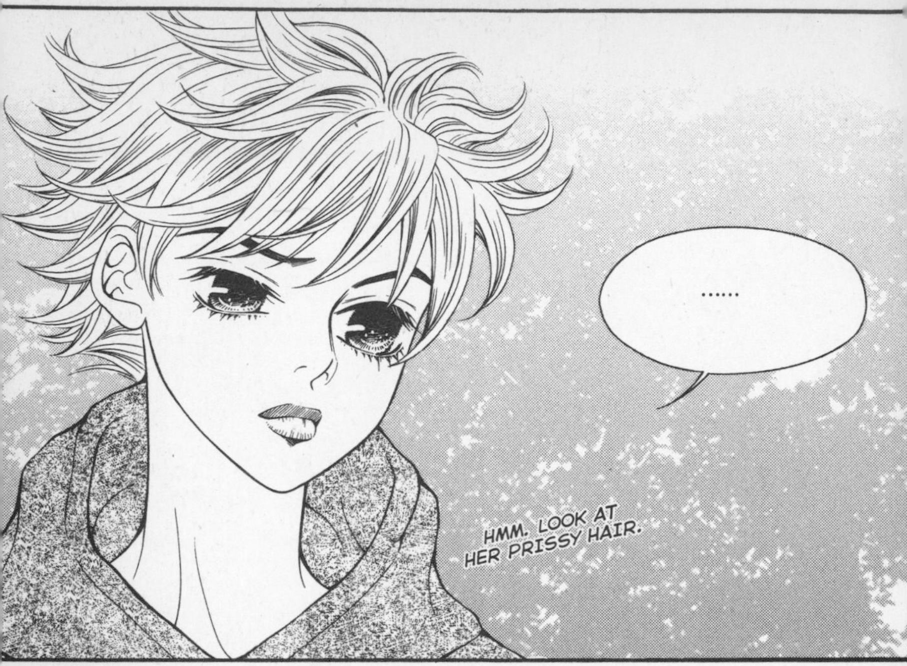
......
HMM. LOOK AT HER PRISSY HAIR.

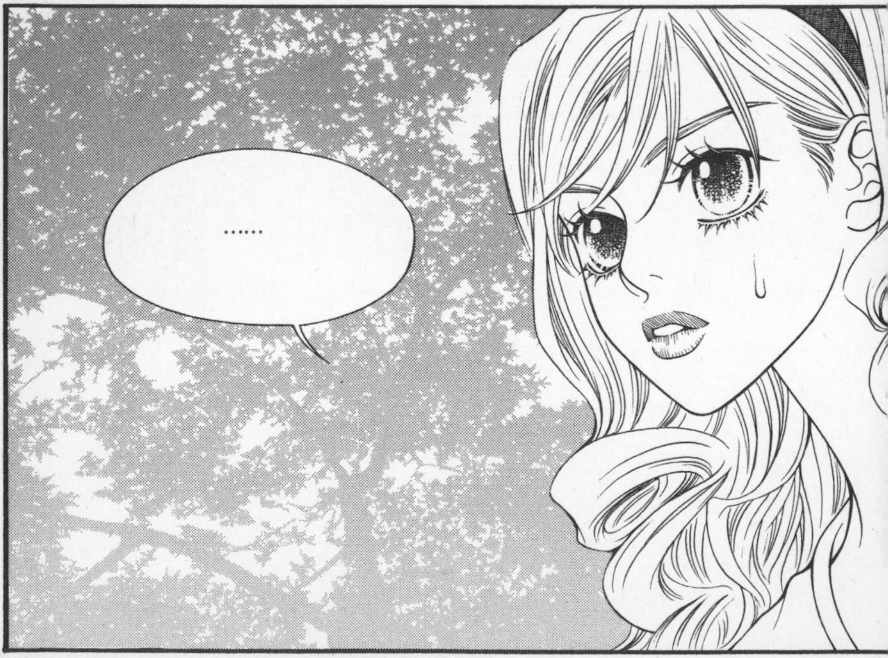
......

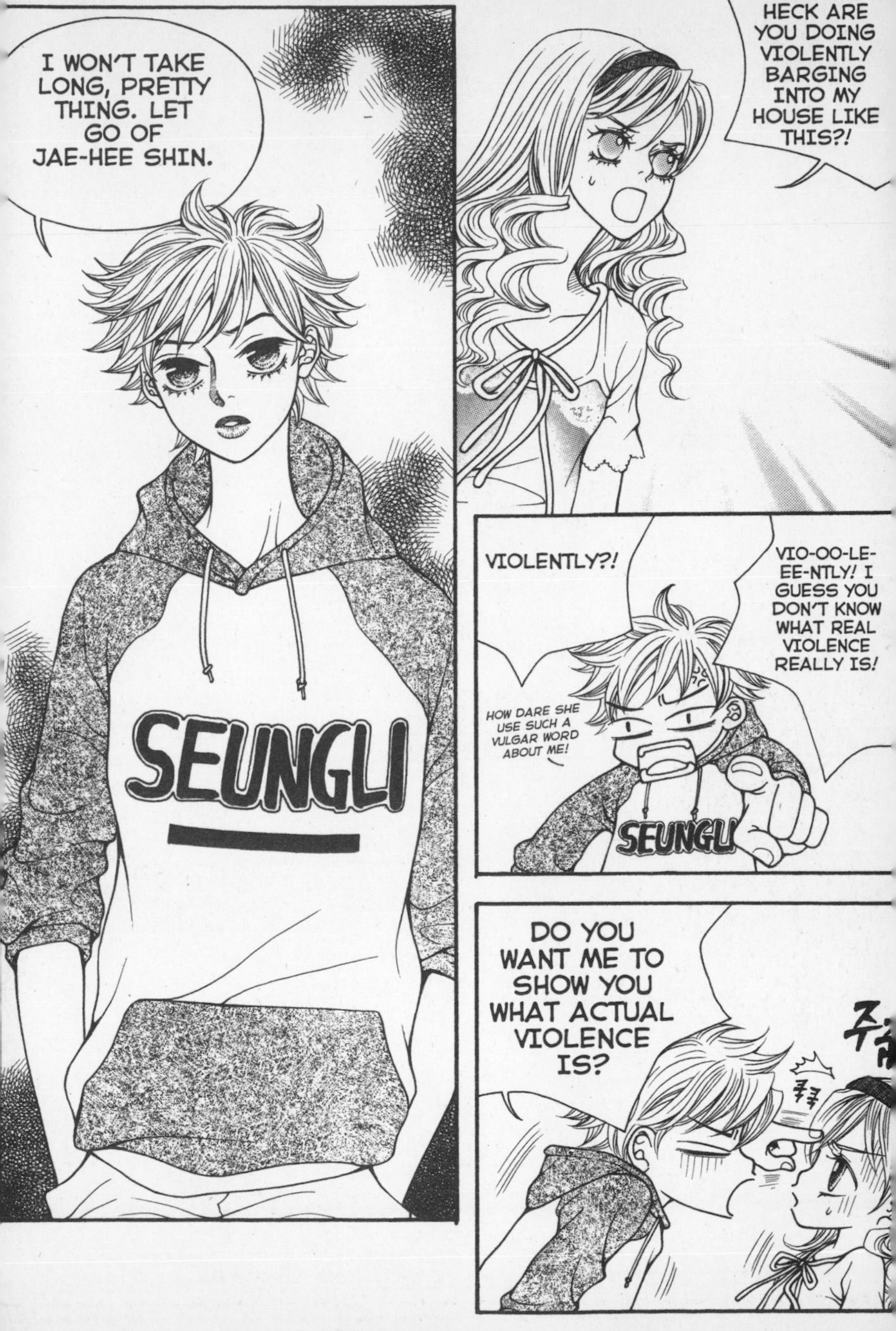
I WON'T TAKE LONG, PRETTY THING. LET GO OF JAE-HEE SHIN.
SEUNGLI
WHAT THE HECK ARE YOU DOING VIOLENTLY BARGING INTO MY HOUSE LIKE THIS?!
VIOLENTLY?!
VIO-OO-LE-EE-NTLY! I GUESS YOU DON'T KNOW WHAT REAL VIOLENCE REALLY IS!
HOW DARE SHE USE SUCH A VULGAR WORD ABOUT ME!
SEUNGLI
DO YOU WANT ME TO SHOW YOU WHAT ACTUAL VIOLENCE IS?

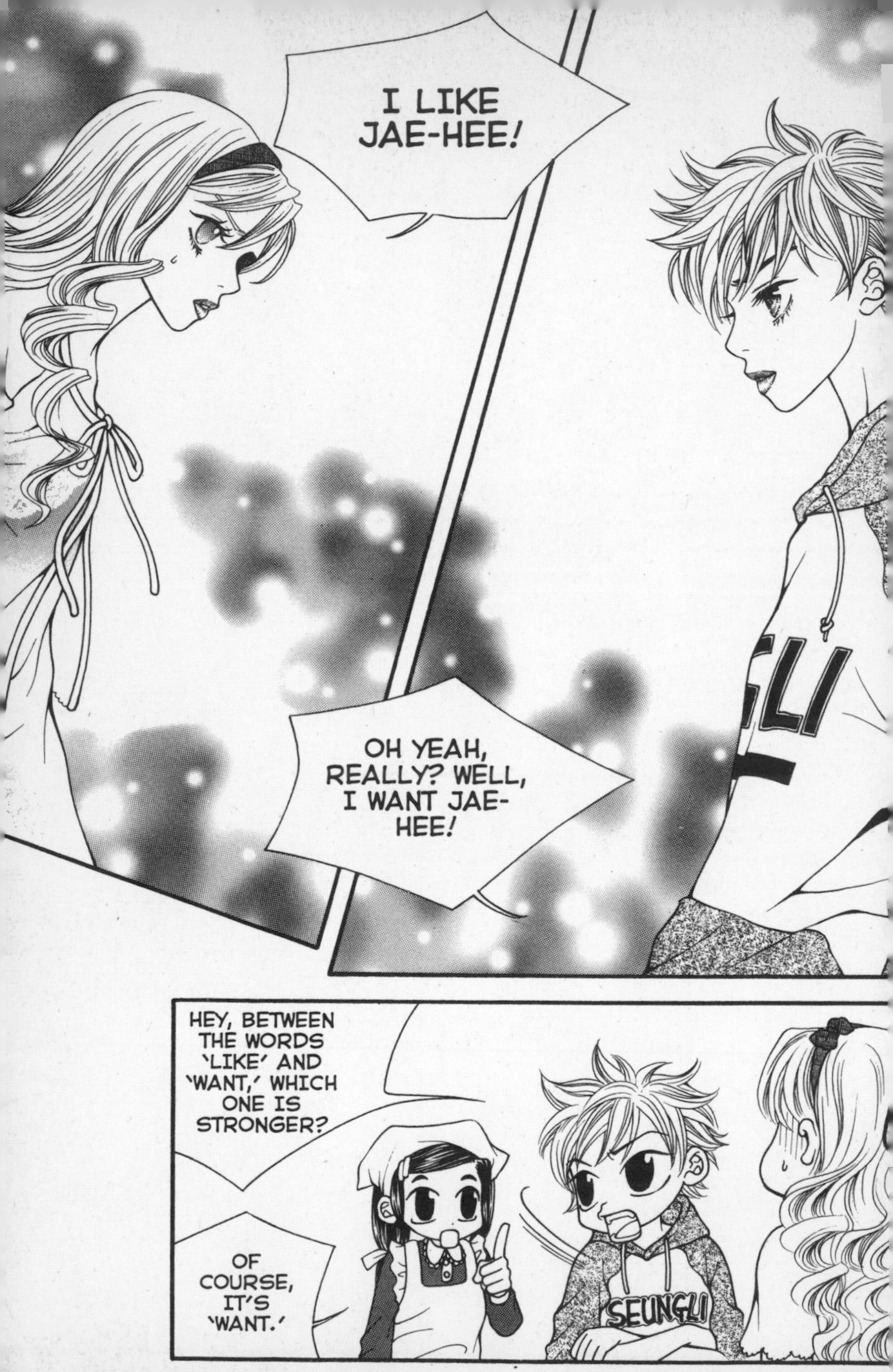
I LIKE JAE-HEE!
OH YEAH, REALLY? WELL, I WANT JAE-HEE!
HEY, BETWEEN THE WORDS 'LIKE' AND 'WANT,' WHICH ONE IS STRONGER?
OF COURSE, IT'S 'WANT.'
SEUNGLI

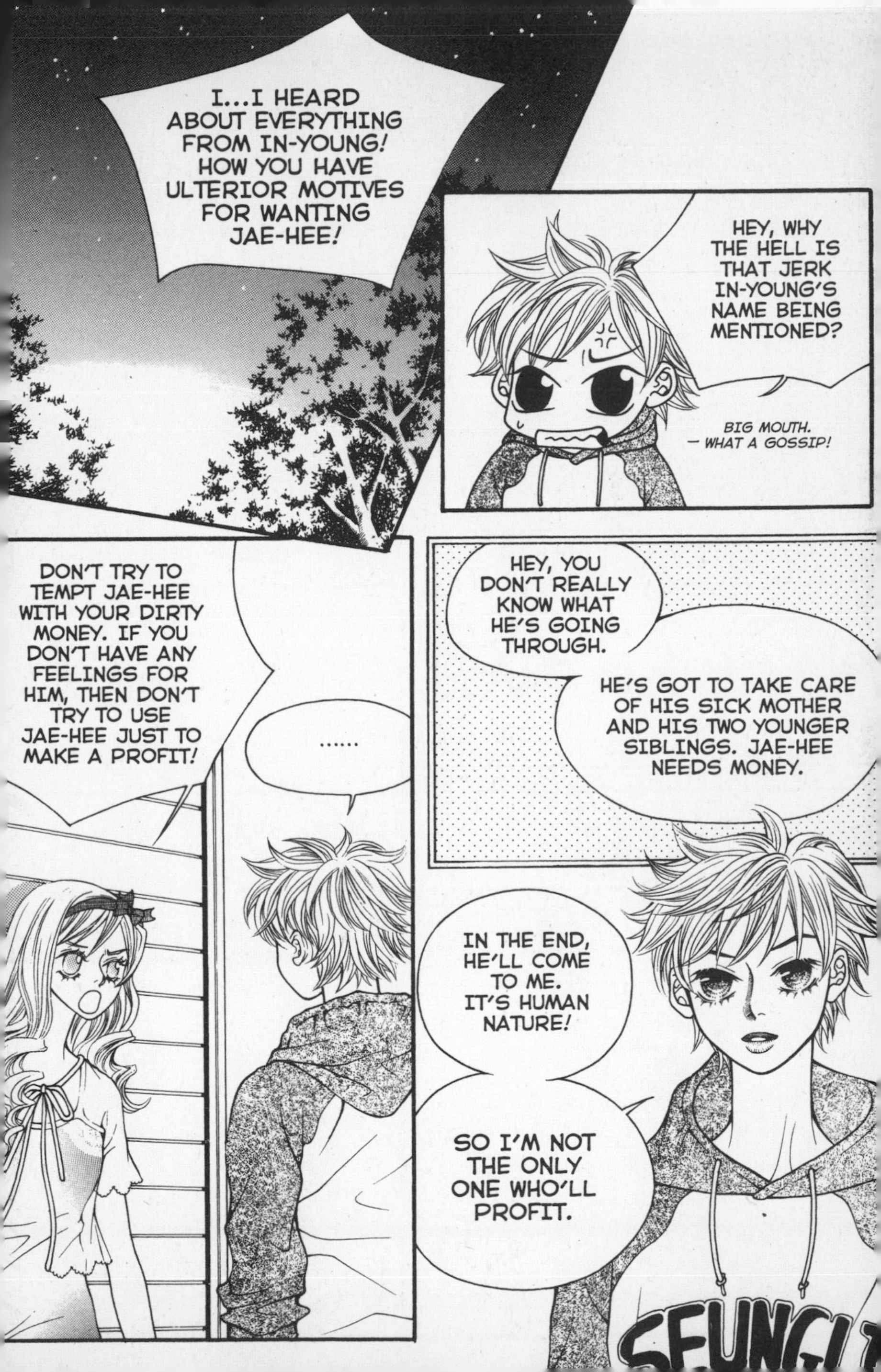
I...I HEARD ABOUT EVERYTHING FROM IN-YOUNG! HOW YOU HAVE ULTERIOR MOTIVES FOR WANTING JAE-HEE!
HEY, WHY THE HELL IS THAT JERK IN-YOUNG'S NAME BEING MENTIONED?
BIG MOUTH. — WHAT A GOSSIP!
DON'T TRY TO TEMPT JAE-HEE WITH YOUR DIRTY MONEY. IF YOU DON'T HAVE ANY FEELINGS FOR HIM, THEN DON'T TRY TO USE JAE-HEE JUST TO MAKE A PROFIT!
......
HEY, YOU DON'T REALLY KNOW WHAT HE'S GOING THROUGH.
HE'S GOT TO TAKE CARE OF HIS SICK MOTHER AND HIS TWO YOUNGER SIBLINGS. JAE-HEE NEEDS MONEY.
IN THE END, HE'LL COME TO ME. IT'S HUMAN NATURE!
SO I'M NOT THE ONLY ONE WHO'LL PROFIT.

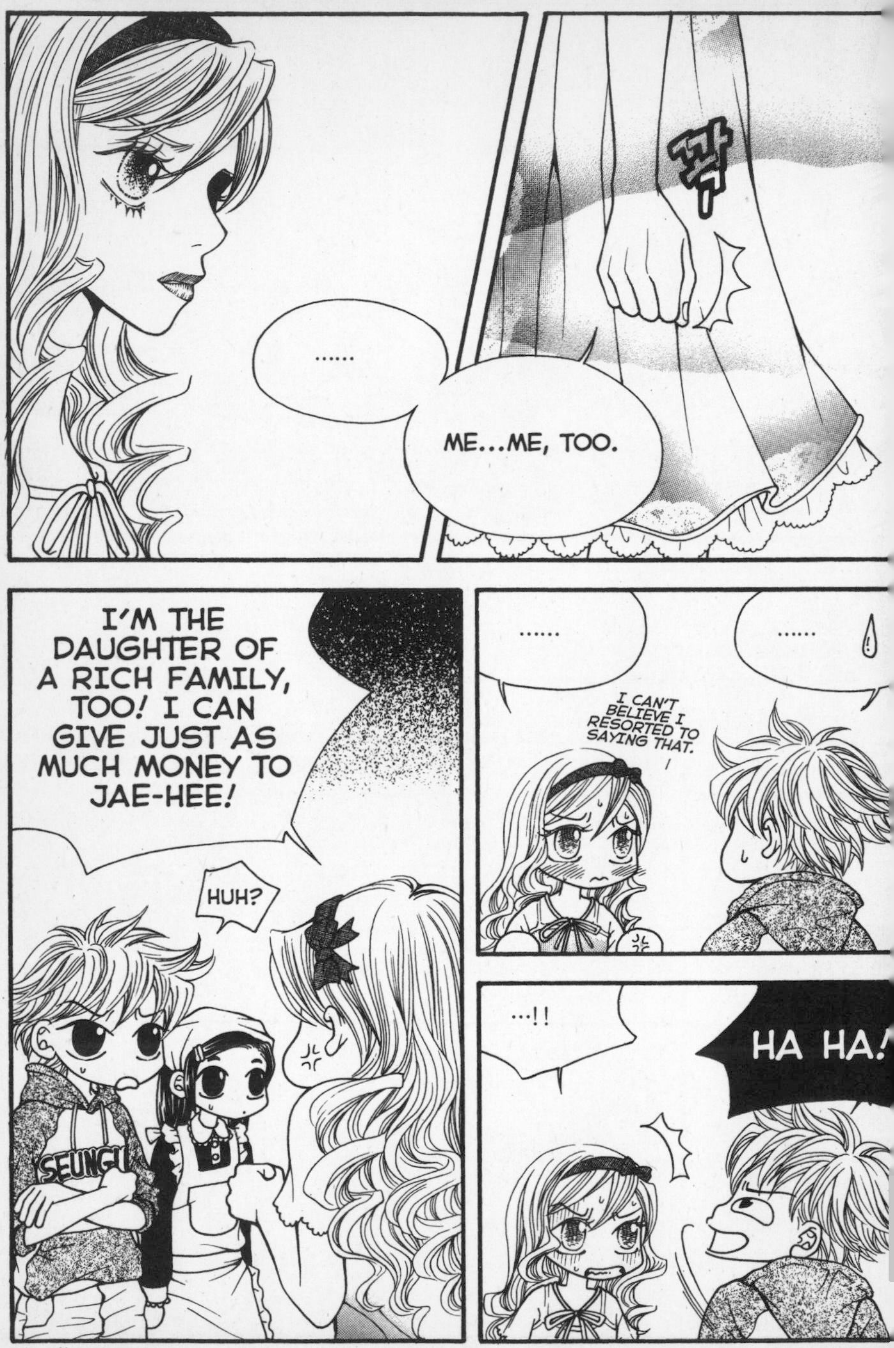
......
꽉
ME...ME, TOO.
I'M THE DAUGHTER OF A RICH FAMILY, TOO! I CAN GIVE JUST AS MUCH MONEY TO JAE-HEE!
HUH?
SEUNGU
......
......
I CAN'T BELIEVE I RESORTED TO SAYING THAT.
...!!
HA HA!

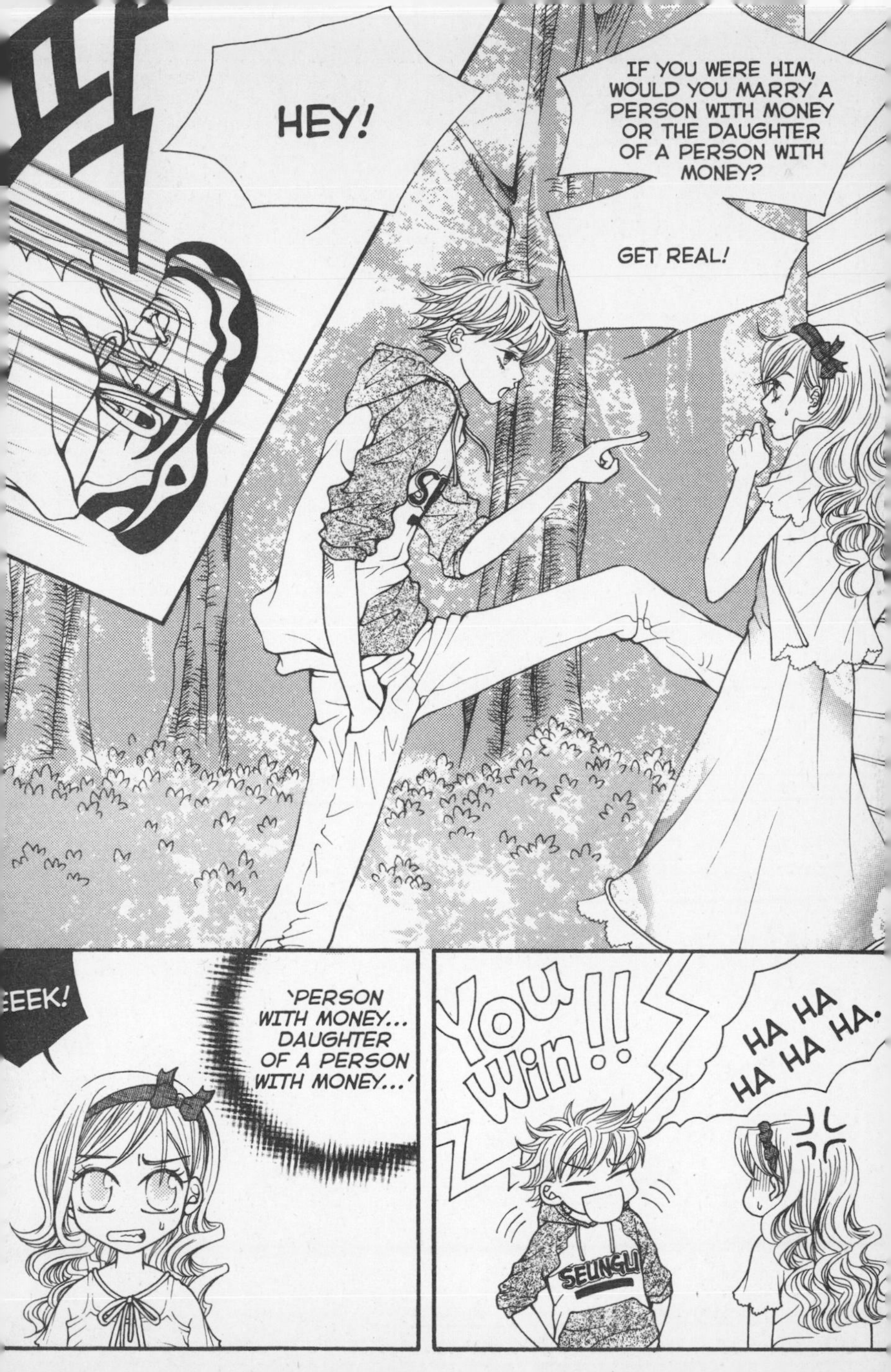
HEY!
IF YOU WERE HIM, WOULD YOU MARRY A PERSON WITH MONEY OR THE DAUGHTER OF A PERSON WITH MONEY?
GET REAL!
EEEK!
'PERSON WITH MONEY... DAUGHTER OF A PERSON WITH MONEY...'
YOU WIN!!
HA HA HA HA HA.
SEUNGLI

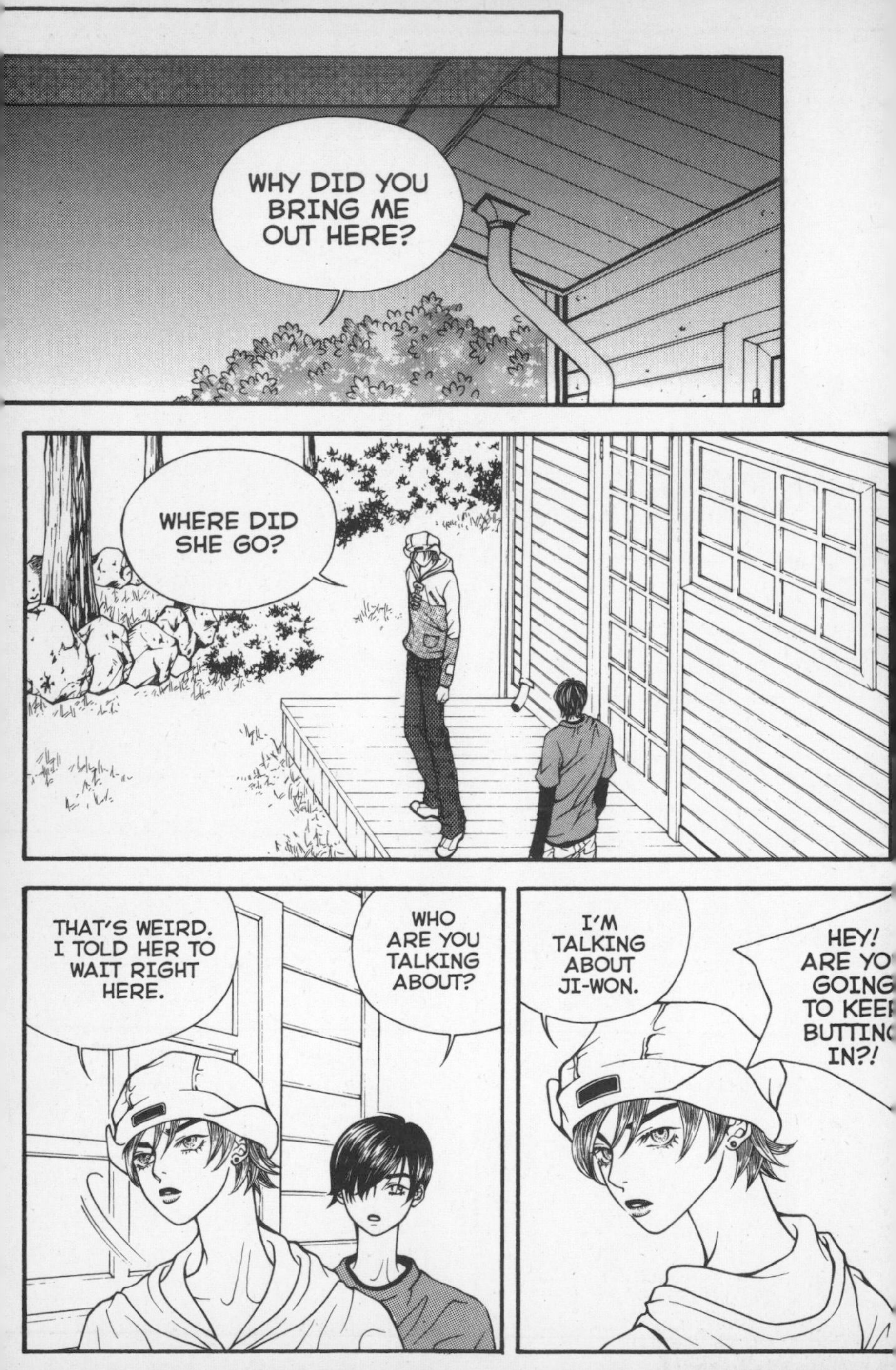
WHY DID YOU BRING ME OUT HERE?
WHERE DID SHE GO?
THAT'S WEIRD. I TOLD HER TO WAIT RIGHT HERE.
WHO ARE YOU TALKING ABOUT?
I'M TALKING ABOUT JI-WON.
HEY! ARE YO GOING TO KEE BUTTIN IN?!

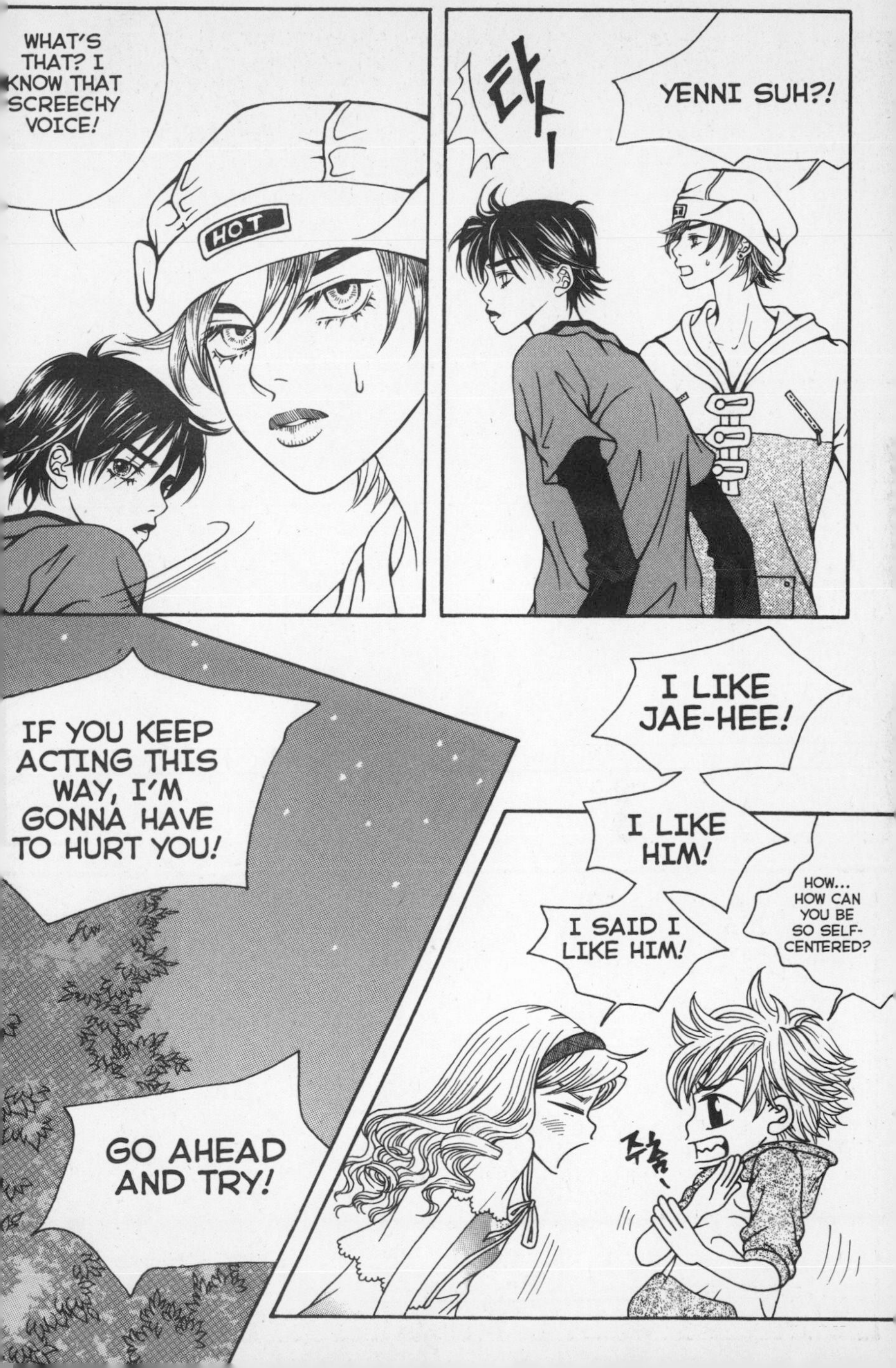
WHAT'S THAT? I KNOW THAT SCREECHY VOICE!
YENNI SUH?!
IF YOU KEEP ACTING THIS WAY, I'M GONNA HAVE TO HURT YOU!
GO AHEAD AND TRY!
I LIKE JAE-HEE!
I LIKE HIM!
I SAID I LIKE HIM!
HOW... HOW CAN YOU BE SO SELF-CENTERED?

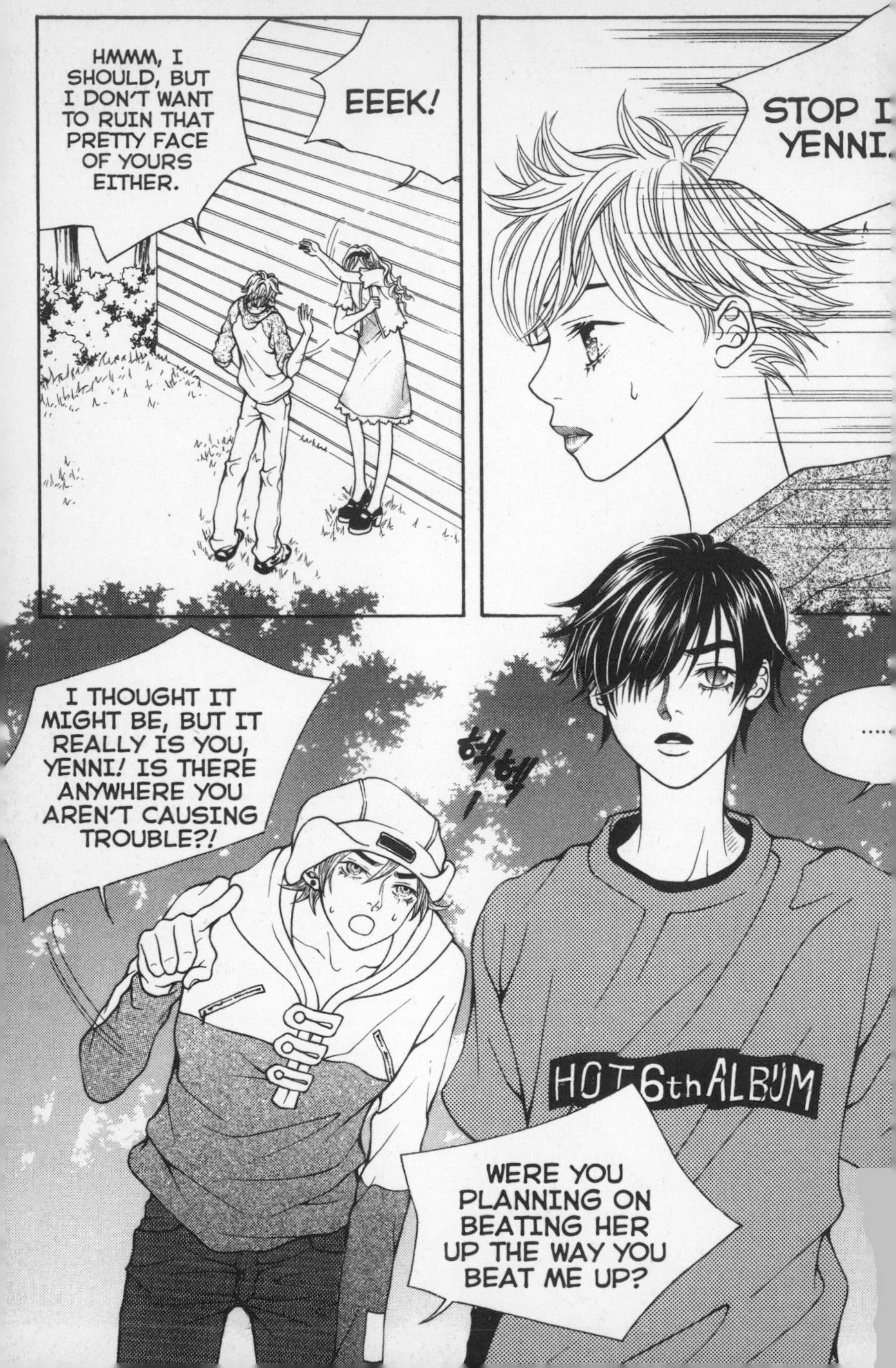
HMMM, I SHOULD, BUT I DON'T WANT TO RUIN THAT PRETTY FACE OF YOURS EITHER.
EEEK!
STOP I
YENNI.
I THOUGHT IT MIGHT BE, BUT IT REALLY IS YOU, YENNI! IS THERE ANYWHERE YOU AREN'T CAUSING TROUBLE?!
헤헤
.....
HOT 6th ALBUM
WERE YOU PLANNING ON BEATING HER UP THE WAY YOU BEAT ME UP?

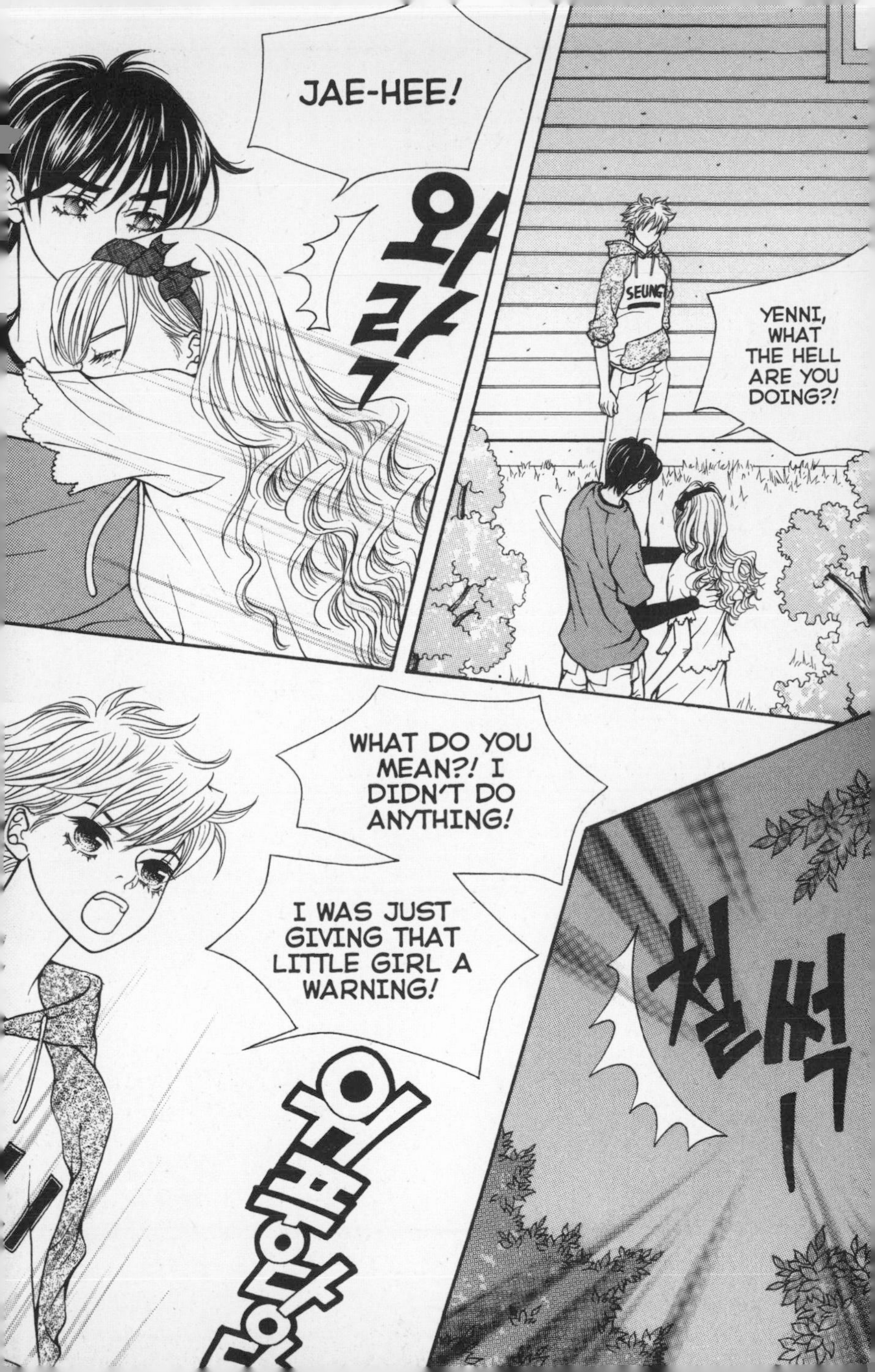
JAE-HEE!
와락
SEUNG
YENNI, WHAT THE HELL ARE YOU DOING?!
WHAT DO YOU MEAN?! I DIDN'T DO ANYTHING!
I WAS JUST GIVING THAT LITTLE GIRL A WARNING!
철썩

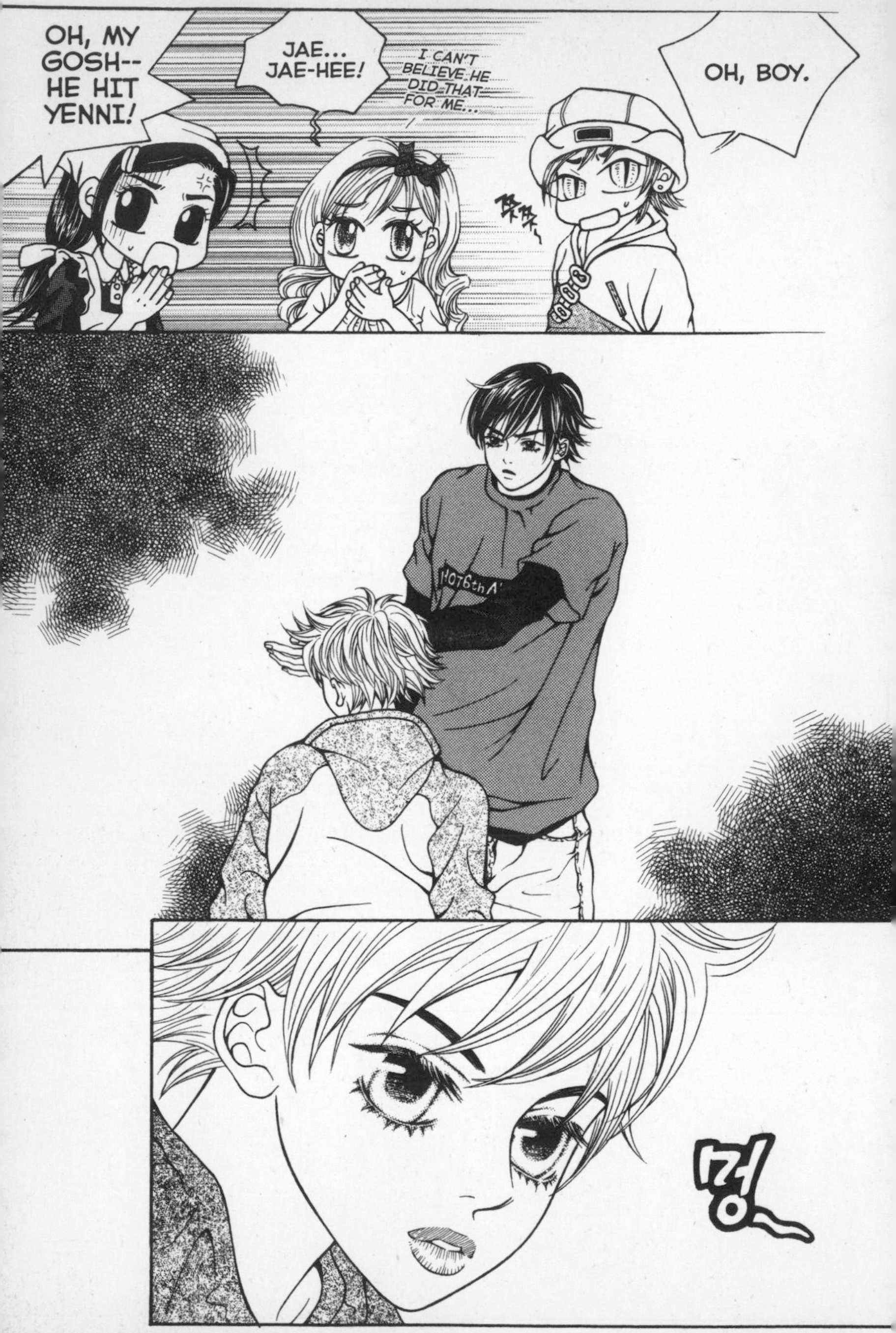
OH, MY GOSH-- HE HIT YENNI!
JAE... JAE-HEE!
I CAN'T BELIEVE HE DID THAT FOR ME...
OH, BOY.
멍~

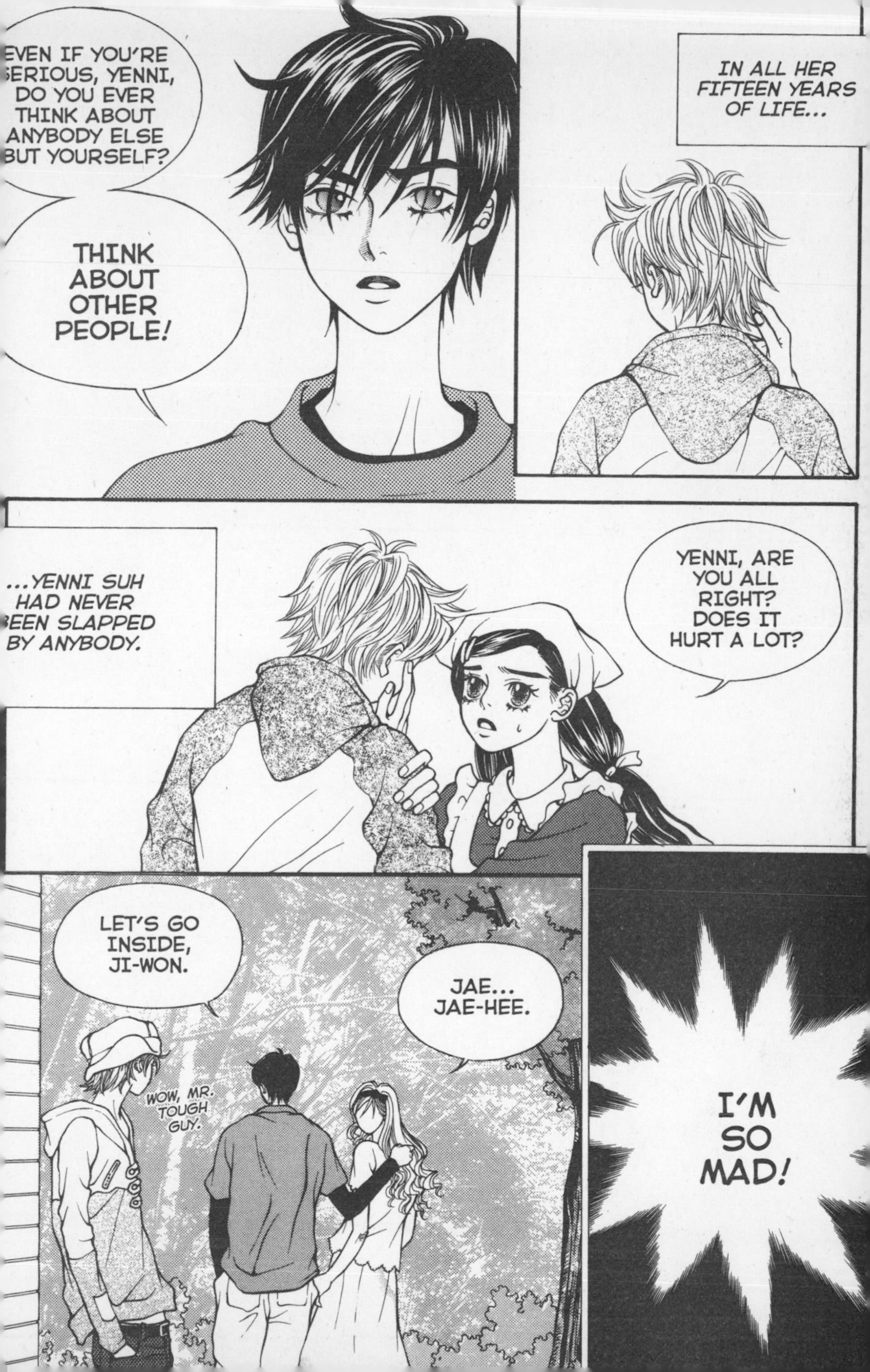
EVEN IF YOU'RE SERIOUS, YENNI, DO YOU EVER THINK ABOUT ANYBODY ELSE BUT YOURSELF?
THINK ABOUT OTHER PEOPLE!
IN ALL HER FIFTEEN YEARS OF LIFE...
...YENNI SUH HAD NEVER BEEN SLAPPED BY ANYBODY.
YENNI, ARE YOU ALL RIGHT? DOES IT HURT A LOT?
LET'S GO INSIDE, JI-WON.
WOW, MR. TOUGH GUY.
JAE... JAE-HEE.
I'M SO MAD!

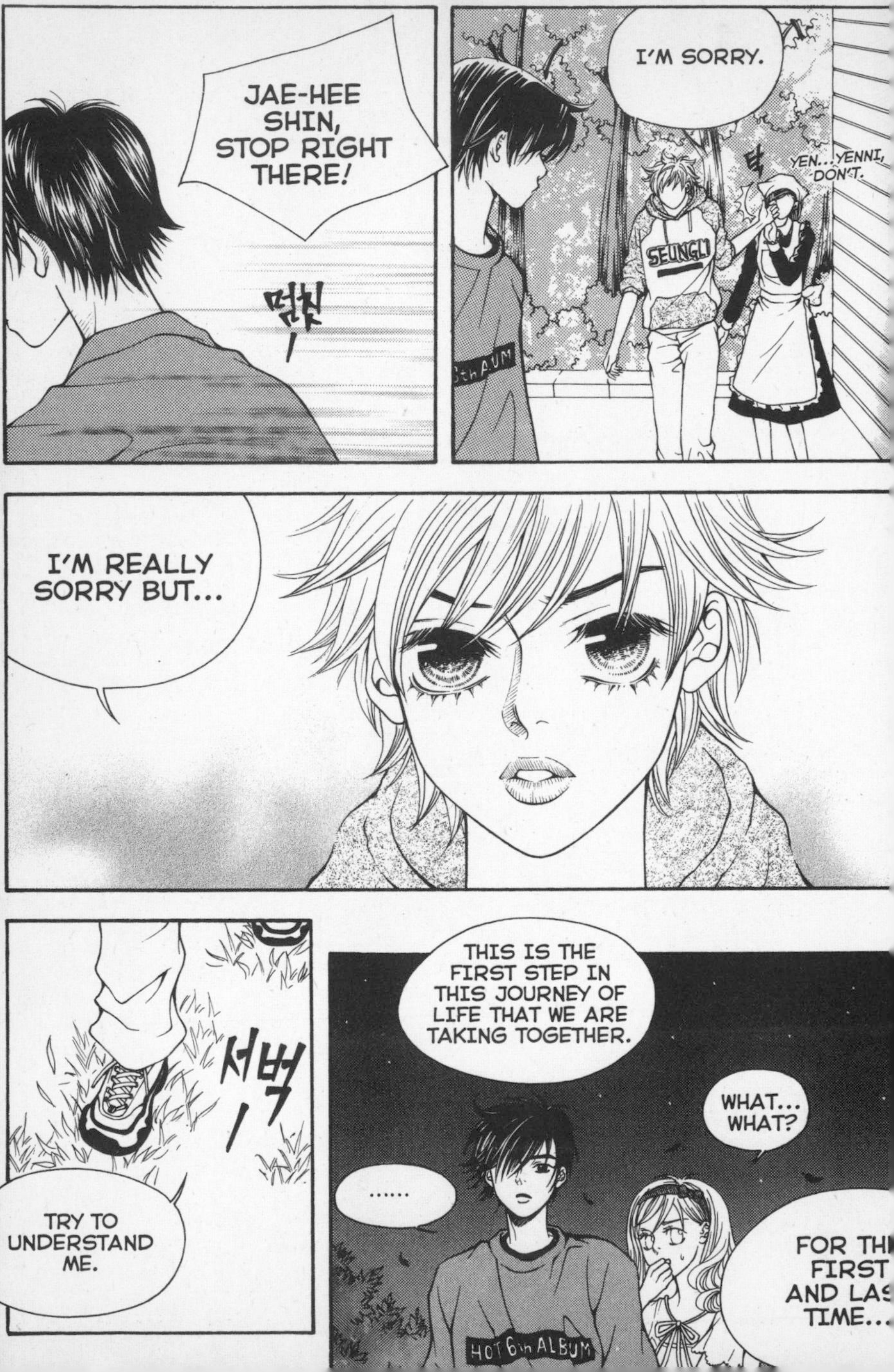
JAE-HEE SHIN, STOP RIGHT THERE!
멈칫
I'M SORRY.
SEUNGLI
탁
YEN... YENNI, DON'T.
I'M REALLY SORRY BUT...
서벅
TRY TO UNDERSTAND ME.
THIS IS THE FIRST STEP IN THIS JOURNEY OF LIFE THAT WE ARE TAKING TOGETHER.
WHAT... WHAT?
......
FOR TH FIRST AND LAS TIME...
HOT 6th ALBUM

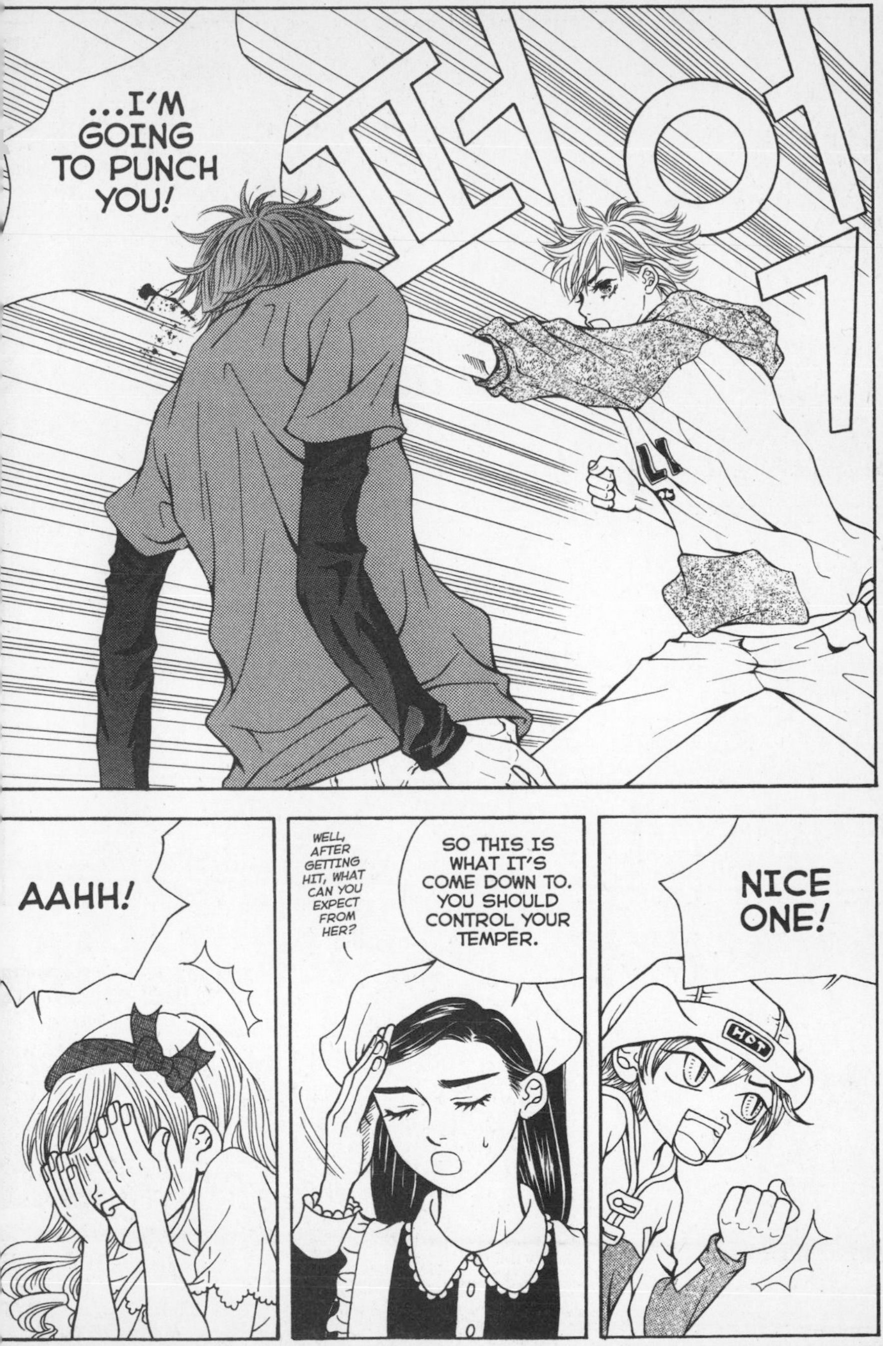
...I'M GOING TO PUNCH YOU!
AAHH!
WELL, AFTER GETTING HIT, WHAT CAN YOU EXPECT FROM HER?
SO THIS IS WHAT IT'S COME DOWN TO. YOU SHOULD CONTROL YOUR TEMPER.
NICE ONE!

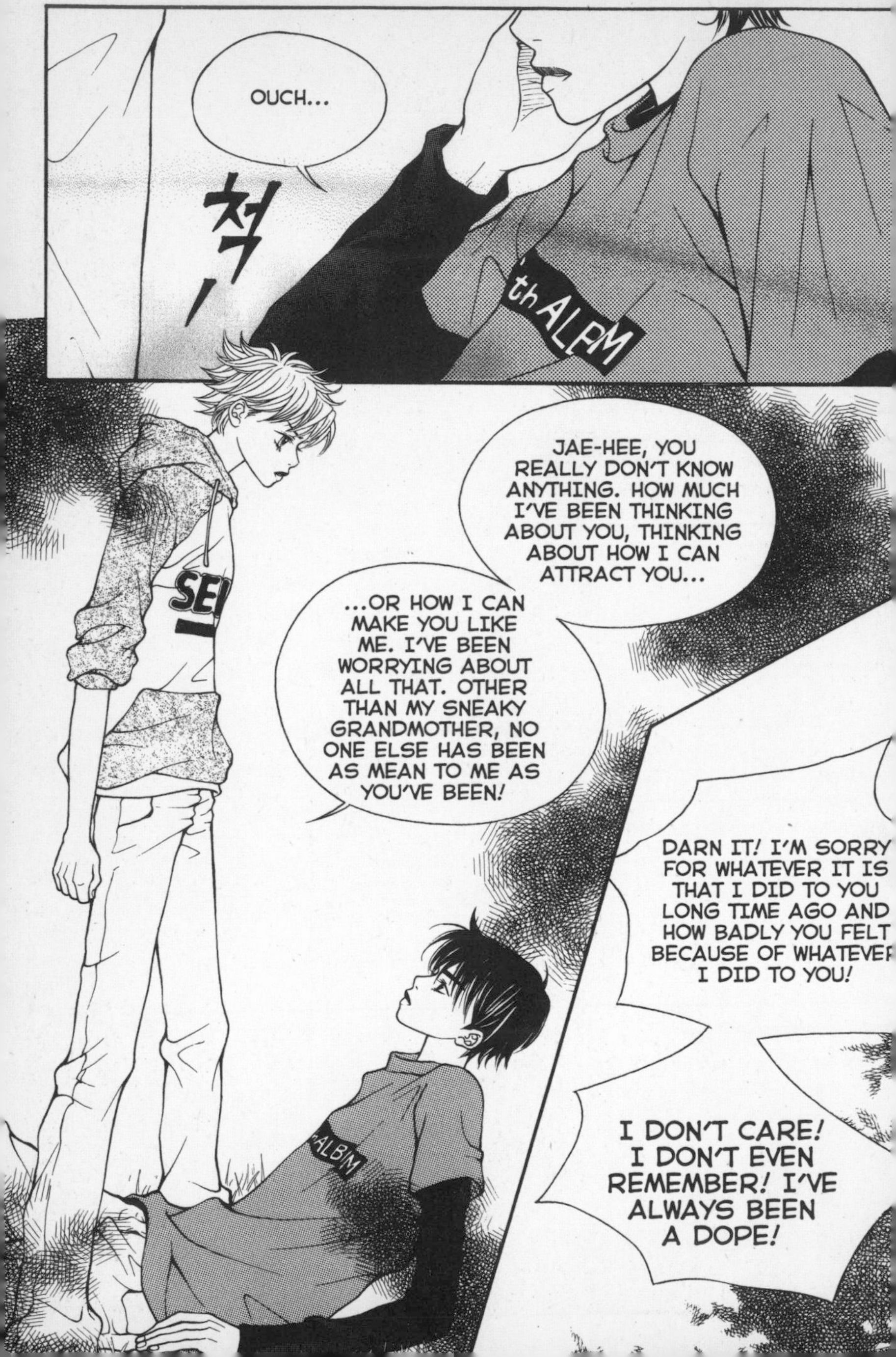
OUCH...
척
JAE-HEE, YOU REALLY DON'T KNOW ANYTHING. HOW MUCH I'VE BEEN THINKING ABOUT YOU, THINKING ABOUT HOW I CAN ATTRACT YOU...
...OR HOW I CAN MAKE YOU LIKE ME. I'VE BEEN WORRYING ABOUT ALL THAT. OTHER THAN MY SNEAKY GRANDMOTHER, NO ONE ELSE HAS BEEN AS MEAN TO ME AS YOU'VE BEEN!
DARN IT! I'M SORRY FOR WHATEVER IT IS THAT I DID TO YOU LONG TIME AGO AND HOW BADLY YOU FELT BECAUSE OF WHATEVER I DID TO YOU!
I DON'T CARE! I DON'T EVEN REMEMBER! I'VE ALWAYS BEEN A DOPE!

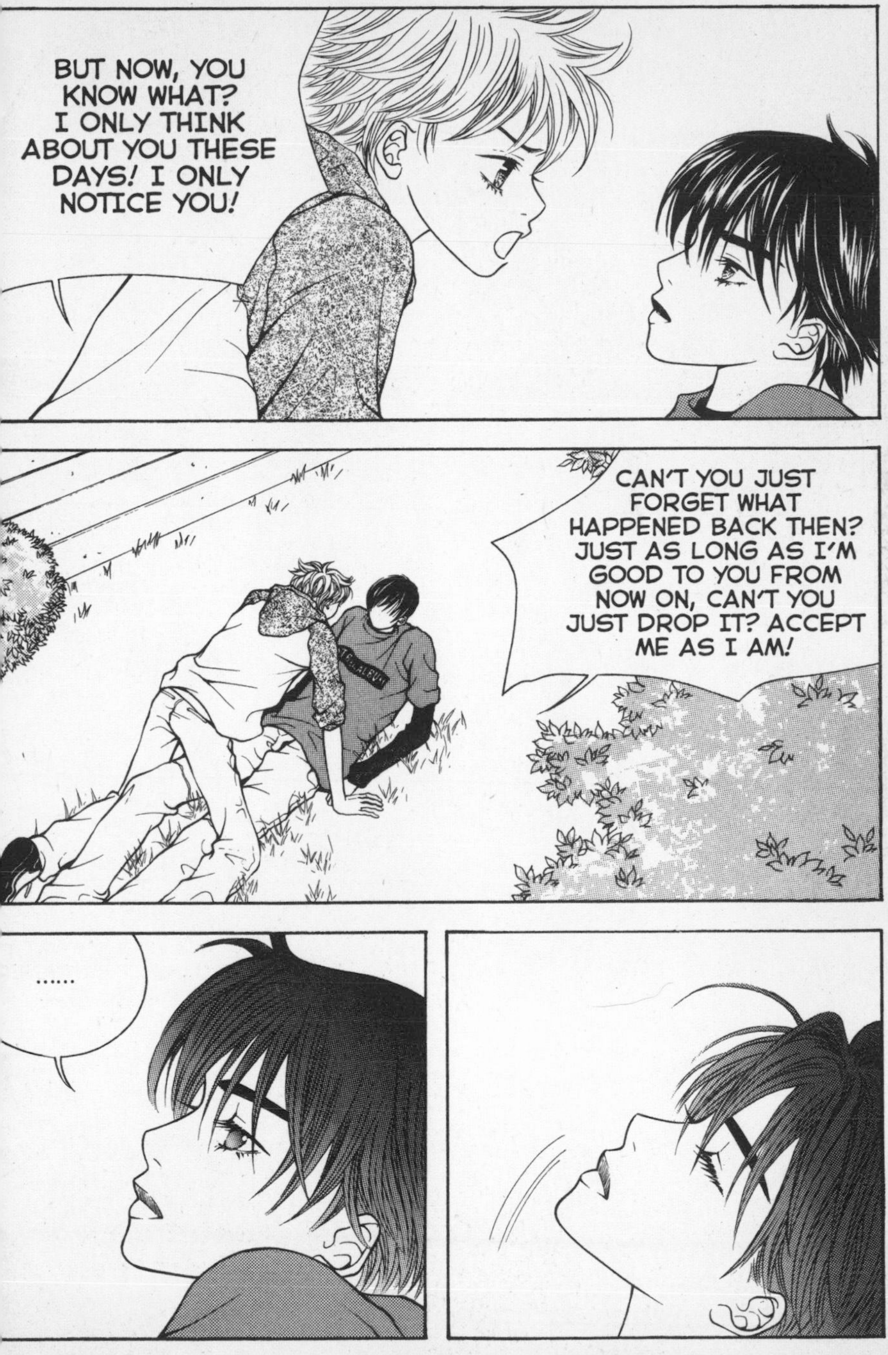
BUT NOW, YOU KNOW WHAT? I ONLY THINK ABOUT YOU THESE DAYS! I ONLY NOTICE YOU!
CAN'T YOU JUST FORGET WHAT HAPPENED BACK THEN? JUST AS LONG AS I'M GOOD TO YOU FROM NOW ON, CAN'T YOU JUST DROP IT? ACCEPT ME AS I AM!
......

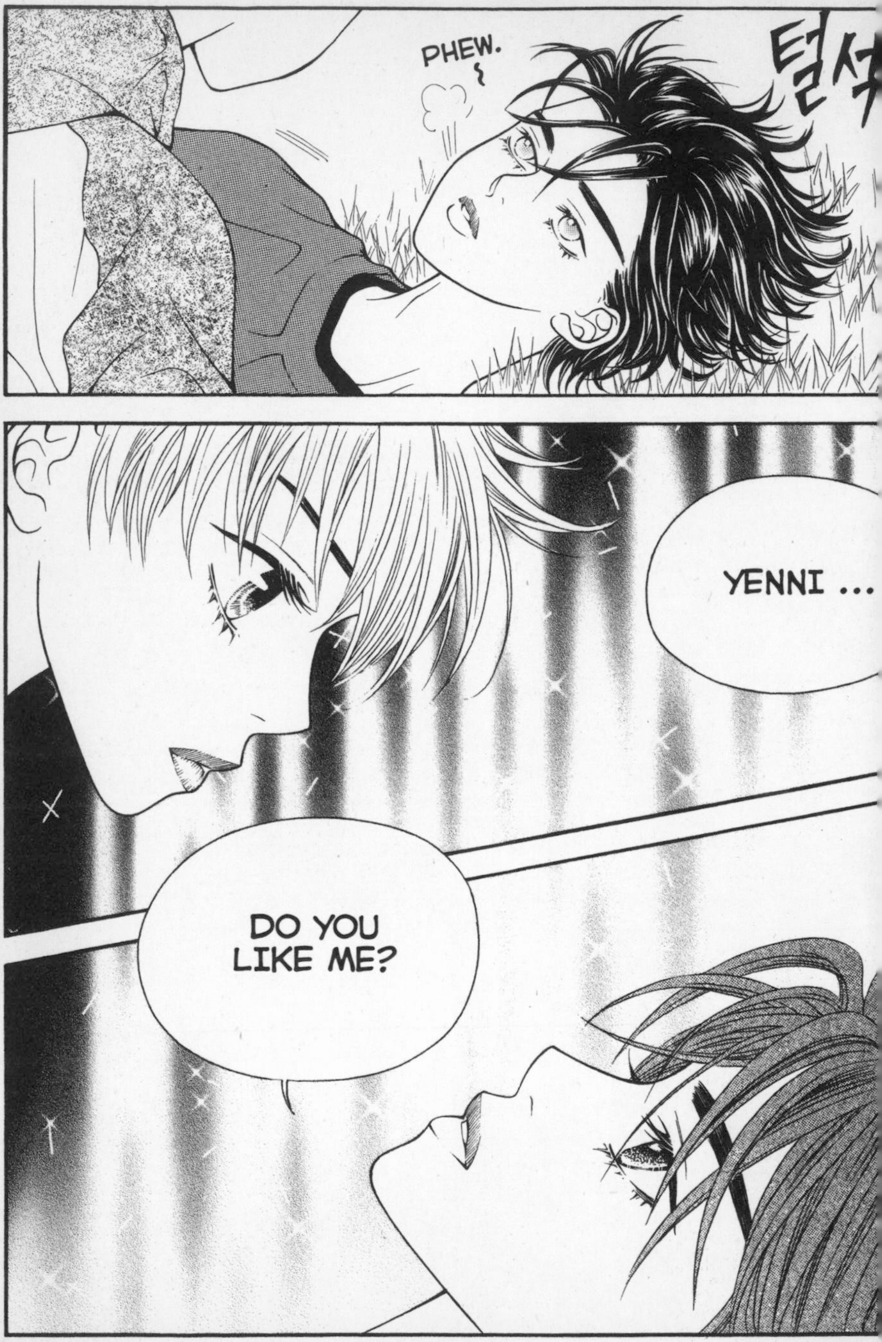
PHEW.
털석
YENNI ...
DO YOU LIKE ME?

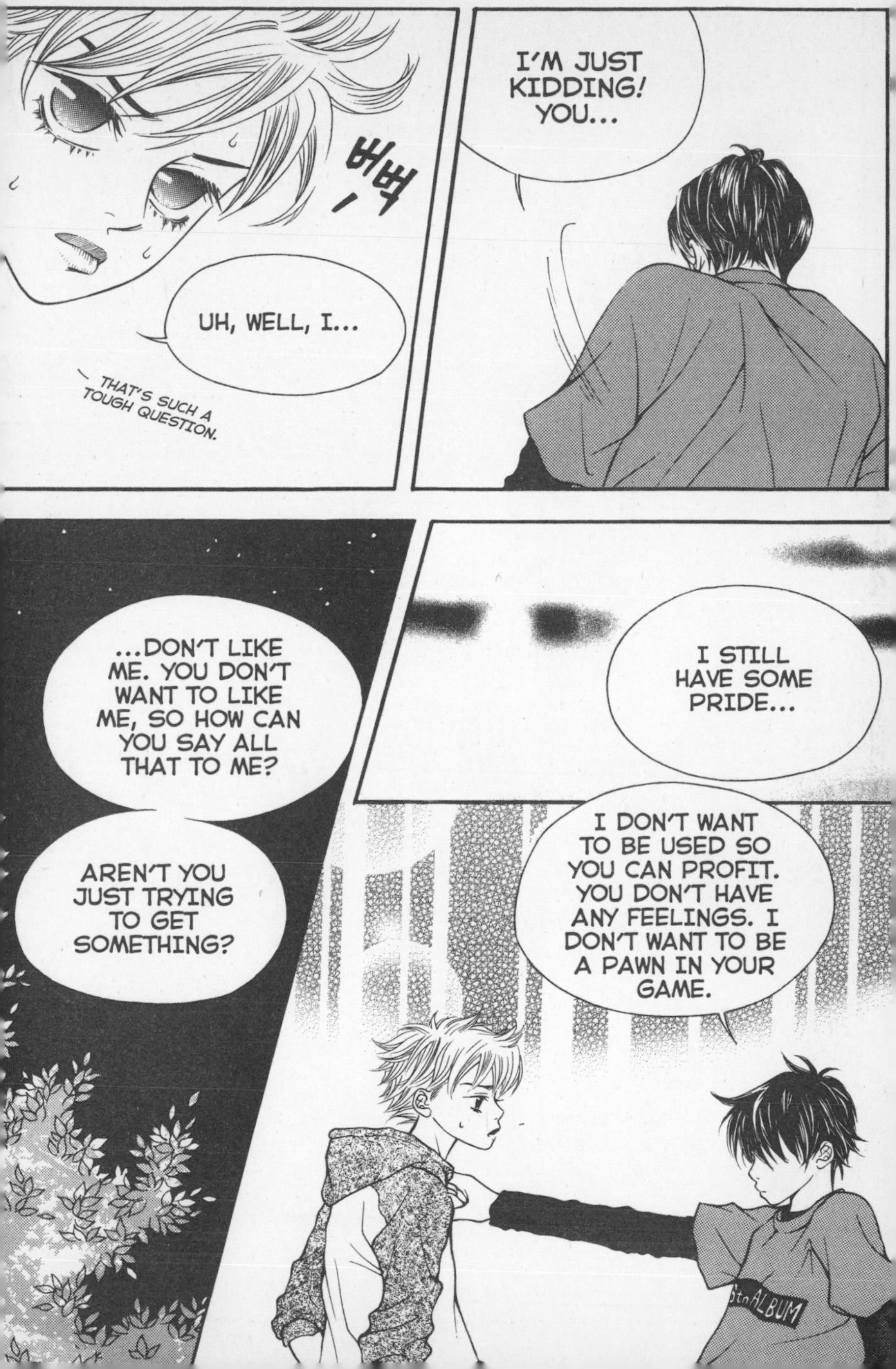
뻐억
UH, WELL, I...
THAT'S SUCH A TOUGH QUESTION.
I'M JUST KIDDING! YOU...
...DON'T LIKE ME. YOU DON'T WANT TO LIKE ME, SO HOW CAN YOU SAY ALL THAT TO ME?
AREN'T YOU JUST TRYING TO GET SOMETHING?
I STILL HAVE SOME PRIDE...
I DON'T WANT TO BE USED SO YOU CAN PROFIT. YOU DON'T HAVE ANY FEELINGS. I DON'T WANT TO BE A PAWN IN YOUR GAME.
5th ALBUM

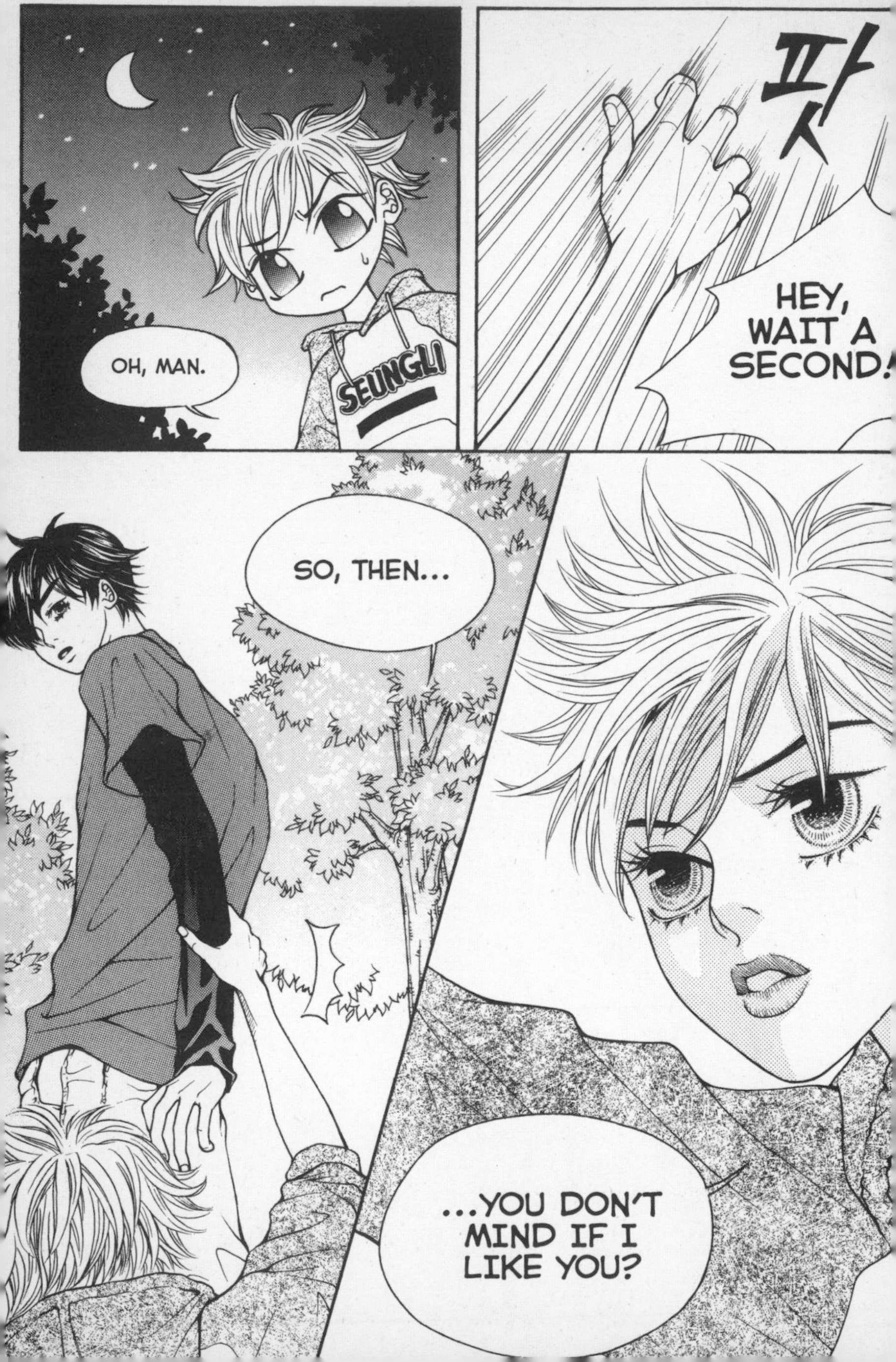
OH, MAN.
파삭
HEY, WAIT A SECOND!
SO, THEN...
...YOU DON'T MIND IF I LIKE YOU?

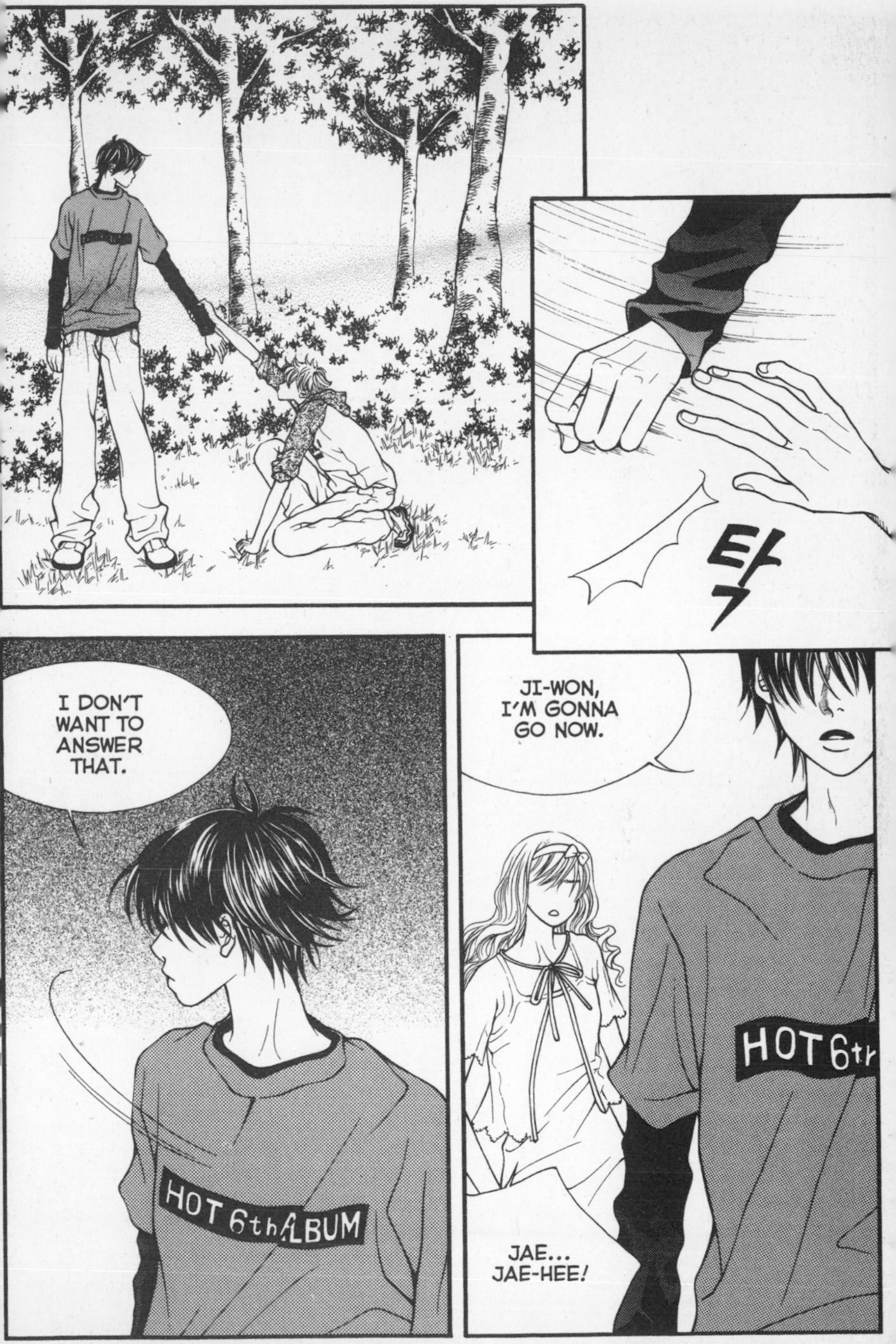
타
I DON'T WANT TO ANSWER THAT.
HOT 6th ALBUM
JI-WON, I'M GONNA GO NOW.
HOT 6th
JAE... JAE-HEE!

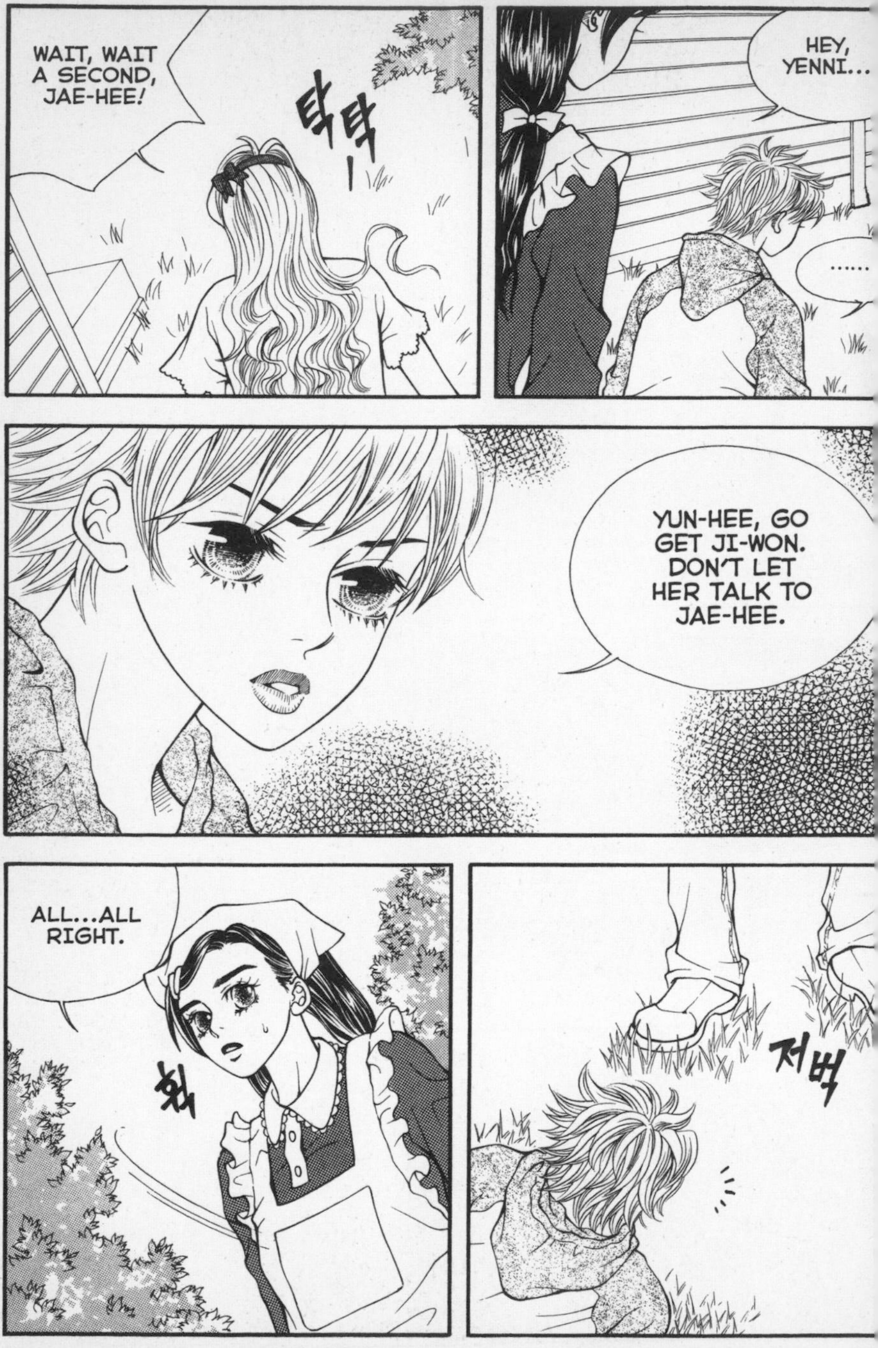
WAIT, WAIT A SECOND, JAE-HEE!
탁탁
HEY, YENNI...
......
YUN-HEE, GO GET JI-WON. DON'T LET HER TALK TO JAE-HEE.
ALL...ALL RIGHT.
휙
저벅

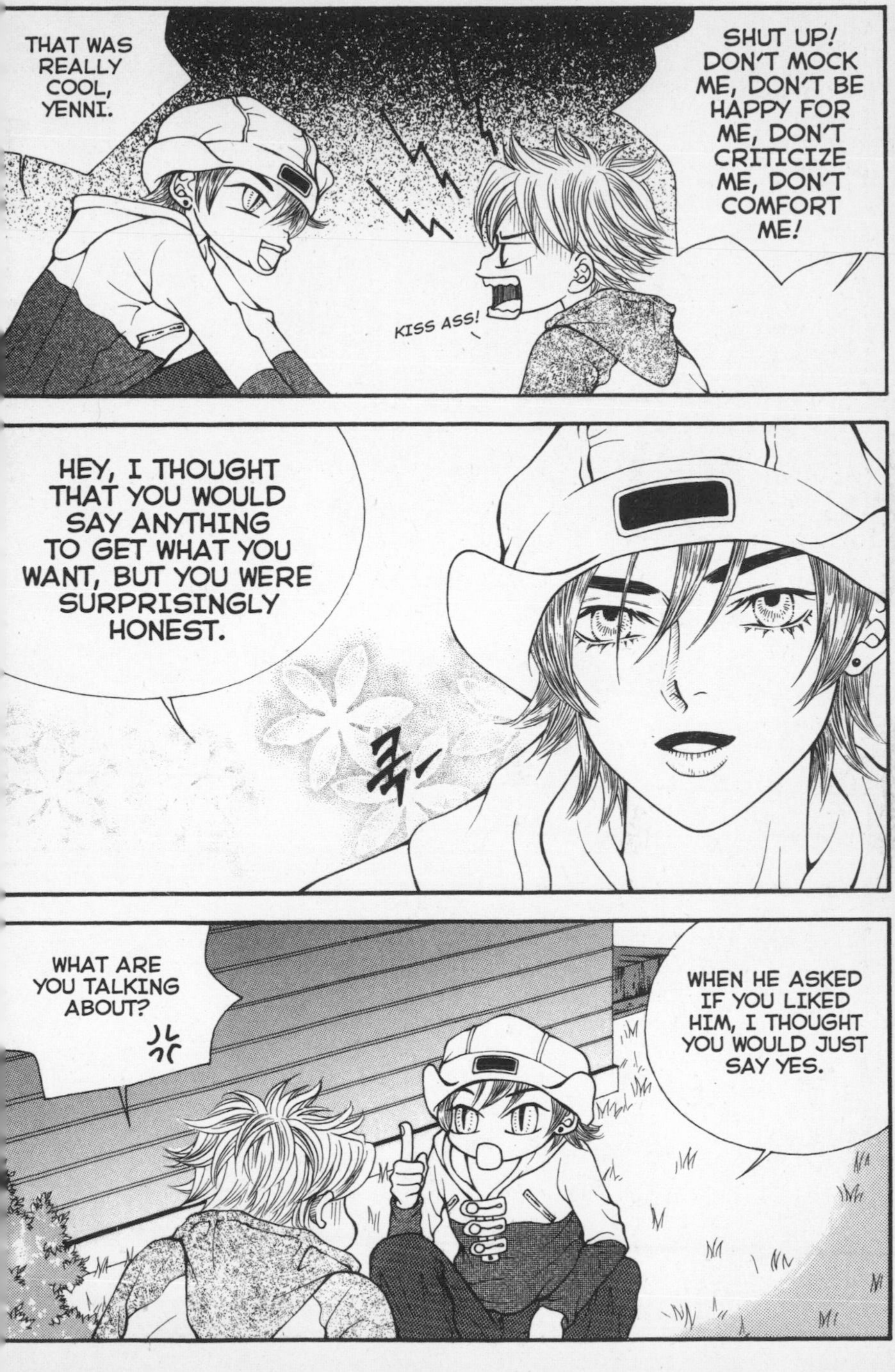
THAT WAS REALLY COOL, YENNI.
SHUT UP! DON'T MOCK ME, DON'T BE HAPPY FOR ME, DON'T CRITICIZE ME, DON'T COMFORT ME!
KISS ASS!
HEY, I THOUGHT THAT YOU WOULD SAY ANYTHING TO GET WHAT YOU WANT, BUT YOU WERE SURPRISINGLY HONEST.
ㅋㅋ
WHAT ARE YOU TALKING ABOUT?
WHEN HE ASKED IF YOU LIKED HIM, I THOUGHT YOU WOULD JUST SAY YES.

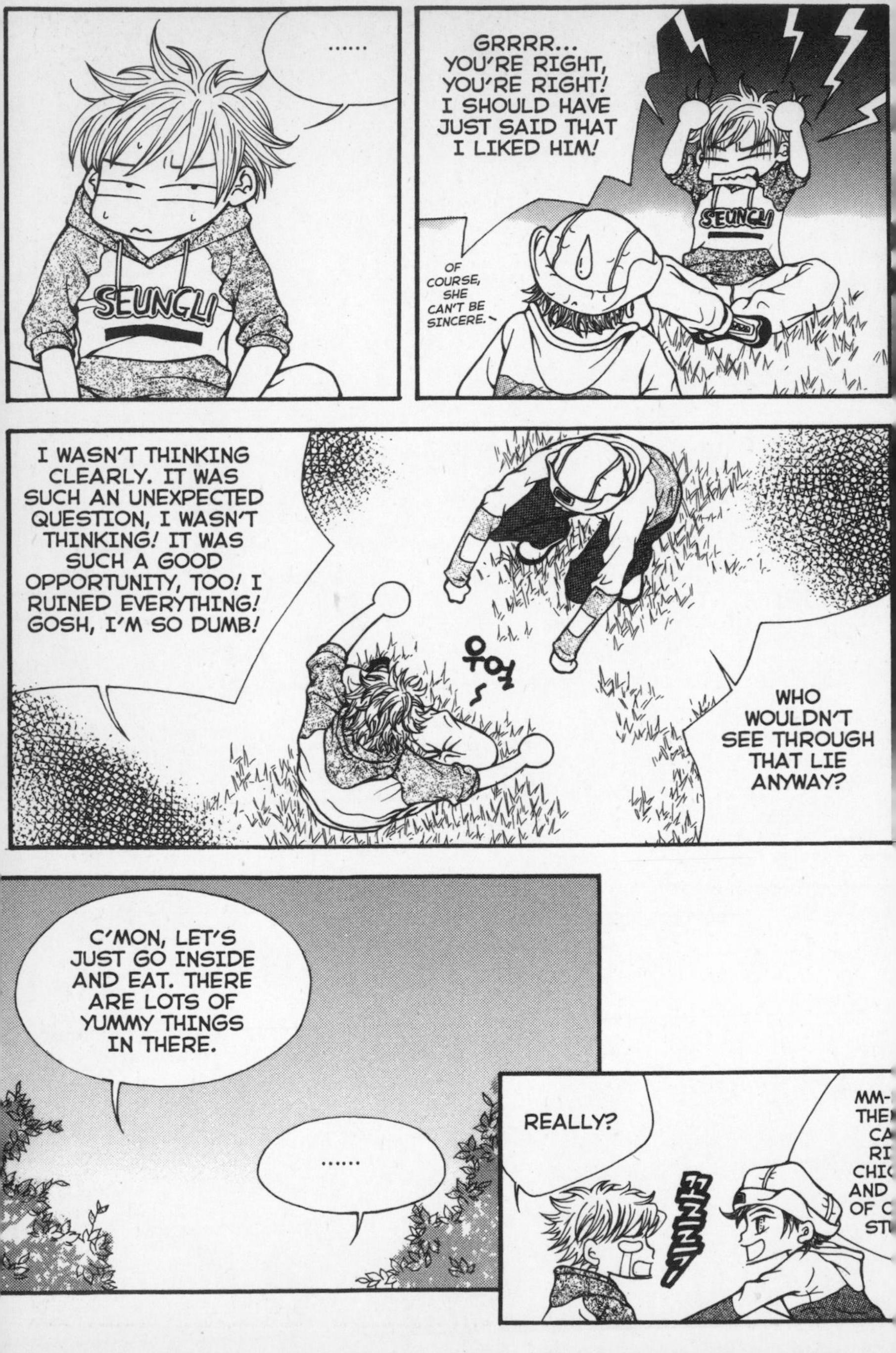
......
GRRRR... YOU'RE RIGHT, YOU'RE RIGHT! I SHOULD HAVE JUST SAID THAT I LIKED HIM!
OF COURSE, SHE CAN'T BE SINCERE.~
I WASN'T THINKING CLEARLY. IT WAS SUCH AN UNEXPECTED QUESTION, I WASN'T THINKING! IT WAS SUCH A GOOD OPPORTUNITY, TOO! I RUINED EVERYTHING! GOSH, I'M SO DUMB!
WHO WOULDN'T SEE THROUGH THAT LIE ANYWAY?
C'MON, LET'S JUST GO INSIDE AND EAT. THERE ARE LOTS OF YUMMY THINGS IN THERE.
......
REALLY?

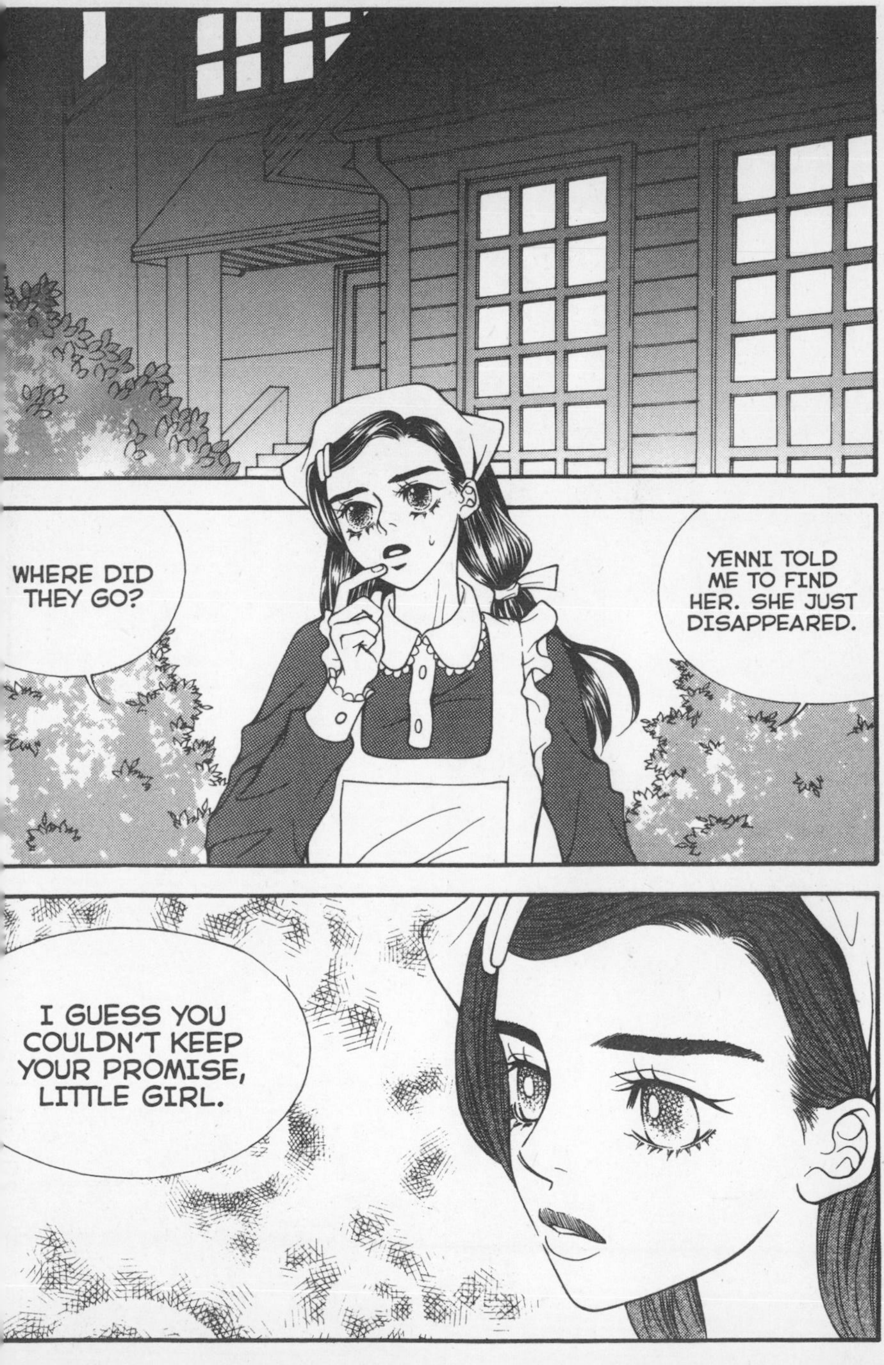
WHERE DID THEY GO?
YENNI TOLD ME TO FIND HER. SHE JUST DISAPPEARED.
I GUESS YOU COULDN'T KEEP YOUR PROMISE, LITTLE GIRL.

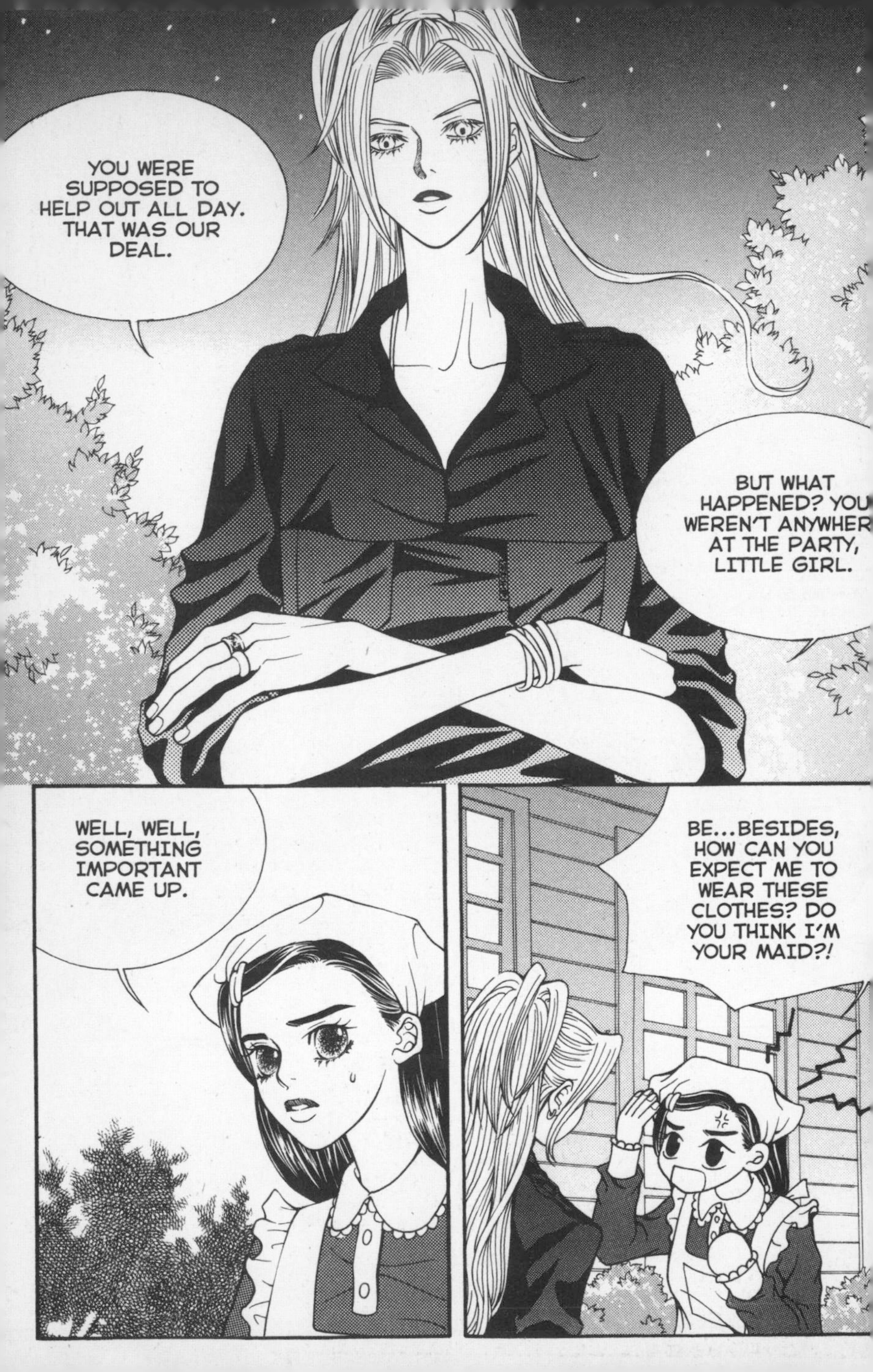
YOU WERE SUPPOSED TO HELP OUT ALL DAY. THAT WAS OUR DEAL.
BUT WHAT HAPPENED? YOU WEREN'T ANYWHER AT THE PARTY, LITTLE GIRL.
WELL, WELL, SOMETHING IMPORTANT CAME UP.
BE...BESIDES, HOW CAN YOU EXPECT ME TO WEAR THESE CLOTHES? DO YOU THINK I'M YOUR MAID?!

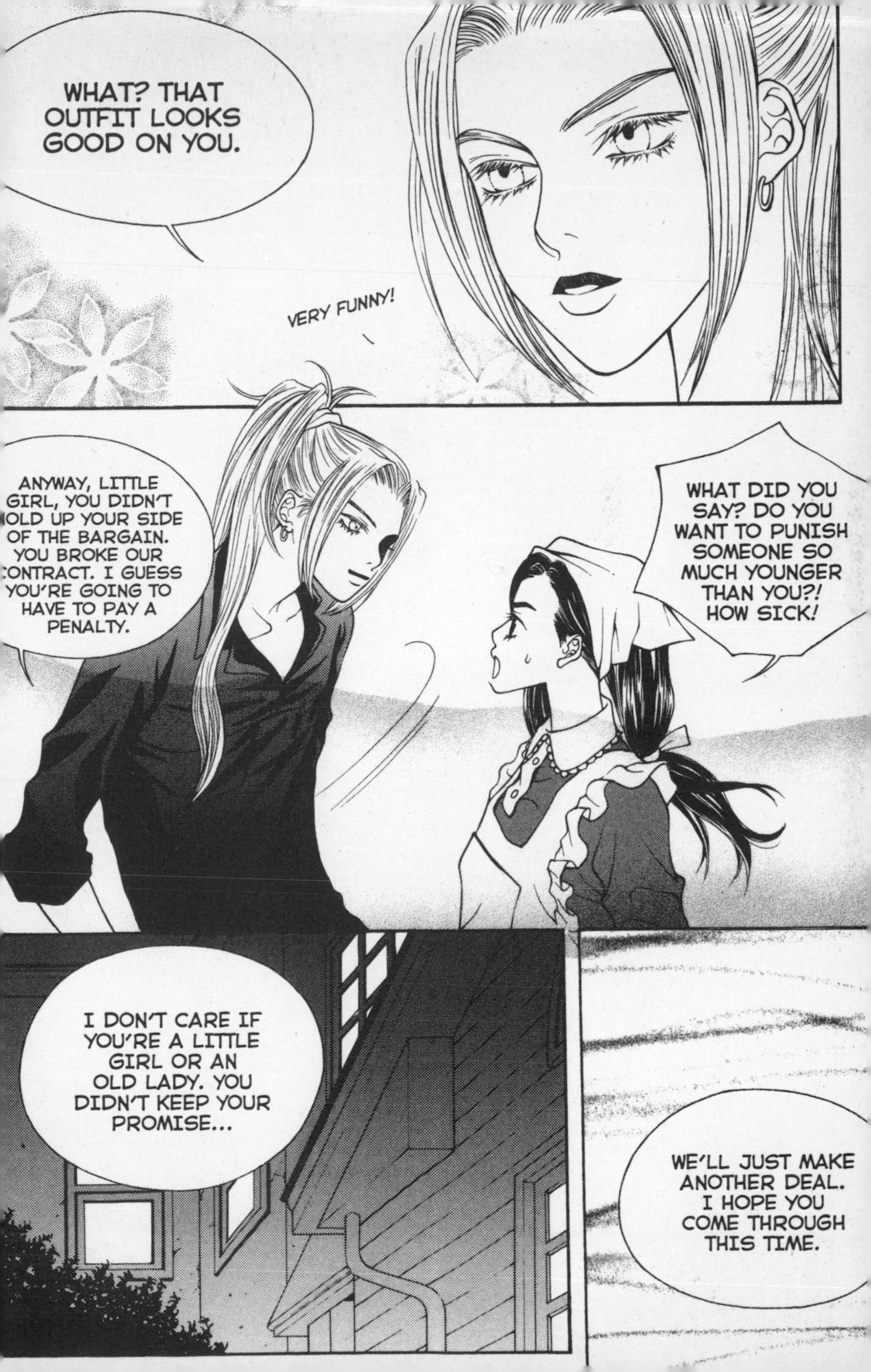
WHAT? THAT OUTFIT LOOKS GOOD ON YOU.
VERY FUNNY!
ANYWAY, LITTLE GIRL, YOU DIDN'T OLD UP YOUR SIDE OF THE BARGAIN. YOU BROKE OUR CONTRACT. I GUESS YOU'RE GOING TO HAVE TO PAY A PENALTY.
WHAT DID YOU SAY? DO YOU WANT TO PUNISH SOMEONE SO MUCH YOUNGER THAN YOU?! HOW SICK!
I DON'T CARE IF YOU'RE A LITTLE GIRL OR AN OLD LADY. YOU DIDN'T KEEP YOUR PROMISE...
WE'LL JUST MAKE ANOTHER DEAL. I HOPE YOU COME THROUGH THIS TIME.

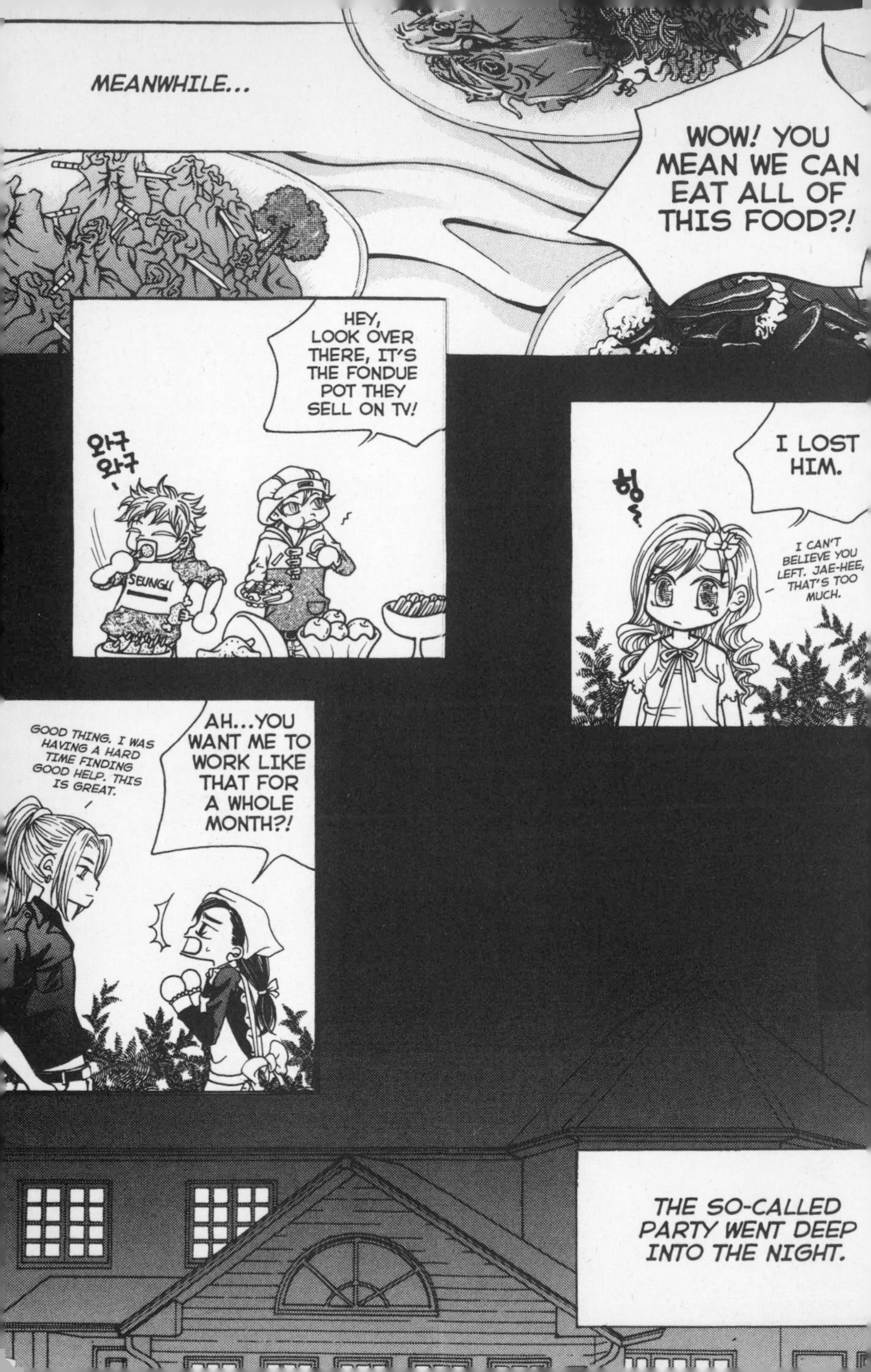
MEANWHILE...
WOW! YOU MEAN WE CAN EAT ALL OF THIS FOOD?!
HEY, LOOK OVER THERE, IT'S THE FONDUE POT THEY SELL ON TV!
와구 와구
SEUNGU
I LOST HIM.
헝
I CAN'T BELIEVE YOU LEFT. JAE-HEE, THAT'S TOO MUCH.
GOOD THING. I WAS HAVING A HARD TIME FINDING GOOD HELP. THIS IS GREAT.
AH...YOU WANT ME TO WORK LIKE THAT FOR A WHOLE MONTH?!
THE SO-CALLED PARTY WENT DEEP INTO THE NIGHT.

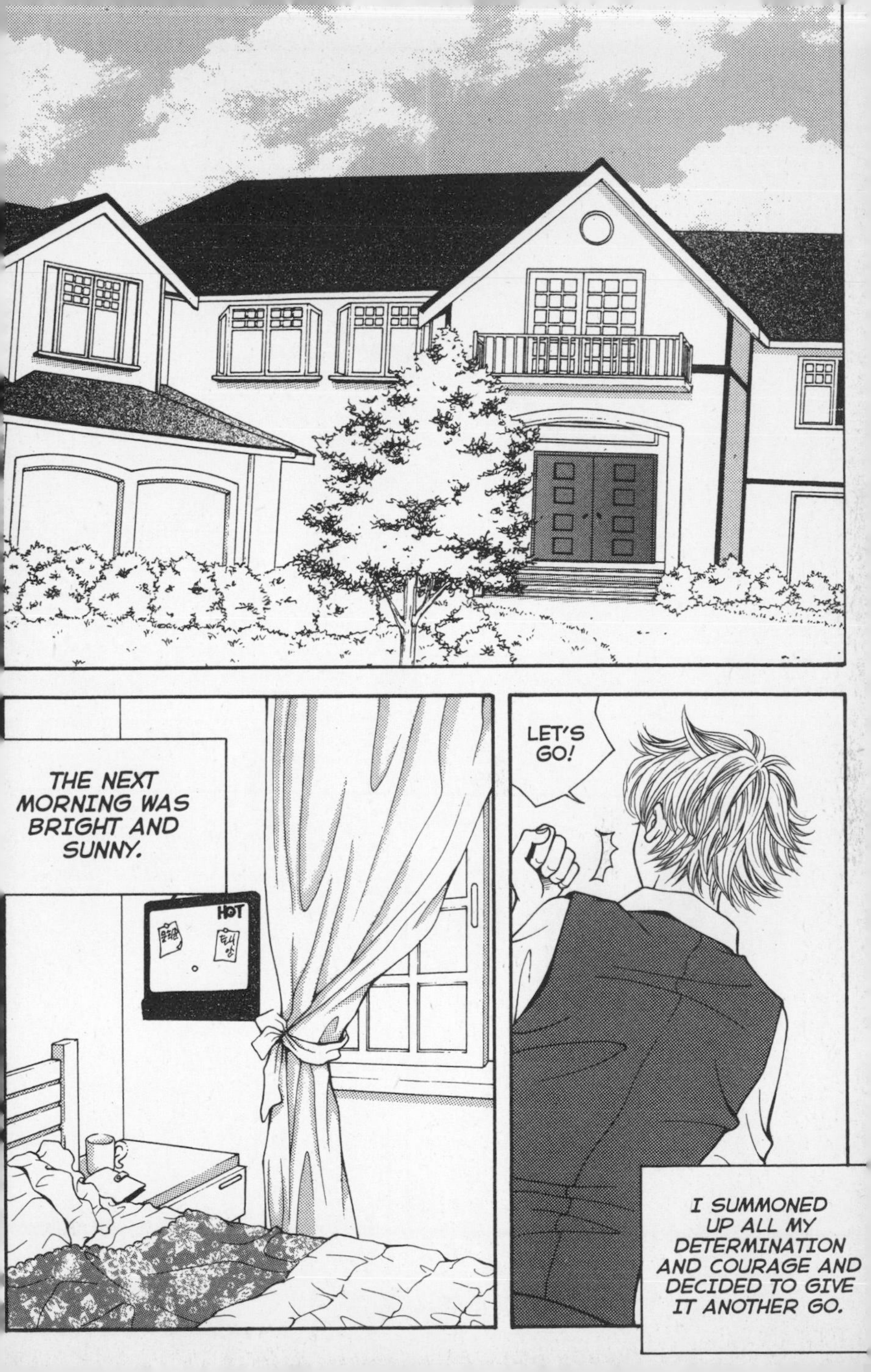
THE NEXT MORNING WAS BRIGHT AND SUNNY.
HOT
LET'S GO!
I SUMMONED UP ALL MY DETERMINATION AND COURAGE AND DECIDED TO GIVE IT ANOTHER GO.

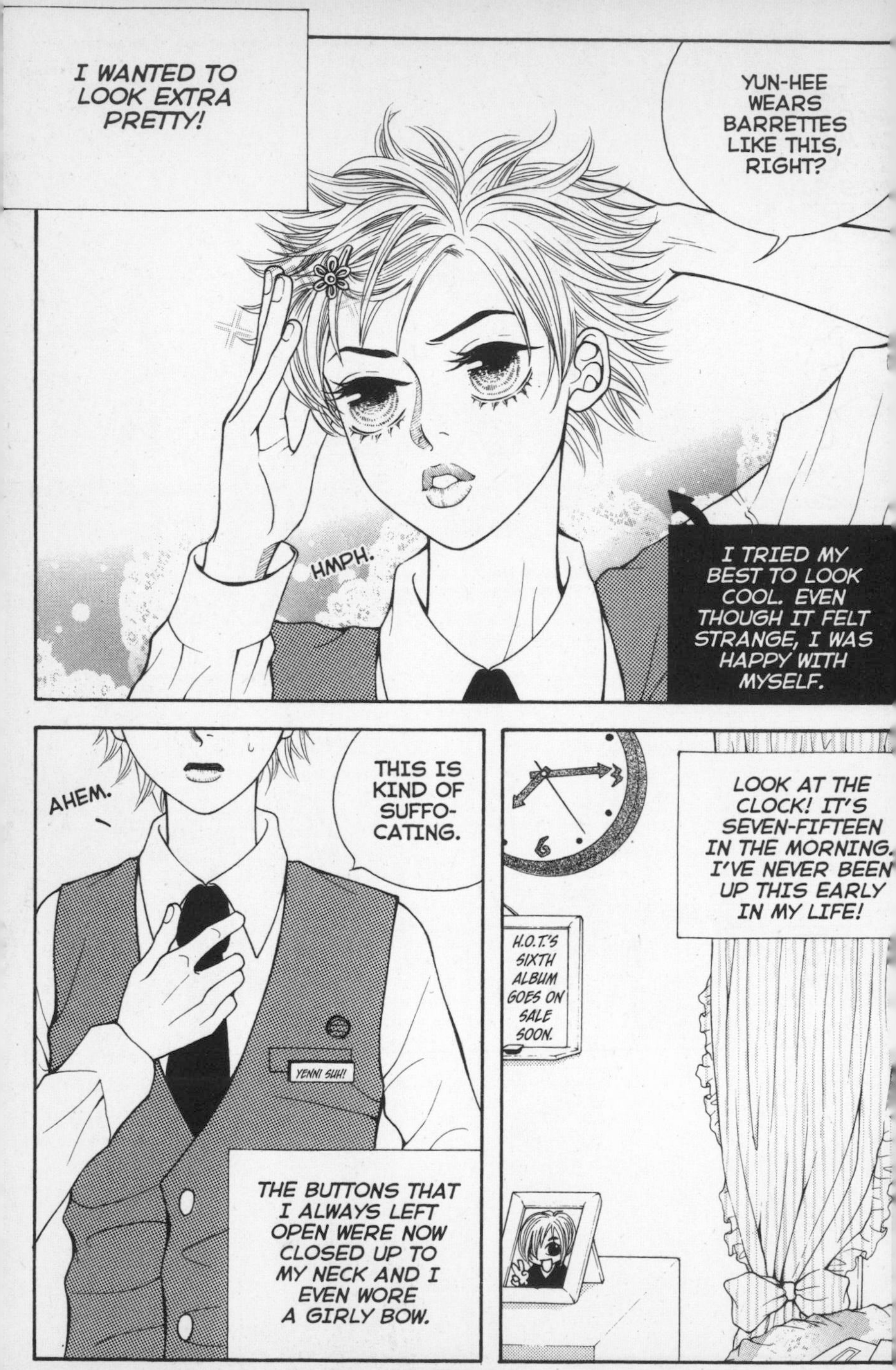
I WANTED TO LOOK EXTRA PRETTY!
YUN-HEE WEARS BARRETTES LIKE THIS, RIGHT?
HMPH.
I TRIED MY BEST TO LOOK COOL. EVEN THOUGH IT FELT STRANGE, I WAS HAPPY WITH MYSELF.
AHEM.
THIS IS KIND OF SUFFO-CATING.
YENNI SUH!
THE BUTTONS THAT I ALWAYS LEFT OPEN WERE NOW CLOSED UP TO MY NECK AND I EVEN WORE A GIRLY BOW.
LOOK AT THE CLOCK! IT'S SEVEN-FIFTEEN IN THE MORNING. I'VE NEVER BEEN UP THIS EARLY IN MY LIFE!
H.O.T.'S SIXTH ALBUM GOES ON SALE SOON.

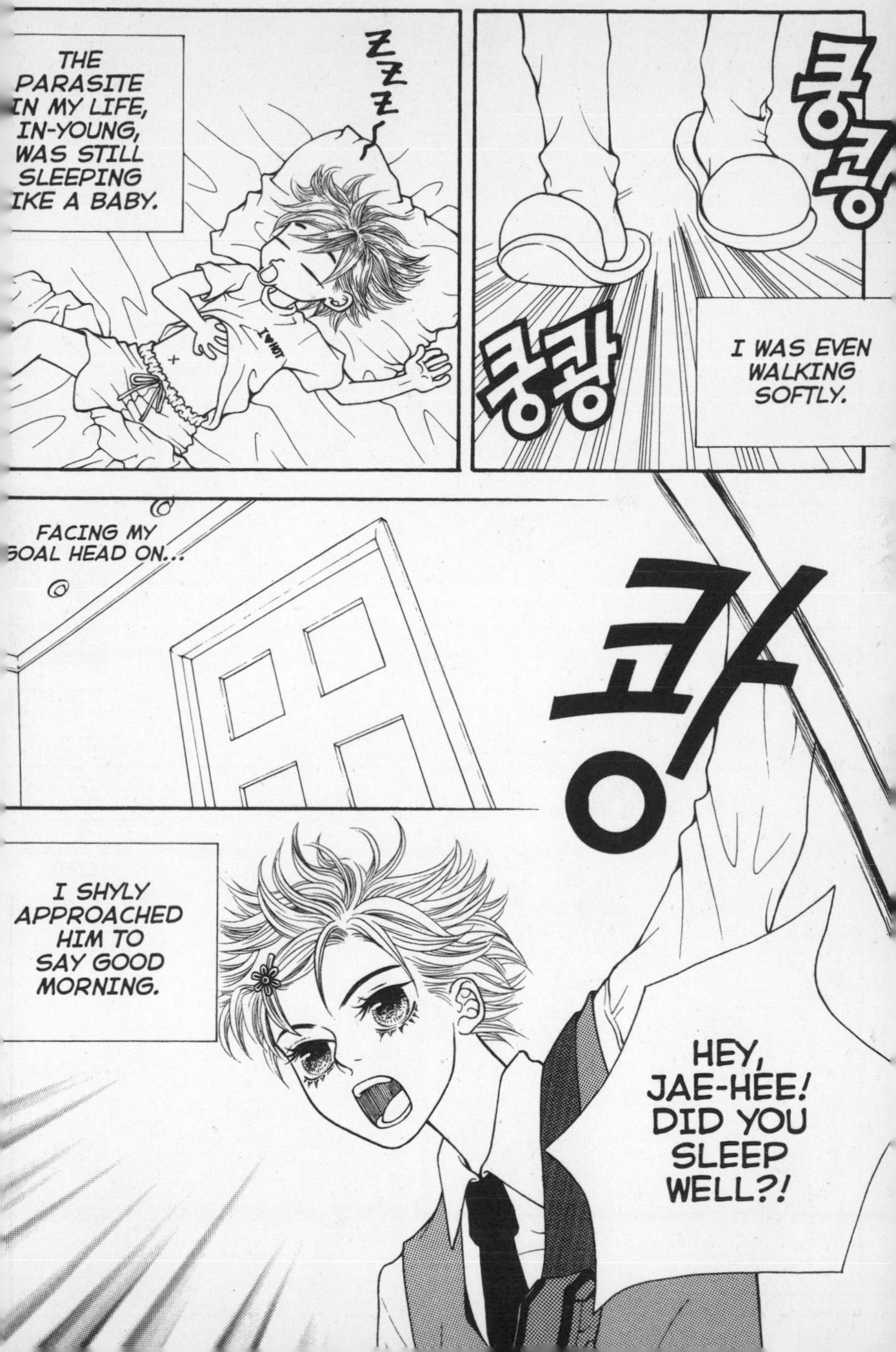
THE PARASITE IN MY LIFE, IN-YOUNG, WAS STILL SLEEPING IKE A BABY.
ZZZ~
쿵쾅
쿵쾅
I WAS EVEN WALKING SOFTLY.
FACING MY GOAL HEAD ON...
쾅
I SHYLY APPROACHED HIM TO SAY GOOD MORNING.
HEY, JAE-HEE! DID YOU SLEEP WELL?!

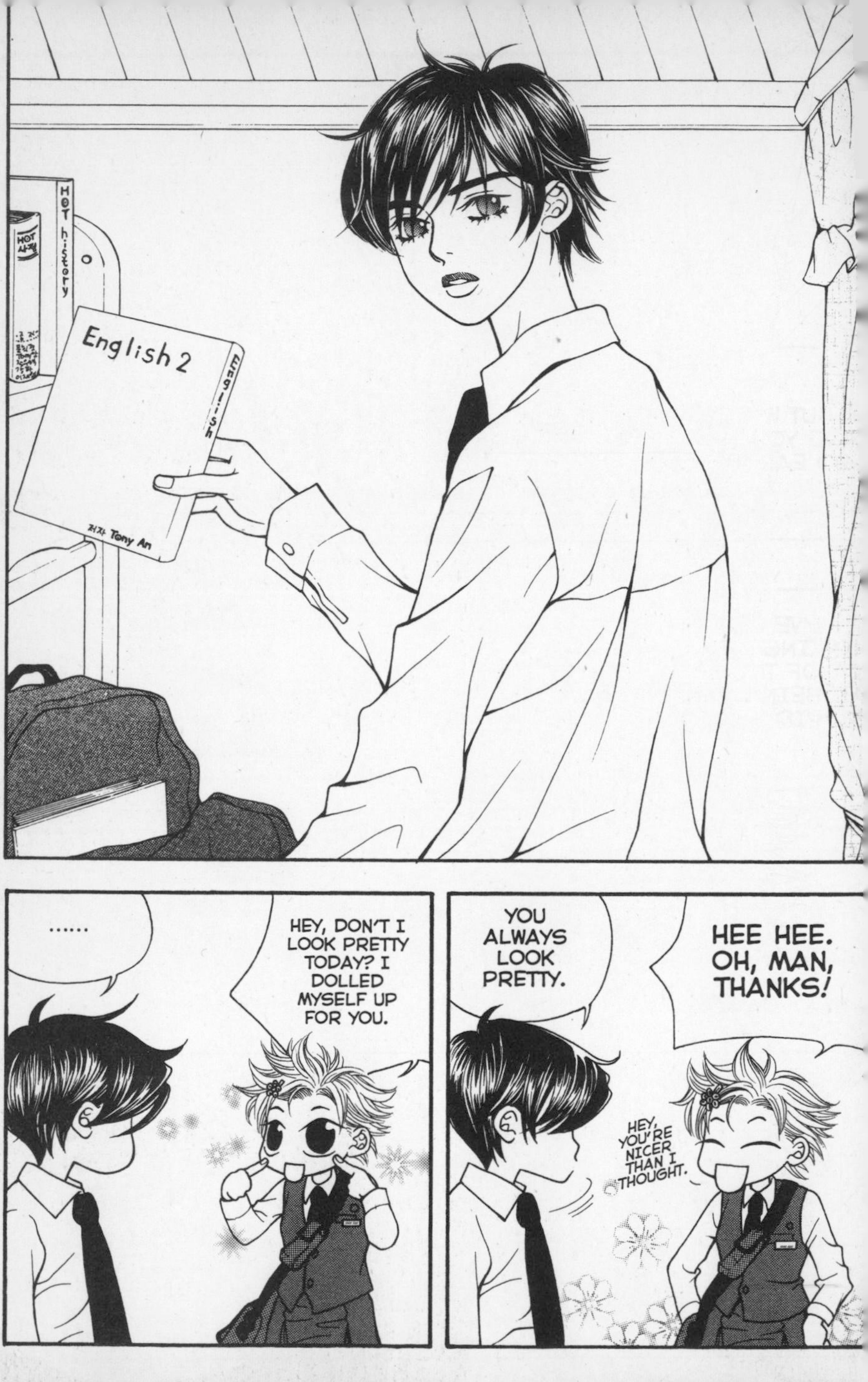
HOT history
English 2
English
Tony An
......
HEY, DON'T I LOOK PRETTY TODAY? I DOLLED MYSELF UP FOR YOU.
YOU ALWAYS LOOK PRETTY.
HEE HEE. OH, MAN, THANKS!
HEY, YOU'RE NICER THAN I THOUGHT.

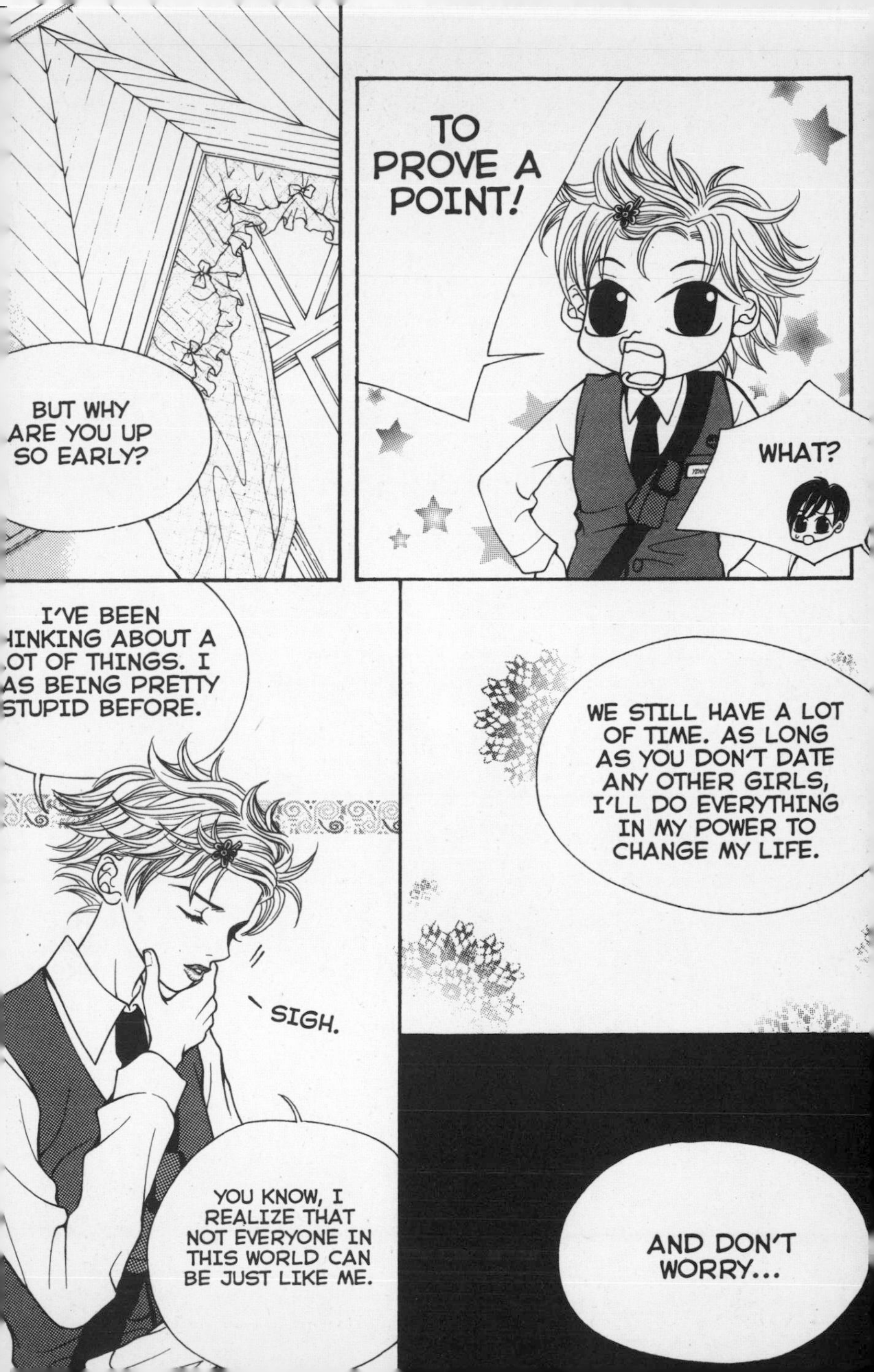
BUT WHY ARE YOU UP SO EARLY?
TO PROVE A POINT!
WHAT?
I'VE BEEN HINKING ABOUT A OT OF THINGS. I AS BEING PRETTY STUPID BEFORE.
SIGH.
YOU KNOW, I REALIZE THAT NOT EVERYONE IN THIS WORLD CAN BE JUST LIKE ME.
WE STILL HAVE A LOT OF TIME. AS LONG AS YOU DON'T DATE ANY OTHER GIRLS, I'LL DO EVERYTHING IN MY POWER TO CHANGE MY LIFE.
AND DON'T WORRY...

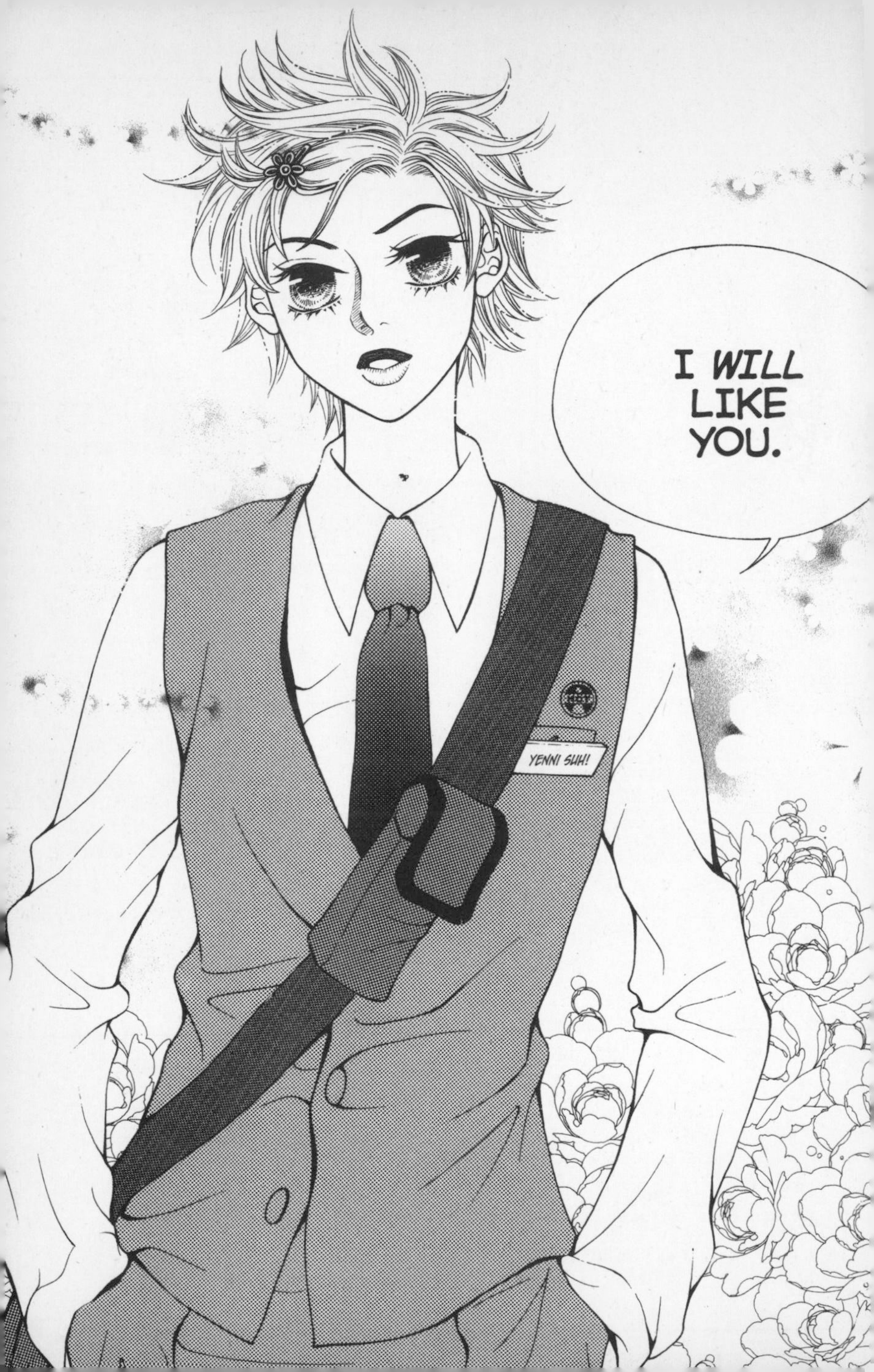
I WILL LIKE YOU.
YENNI SUH!

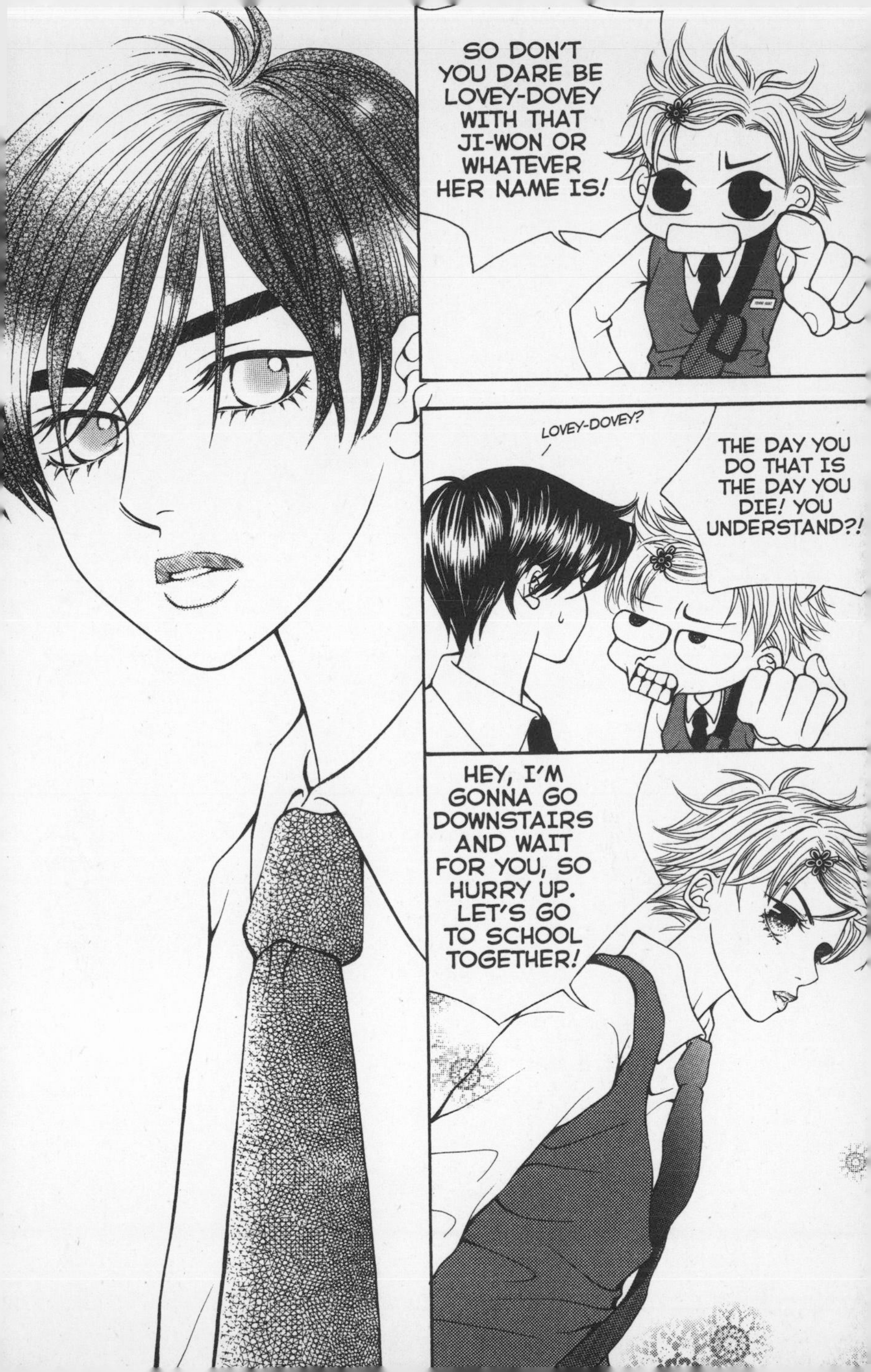
SO DON'T YOU DARE BE LOVEY-DOVEY WITH THAT JI-WON OR WHATEVER HER NAME IS!
LOVEY-DOVEY?
THE DAY YOU DO THAT IS THE DAY YOU DIE! YOU UNDERSTAND?!
HEY, I'M GONNA GO DOWNSTAIRS AND WAIT FOR YOU, SO HURRY UP. LET'S GO TO SCHOOL TOGETHER!

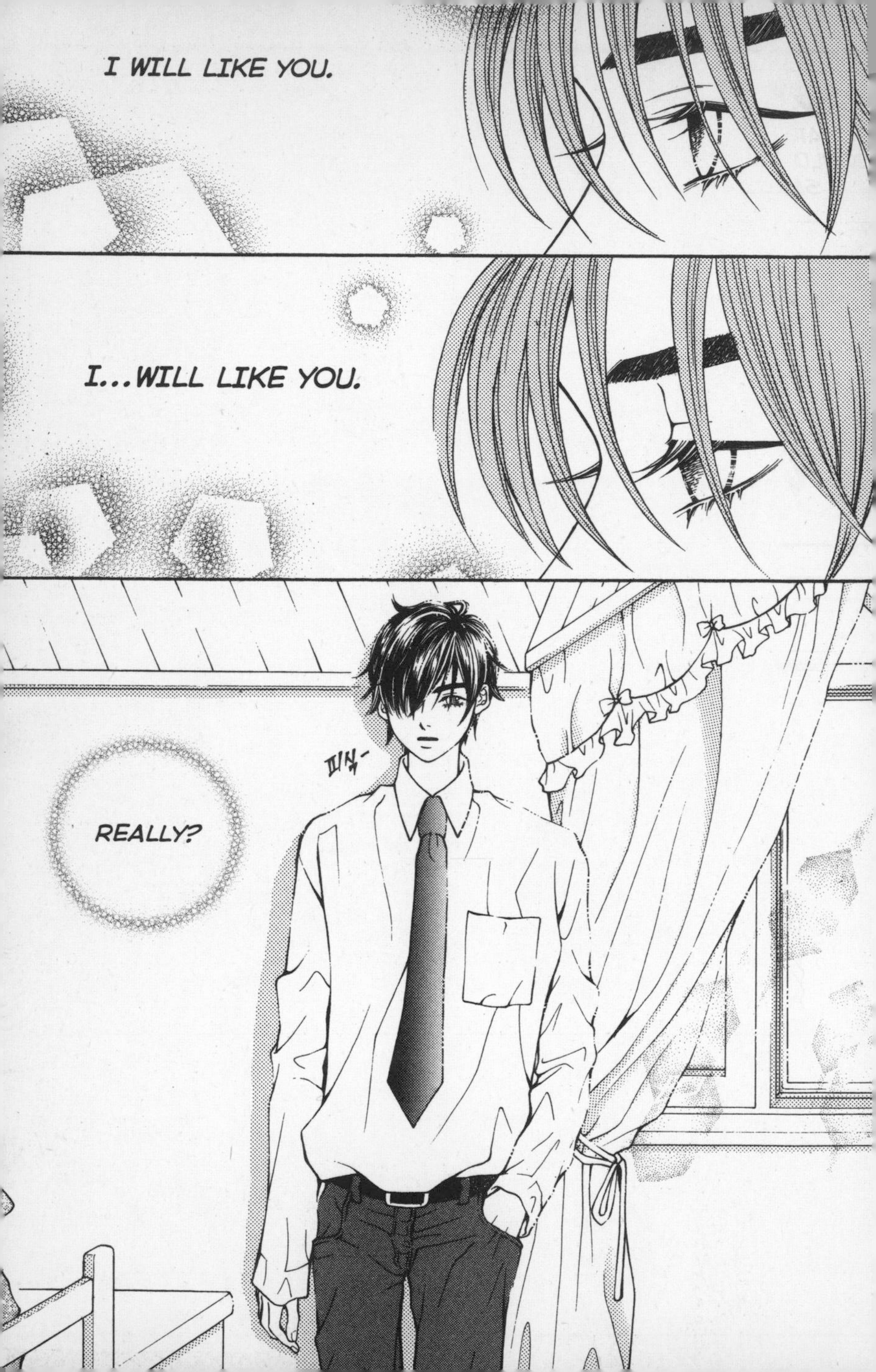
I WILL LIKE YOU.
I...WILL LIKE YOU.
REALLY?

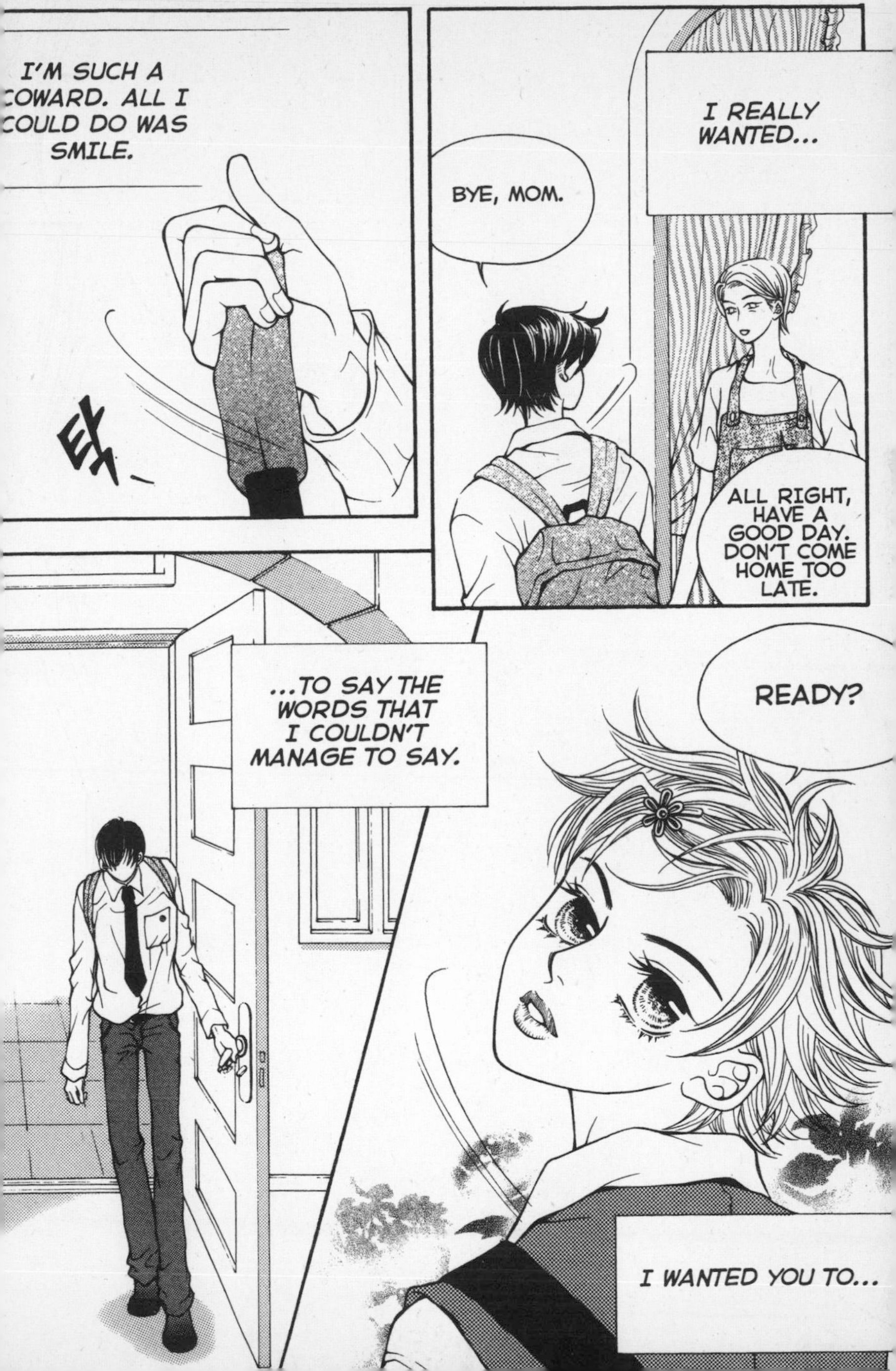
I'M SUCH A COWARD. ALL I COULD DO WAS SMILE.
탁
I REALLY WANTED...
BYE, MOM.
ALL RIGHT, HAVE A GOOD DAY. DON'T COME HOME TOO LATE.
...TO SAY THE WORDS THAT I COULDN'T MANAGE TO SAY.
READY?
I WANTED YOU TO...

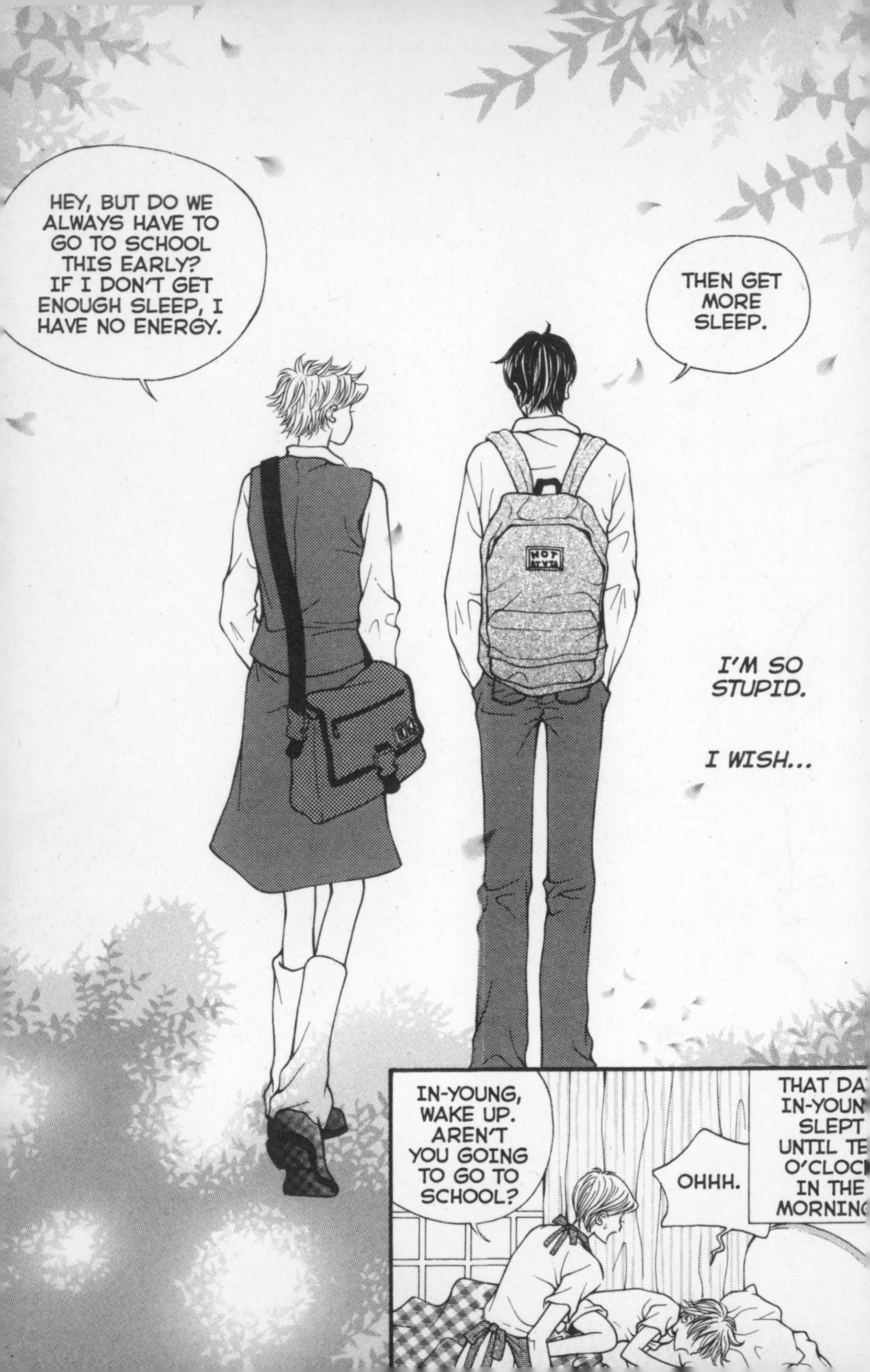
HEY, BUT DO WE ALWAYS HAVE TO GO TO SCHOOL THIS EARLY? IF I DON'T GET ENOUGH SLEEP, I HAVE NO ENERGY.
THEN GET MORE SLEEP.
I'M SO STUPID.
I WISH...
IN-YOUNG, WAKE UP. AREN'T YOU GOING TO GO TO SCHOOL?
OHHH.
THAT DA IN-YOUN SLEPT UNTIL TE O'CLOC IN THE MORNIN

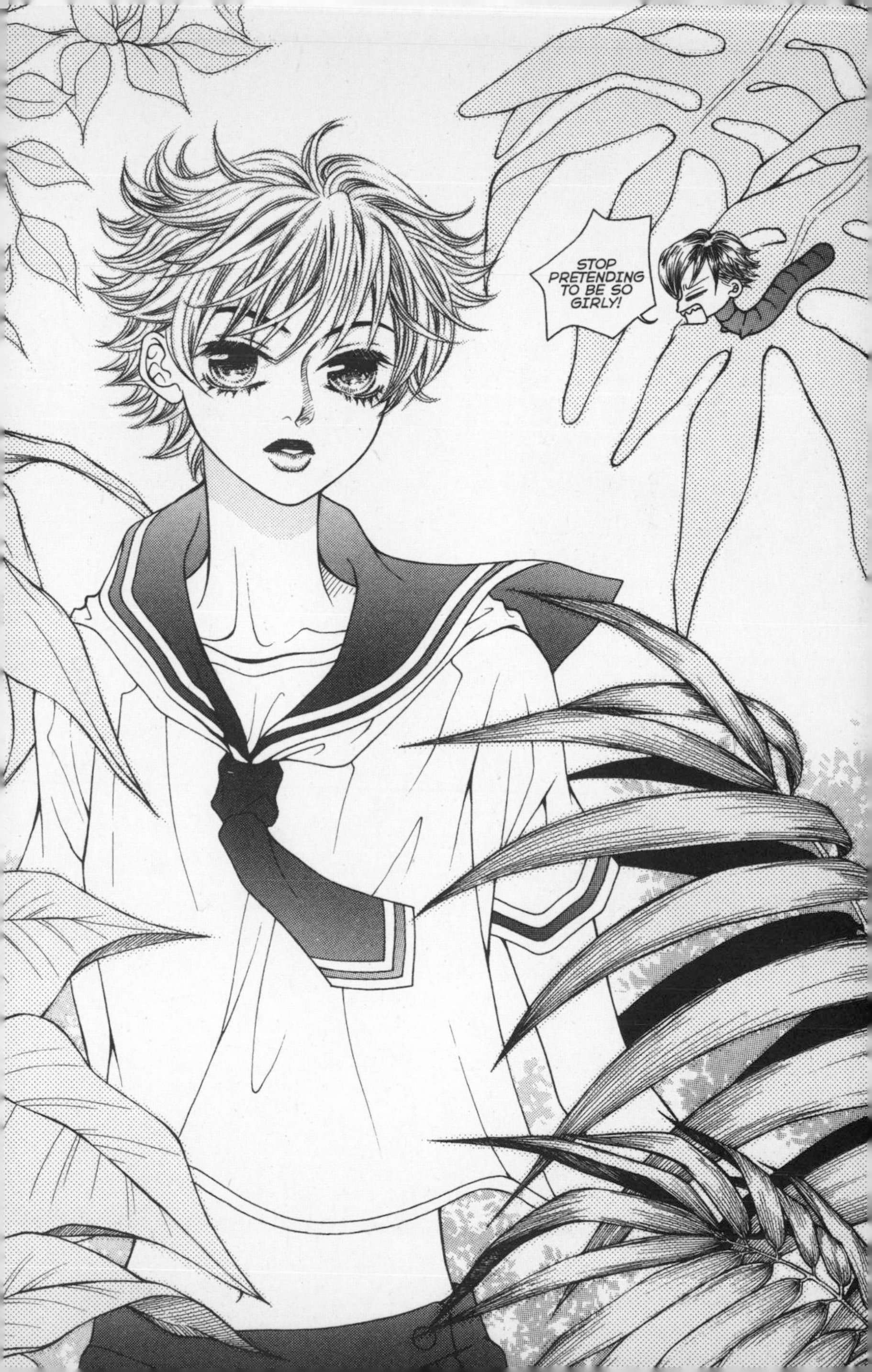
STOP PRETENDING TO BE SO GIRLY!

YOU POOR LITTLE PAUPER...
IF YOUR FAMILY IS BANKRUPT, THEN SHOULDN'T YOU BE DOING EVERYTHING YOU CAN TO MAKE SOME MONEY? DON'T YOU HAVE SOMETHING ELSE TO DO INSTEAD OF BUTTING IN?
DON'T TRY TO HANG ONTO SOMEONE ELSE. JUST MAKE SURE YOU DO WHAT YOU GOTTA DO!
H.O.T. LOVE
6th ALBUM COMING SOON
FOREVER H.O.T.

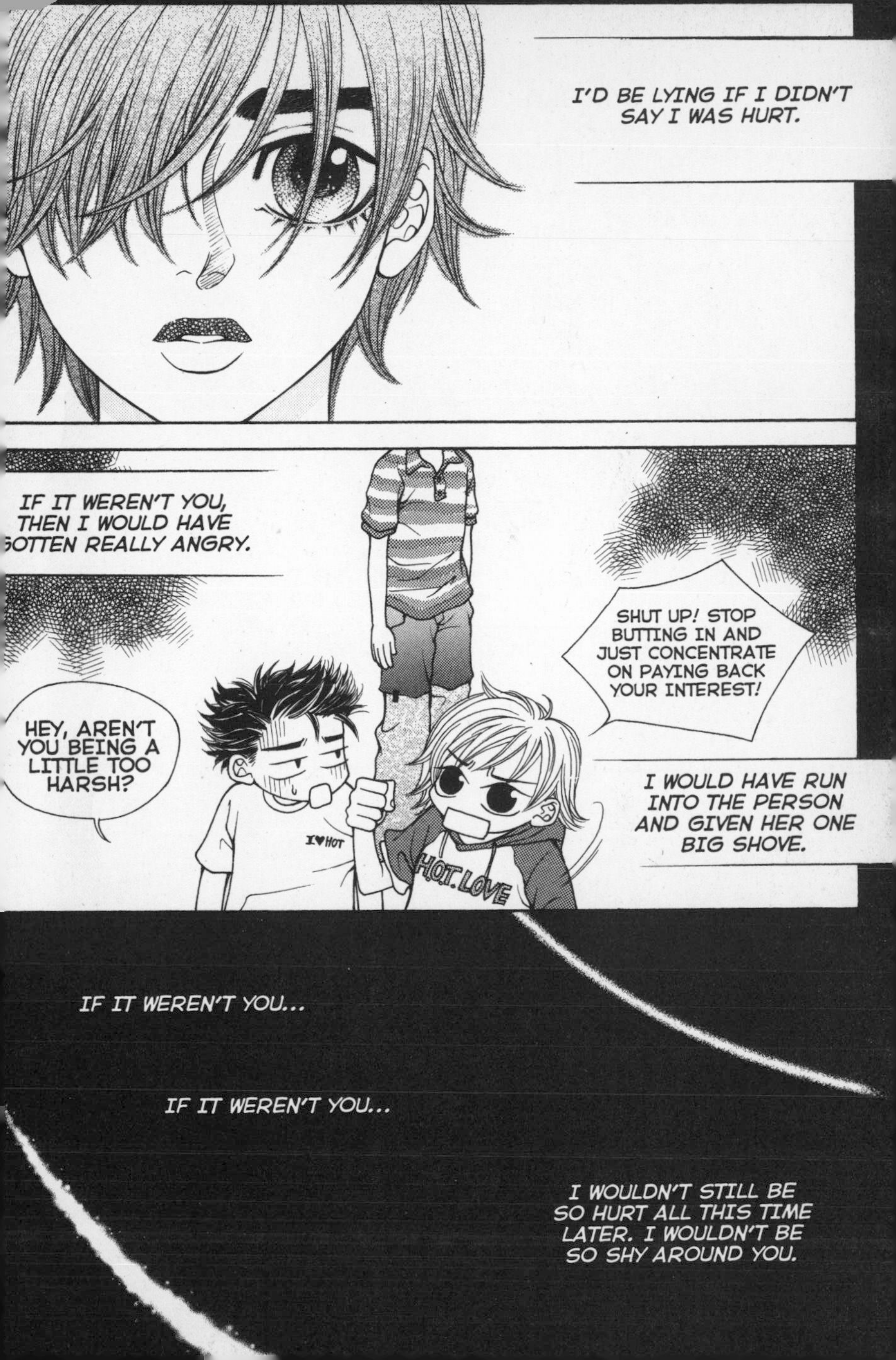

I'D BE LYING IF I DIDN'T SAY I WAS HURT.
IF IT WEREN'T YOU, THEN I WOULD HAVE GOTTEN REALLY ANGRY.
HEY, AREN'T YOU BEING A LITTLE TOO HARSH?
SHUT UP! STOP BUTTING IN AND JUST CONCENTRATE ON PAYING BACK YOUR INTEREST!
I♥HOT
H.O.T. LOVE
I WOULD HAVE RUN INTO THE PERSON AND GIVEN HER ONE BIG SHOVE.
IF IT WEREN'T YOU...
IF IT WEREN'T YOU...
I WOULDN'T STILL BE SO HURT ALL THIS TIME LATER. I WOULDN'T BE SO SHY AROUND YOU.

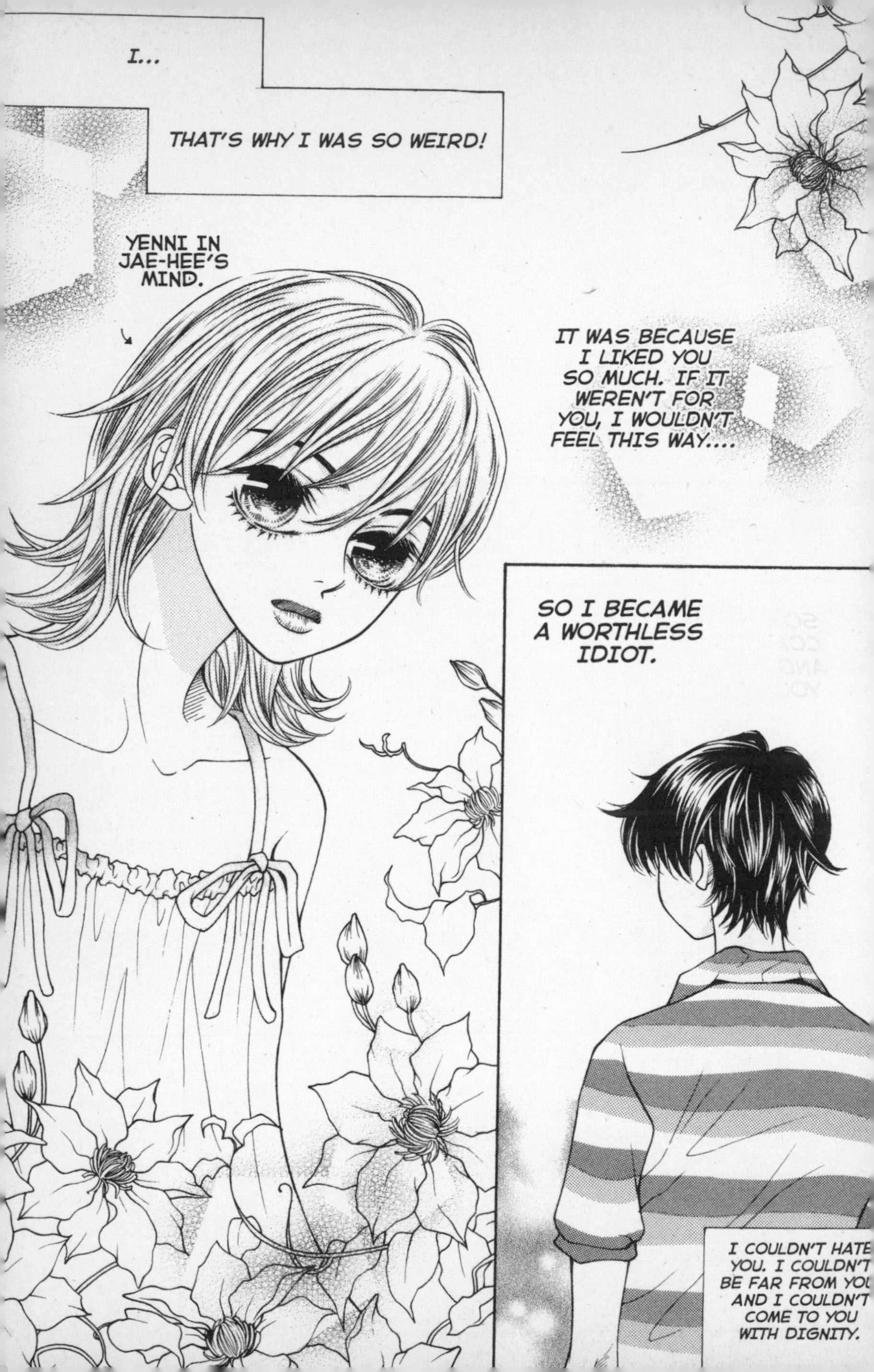
I...
THAT'S WHY I WAS SO WEIRD!
YENNI IN JAE-HEE'S MIND.
IT WAS BECAUSE I LIKED YOU SO MUCH. IF IT WEREN'T FOR YOU, I WOULDN'T FEEL THIS WAY....
SO I BECAME A WORTHLESS IDIOT.
I COULDN'T HATE YOU. I COULDN'T BE FAR FROM YOU AND I COULDN'T COME TO YOU WITH DIGNITY.

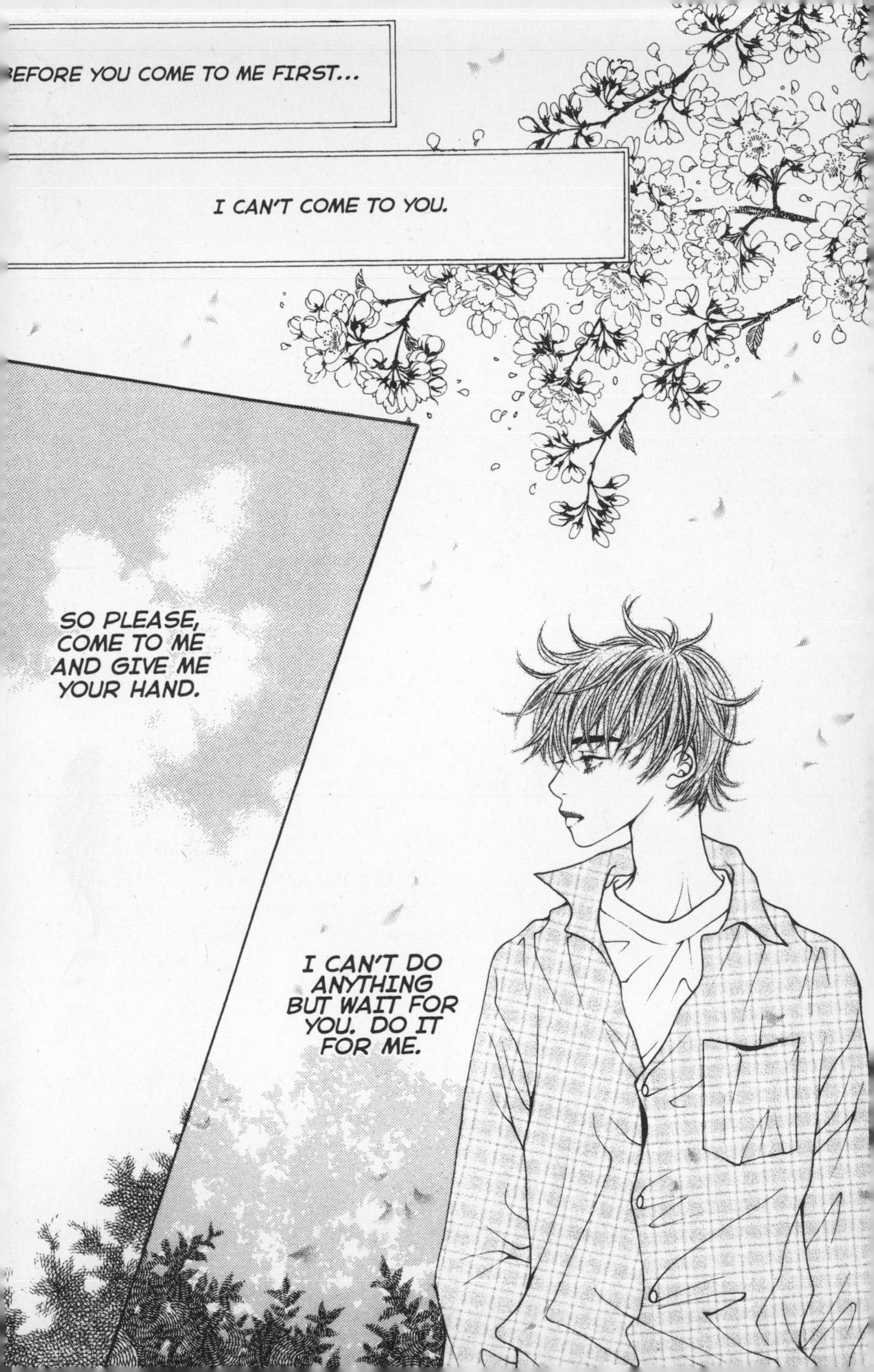
EFORE YOU COME TO ME FIRST...
I CAN'T COME TO YOU.
SO PLEASE, COME TO ME AND GIVE ME YOUR HAND.
I CAN'T DO ANYTHING BUT WAIT FOR YOU. DO IT FOR ME.

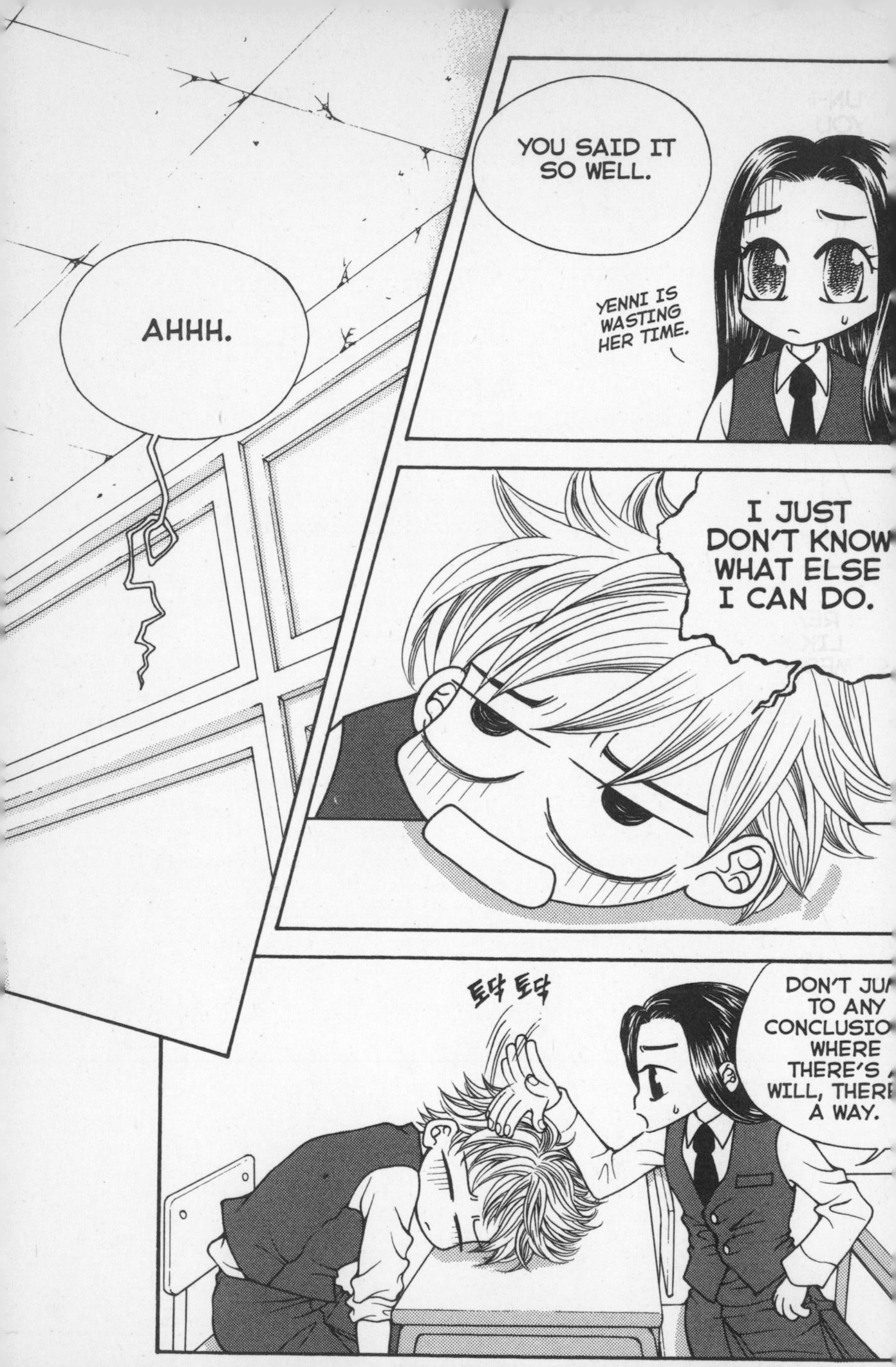
AHHH.
YOU SAID IT SO WELL.
YENNI IS WASTING HER TIME.
I JUST DON'T KNOW WHAT ELSE I CAN DO.
토닥 토닥
DON'T JU TO ANY CONCLUSIO WHERE THERE'S WILL, THER A WAY.

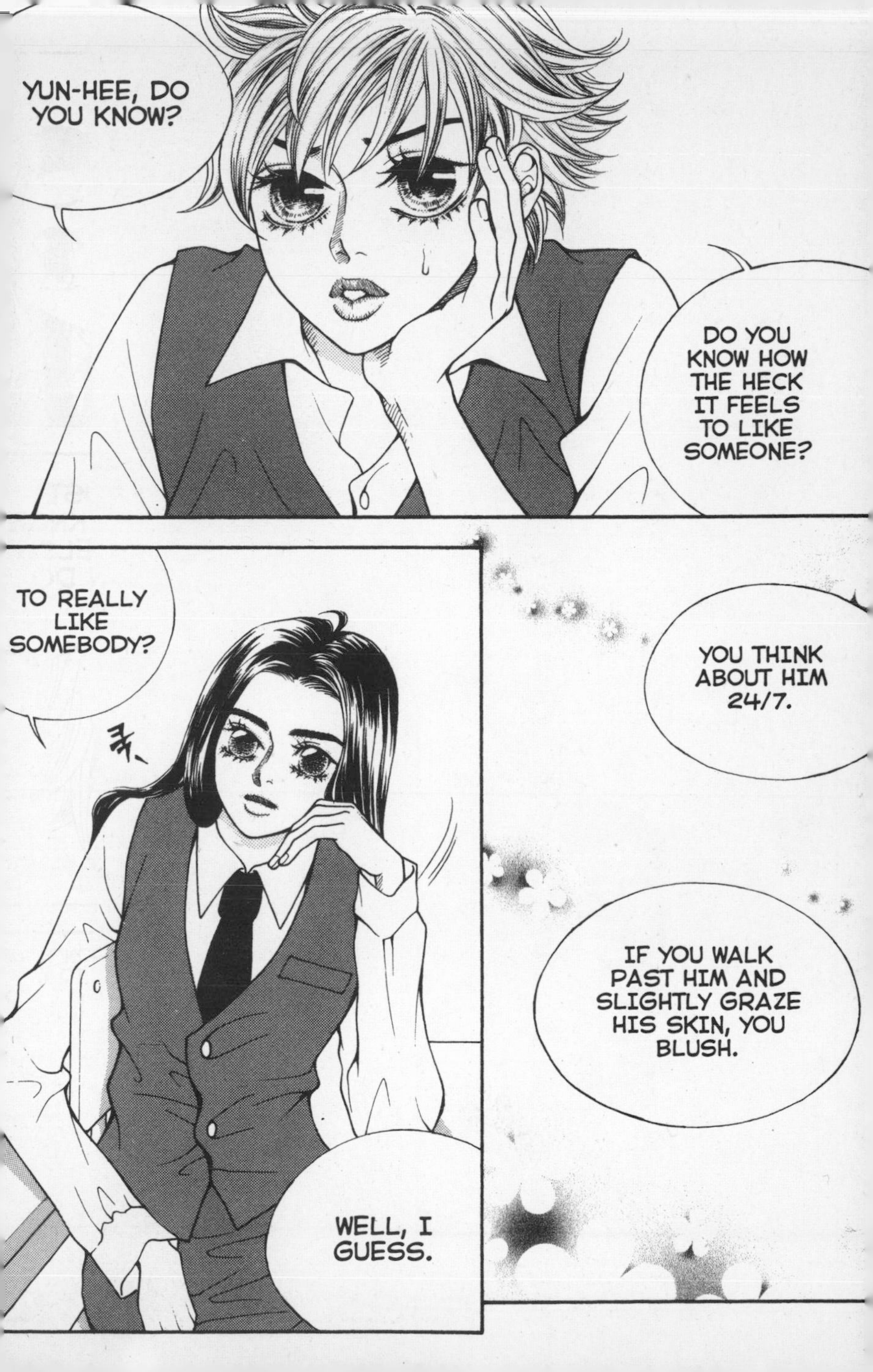
YUN-HEE, DO YOU KNOW?
DO YOU KNOW HOW THE HECK IT FEELS TO LIKE SOMEONE?
TO REALLY LIKE SOMEBODY?
크
WELL, I GUESS.
YOU THINK ABOUT HIM 24/7.
IF YOU WALK PAST HIM AND SLIGHTLY GRAZE HIS SKIN, YOU BLUSH.

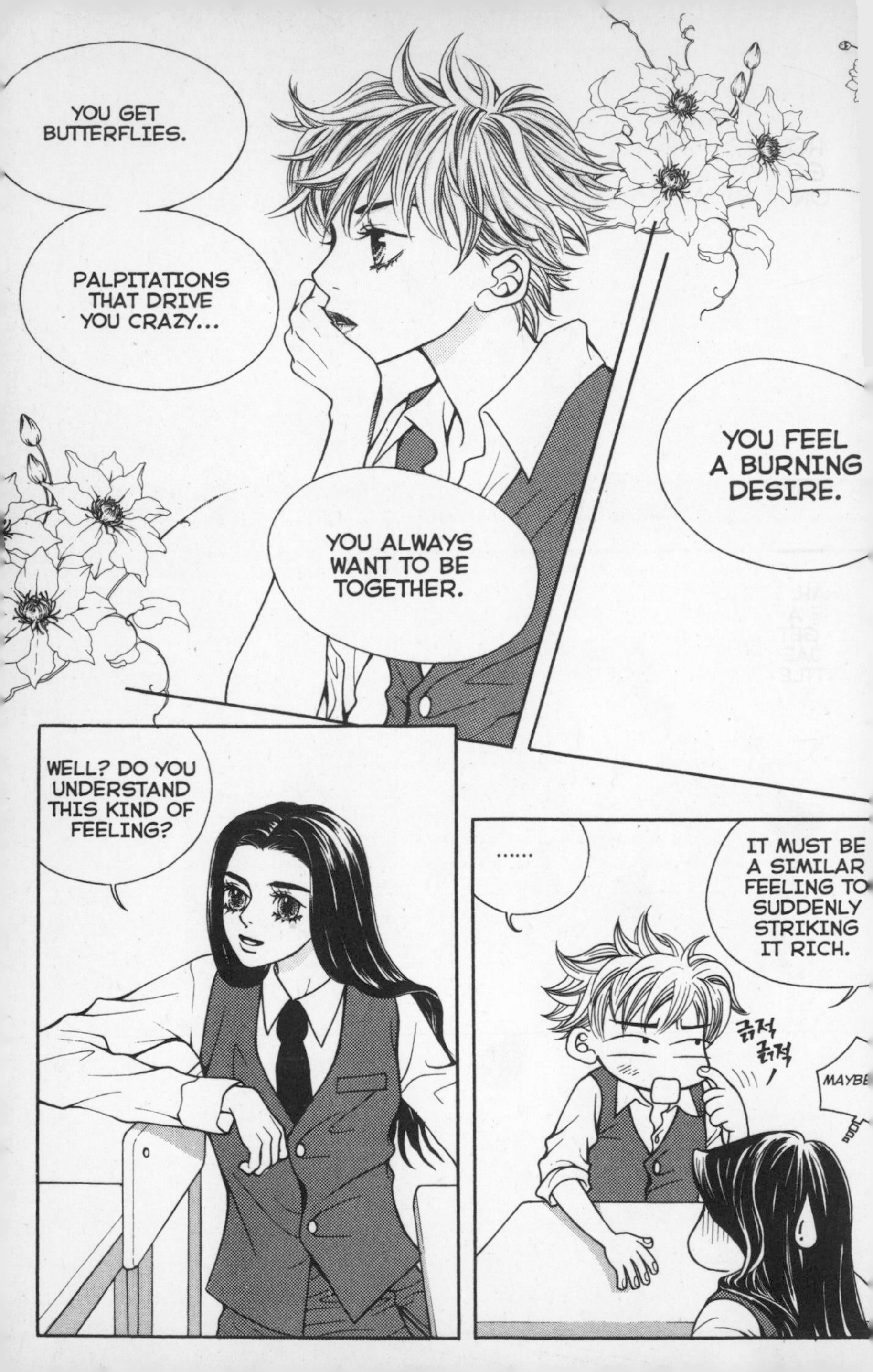
YOU GET BUTTERFLIES.
PALPITATIONS THAT DRIVE YOU CRAZY...
YOU ALWAYS WANT TO BE TOGETHER.
YOU FEEL A BURNING DESIRE.
WELL? DO YOU UNDERSTAND THIS KIND OF FEELING?
......
IT MUST BE A SIMILAR FEELING TO SUDDENLY STRIKING IT RICH.
긁적 긁적
MAYBE

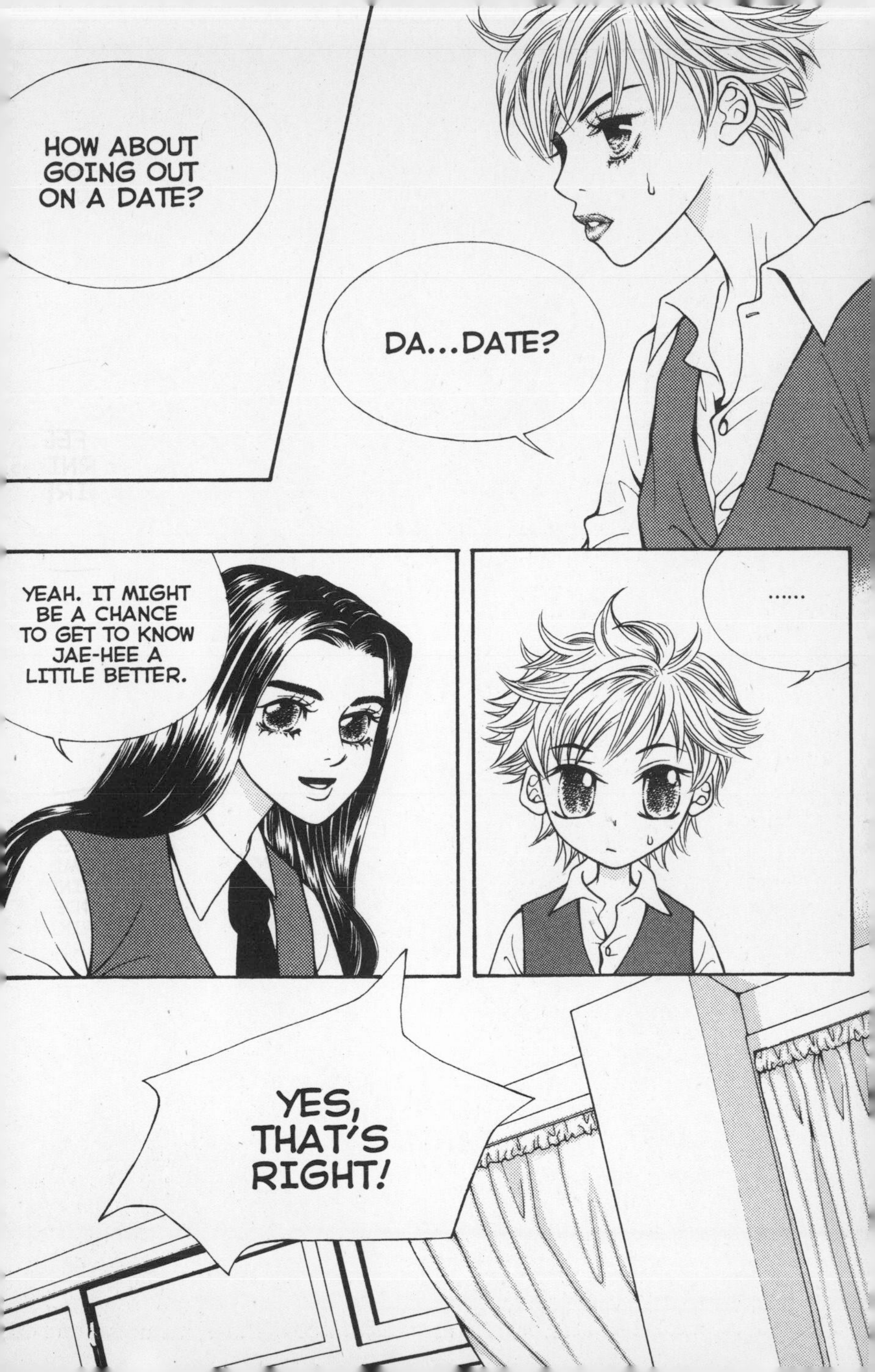
HOW ABOUT GOING OUT ON A DATE?
DA...DATE?
YEAH. IT MIGHT BE A CHANCE TO GET TO KNOW JAE-HEE A LITTLE BETTER.
......
YES, THAT'S RIGHT!

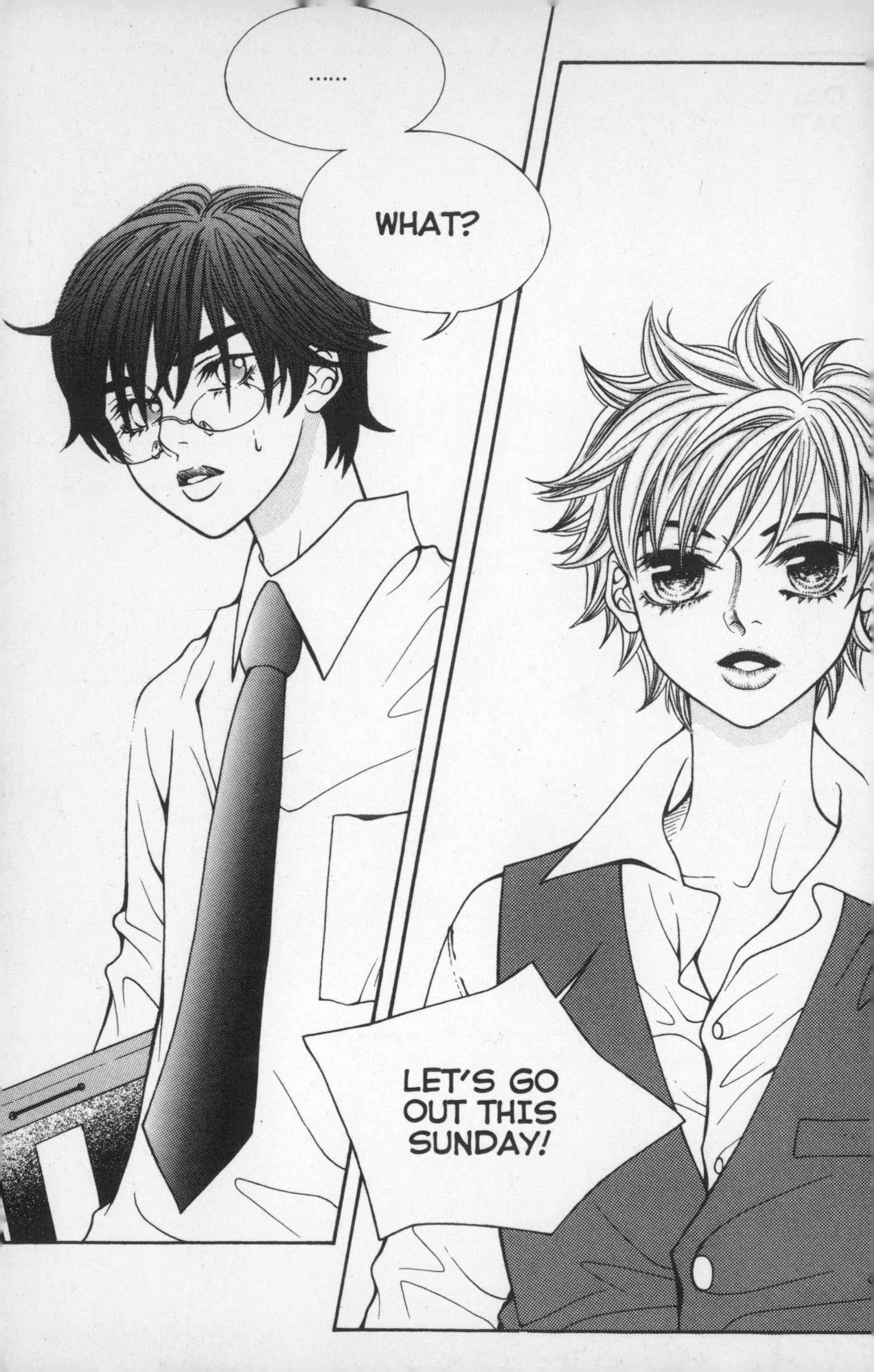
......
WHAT?
LET'S GO OUT THIS SUNDAY!

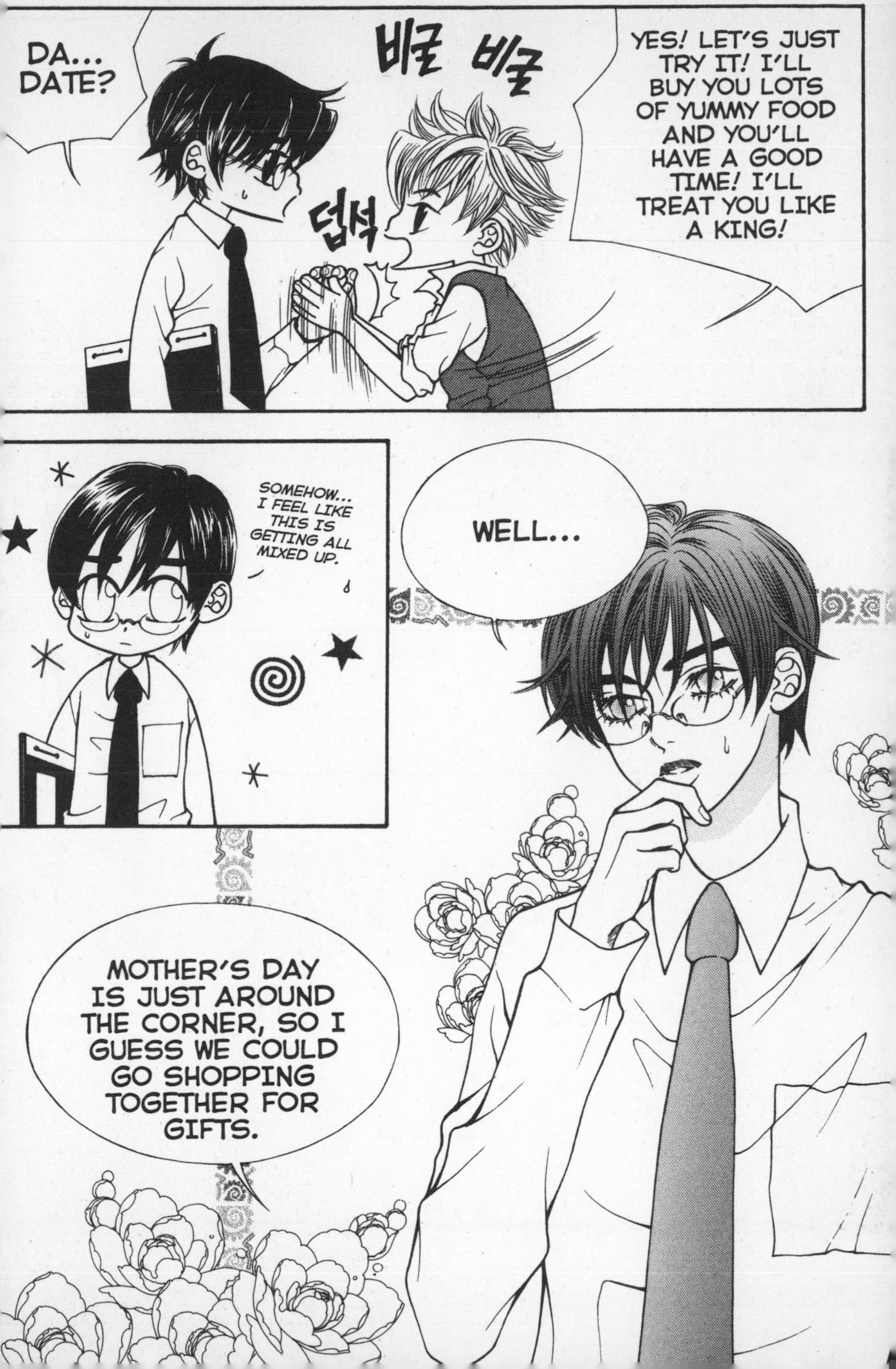
DA... DATE?
비굴 비굴
덥석
YES! LET'S JUST TRY IT! I'LL BUY YOU LOTS OF YUMMY FOOD AND YOU'LL HAVE A GOOD TIME! I'LL TREAT YOU LIKE A KING!
SOMEHOW... I FEEL LIKE THIS IS GETTING ALL MIXED UP.
WELL...
MOTHER'S DAY IS JUST AROUND THE CORNER, SO I GUESS WE COULD GO SHOPPING TOGETHER FOR GIFTS.

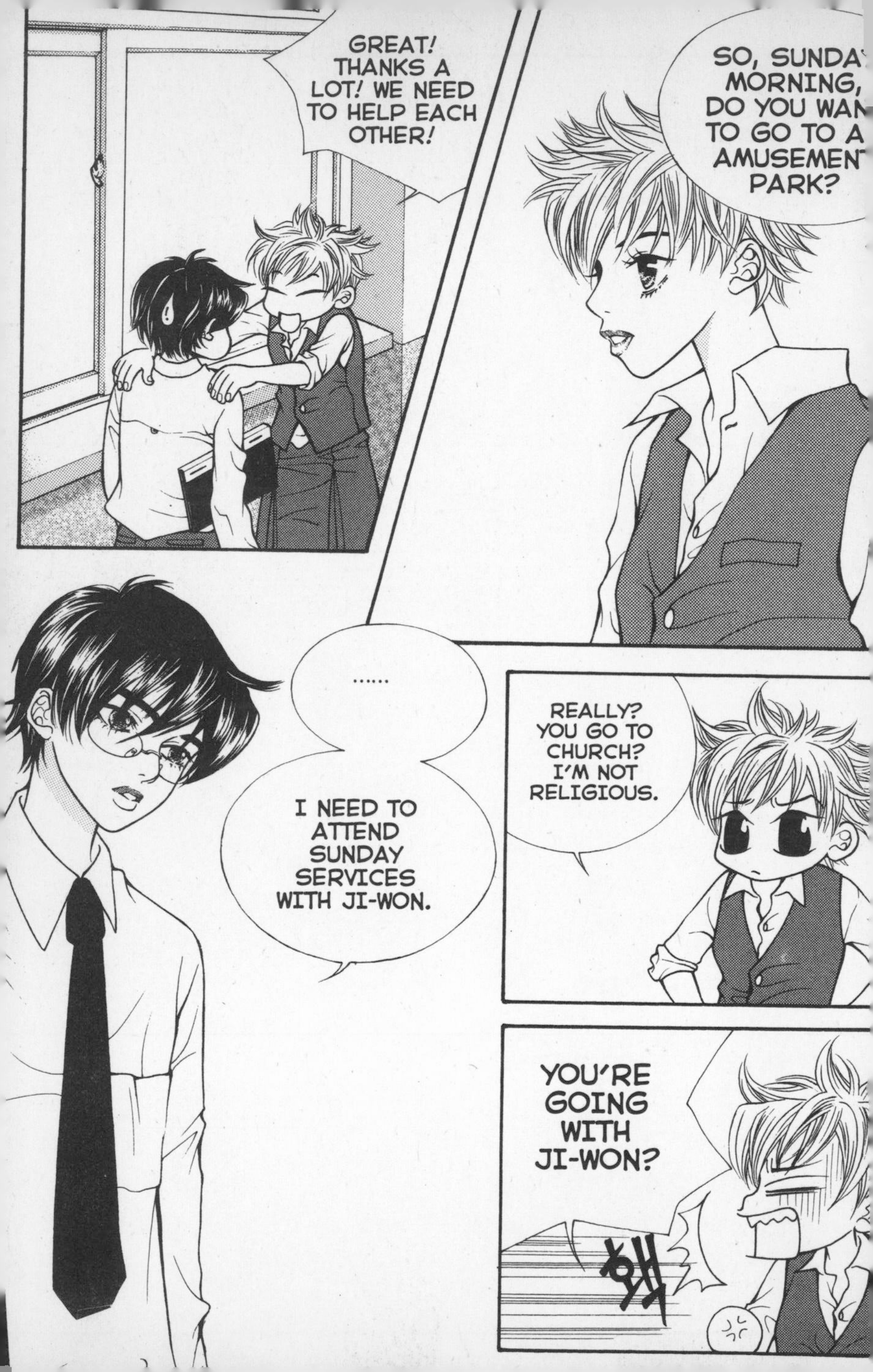
GREAT! THANKS A LOT! WE NEED TO HELP EACH OTHER!
SO, SUNDA MORNING, DO YOU WAN TO GO TO A AMUSEMEN PARK?
......
I NEED TO ATTEND SUNDAY SERVICES WITH JI-WON.
REALLY? YOU GO TO CHURCH? I'M NOT RELIGIOUS.
YOU'RE GOING WITH JI-WON?

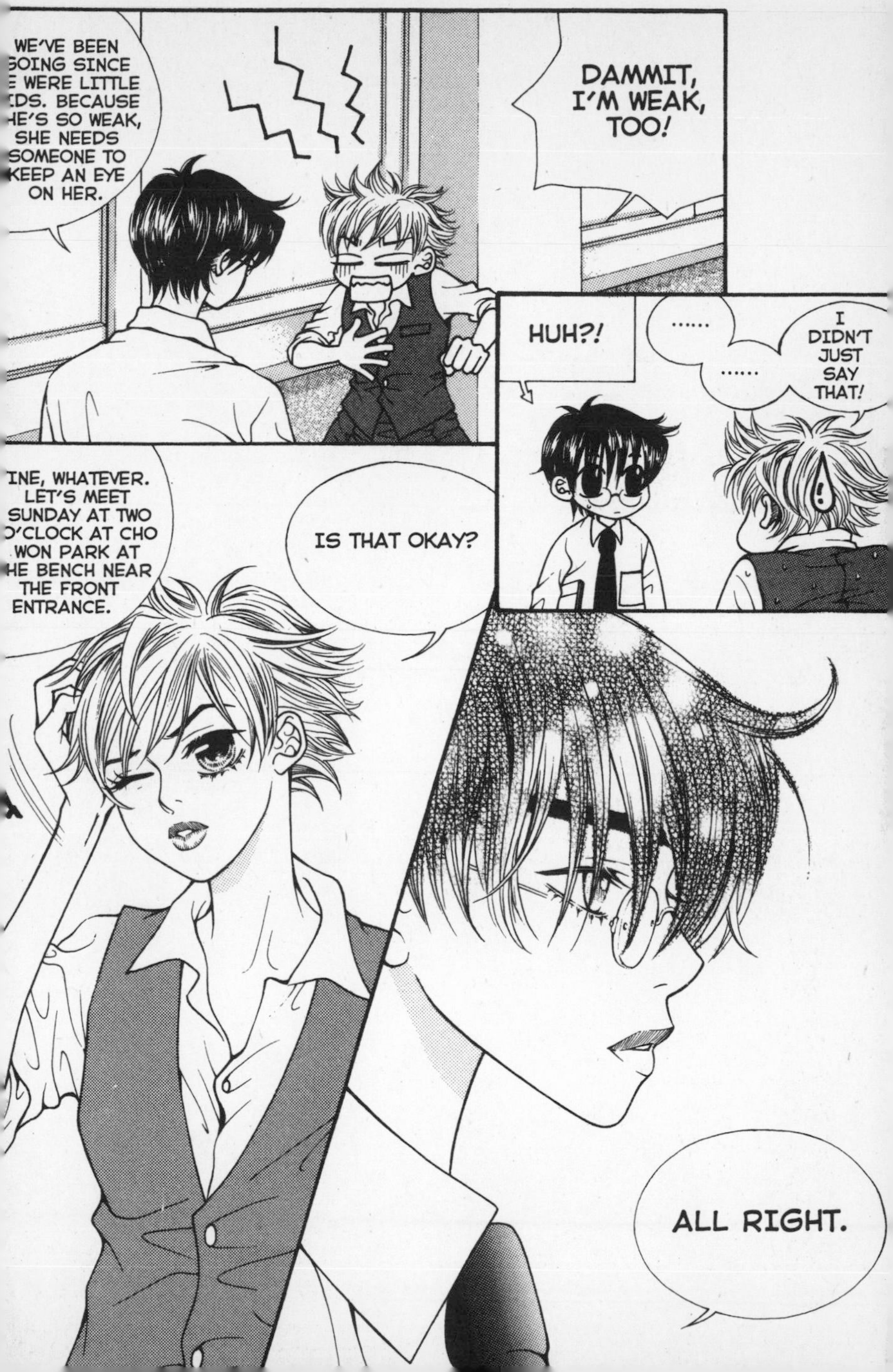
WE'VE BEEN GOING SINCE E WERE LITTLE IDS. BECAUSE HE'S SO WEAK, SHE NEEDS SOMEONE TO KEEP AN EYE ON HER.
DAMMIT, I'M WEAK, TOO!
HUH?!
......
......
I DIDN'T JUST SAY THAT!
INE, WHATEVER. LET'S MEET SUNDAY AT TWO O'CLOCK AT CHO WON PARK AT HE BENCH NEAR THE FRONT ENTRANCE.
IS THAT OKAY?
ALL RIGHT.

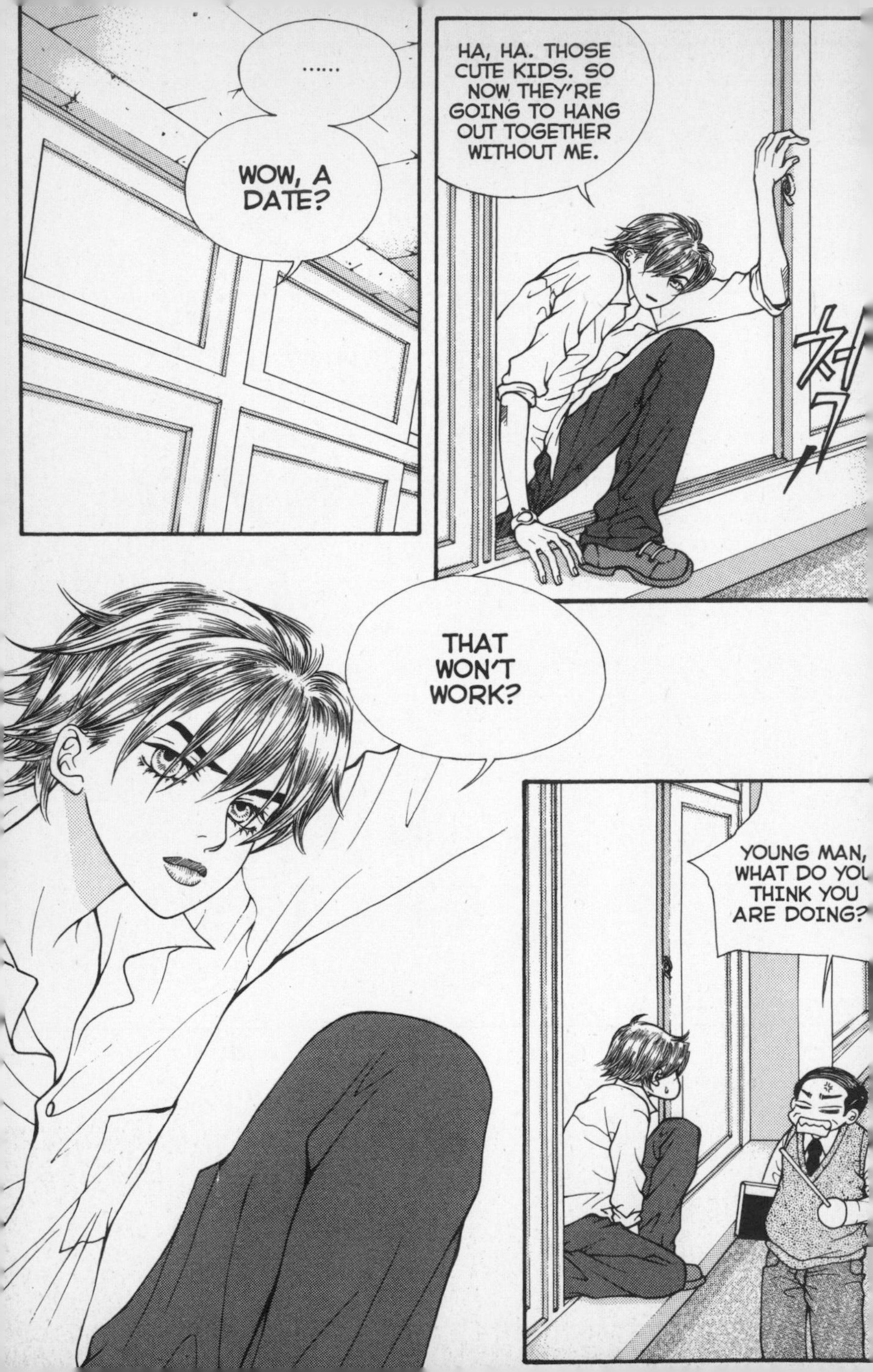
......
WOW, A DATE?
HA, HA. THOSE CUTE KIDS. SO NOW THEY'RE GOING TO HANG OUT TOGETHER WITHOUT ME.
THAT WON'T WORK?
YOUNG MAN, WHAT DO YOU THINK YOU ARE DOING?

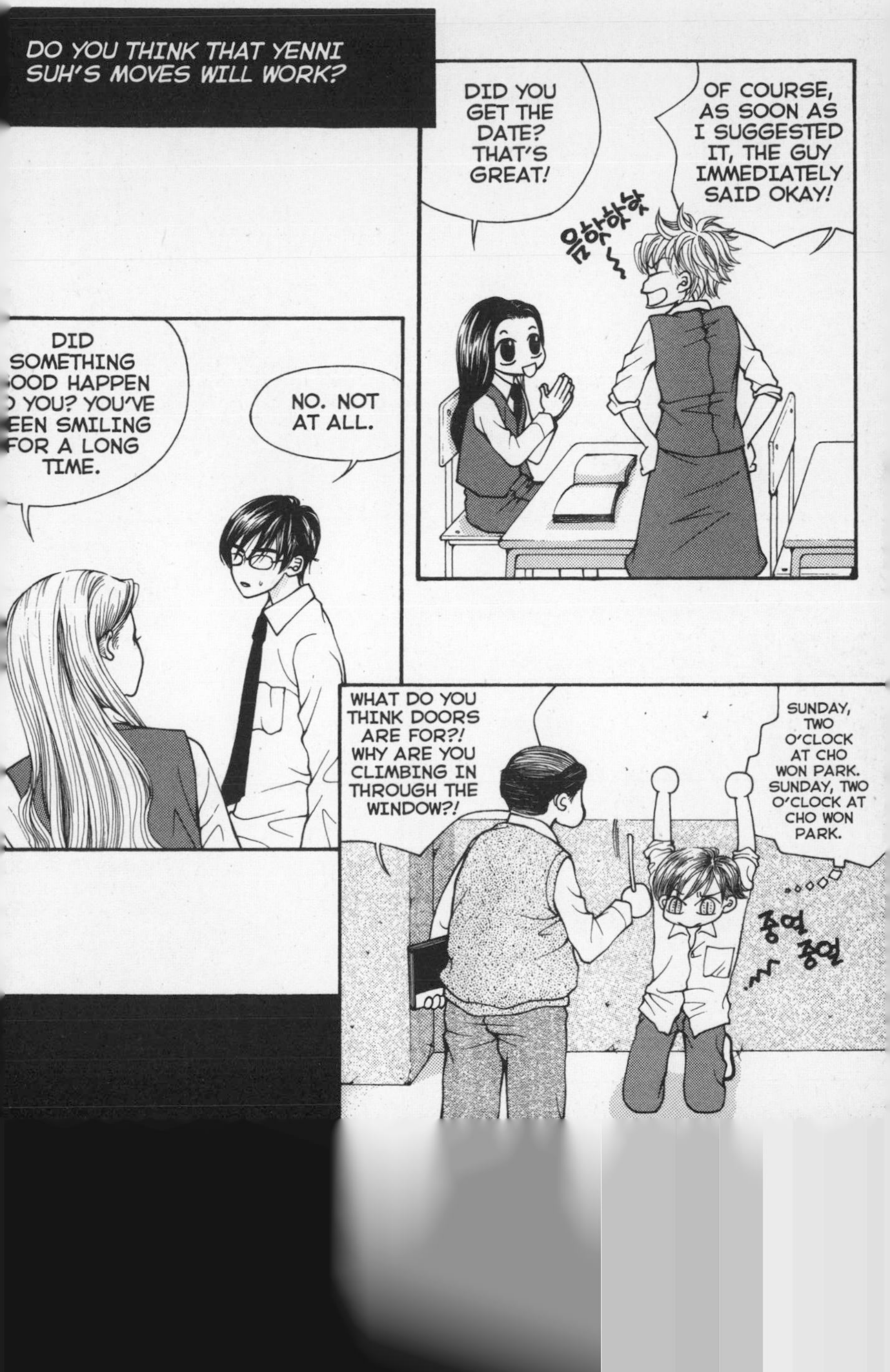
DO YOU THINK THAT YENNI SUH'S MOVES WILL WORK?
DID YOU GET THE DATE? THAT'S GREAT!
OF COURSE, AS SOON AS I SUGGESTED IT, THE GUY IMMEDIATELY SAID OKAY!
음핫핫핫~
DID SOMETHING OOD HAPPEN O YOU? YOU'VE EEN SMILING FOR A LONG TIME.
NO. NOT AT ALL.
WHAT DO YOU THINK DOORS ARE FOR?! WHY ARE YOU CLIMBING IN THROUGH THE WINDOW?!
SUNDAY, TWO O'CLOCK AT CHO WON PARK. SUNDAY, TWO O'CLOCK AT CHO WON PARK.
중얼중얼~

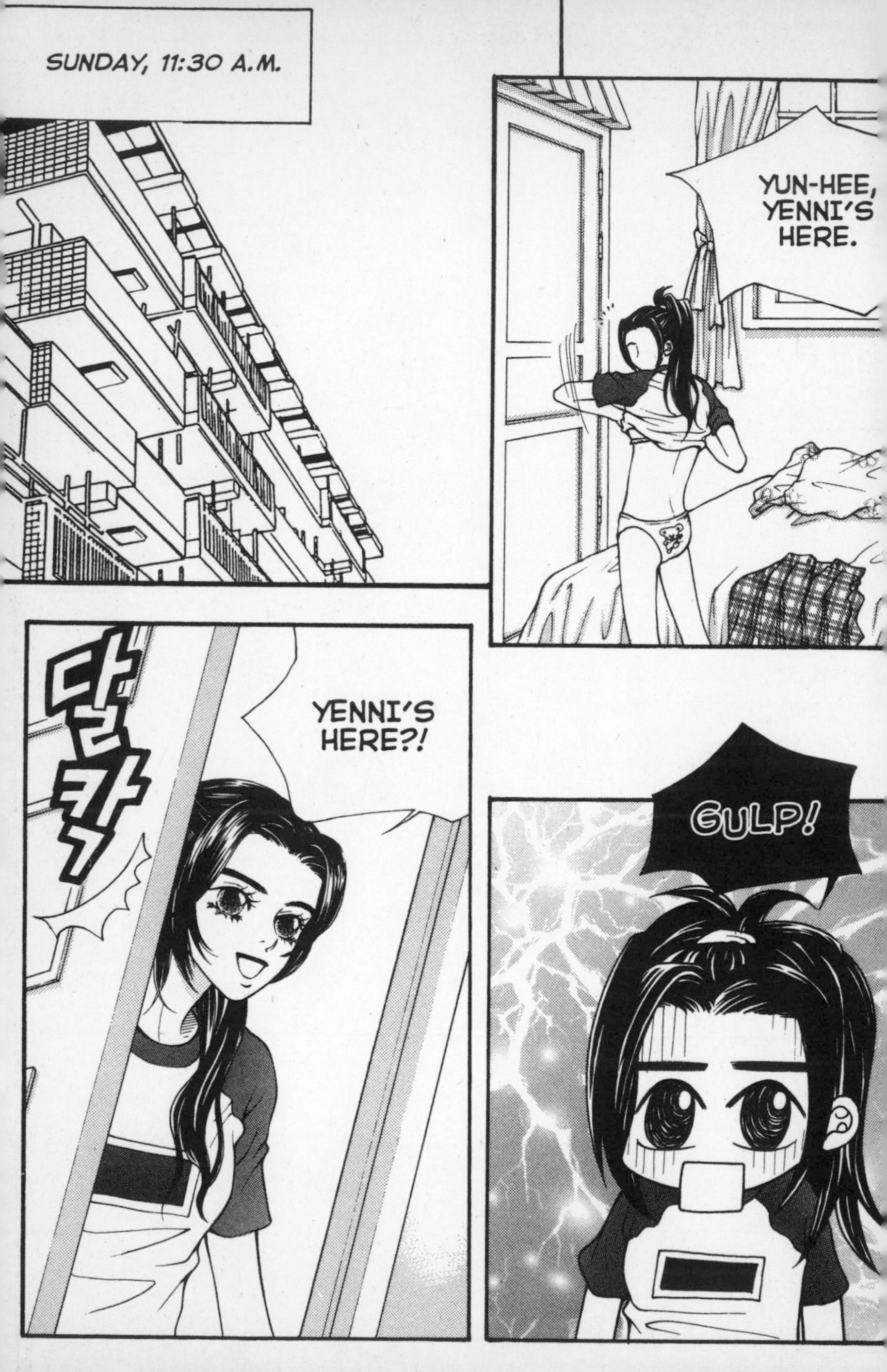
SUNDAY, 11:30 A.M.
YUN-HEE, YENNI'S HERE.
YENNI'S HERE?!
GULP!

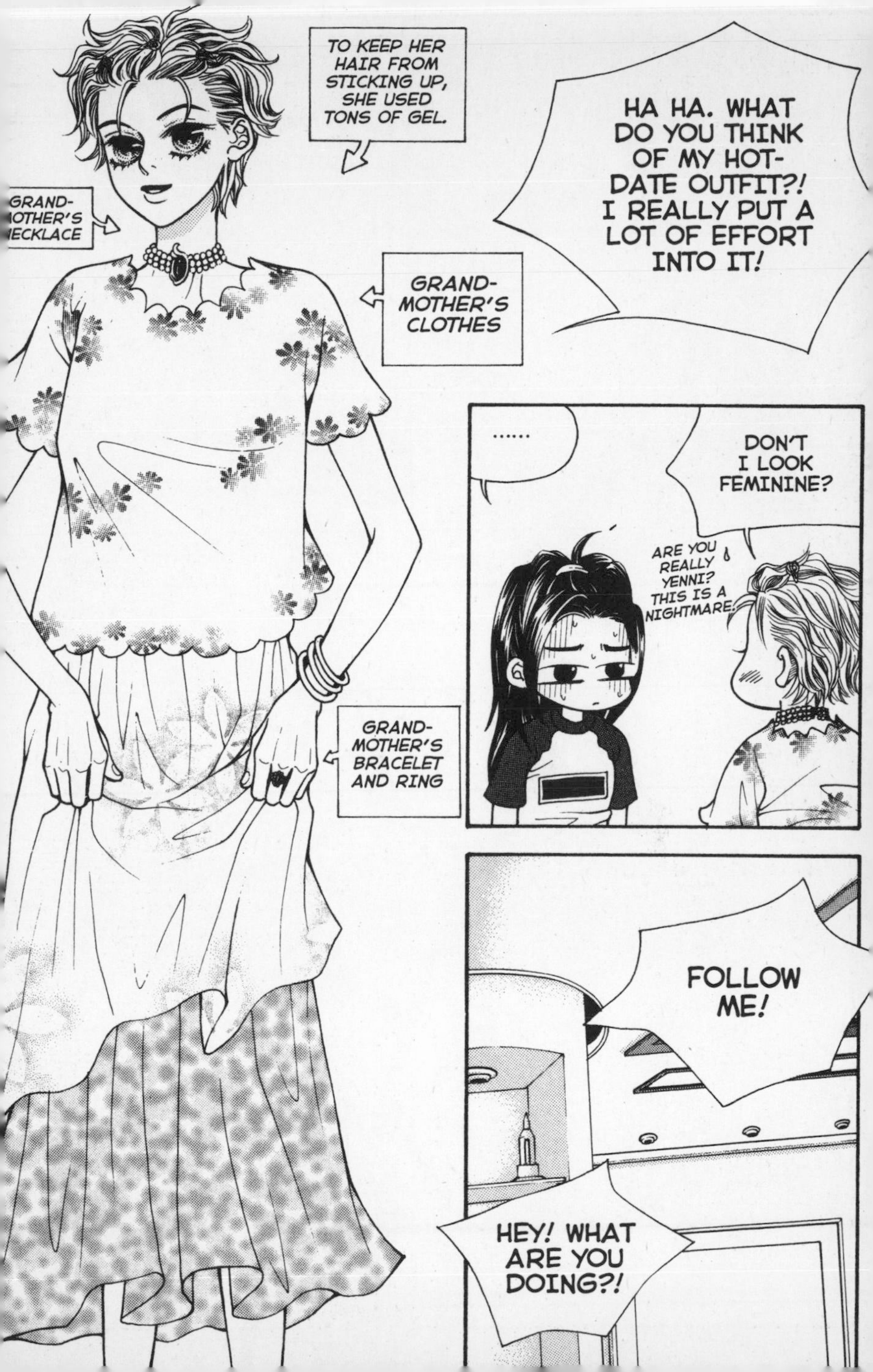

TO KEEP HER HAIR FROM STICKING UP, SHE USED TONS OF GEL.
GRAND- OTHER'S ECKLACE
GRAND-MOTHER'S CLOTHES
GRAND-MOTHER'S BRACELET AND RING
HA HA. WHAT DO YOU THINK OF MY HOT-DATE OUTFIT?! I REALLY PUT A LOT OF EFFORT INTO IT!
......
DON'T I LOOK FEMININE?
ARE YOU REALLY YENNI? THIS IS A NIGHTMARE.
FOLLOW ME!
HEY! WHAT ARE YOU DOING?!

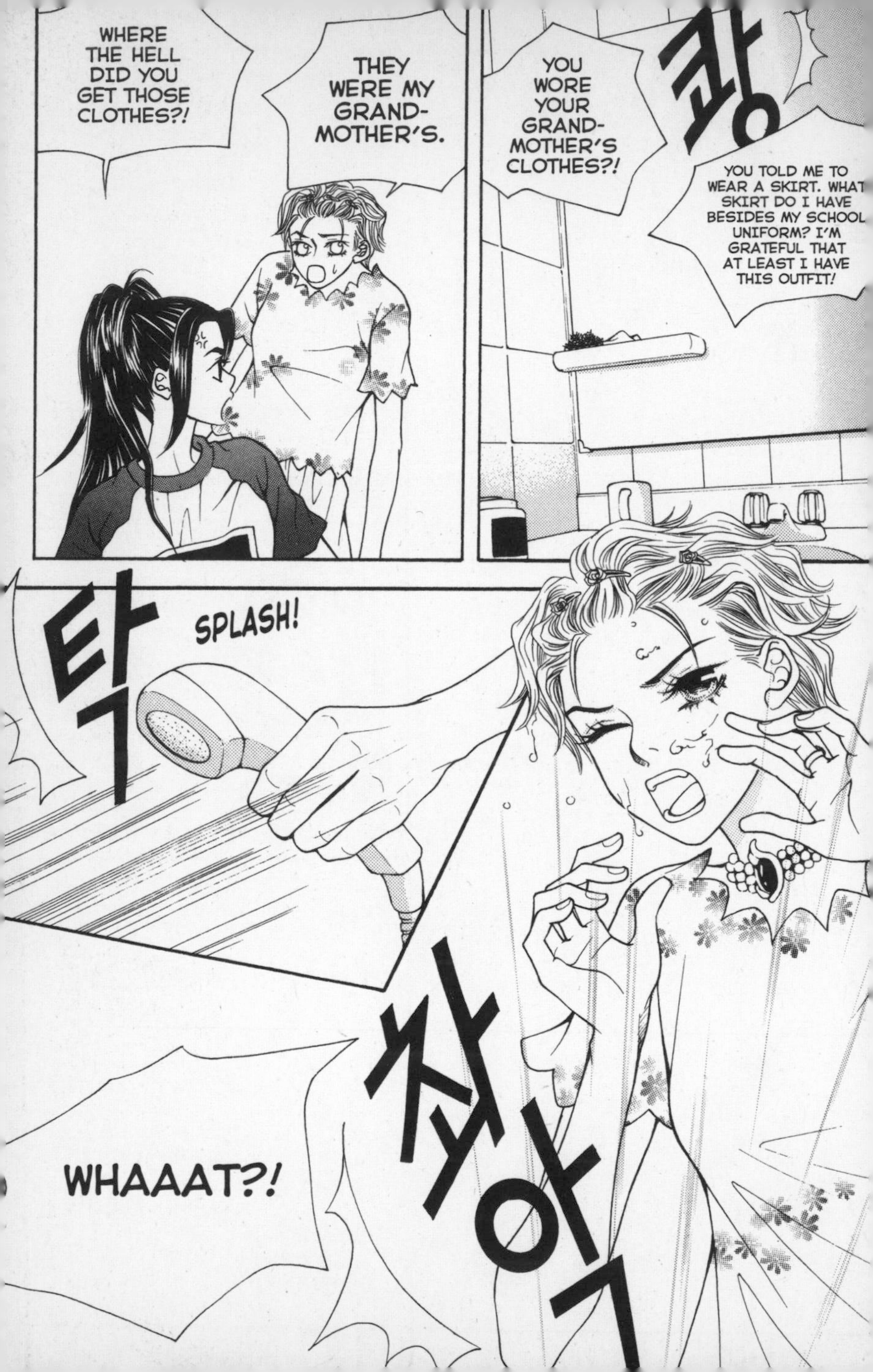
WHERE THE HELL DID YOU GET THOSE CLOTHES?!
THEY WERE MY GRAND-MOTHER'S.
YOU WORE YOUR GRAND-MOTHER'S CLOTHES?!
쾅
YOU TOLD ME TO WEAR A SKIRT. WHAT SKIRT DO I HAVE BESIDES MY SCHOOL UNIFORM? I'M GRATEFUL THAT AT LEAST I HAVE THIS OUTFIT!
탁
SPLASH!
WHAAAT?!

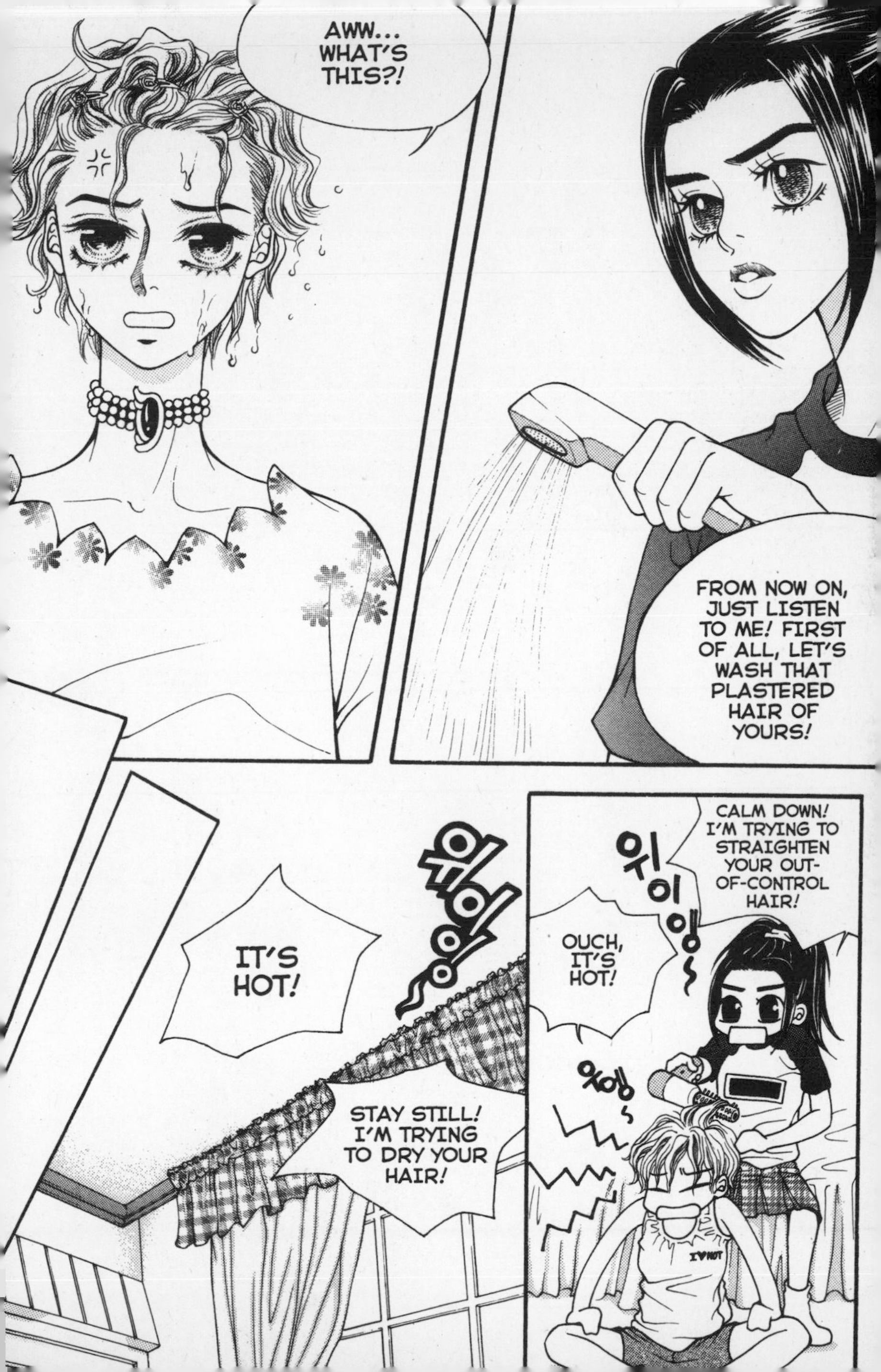
AWW... WHAT'S THIS?!
FROM NOW ON, JUST LISTEN TO ME! FIRST OF ALL, LET'S WASH THAT PLASTERED HAIR OF YOURS!
IT'S HOT!
위잉~
STAY STILL! I'M TRYING TO DRY YOUR HAIR!
CALM DOWN! I'M TRYING TO STRAIGHTEN YOUR OUT-OF-CONTROL HAIR!
위이잉~
OUCH, IT'S HOT!
I♥HOT

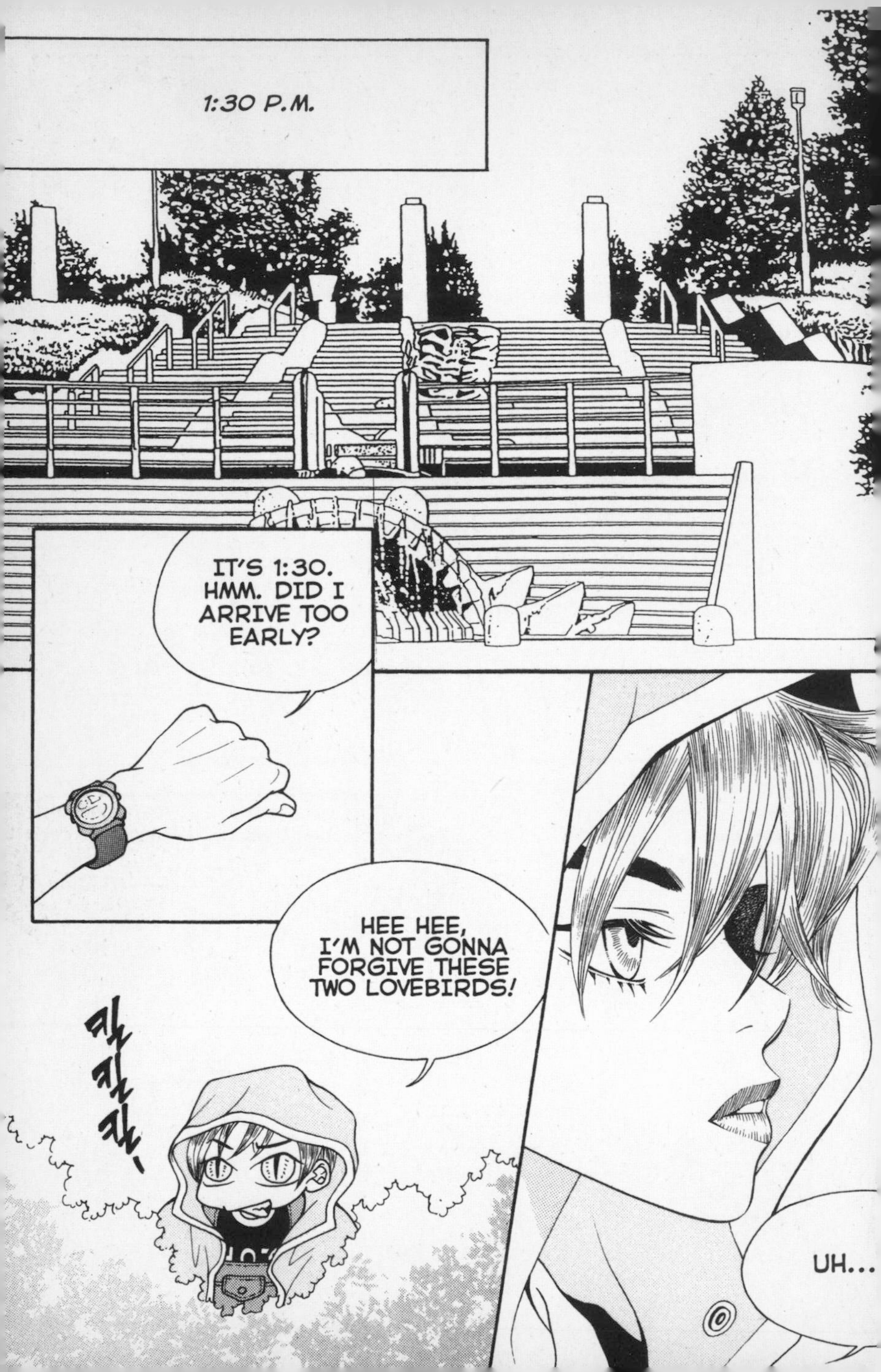
1:30 P.M.
IT'S 1:30. HMM. DID I ARRIVE TOO EARLY?
HEE HEE, I'M NOT GONNA FORGIVE THESE TWO LOVEBIRDS!
UH...

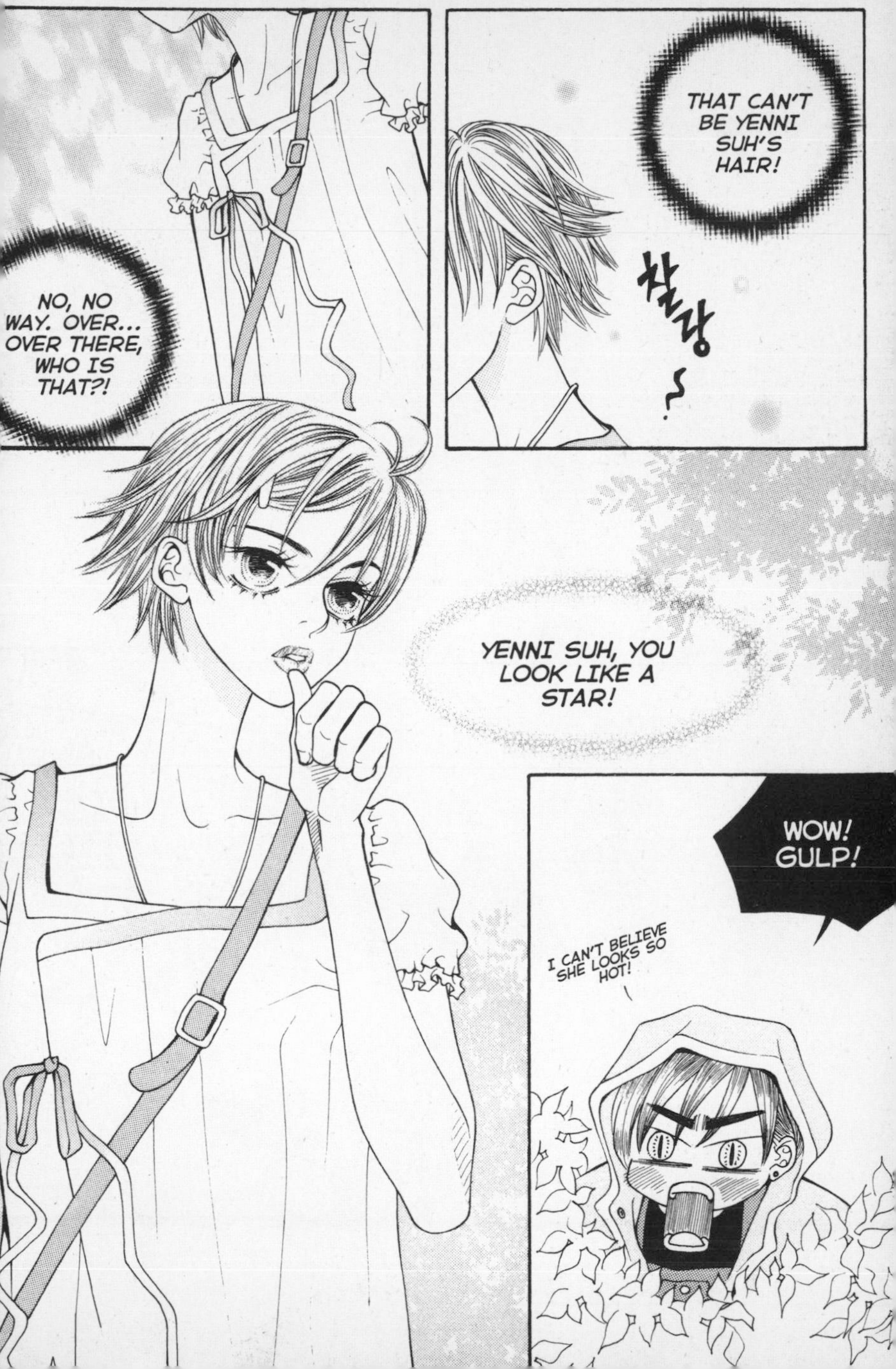
NO, NO WAY. OVER... OVER THERE, WHO IS THAT?!
THAT CAN'T BE YENNI SUH'S HAIR!
찰랑~
YENNI SUH, YOU LOOK LIKE A STAR!
WOW! GULP!
I CAN'T BELIEVE SHE LOOKS SO HOT!

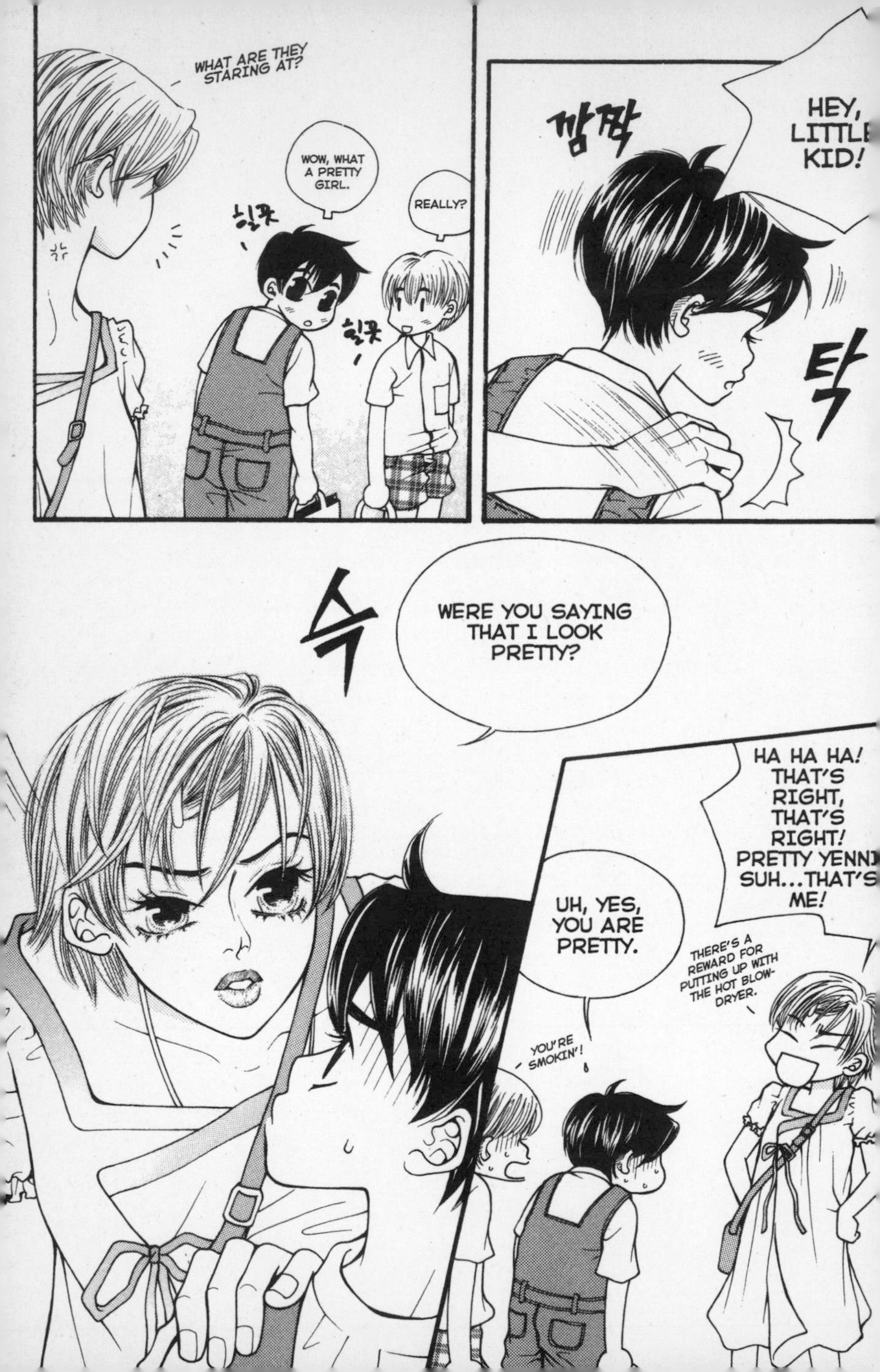
WHAT ARE THEY STARING AT?
WOW, WHAT A PRETTY GIRL.
힐끗
REALLY?
힐끗
깜짝
HEY, LITTLE KID!
탁
슥
WERE YOU SAYING THAT I LOOK PRETTY?
UH, YES, YOU ARE PRETTY.
YOU'RE SMOKIN'!
HA HA HA! THAT'S RIGHT, THAT'S RIGHT! PRETTY YENNI SUH...THAT'S ME!
THERE'S A REWARD FOR PUTTING UP WITH THE HOT BLOW-DRYER.

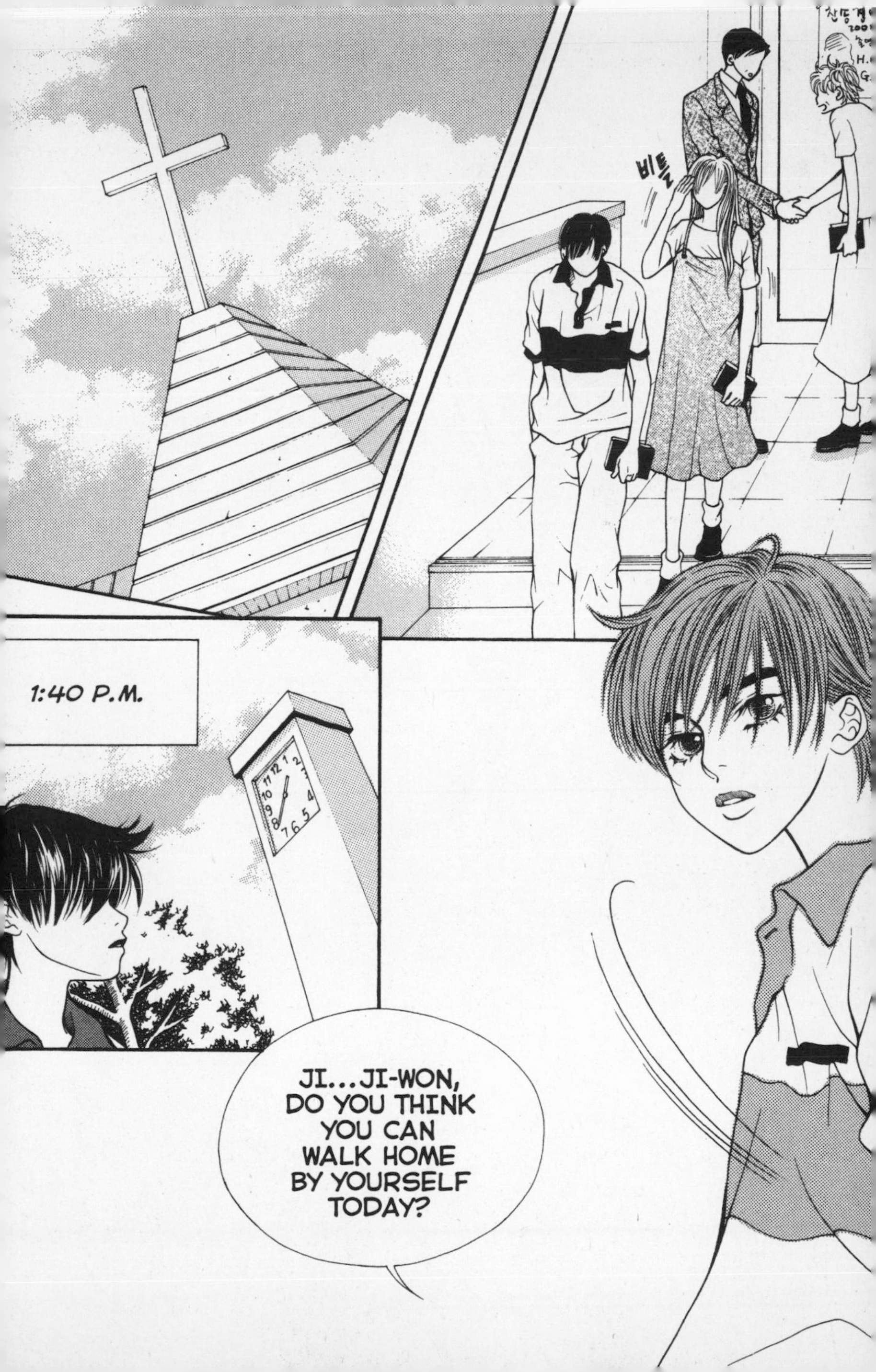
비틀
1:40 P.M.
JI...JI-WON, DO YOU THINK YOU CAN WALK HOME BY YOURSELF TODAY?

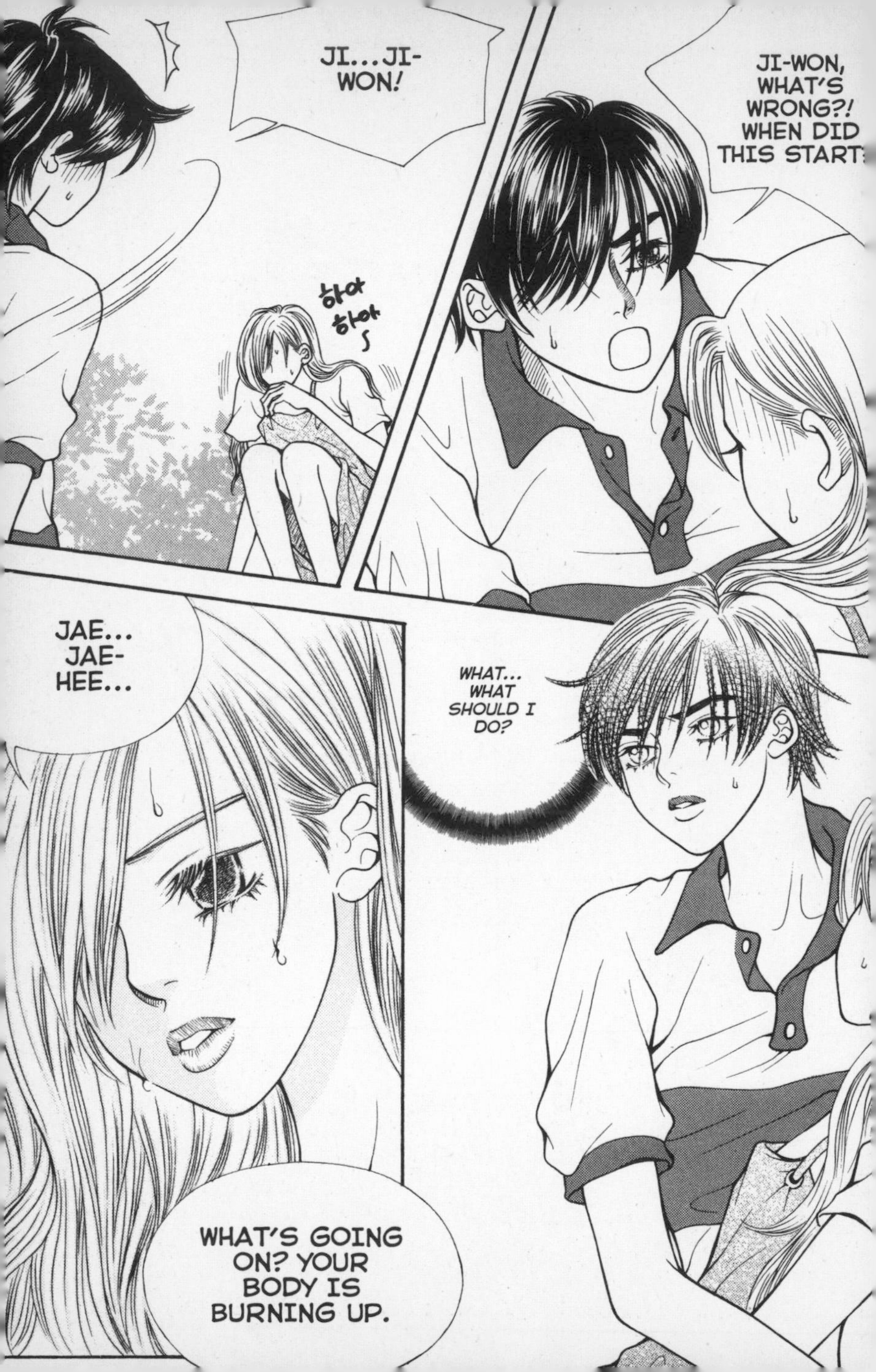
JI...JI-WON!
하아 하아
JI-WON, WHAT'S WRONG?! WHEN DID THIS START
JAE... JAE-HEE...
WHAT'S GOING ON? YOUR BODY IS BURNING UP.
WHAT... WHAT SHOULD I DO?

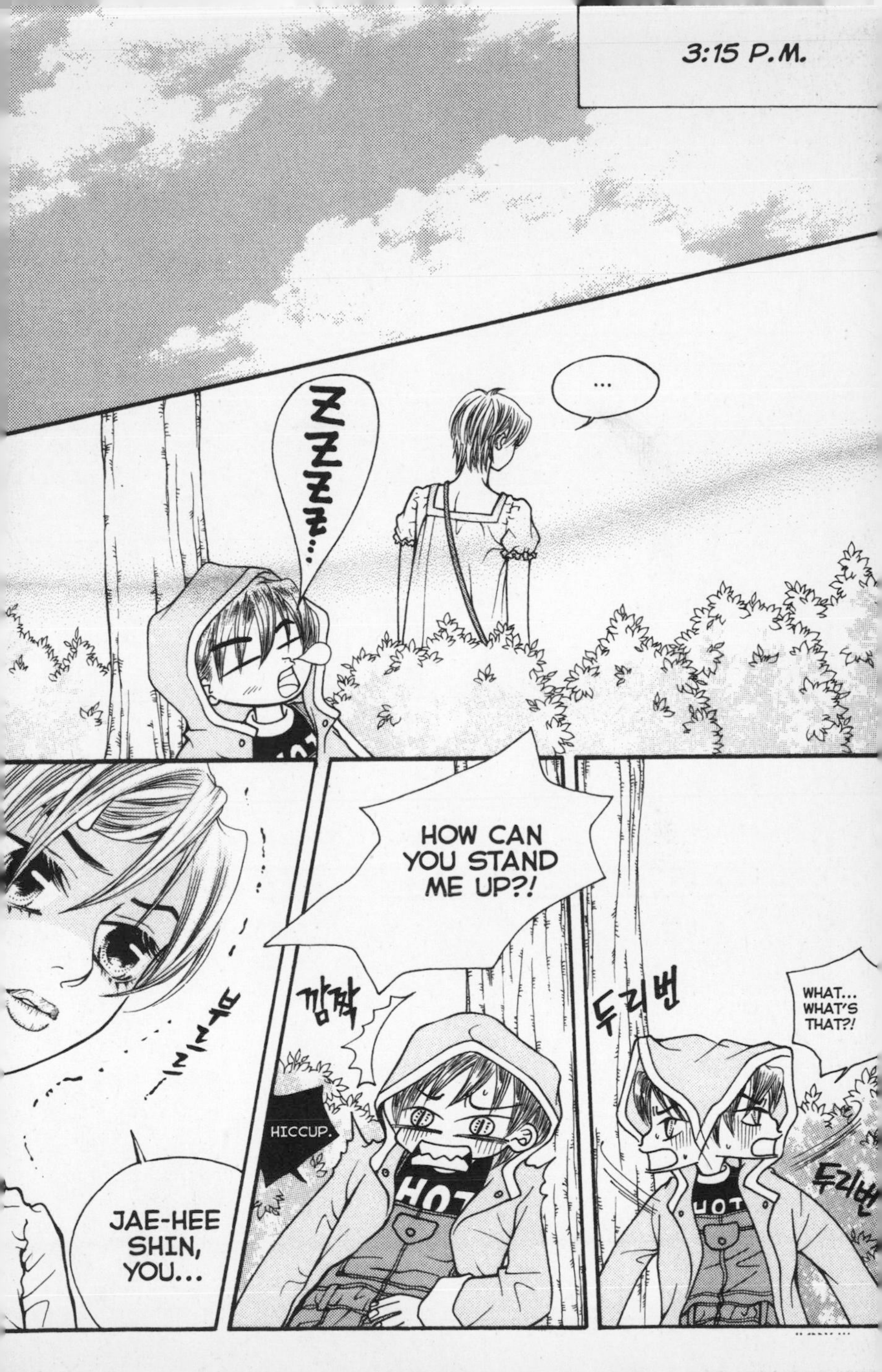
3:15 P.M.
즈즈즈즈...
...
부르르
JAE-HEE SHIN, YOU...
HOW CAN YOU STAND ME UP?!
깜짝
HICCUP.
두리번
WHAT... WHAT'S THAT?!
두리번

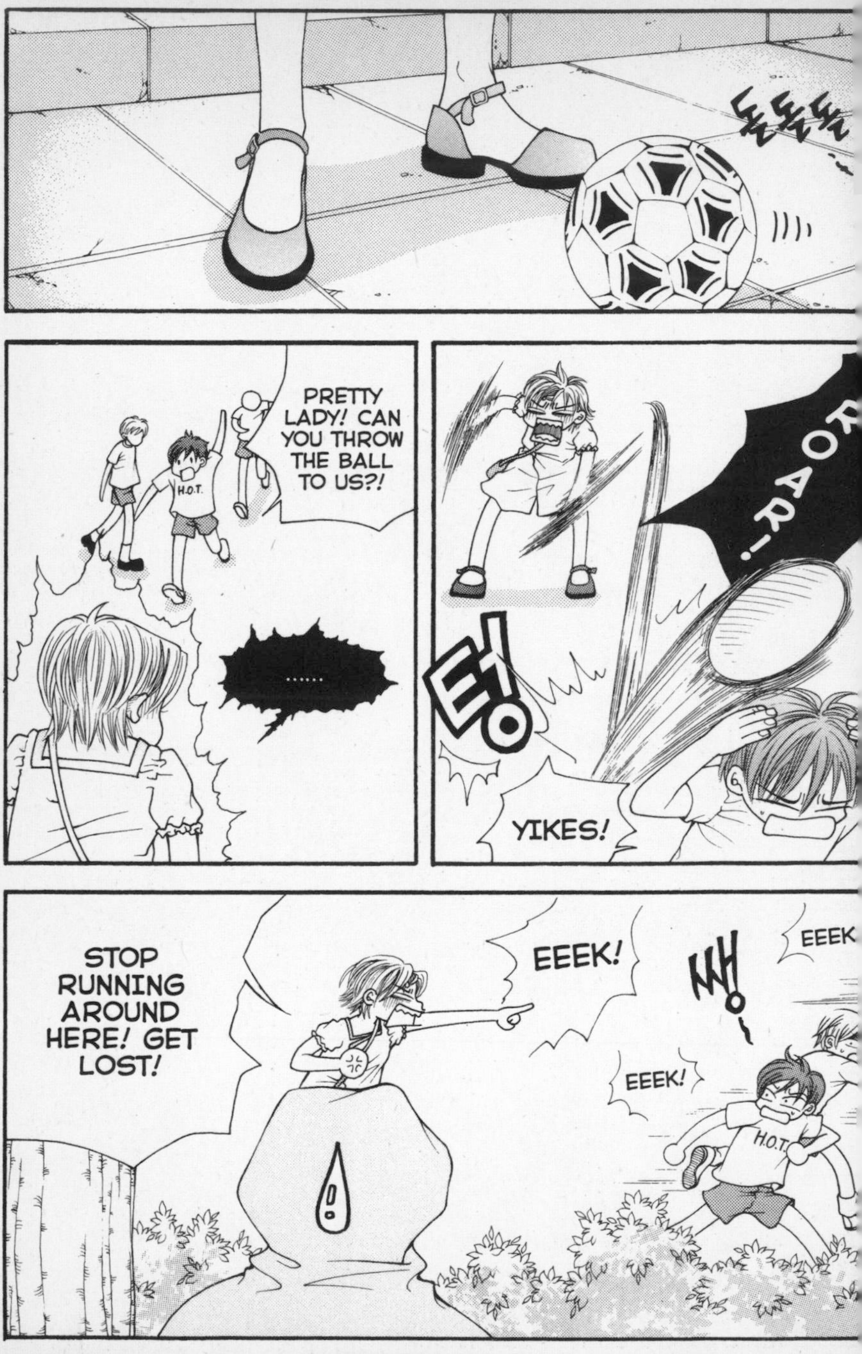
PRETTY LADY! CAN YOU THROW THE BALL TO US?!
......
ROAR!
YIKES!
STOP RUNNING AROUND HERE! GET LOST!
EEEK!
EEEK!
EEEK

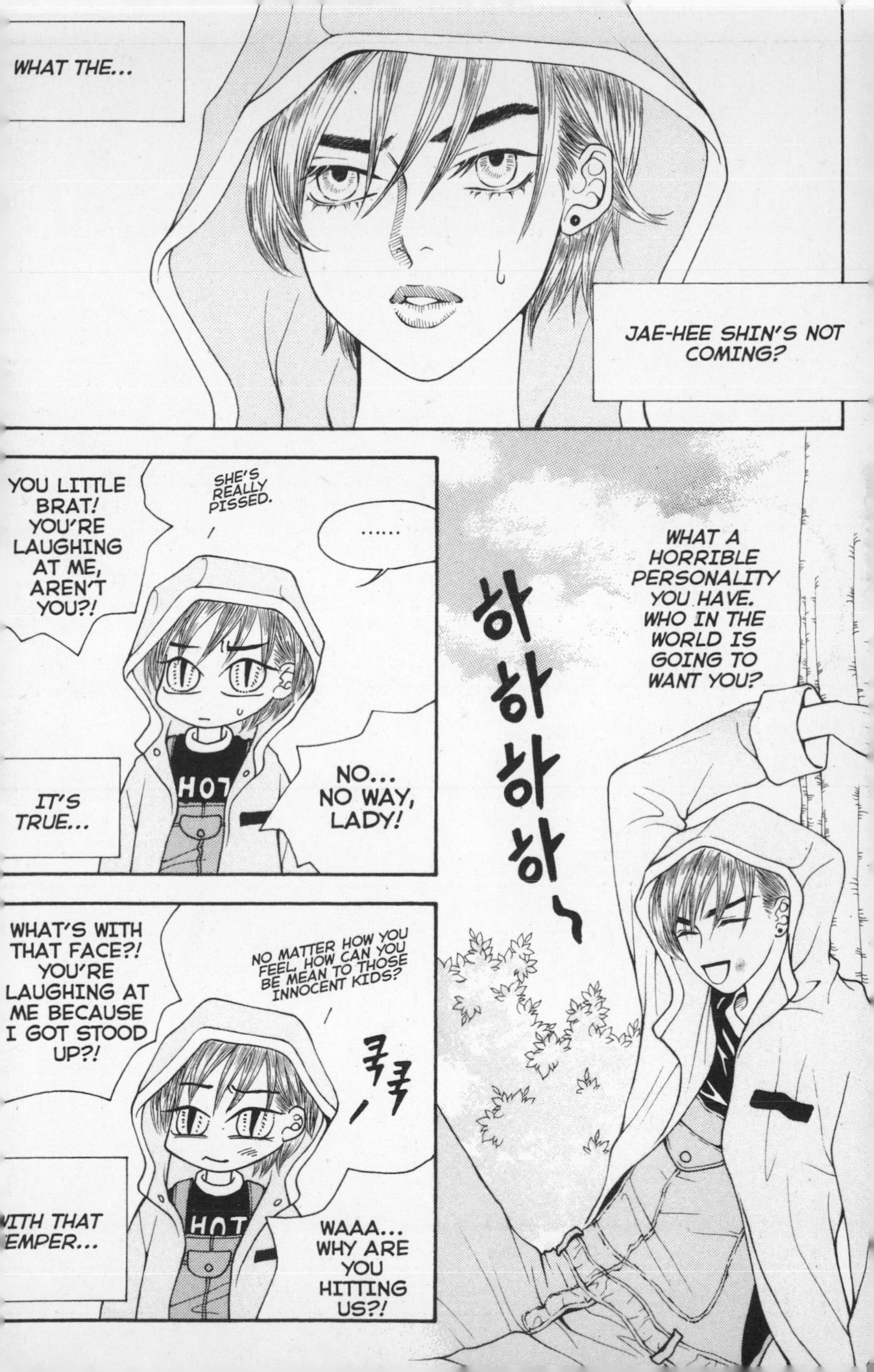
WHAT THE...
JAE-HEE SHIN'S NOT COMING?
YOU LITTLE BRAT! YOU'RE LAUGHING AT ME, AREN'T YOU?!
SHE'S REALLY PISSED.
......
IT'S TRUE...
NO... NO WAY, LADY!
WHAT'S WITH THAT FACE?! YOU'RE LAUGHING AT ME BECAUSE I GOT STOOD UP?!
NO MATTER HOW YOU FEEL, HOW CAN YOU BE MEAN TO THOSE INNOCENT KIDS?
쿡쿡
WITH THAT EMPER...
WAAA... WHY ARE YOU HITTING US?!
하하하하~
WHAT A HORRIBLE PERSONALITY YOU HAVE. WHO IN THE WORLD IS GOING TO WANT YOU?

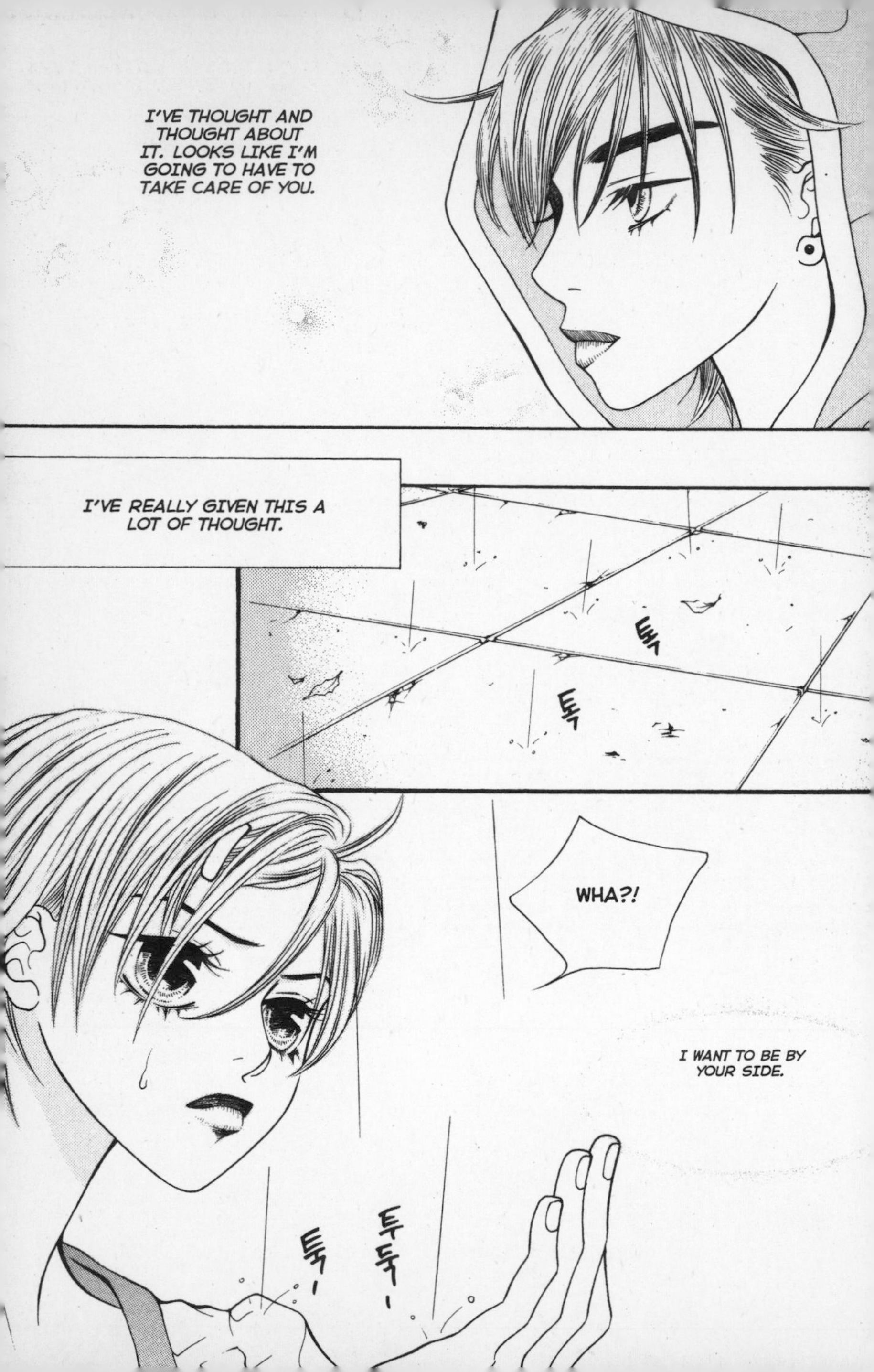

I'VE THOUGHT AND THOUGHT ABOUT IT. LOOKS LIKE I'M GOING TO HAVE TO TAKE CARE OF YOU.
I'VE REALLY GIVEN THIS A LOT OF THOUGHT.
툭
툭
WHA?!
I WANT TO BE BY YOUR SIDE.
툭
투두

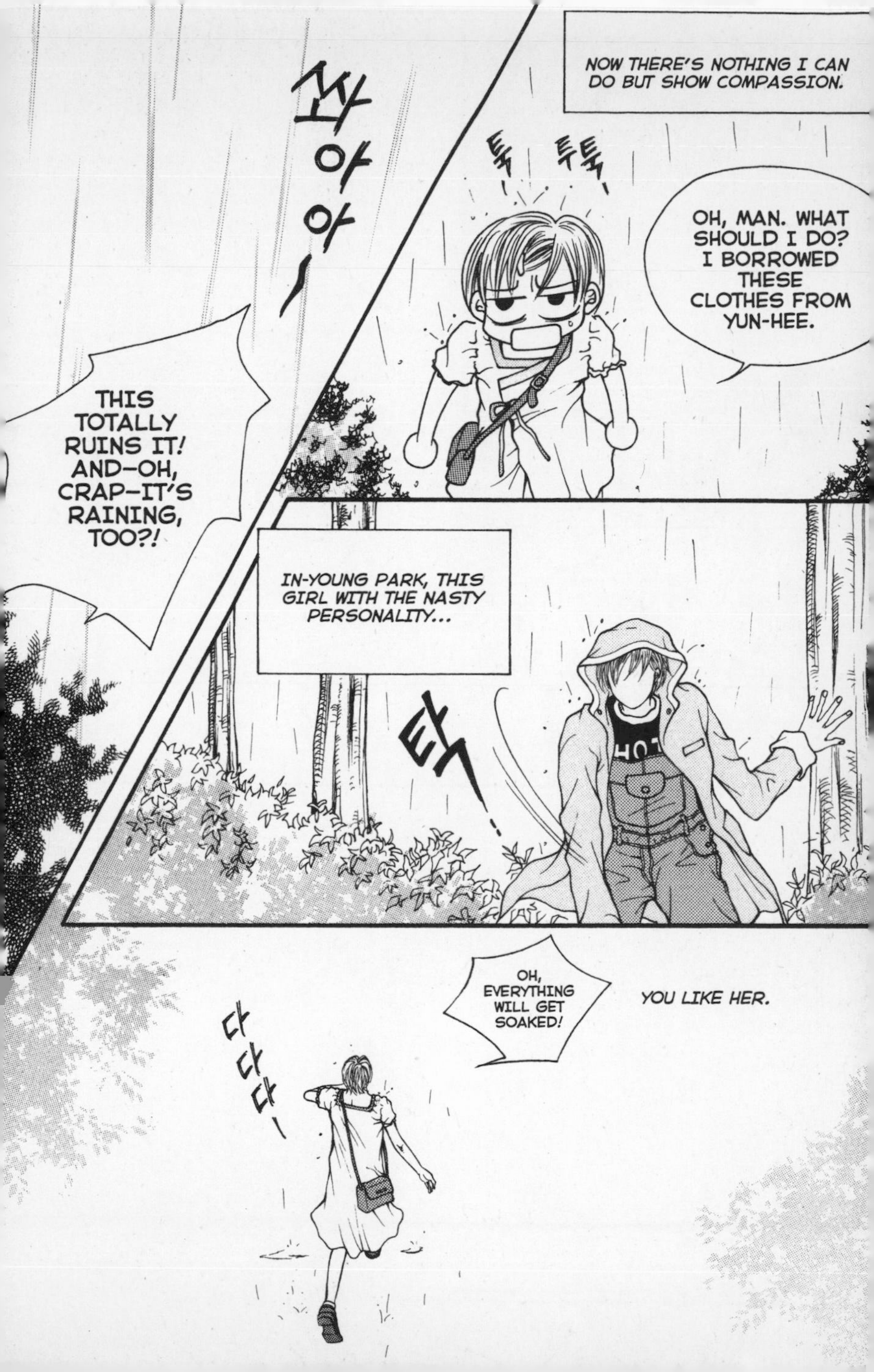
쏴아아
THIS TOTALLY RUINS IT! AND—OH, CRAP—IT'S RAINING, TOO?!
NOW THERE'S NOTHING I CAN DO BUT SHOW COMPASSION.
툭 투툭
OH, MAN. WHAT SHOULD I DO? I BORROWED THESE CLOTHES FROM YUN-HEE.
IN-YOUNG PARK, THIS GIRL WITH THE NASTY PERSONALITY...
탁
다다다
OH, EVERYTHING WILL GET SOAKED!
YOU LIKE HER.

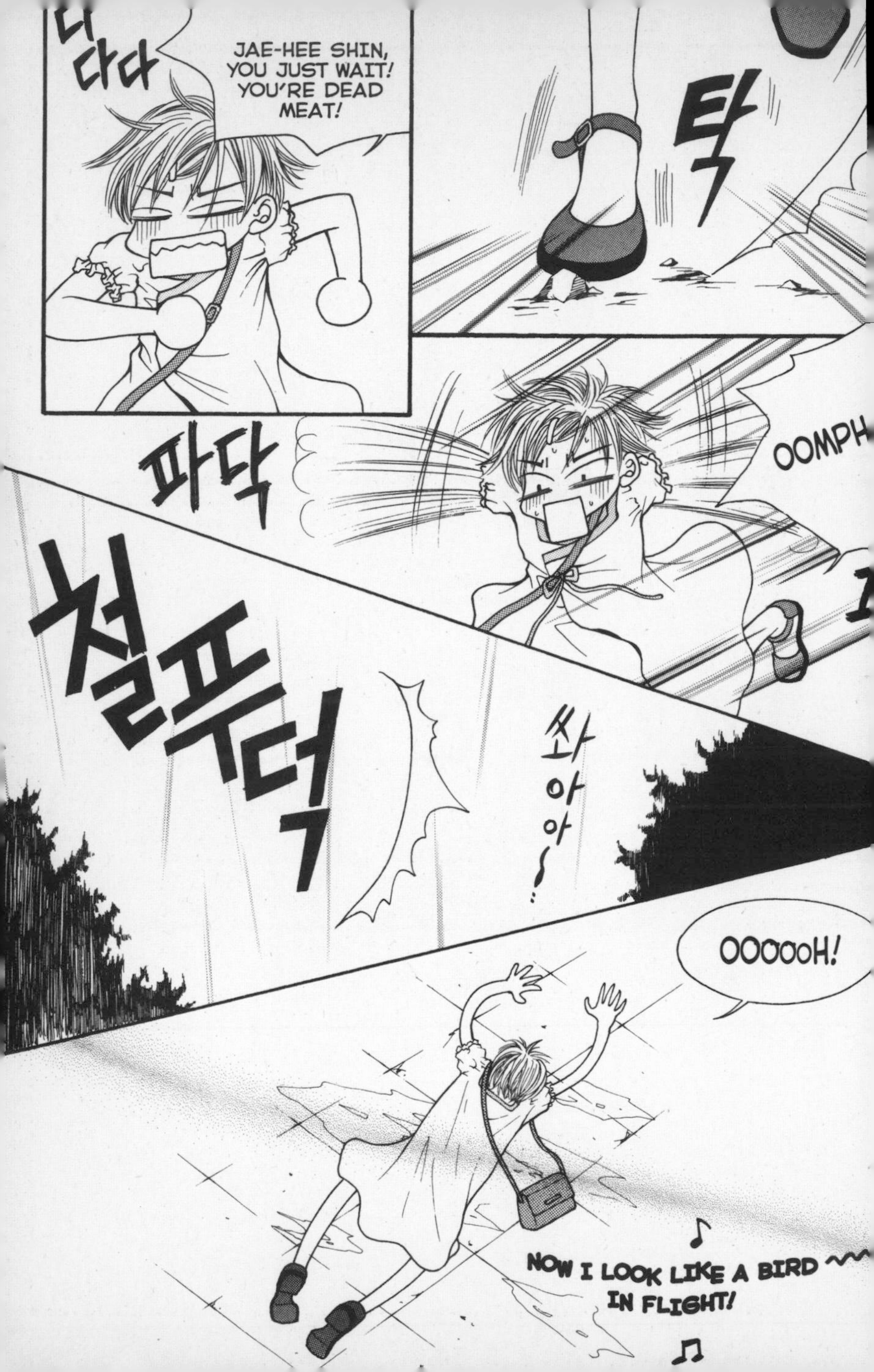
다다다
JAE-HEE SHIN, YOU JUST WAIT! YOU'RE DEAD MEAT!
탁
파닥
OOMPH
철푸덕
좌아아~!
OOOOOH!
NOW I LOOK LIKE A BIRD IN FLIGHT!

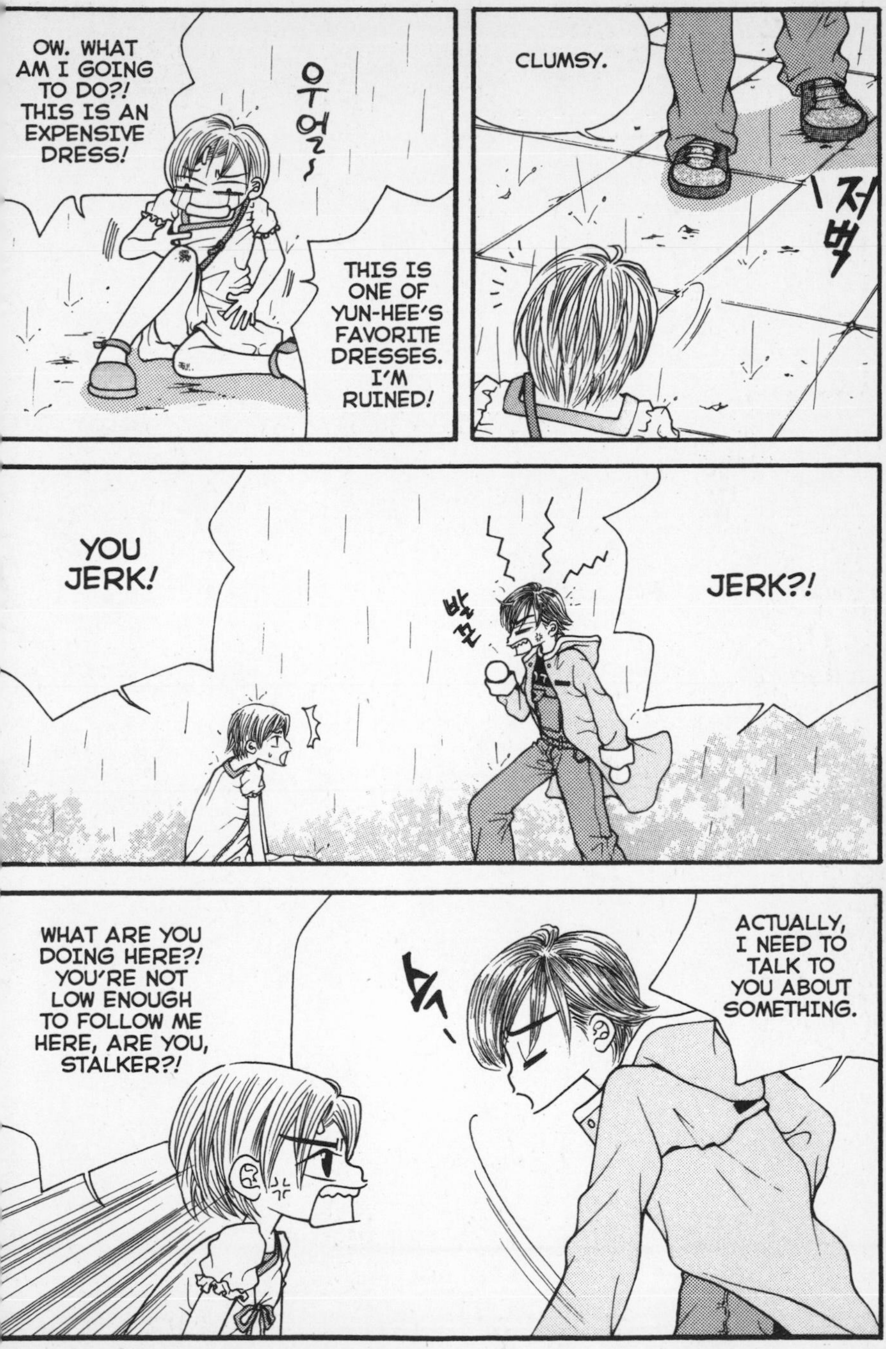
OW. WHAT AM I GOING TO DO?! THIS IS AN EXPENSIVE DRESS!
우얼~
THIS IS ONE OF YUN-HEE'S FAVORITE DRESSES. I'M RUINED!
CLUMSY.
저벅
YOU JERK!
발끈
JERK?!
WHAT ARE YOU DOING HERE?! YOU'RE NOT LOW ENOUGH TO FOLLOW ME HERE, ARE YOU, STALKER?!
ACTUALLY, I NEED TO TALK TO YOU ABOUT SOMETHING.

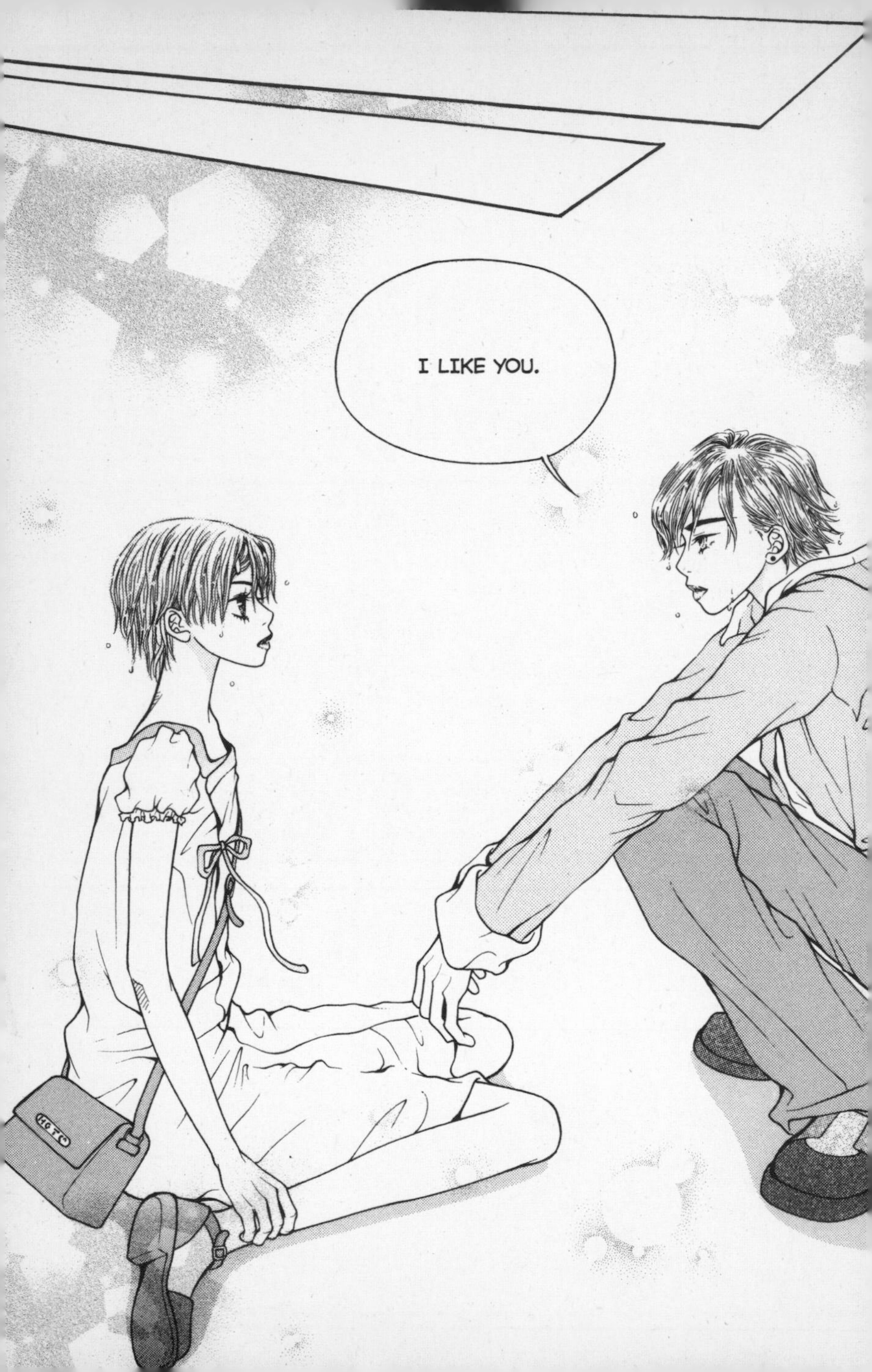
I LIKE YOU.

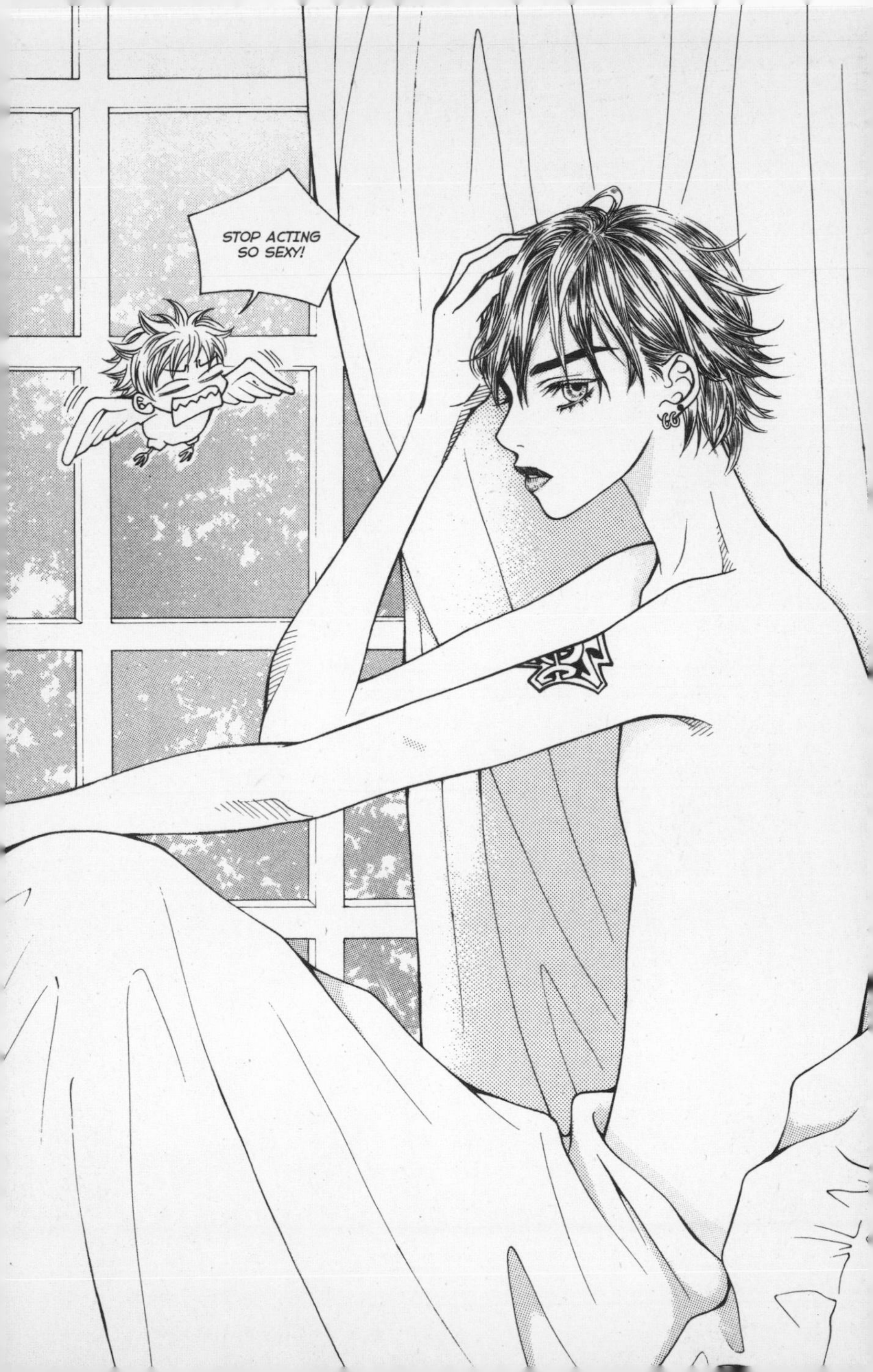
STOP ACTING SO SEXY!

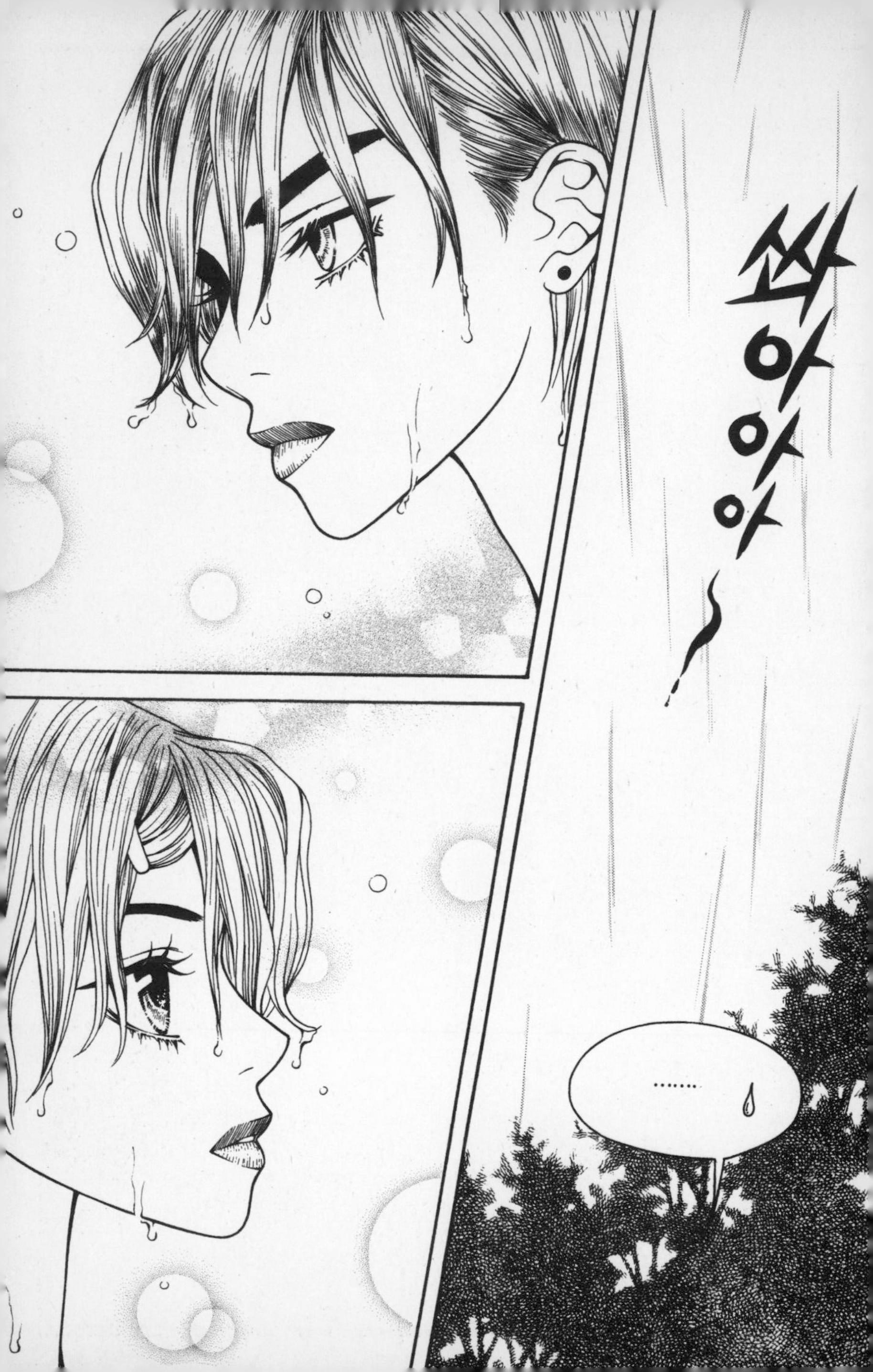
쏴아아아
....

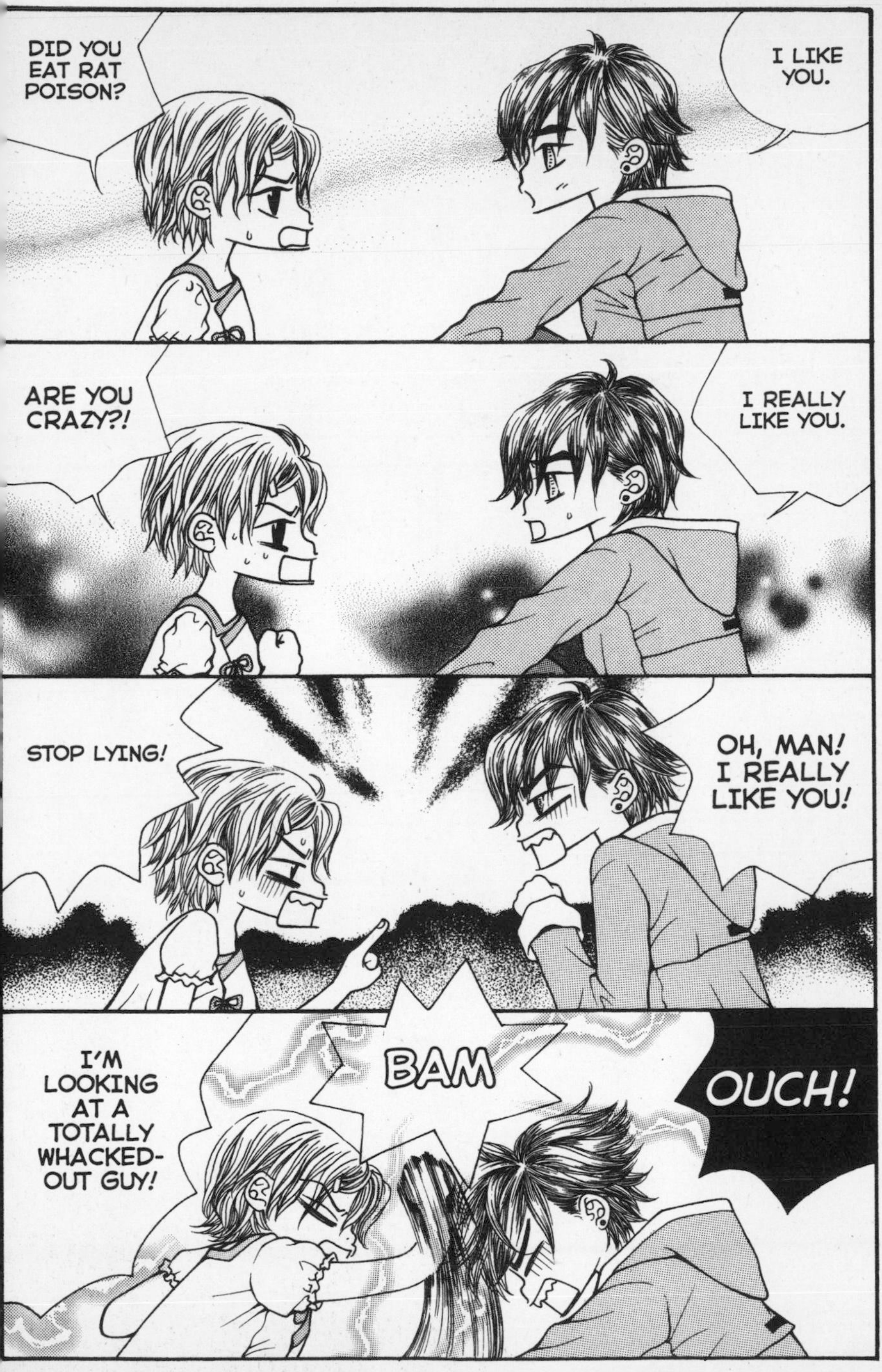

DID YOU EAT RAT POISON?
I LIKE YOU.
ARE YOU CRAZY?!
I REALLY LIKE YOU.
STOP LYING!
OH, MAN! I REALLY LIKE YOU!
I'M LOOKING AT A TOTALLY WHACKED-OUT GUY!
BAM
OUCH!

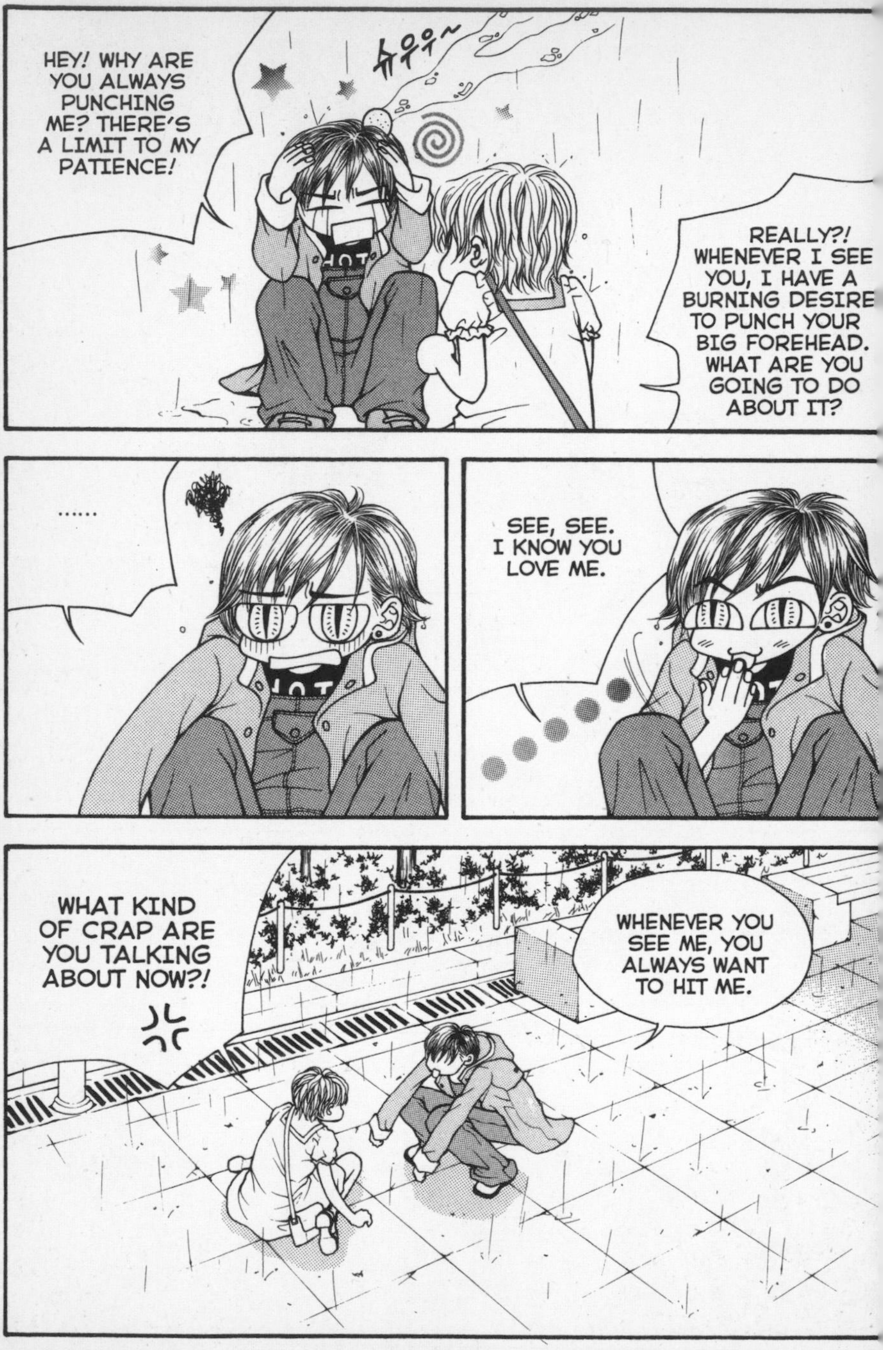
HEY! WHY ARE YOU ALWAYS PUNCHING ME? THERE'S A LIMIT TO MY PATIENCE!
슈우우~
REALLY?! WHENEVER I SEE YOU, I HAVE A BURNING DESIRE TO PUNCH YOUR BIG FOREHEAD. WHAT ARE YOU GOING TO DO ABOUT IT?
......
SEE, SEE. I KNOW YOU LOVE ME.
WHAT KIND OF CRAP ARE YOU TALKING ABOUT NOW?!
WHENEVER YOU SEE ME, YOU ALWAYS WANT TO HIT ME.

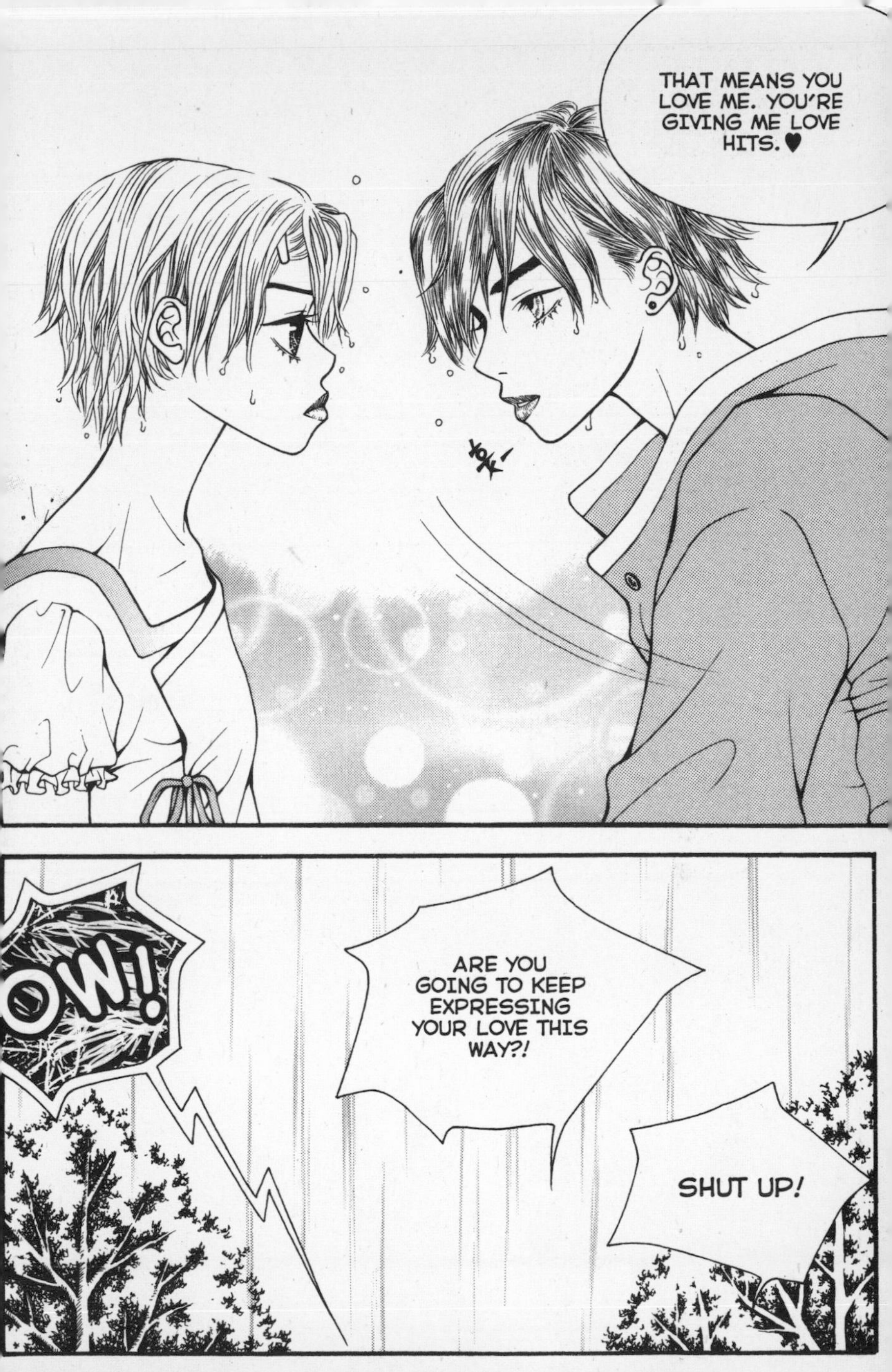
THAT MEANS YOU LOVE ME. YOU'RE GIVING ME LOVE HITS.♥
OW!
ARE YOU GOING TO KEEP EXPRESSING YOUR LOVE THIS WAY?!
SHUT UP!

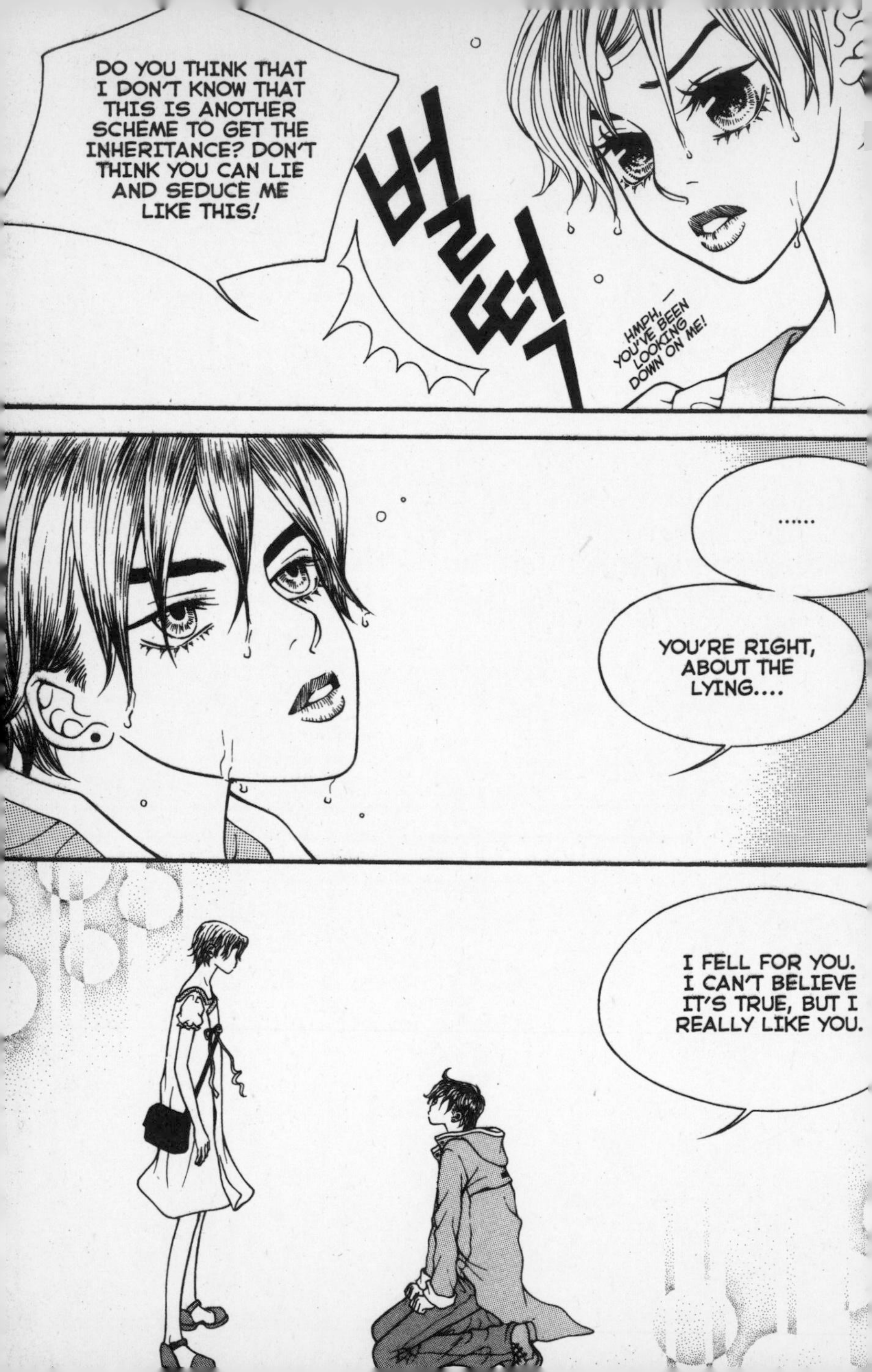
DO YOU THINK THAT I DON'T KNOW THAT THIS IS ANOTHER SCHEME TO GET THE INHERITANCE? DON'T THINK YOU CAN LIE AND SEDUCE ME LIKE THIS!
벌떡
HMPH, YOU'VE BEEN LOOKING DOWN ON ME!
......
YOU'RE RIGHT, ABOUT THE LYING....
I FELL FOR YOU. I CAN'T BELIEVE IT'S TRUE, BUT I REALLY LIKE YOU.

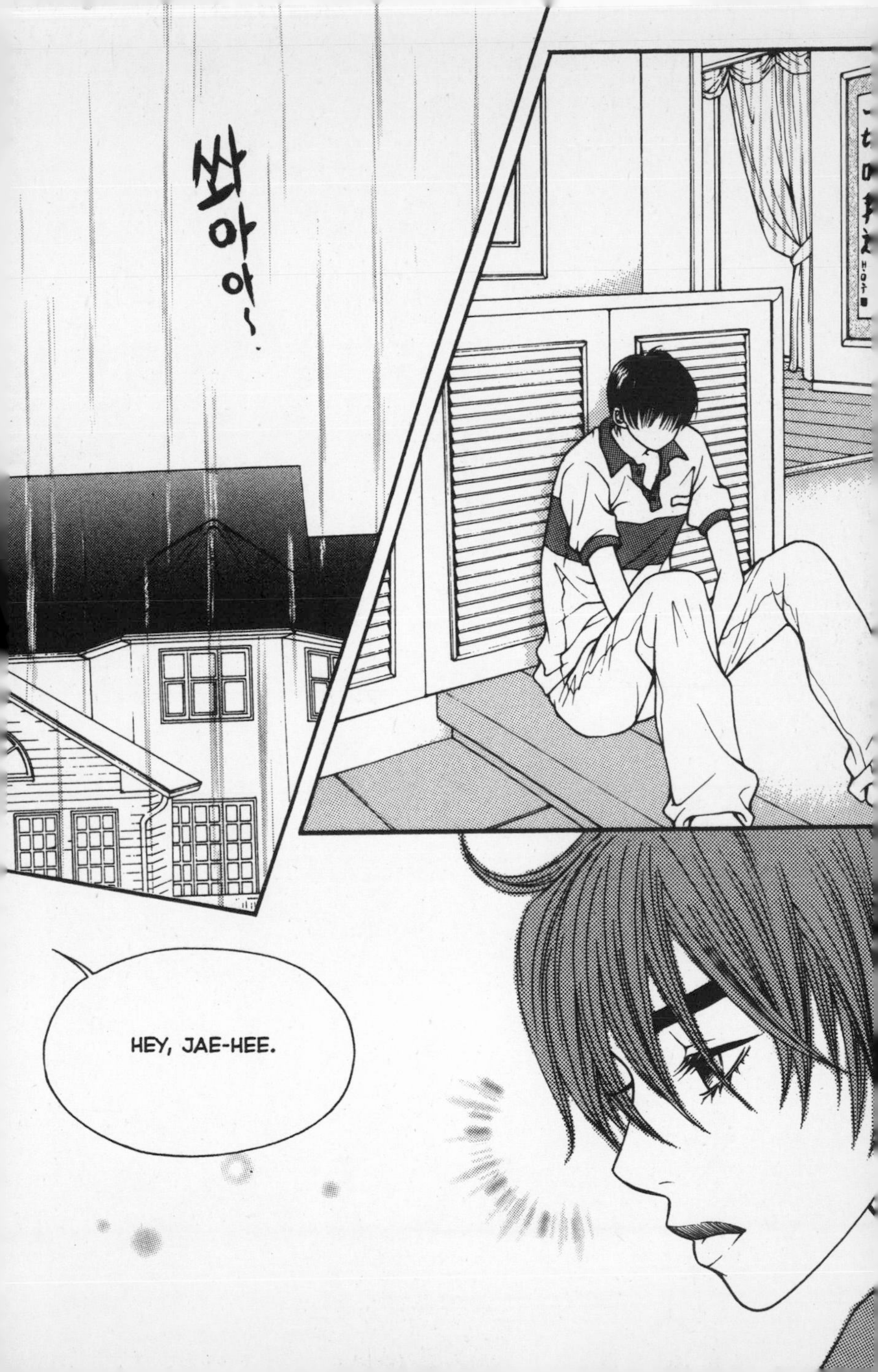
쏴아아~
HEY, JAE-HEE.

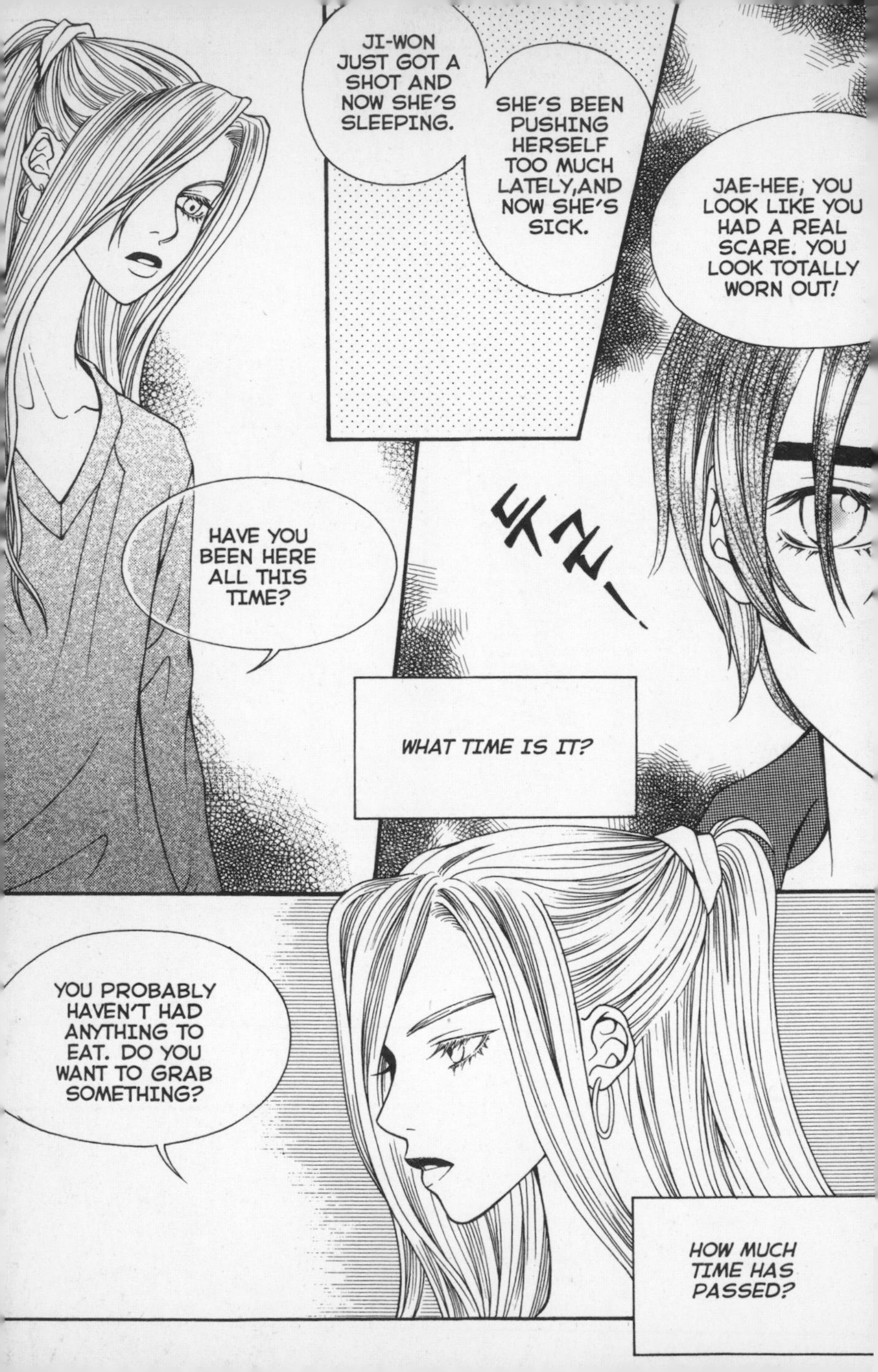
HAVE YOU BEEN HERE ALL THIS TIME?
JI-WON JUST GOT A SHOT AND NOW SHE'S SLEEPING.
SHE'S BEEN PUSHING HERSELF TOO MUCH LATELY,AND NOW SHE'S SICK.
JAE-HEE, YOU LOOK LIKE YOU HAD A REAL SCARE. YOU LOOK TOTALLY WORN OUT!
WHAT TIME IS IT?
YOU PROBABLY HAVEN'T HAD ANYTHING TO EAT. DO YOU WANT TO GRAB SOMETHING?
HOW MUCH TIME HAS PASSED?

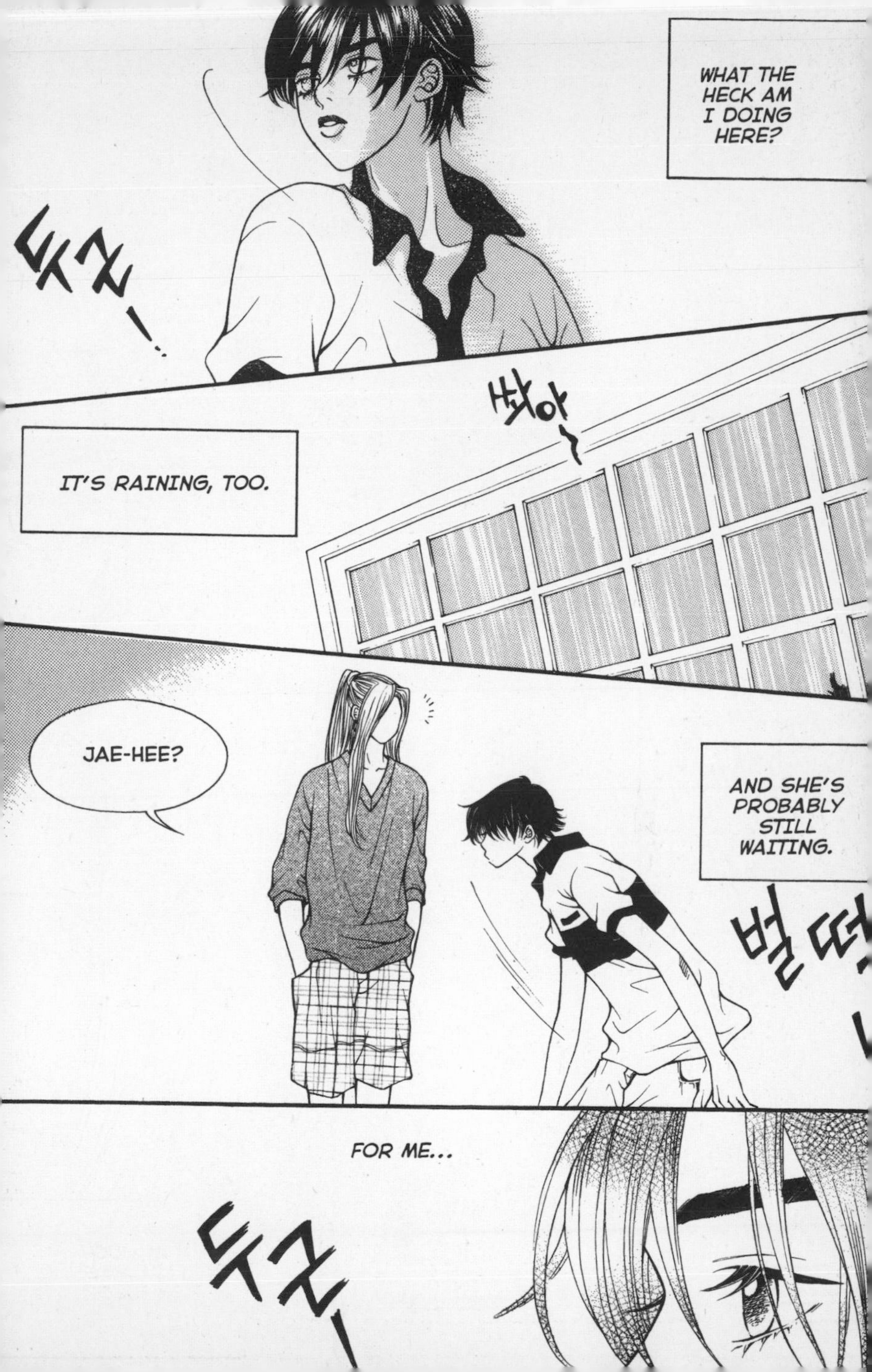
WHAT THE HECK AM I DOING HERE?
IT'S RAINING, TOO.
JAE-HEE?
AND SHE'S PROBABLY STILL WAITING.
FOR ME...
두근

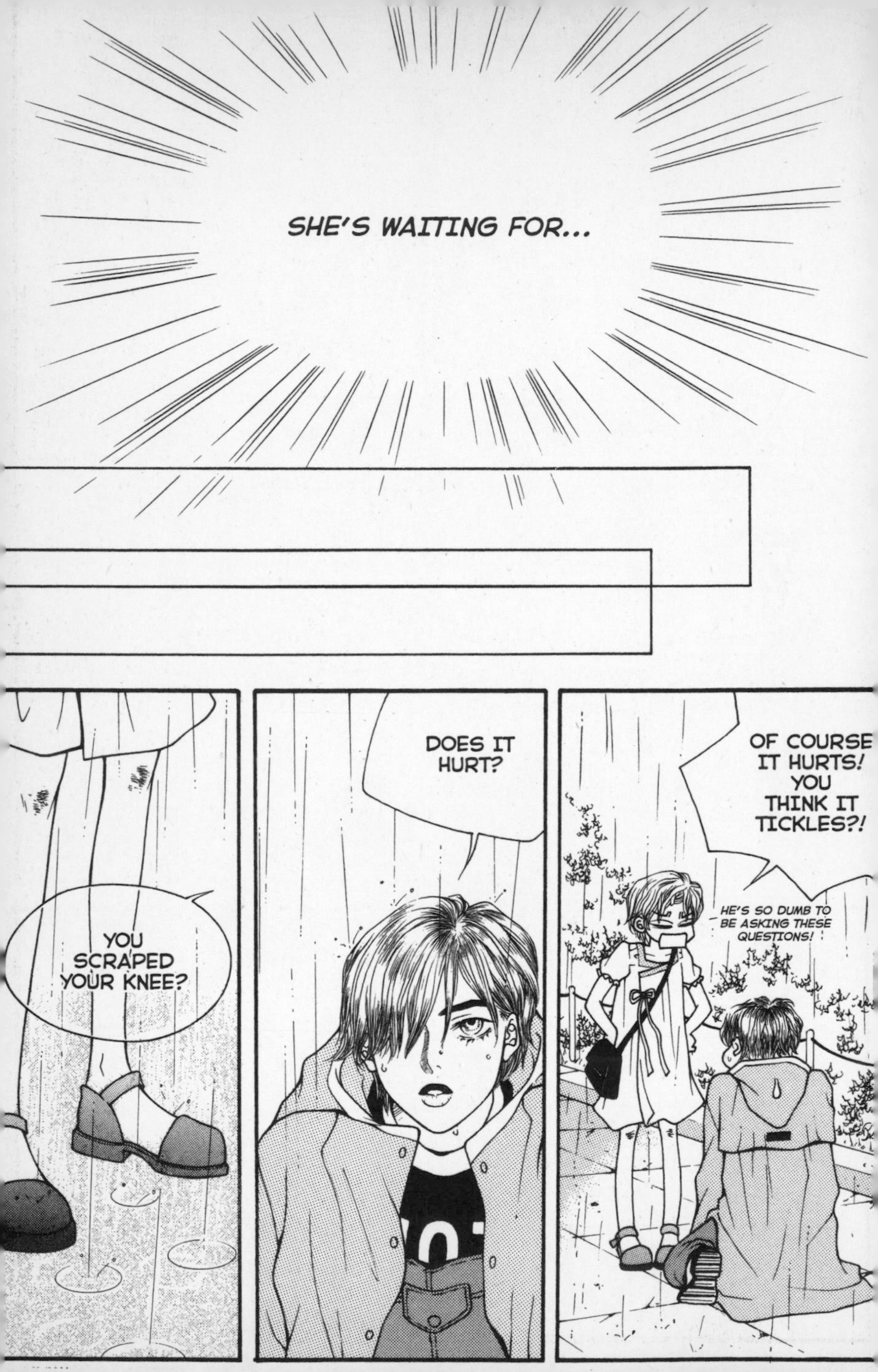
SHE'S WAITING FOR...
YOU SCRAPED YOUR KNEE?
DOES IT HURT?
OF COURSE IT HURTS! YOU THINK IT TICKLES?!
HE'S SO DUMB TO BE ASKING THESE QUESTIONS!

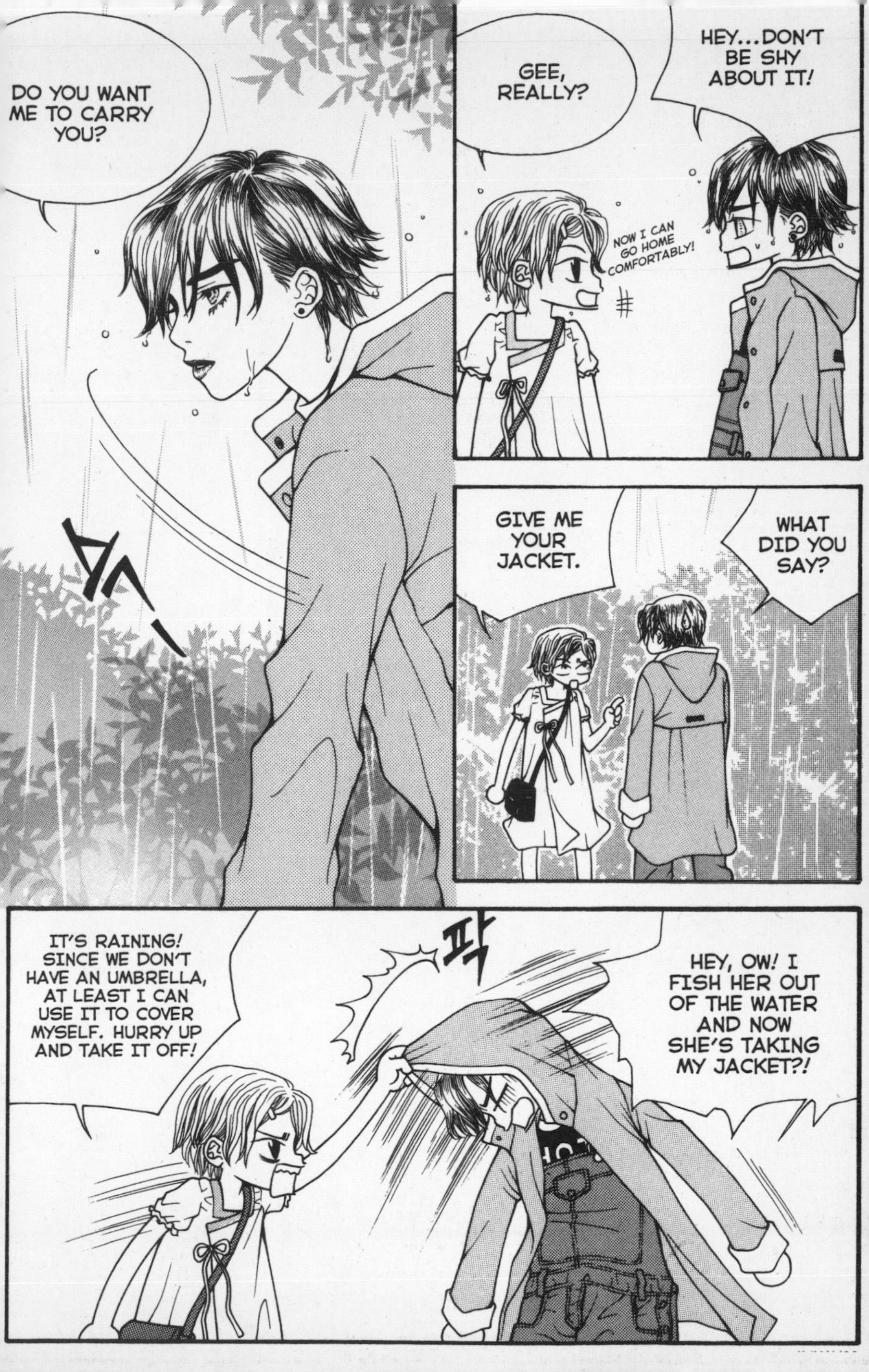
DO YOU WANT ME TO CARRY YOU?
GEE, REALLY?
HEY...DON'T BE SHY ABOUT IT!
NOW I CAN GO HOME COMFORTABLY!
GIVE ME YOUR JACKET.
WHAT DID YOU SAY?
IT'S RAINING! SINCE WE DON'T HAVE AN UMBRELLA, AT LEAST I CAN USE IT TO COVER MYSELF. HURRY UP AND TAKE IT OFF!
HEY, OW! I FISH HER OUT OF THE WATER AND NOW SHE'S TAKING MY JACKET?!

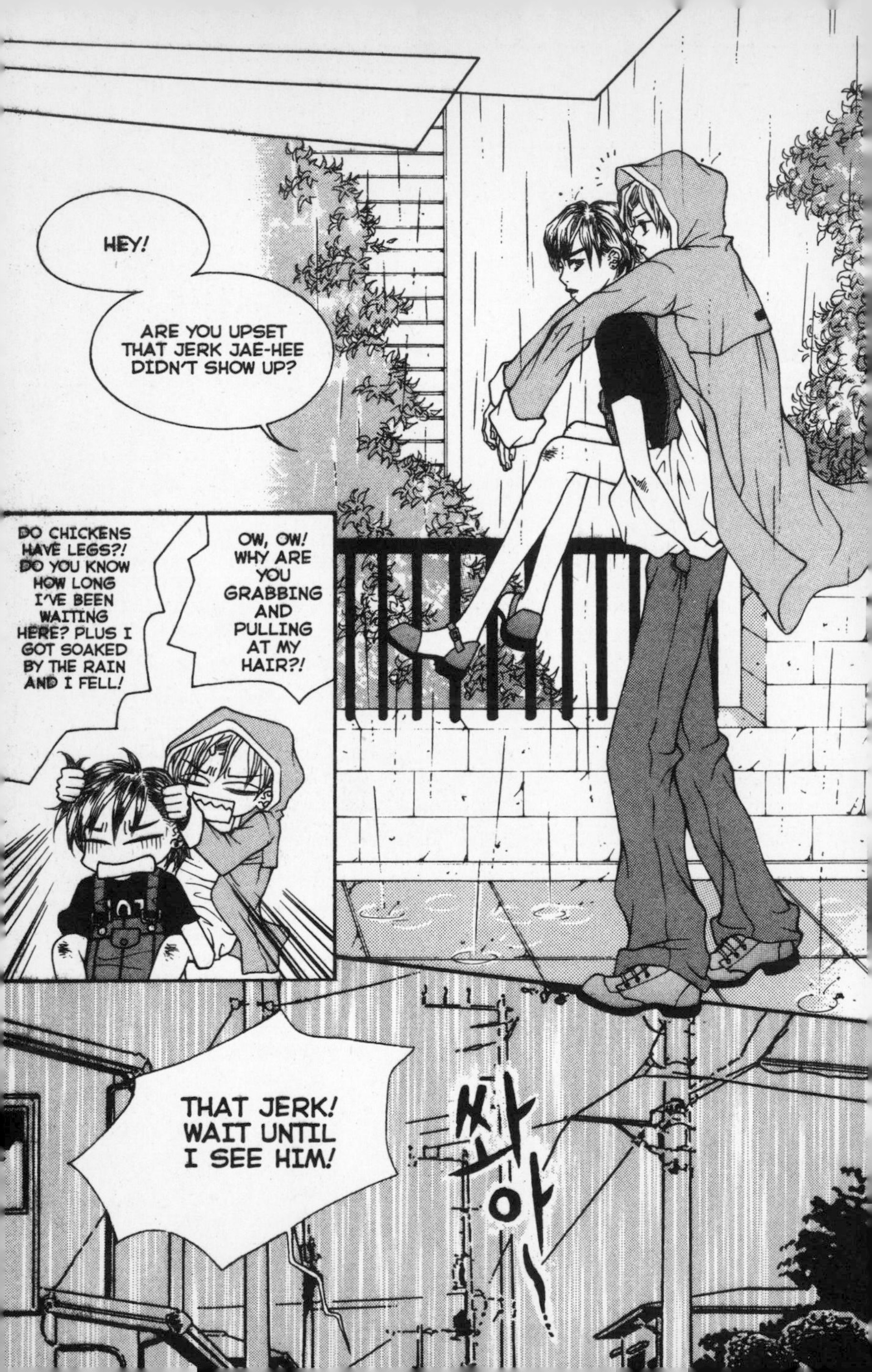
HEY!
ARE YOU UPSET THAT JERK JAE-HEE DIDN'T SHOW UP?
DO CHICKENS HAVE LEGS?! DO YOU KNOW HOW LONG I'VE BEEN WAITING HERE? PLUS I GOT SOAKED BY THE RAIN AND I FELL!
OW, OW! WHY ARE YOU GRABBING AND PULLING AT MY HAIR?!
THAT JERK! WAIT UNTIL I SEE HIM!
쏴아

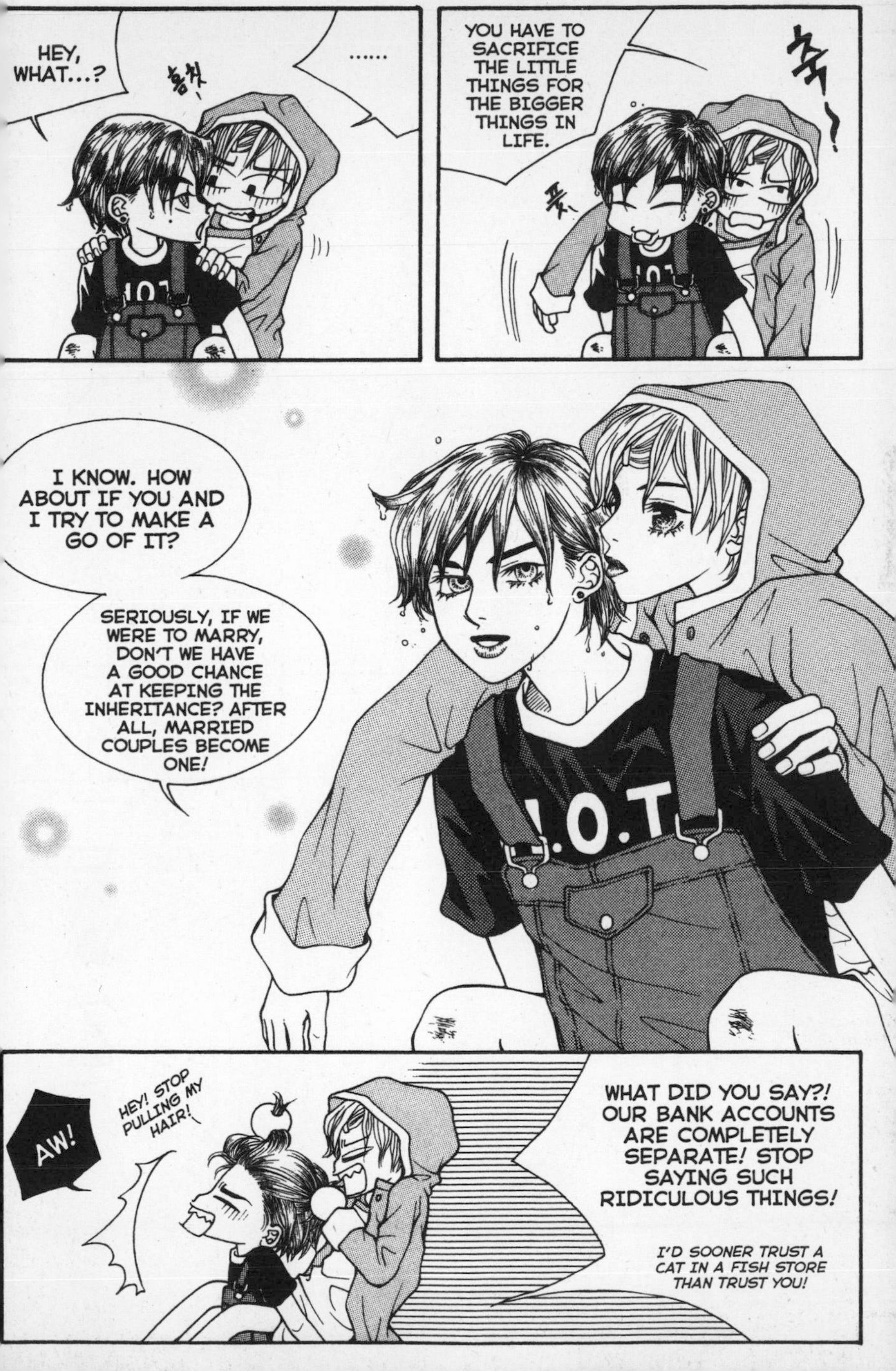
HEY, WHAT...?
흠칫
......
YOU HAVE TO SACRIFICE THE LITTLE THINGS FOR THE BIGGER THINGS IN LIFE.
I KNOW. HOW ABOUT IF YOU AND I TRY TO MAKE A GO OF IT?
SERIOUSLY, IF WE WERE TO MARRY, DON'T WE HAVE A GOOD CHANCE AT KEEPING THE INHERITANCE? AFTER ALL, MARRIED COUPLES BECOME ONE!
AW!
HEY! STOP PULLING MY HAIR!
WHAT DID YOU SAY?! OUR BANK ACCOUNTS ARE COMPLETELY SEPARATE! STOP SAYING SUCH RIDICULOUS THINGS!
I'D SOONER TRUST A CAT IN A FISH STORE THAN TRUST YOU!

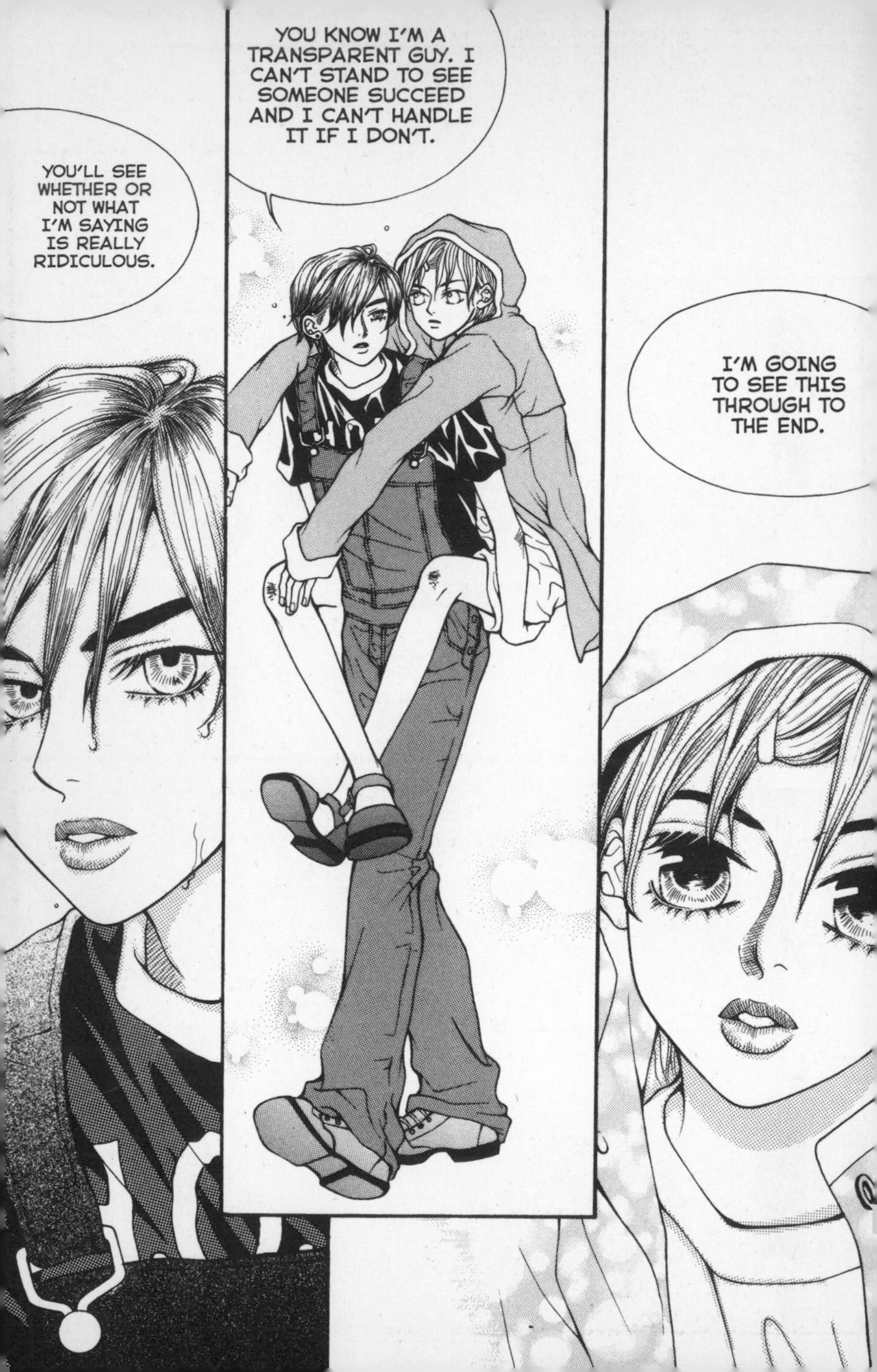
YOU'LL SEE WHETHER OR NOT WHAT I'M SAYING IS REALLY RIDICULOUS.
YOU KNOW I'M A TRANSPARENT GUY. I CAN'T STAND TO SEE SOMEONE SUCCEED AND I CAN'T HANDLE IT IF I DON'T.
I'M GOING TO SEE THIS THROUGH TO THE END.

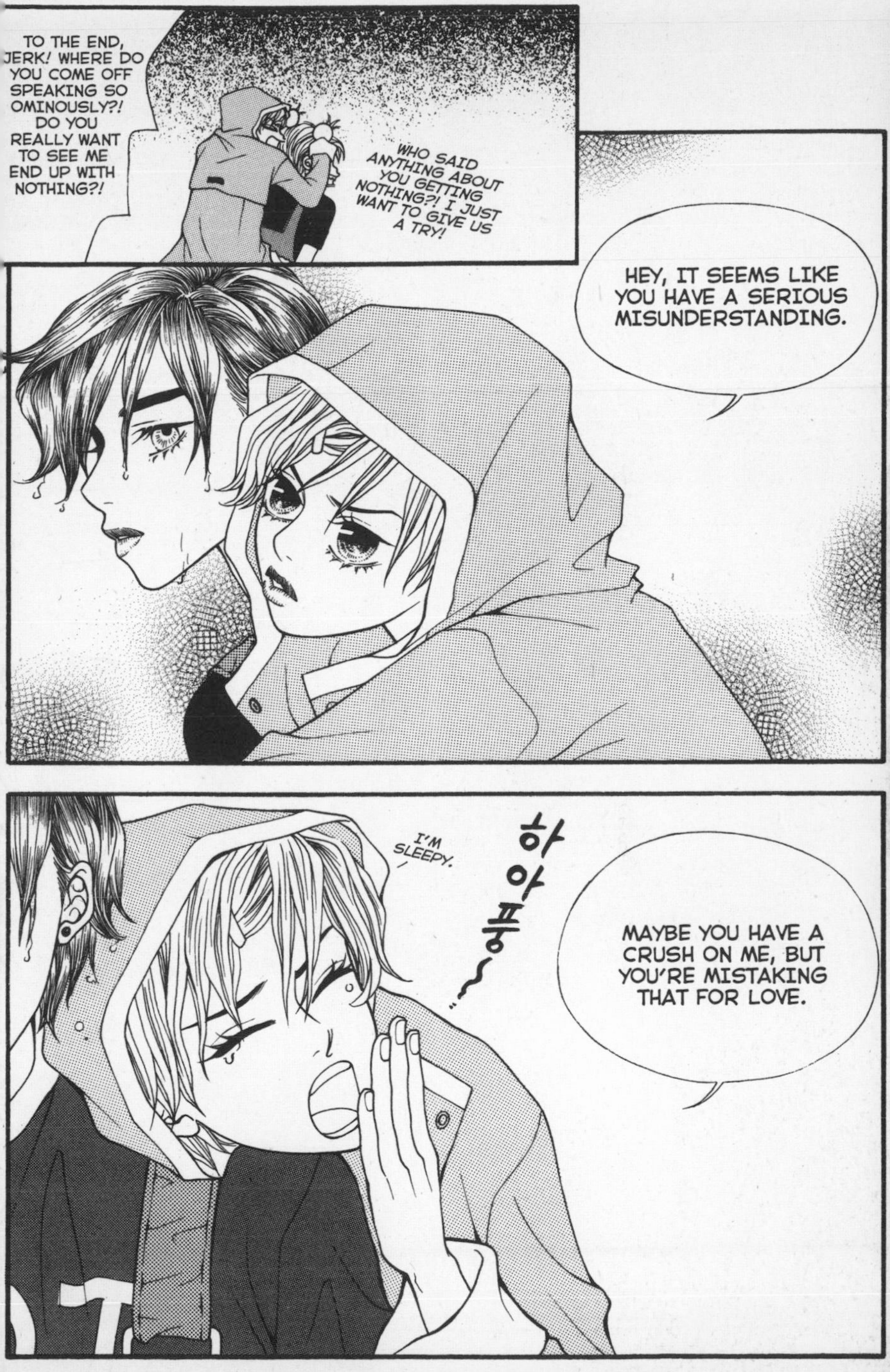
TO THE END, JERK! WHERE DO YOU COME OFF SPEAKING SO OMINOUSLY?! DO YOU REALLY WANT TO SEE ME END UP WITH NOTHING?!
WHO SAID ANYTHING ABOUT YOU GETTING NOTHING?! I JUST WANT TO GIVE US A TRY!
HEY, IT SEEMS LIKE YOU HAVE A SERIOUS MISUNDERSTANDING.
I'M SLEEPY.
하아품~
MAYBE YOU HAVE A CRUSH ON ME, BUT YOU'RE MISTAKING THAT FOR LOVE.

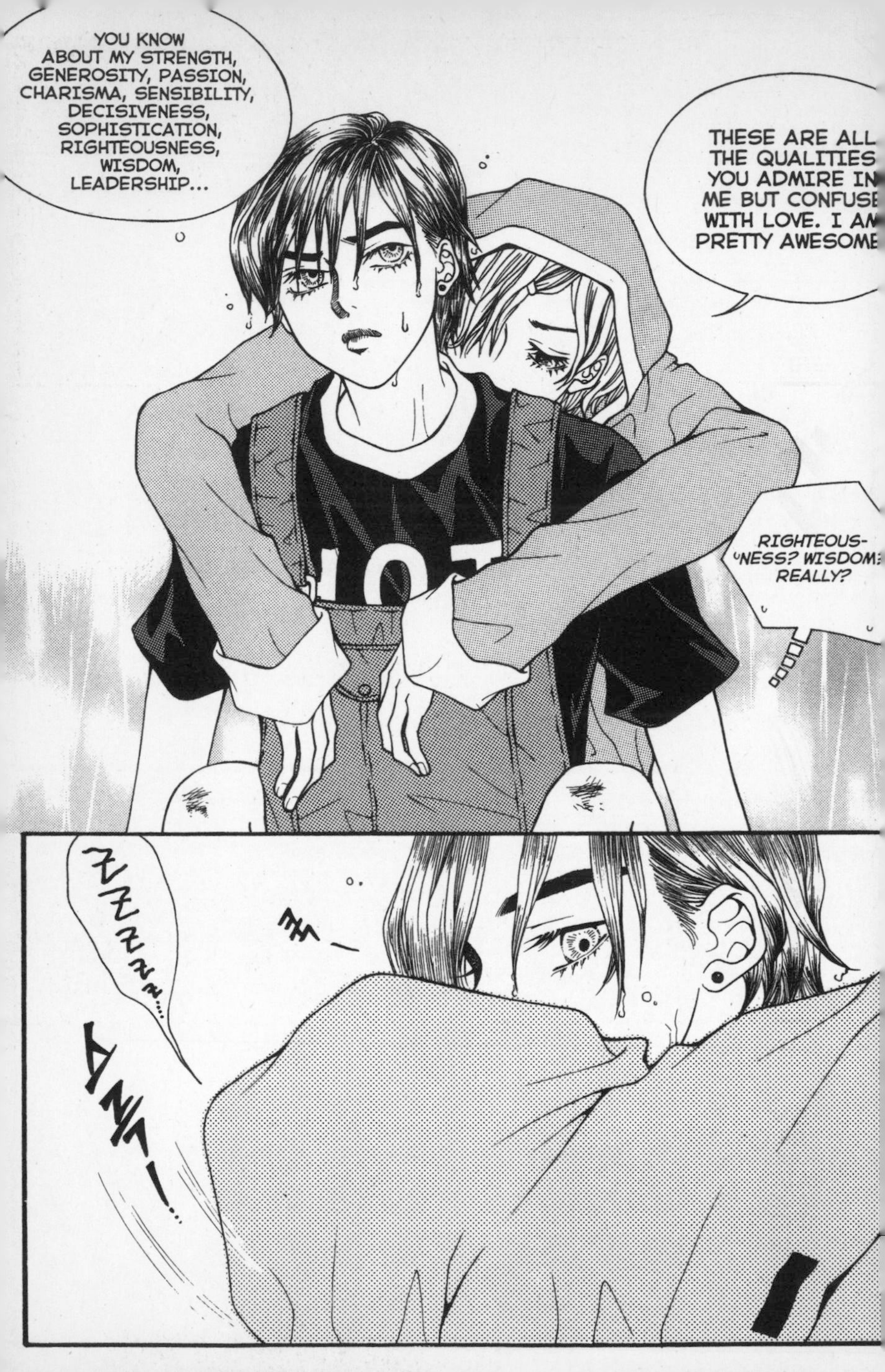
YOU KNOW ABOUT MY STRENGTH, GENEROSITY, PASSION, CHARISMA, SENSIBILITY, DECISIVENESS, SOPHISTICATION, RIGHTEOUSNESS, WISDOM, LEADERSHIP...
THESE ARE ALL THE QUALITIES YOU ADMIRE IN ME BUT CONFUSE WITH LOVE. I AM PRETTY AWESOME
RIGHTEOUSNESS? WISDOM? REALLY?
ZZZZZZ...

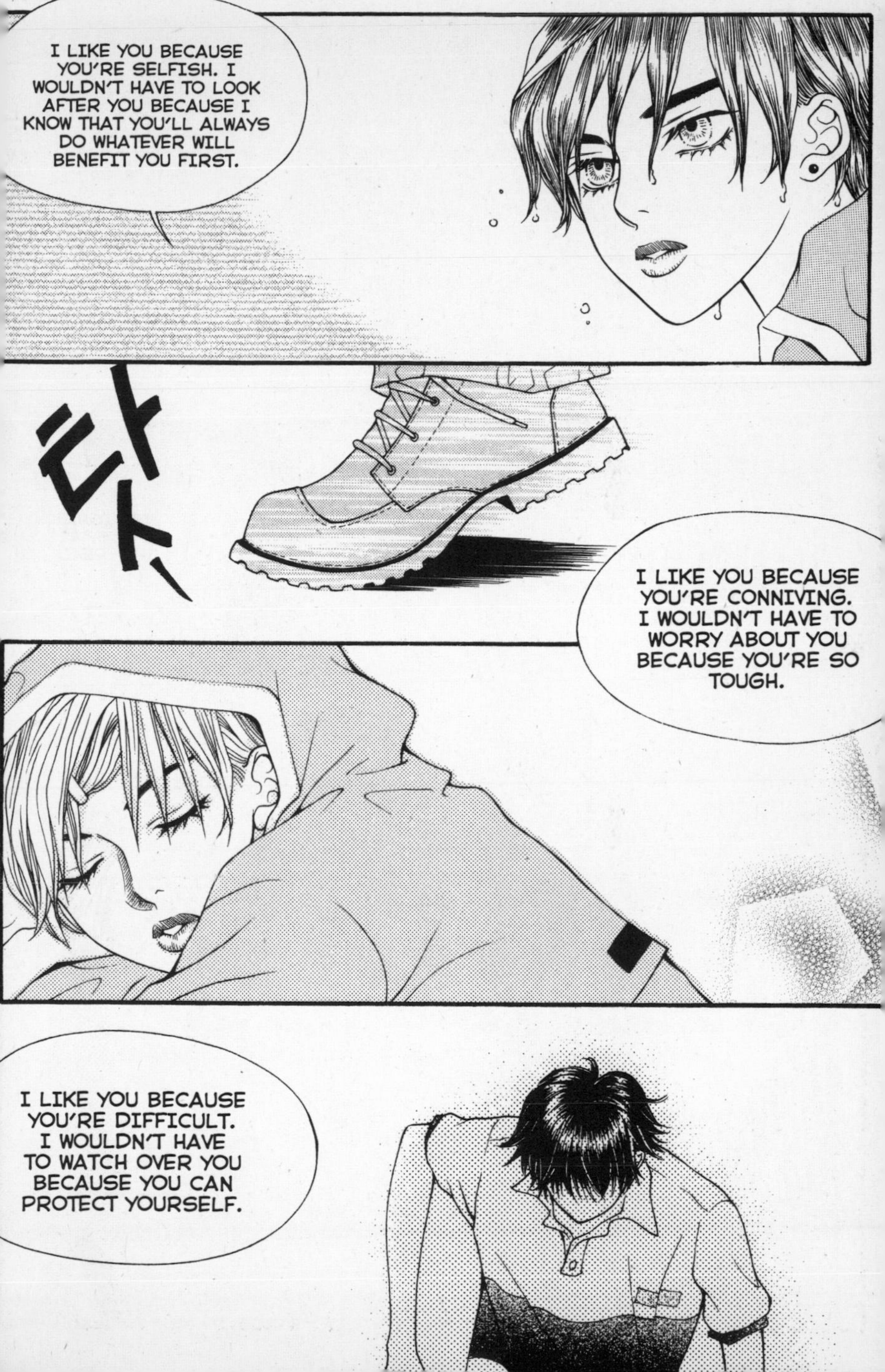
I LIKE YOU BECAUSE YOU'RE SELFISH. I WOULDN'T HAVE TO LOOK AFTER YOU BECAUSE I KNOW THAT YOU'LL ALWAYS DO WHATEVER WILL BENEFIT YOU FIRST.
I LIKE YOU BECAUSE YOU'RE CONNIVING. I WOULDN'T HAVE TO WORRY ABOUT YOU BECAUSE YOU'RE SO TOUGH.
I LIKE YOU BECAUSE YOU'RE DIFFICULT. I WOULDN'T HAVE TO WATCH OVER YOU BECAUSE YOU CAN PROTECT YOURSELF.

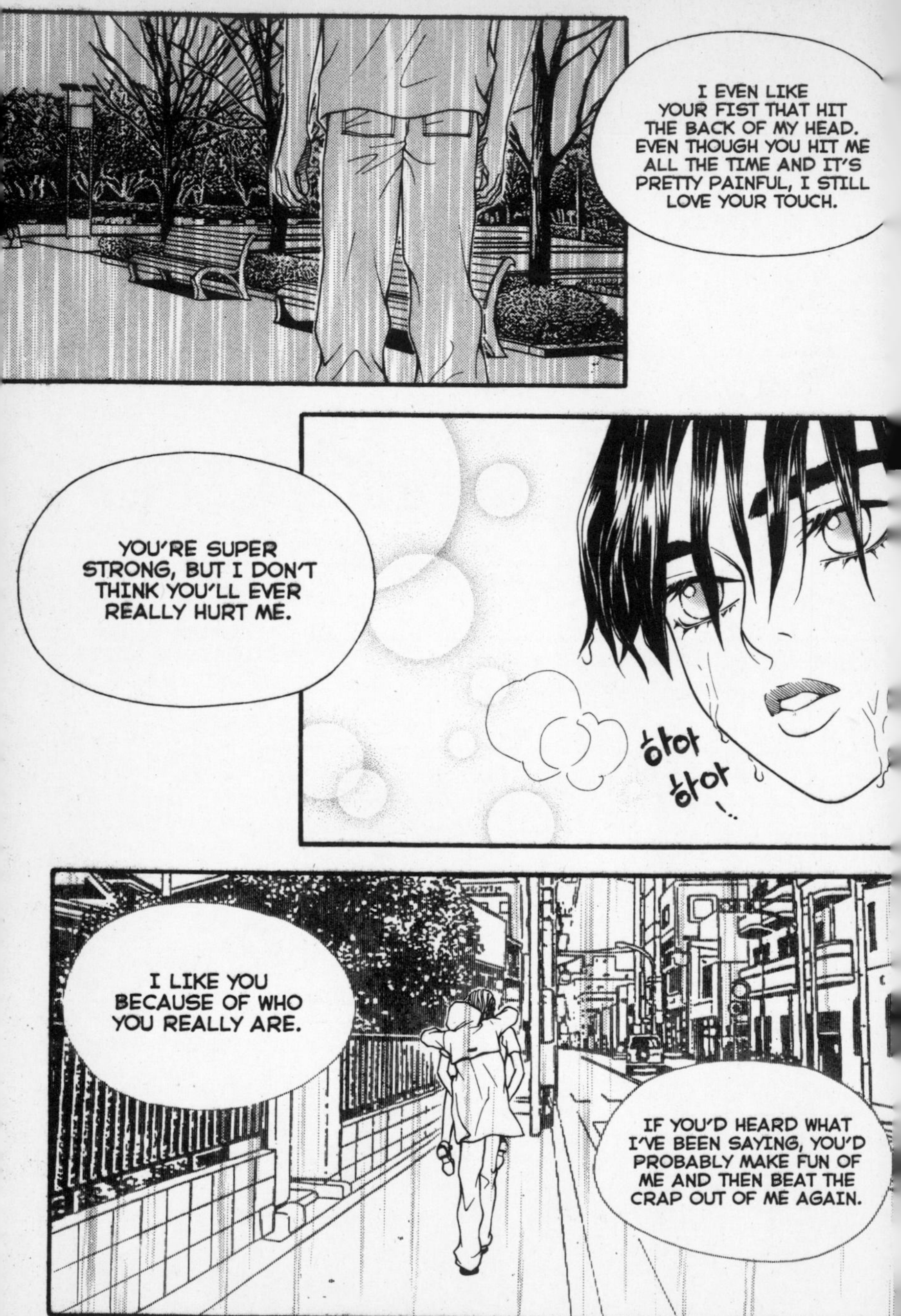
I EVEN LIKE YOUR FIST THAT HIT THE BACK OF MY HEAD. EVEN THOUGH YOU HIT ME ALL THE TIME AND IT'S PRETTY PAINFUL, I STILL LOVE YOUR TOUCH.
YOU'RE SUPER STRONG, BUT I DON'T THINK YOU'LL EVER REALLY HURT ME.
하아 하아
I LIKE YOU BECAUSE OF WHO YOU REALLY ARE.
IF YOU'D HEARD WHAT I'VE BEEN SAYING, YOU'D PROBABLY MAKE FUN OF ME AND THEN BEAT THE CRAP OUT OF ME AGAIN.

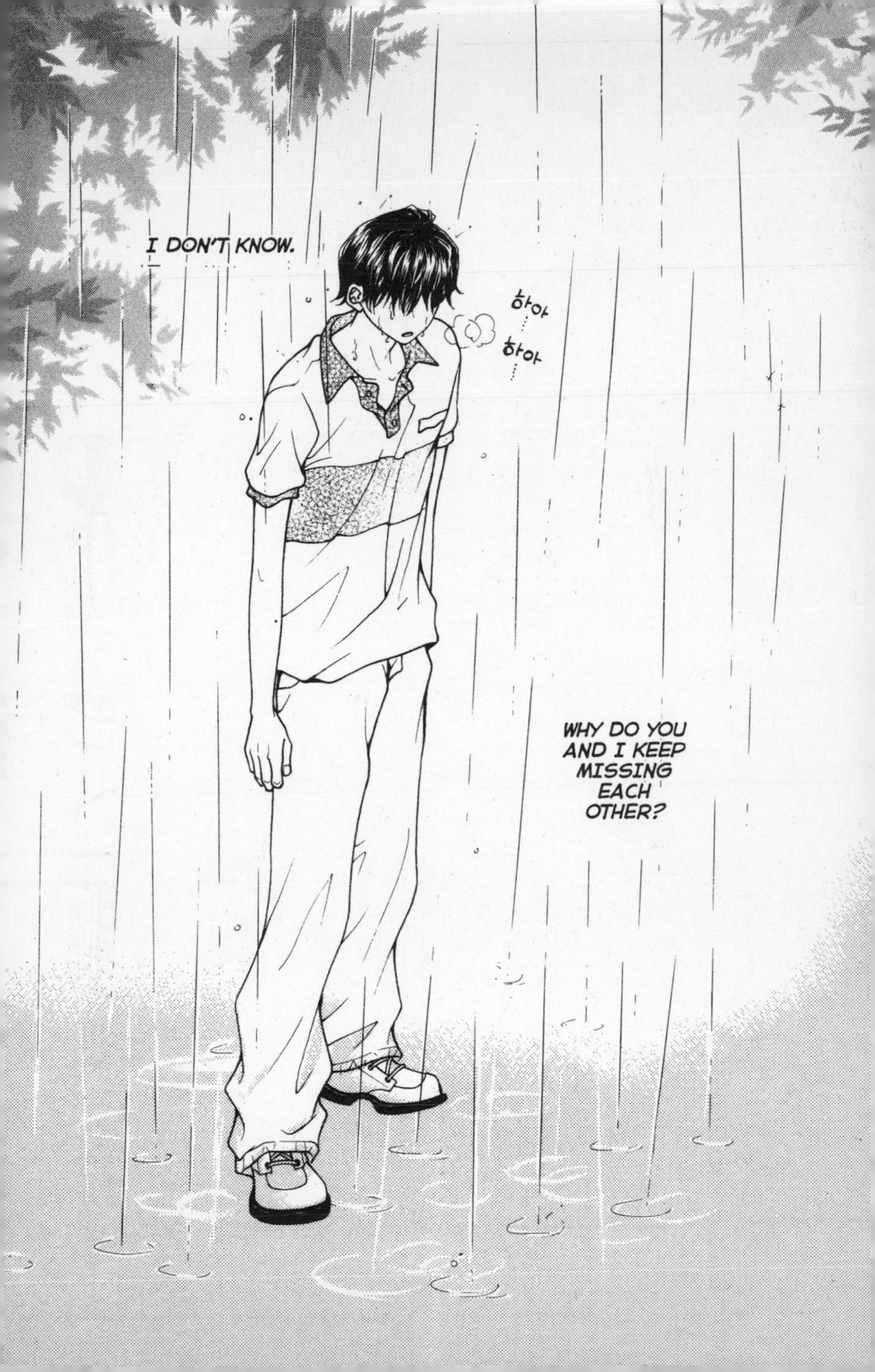
I DON'T KNOW.
하아…… 하아……
WHY DO YOU AND I KEEP MISSING EACH OTHER?

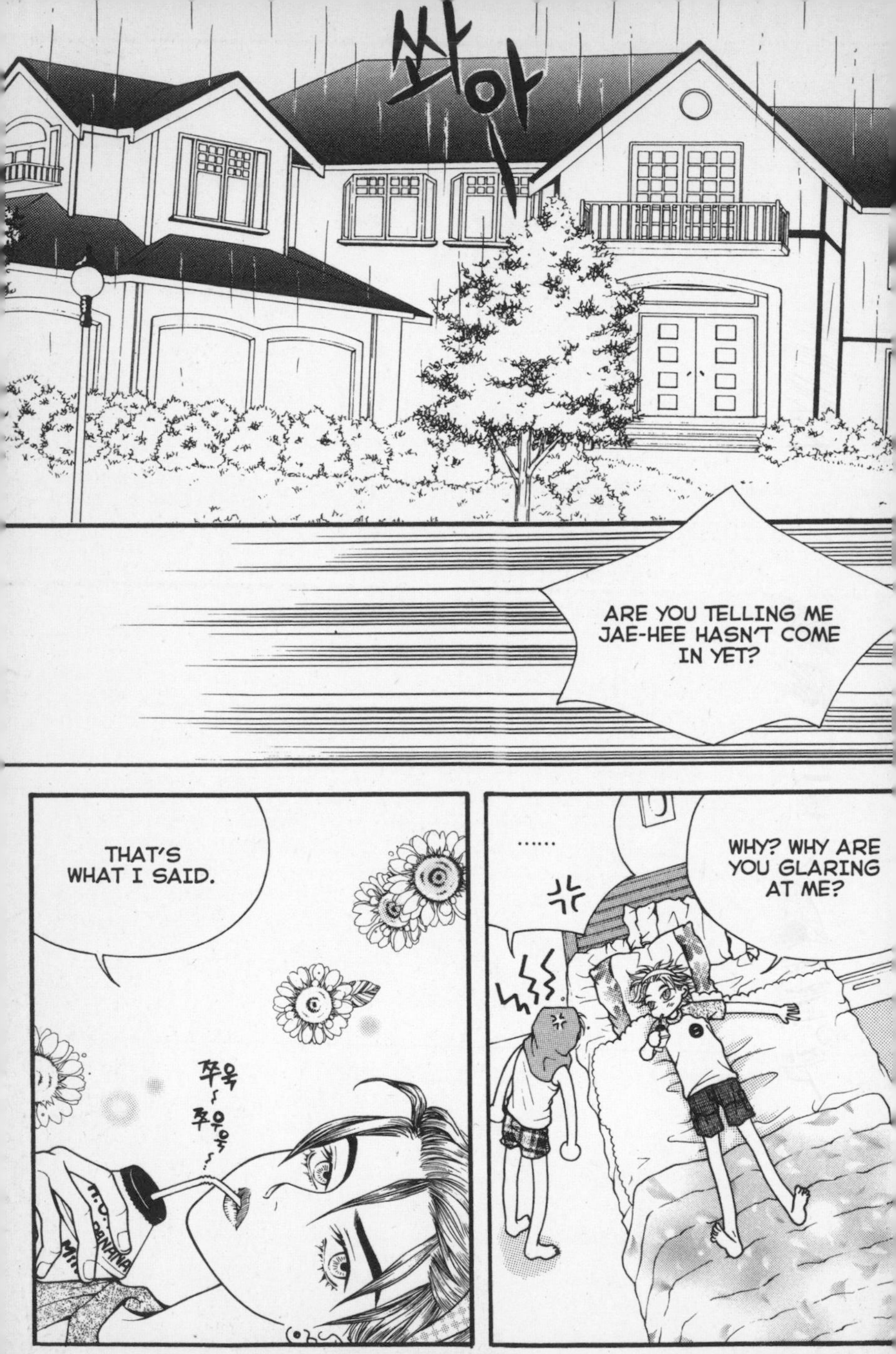
쏴아
ARE YOU TELLING ME JAE-HEE HASN'T COME IN YET?
THAT'S WHAT I SAID.
쭈욱~
쭈우욱~
......
WHY? WHY ARE YOU GLARING AT ME?

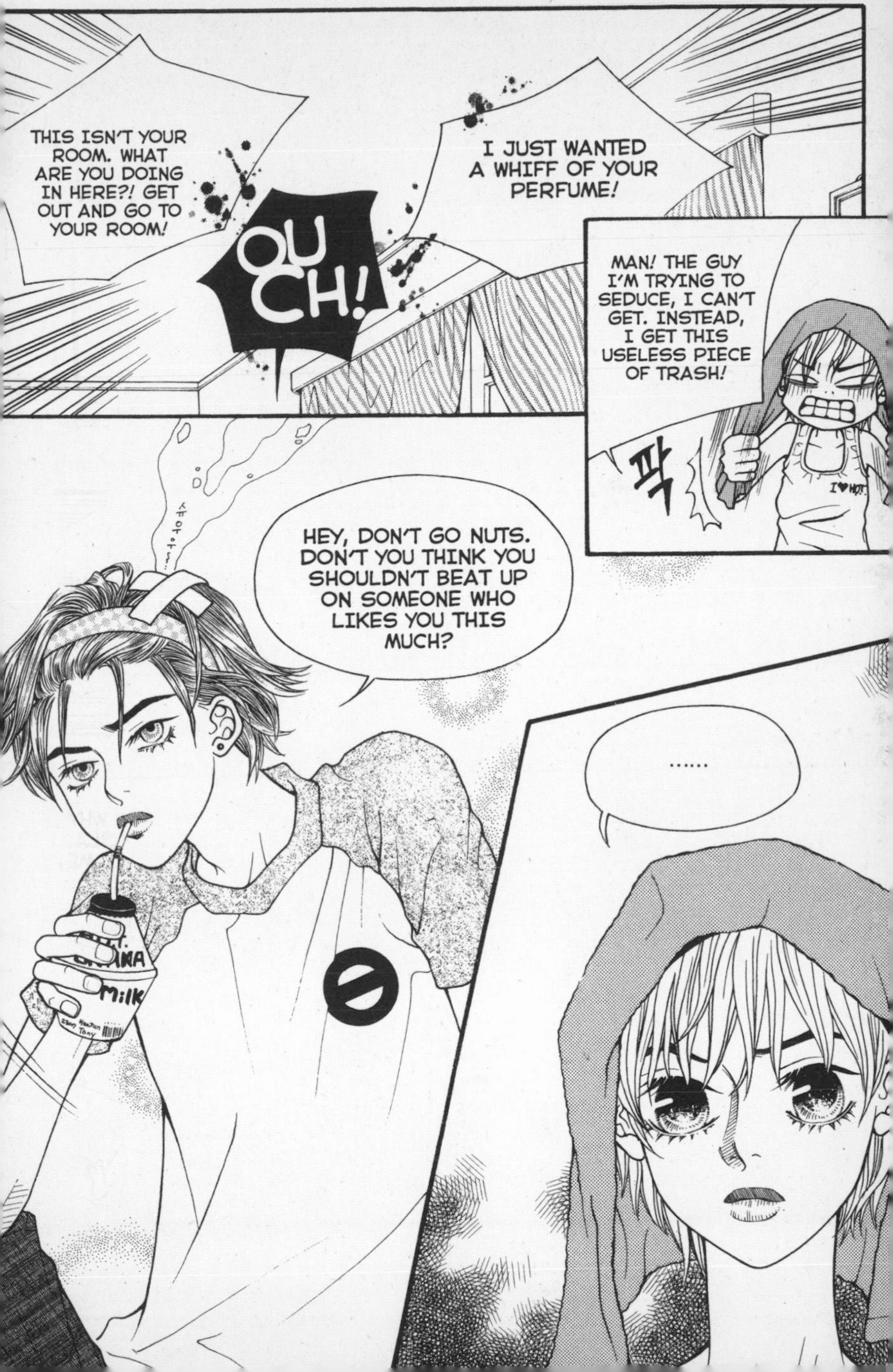
THIS ISN'T YOUR ROOM. WHAT ARE YOU DOING IN HERE?! GET OUT AND GO TO YOUR ROOM!
OUCH!
I JUST WANTED A WHIFF OF YOUR PERFUME!
MAN! THE GUY I'M TRYING TO SEDUCE, I CAN'T GET. INSTEAD, I GET THIS USELESS PIECE OF TRASH!
팍
HEY, DON'T GO NUTS. DON'T YOU THINK YOU SHOULDN'T BEAT UP ON SOMEONE WHO LIKES YOU THIS MUCH?
......

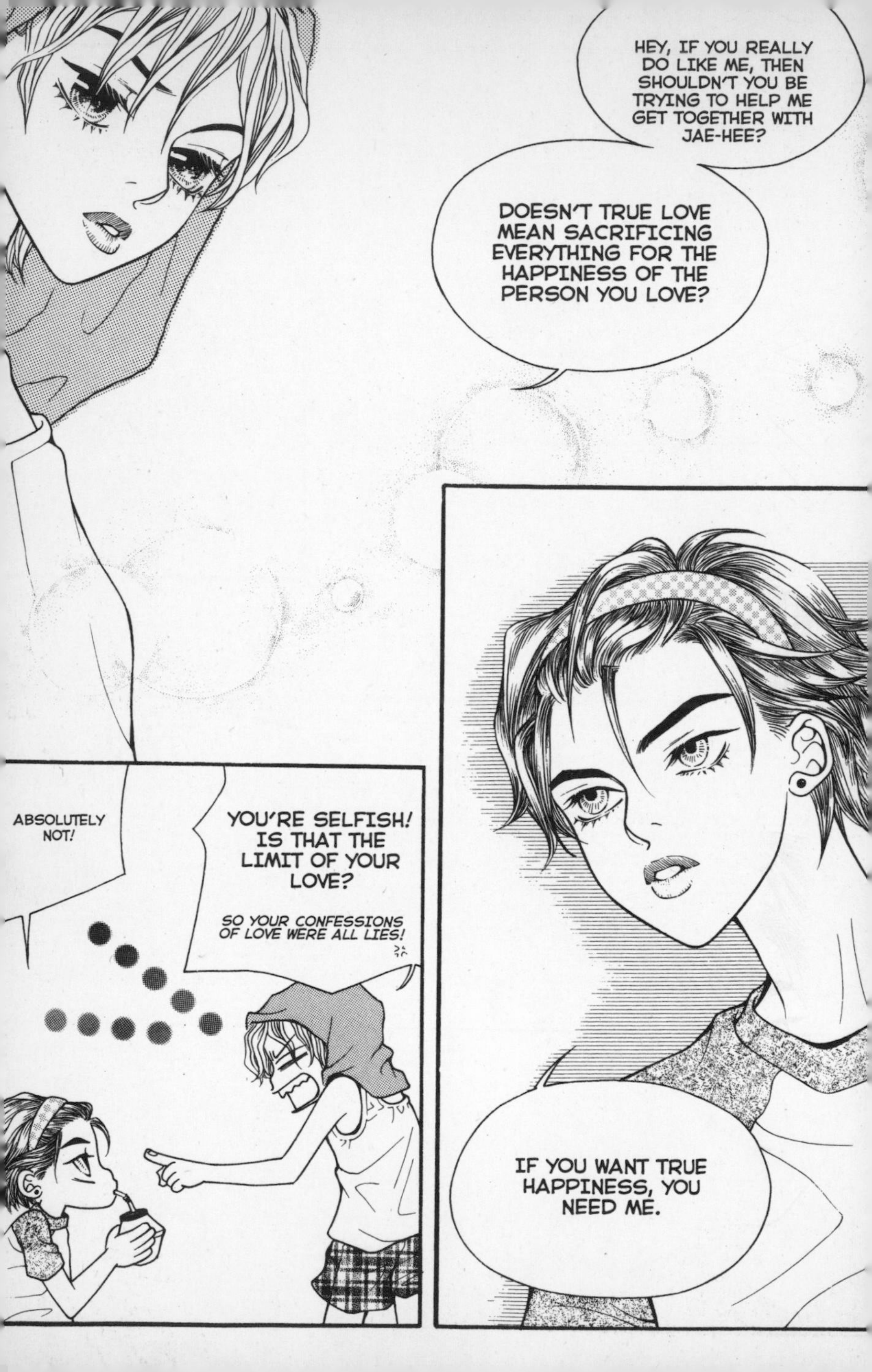
HEY, IF YOU REALLY DO LIKE ME, THEN SHOULDN'T YOU BE TRYING TO HELP ME GET TOGETHER WITH JAE-HEE?
DOESN'T TRUE LOVE MEAN SACRIFICING EVERYTHING FOR THE HAPPINESS OF THE PERSON YOU LOVE?
ABSOLUTELY NOT!
YOU'RE SELFISH! IS THAT THE LIMIT OF YOUR LOVE?
SO YOUR CONFESSIONS OF LOVE WERE ALL LIES!
IF YOU WANT TRUE HAPPINESS, YOU NEED ME.

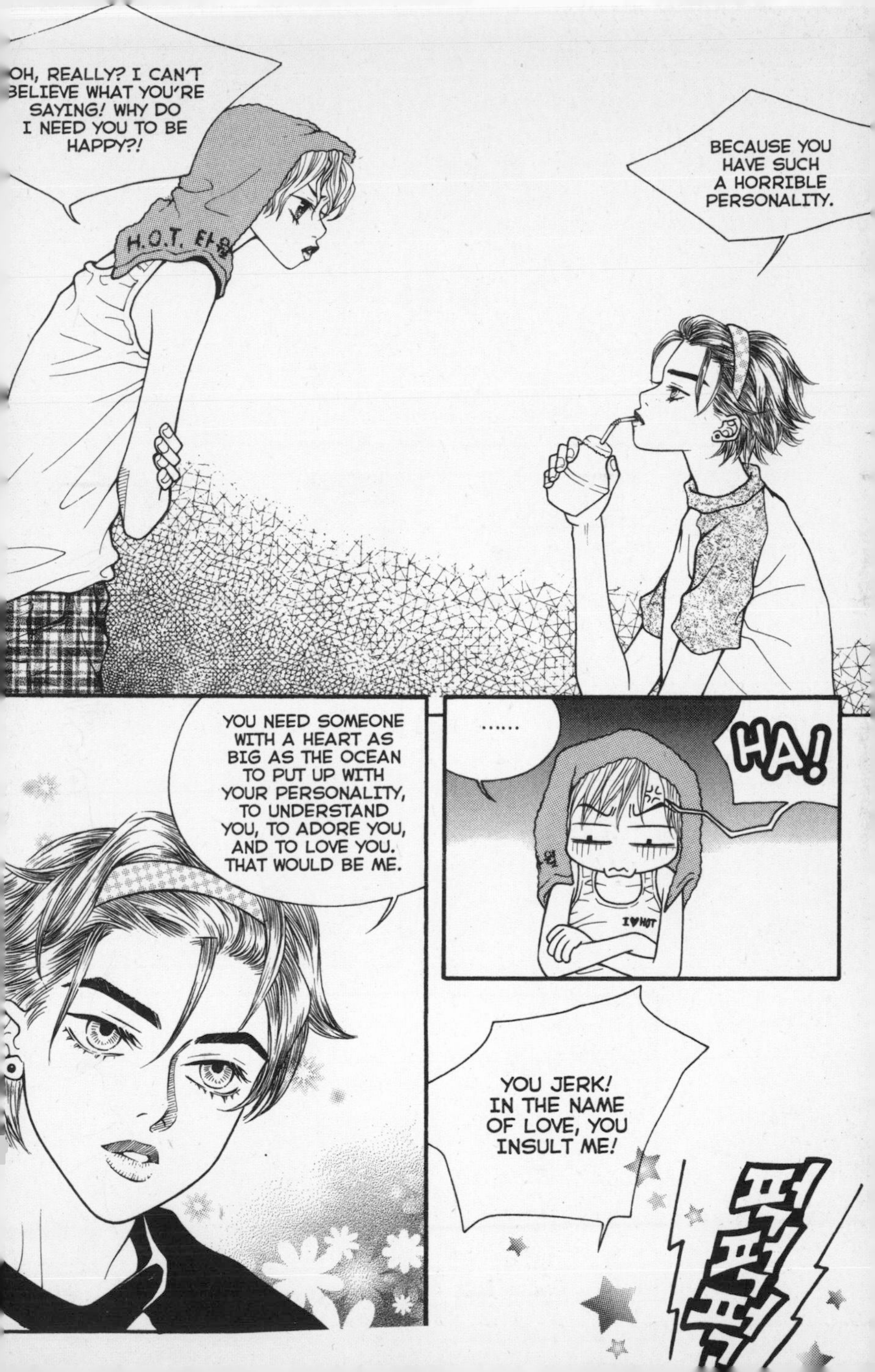
OH, REALLY? I CAN'T BELIEVE WHAT YOU'RE SAYING! WHY DO I NEED YOU TO BE HAPPY?!
BECAUSE YOU HAVE SUCH A HORRIBLE PERSONALITY.
YOU NEED SOMEONE WITH A HEART AS BIG AS THE OCEAN TO PUT UP WITH YOUR PERSONALITY, TO UNDERSTAND YOU, TO ADORE YOU, AND TO LOVE YOU. THAT WOULD BE ME.
......
HA!
YOU JERK! IN THE NAME OF LOVE, YOU INSULT ME!

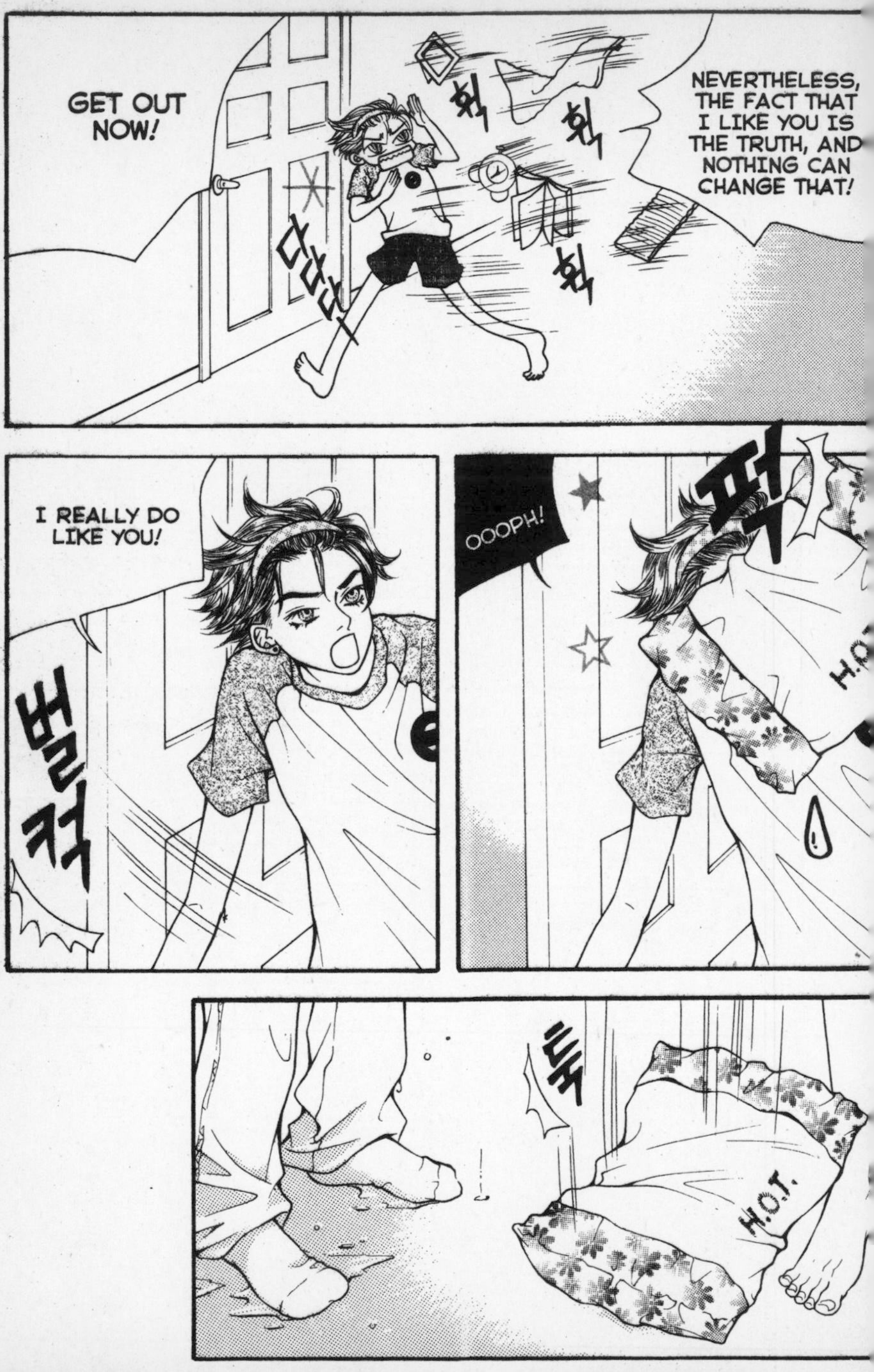
GET OUT NOW!
휙
휙
휙
다다다
NEVERTHELESS, THE FACT THAT I LIKE YOU IS THE TRUTH, AND NOTHING CAN CHANGE THAT!
I REALLY DO LIKE YOU!
벌컥
OOOPH!
퍽
H.O.T.
툭
H.O.T.

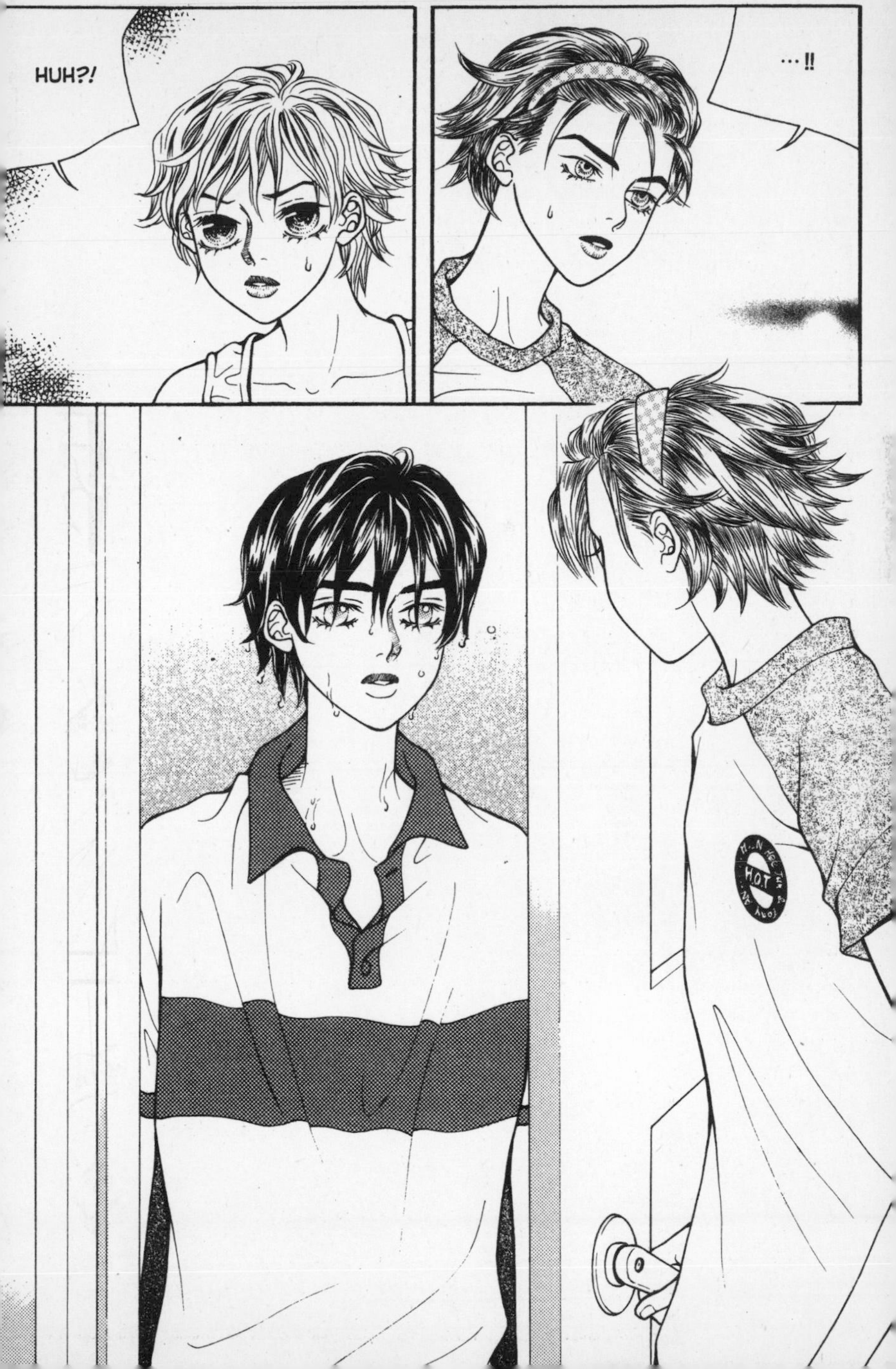
HUH?!
...!!
H.O.T

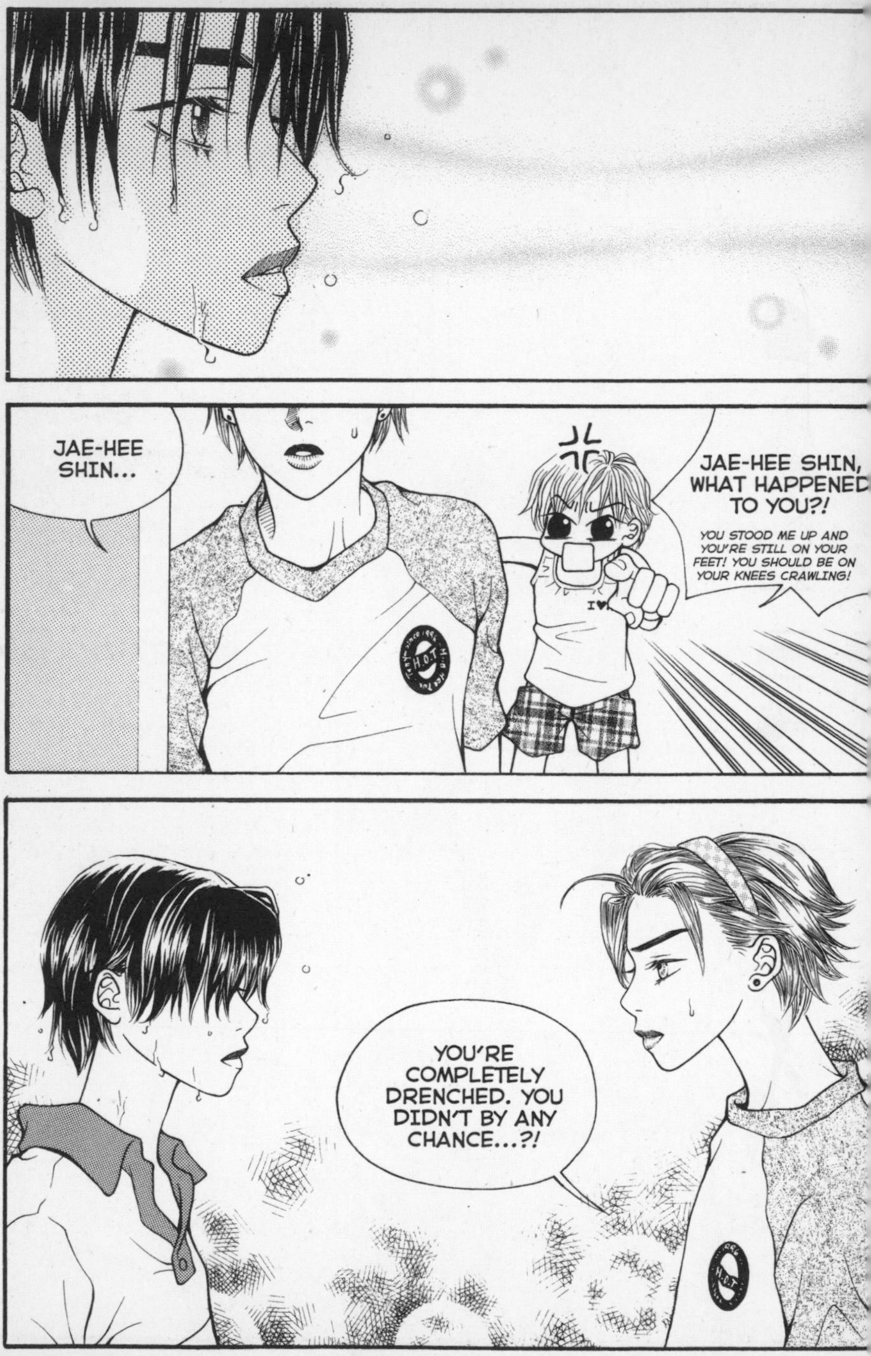
JAE-HEE SHIN...
JAE-HEE SHIN, WHAT HAPPENED TO YOU?!
YOU STOOD ME UP AND YOU'RE STILL ON YOUR FEET! YOU SHOULD BE ON YOUR KNEES CRAWLING!
YOU'RE COMPLETELY DRENCHED. YOU DIDN'T BY ANY CHANCE...?!

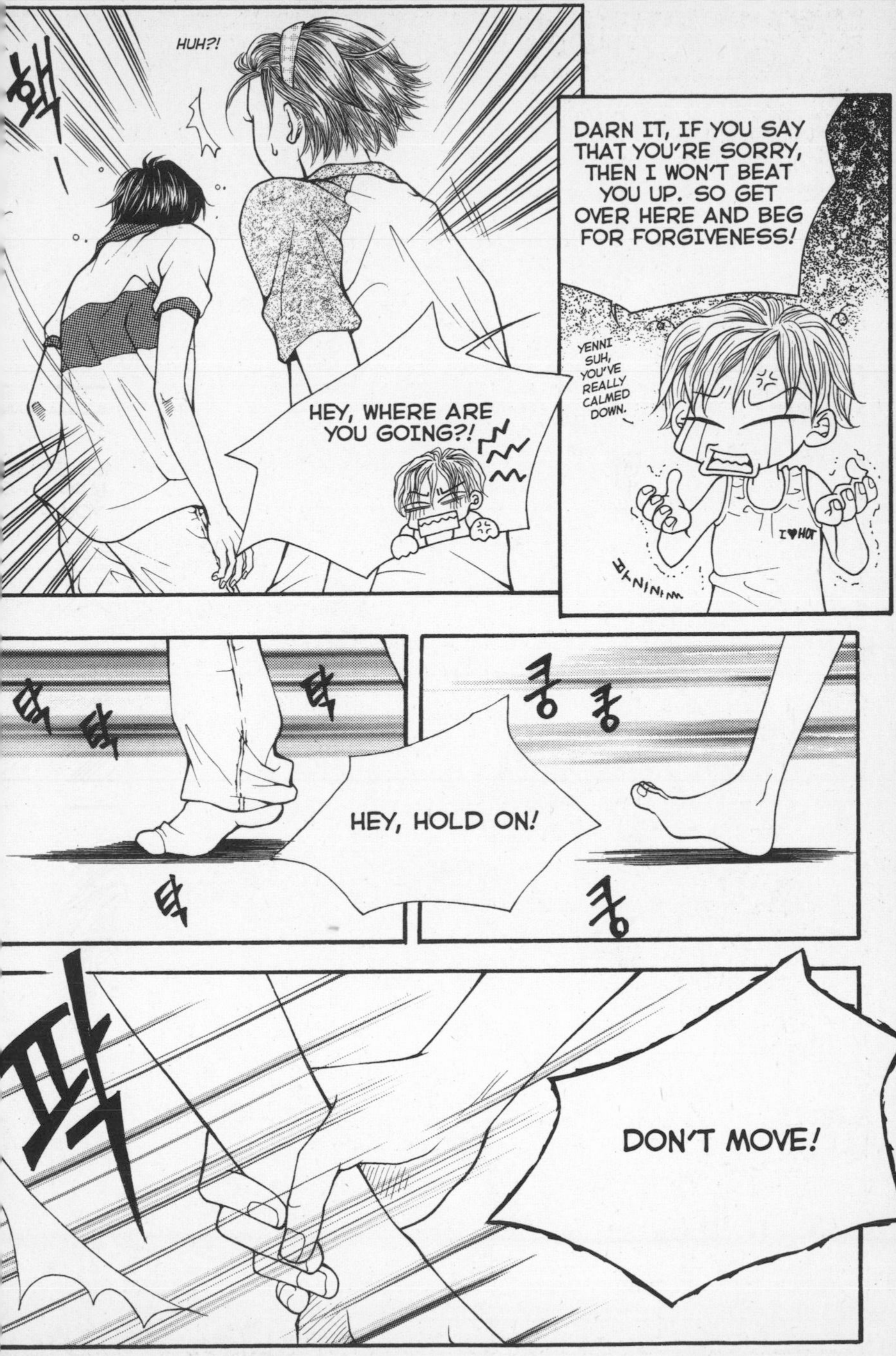
홱
HUH?!
HEY, WHERE ARE YOU GOING?!
DARN IT, IF YOU SAY THAT YOU'RE SORRY, THEN I WON'T BEAT YOU UP. SO GET OVER HERE AND BEG FOR FORGIVENESS!
YENNI SUH, YOU'VE REALLY CALMED DOWN.
탁 탁 탁
탁
HEY, HOLD ON!
쿵 쿵
쿵
팍
DON'T MOVE!

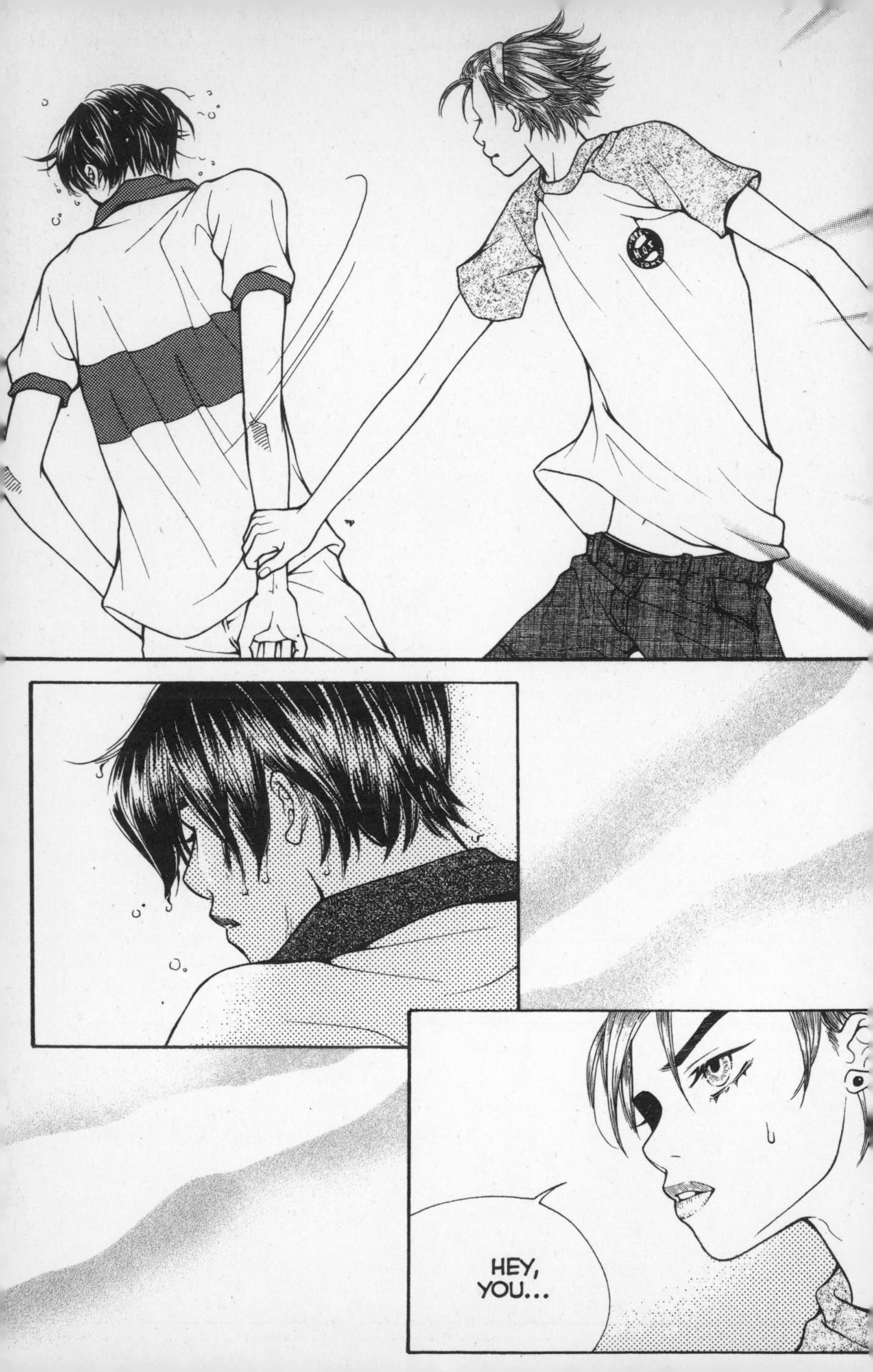
HEY, YOU...

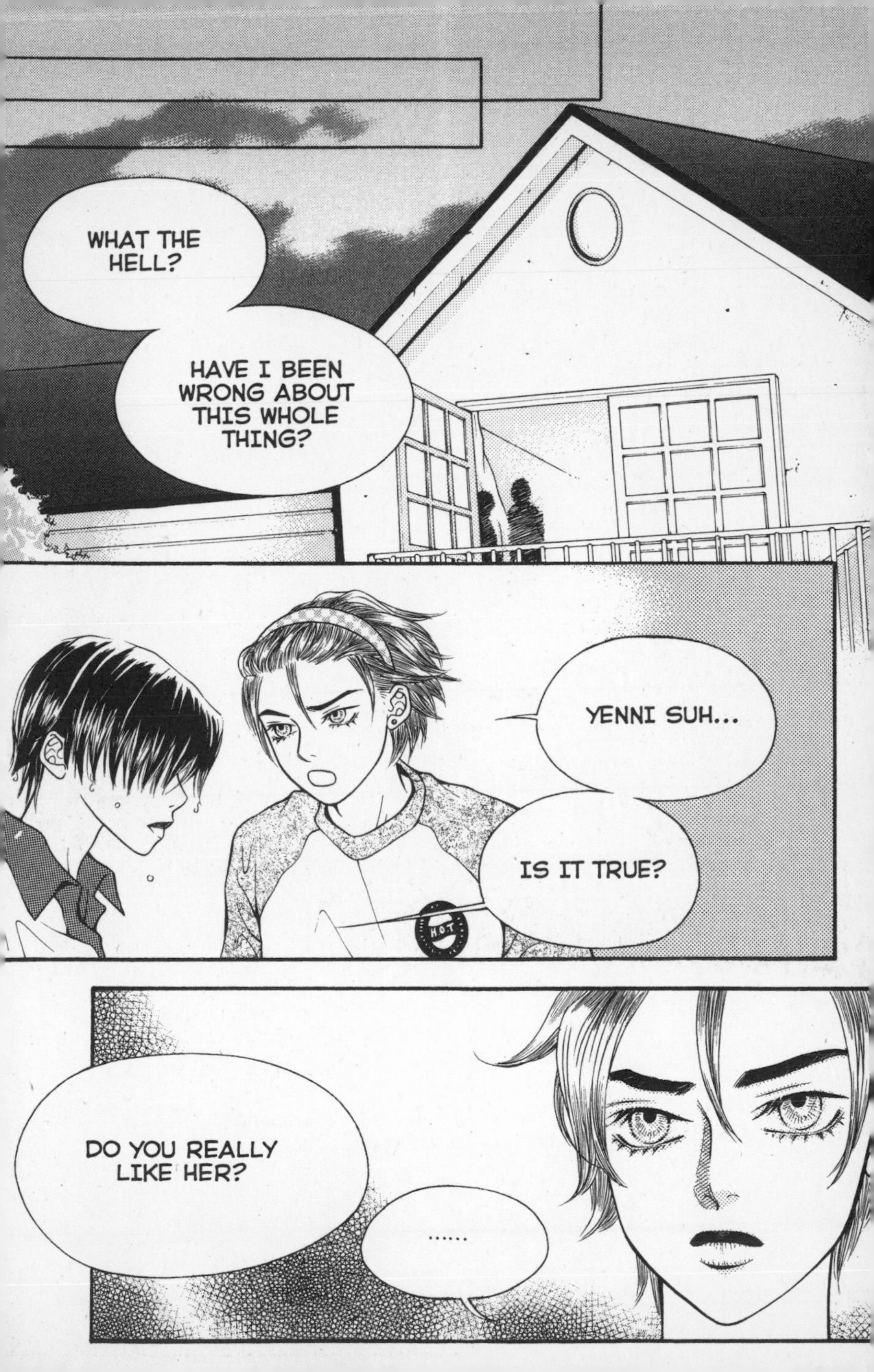
WHAT THE HELL?
HAVE I BEEN WRONG ABOUT THIS WHOLE THING?
YENNI SUH...
IS IT TRUE?
H.O.T.
DO YOU REALLY LIKE HER?
......

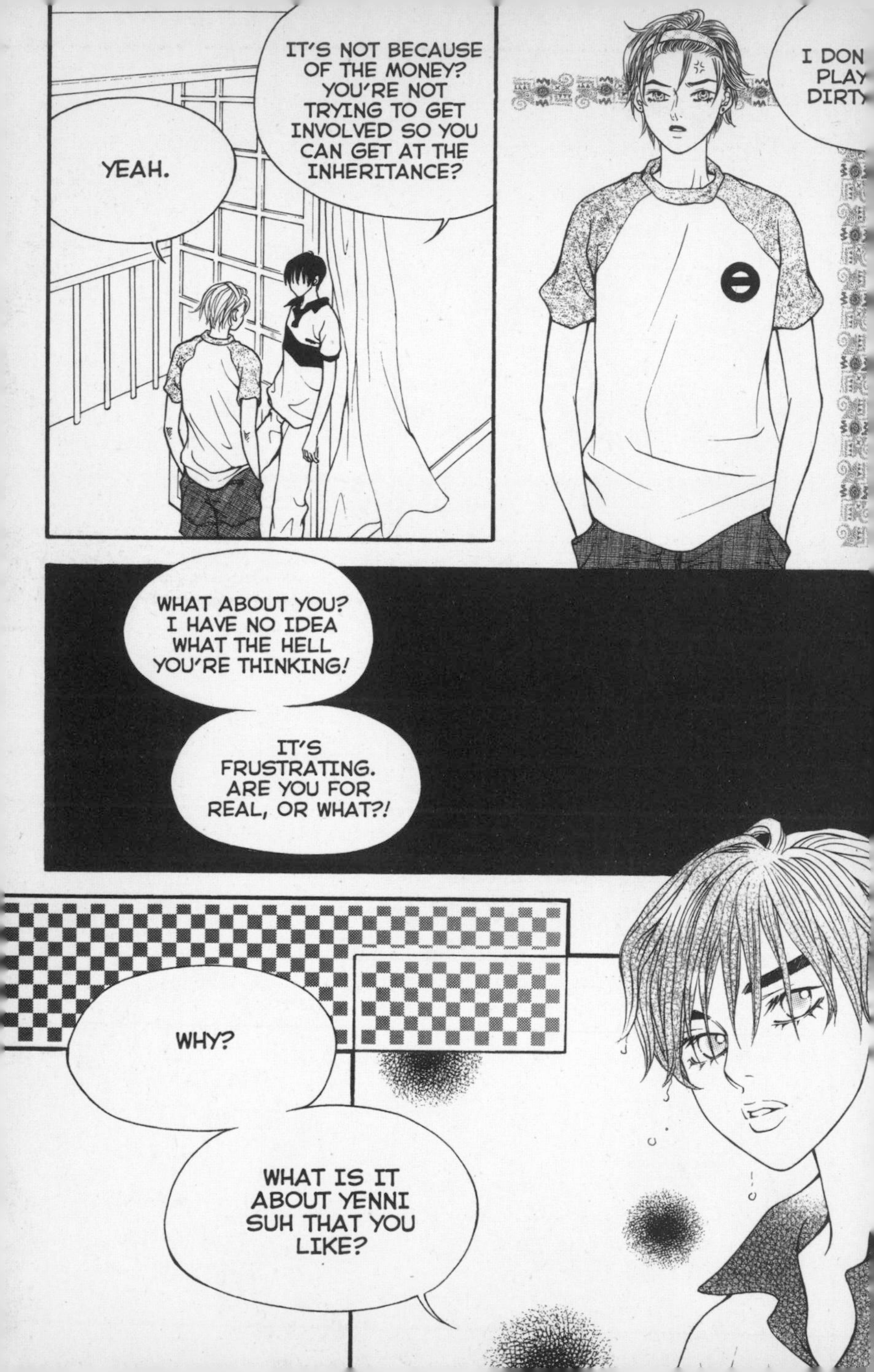
IT'S NOT BECAUSE OF THE MONEY? YOU'RE NOT TRYING TO GET INVOLVED SO YOU CAN GET AT THE INHERITANCE?
YEAH.
I DON PLAY DIRT
WHAT ABOUT YOU? I HAVE NO IDEA WHAT THE HELL YOU'RE THINKING!
IT'S FRUSTRATING. ARE YOU FOR REAL, OR WHAT?!
WHY?
WHAT IS IT ABOUT YENNI SUH THAT YOU LIKE?

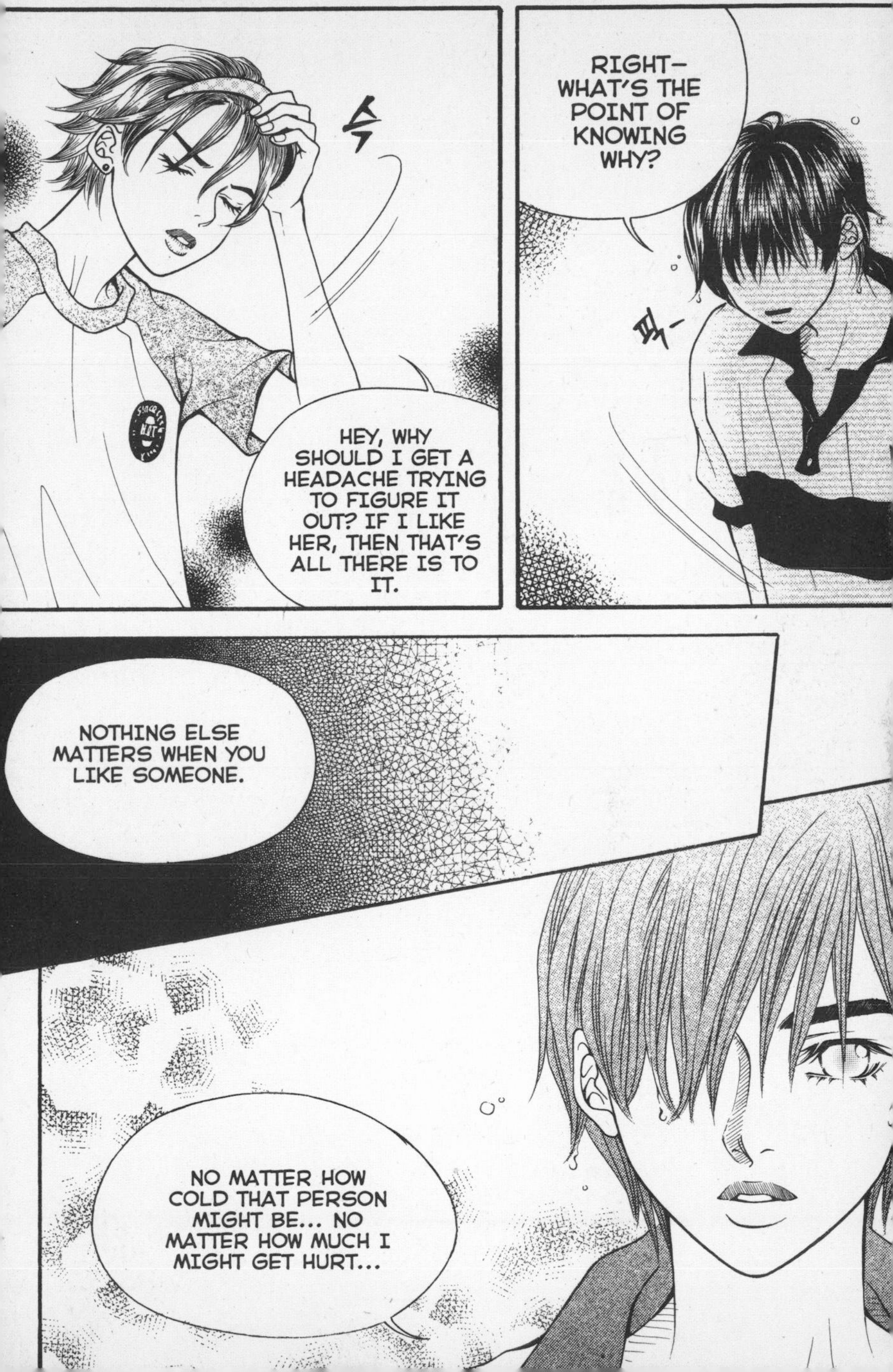
HEY, WHY SHOULD I GET A HEADACHE TRYING TO FIGURE IT OUT? IF I LIKE HER, THEN THAT'S ALL THERE IS TO IT.
RIGHT— WHAT'S THE POINT OF KNOWING WHY?
NOTHING ELSE MATTERS WHEN YOU LIKE SOMEONE.
NO MATTER HOW COLD THAT PERSON MIGHT BE... NO MATTER HOW MUCH I MIGHT GET HURT...

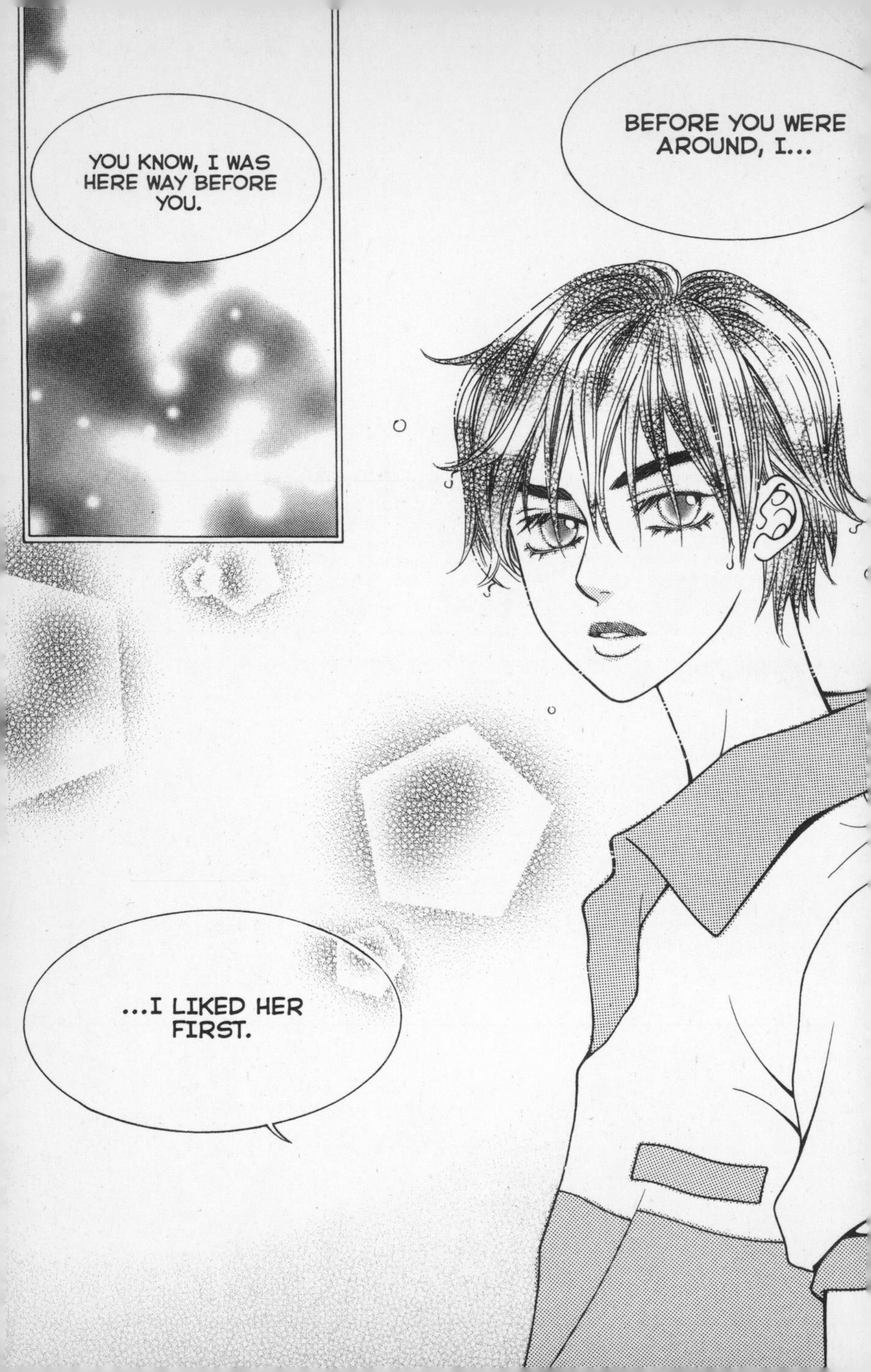
YOU KNOW, I WAS HERE WAY BEFORE YOU.
BEFORE YOU WERE AROUND, I...
...I LIKED HER FIRST.

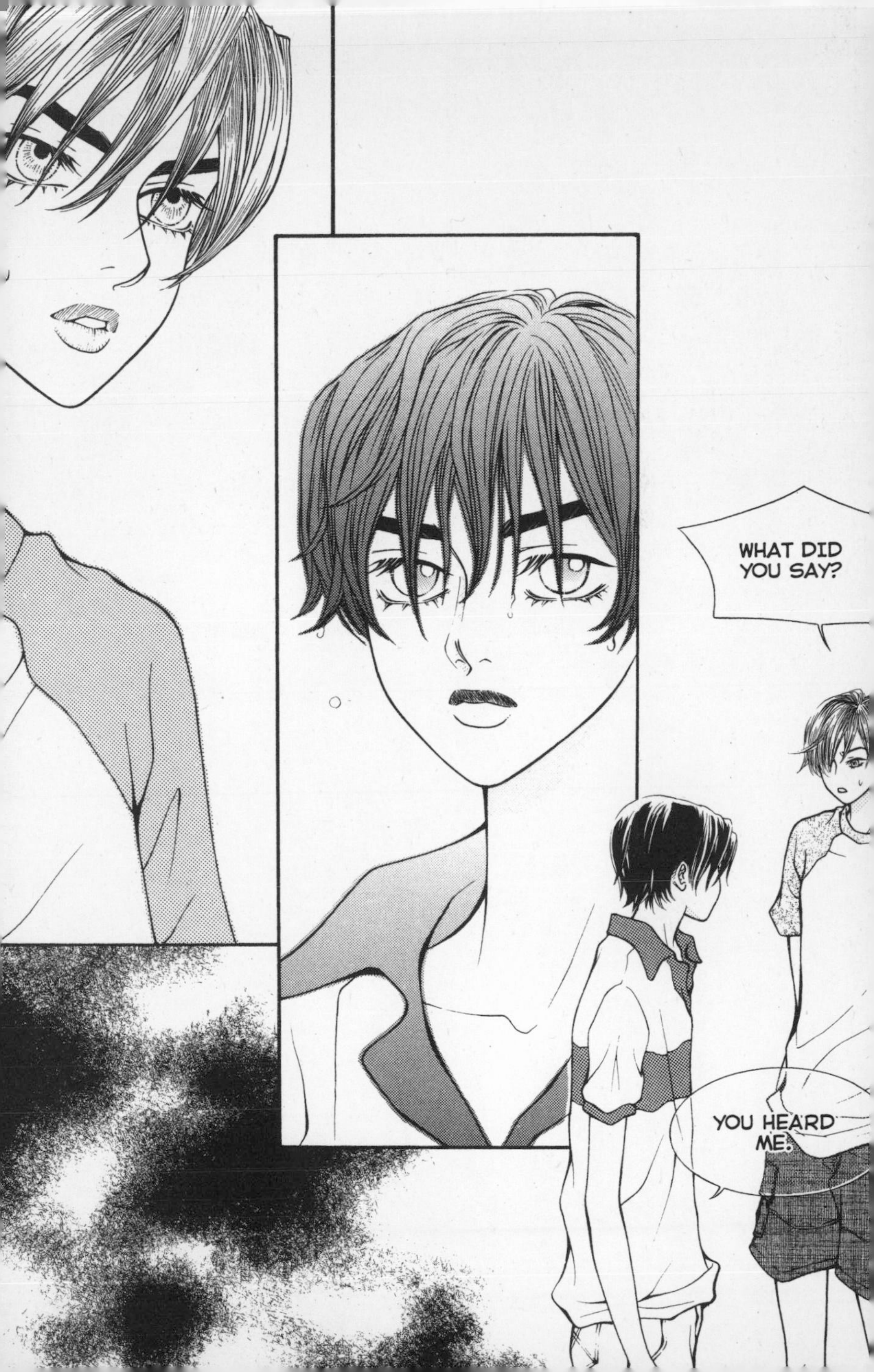
WHAT DID YOU SAY?
YOU HEARD ME.

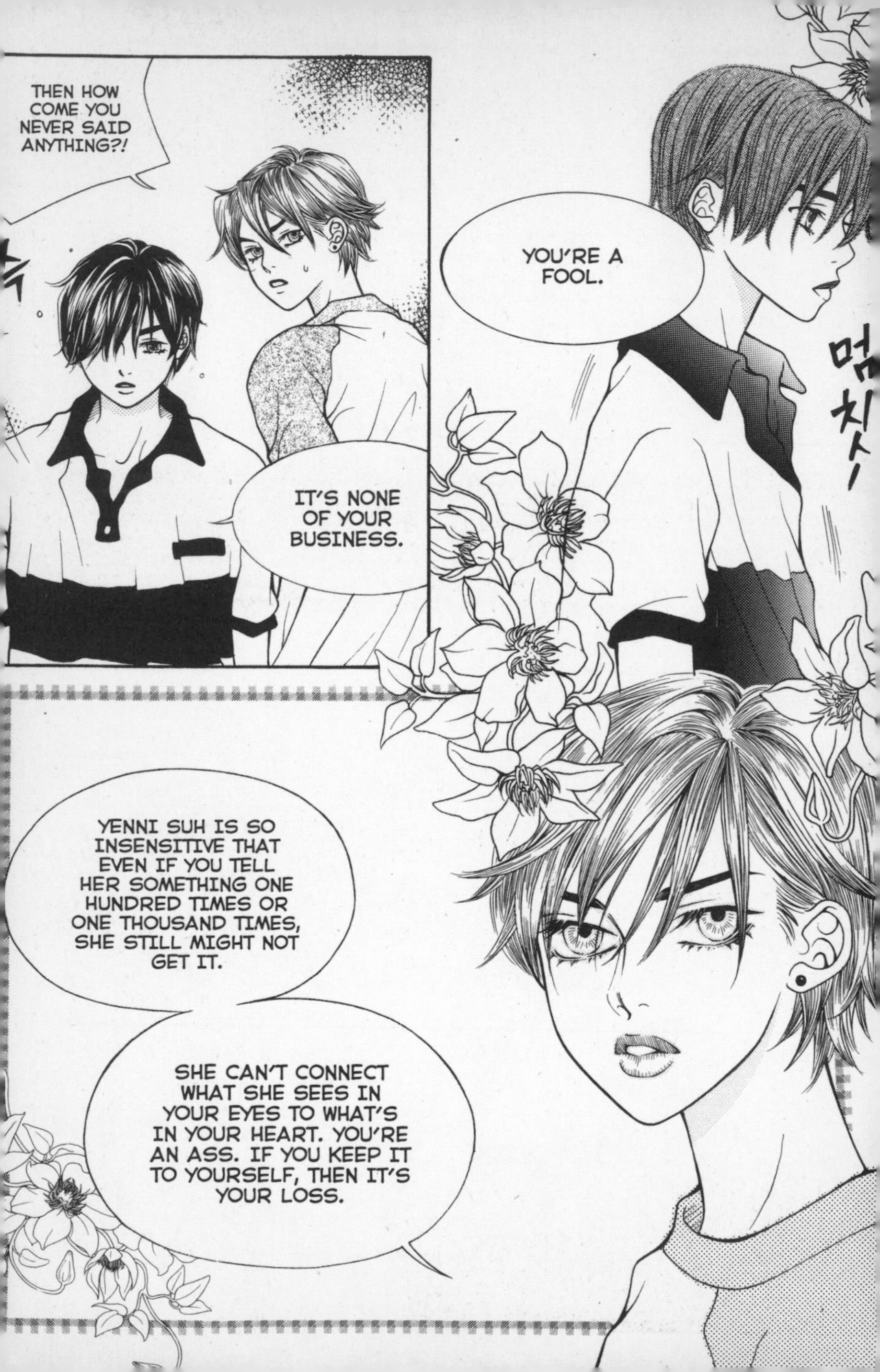
THEN HOW COME YOU NEVER SAID ANYTHING?!
IT'S NONE OF YOUR BUSINESS.
YOU'RE A FOOL.
멈칫!
YENNI SUH IS SO INSENSITIVE THAT EVEN IF YOU TELL HER SOMETHING ONE HUNDRED TIMES OR ONE THOUSAND TIMES, SHE STILL MIGHT NOT GET IT.
SHE CAN'T CONNECT WHAT SHE SEES IN YOUR EYES TO WHAT'S IN YOUR HEART. YOU'RE AN ASS. IF YOU KEEP IT TO YOURSELF, THEN IT'S YOUR LOSS.

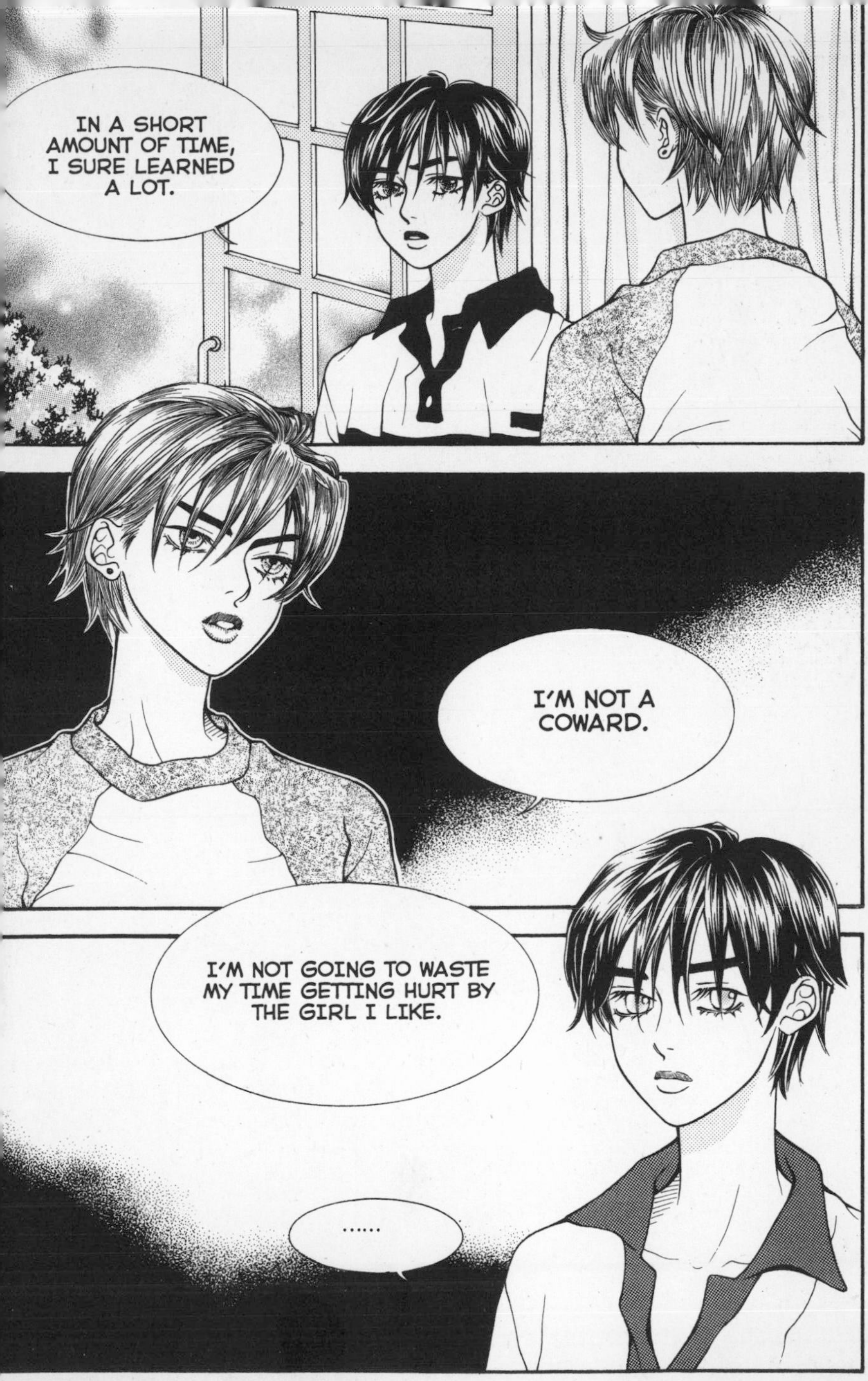
IN A SHORT AMOUNT OF TIME, I SURE LEARNED A LOT.
I'M NOT A COWARD.
I'M NOT GOING TO WASTE MY TIME GETTING HURT BY THE GIRL I LIKE.
......

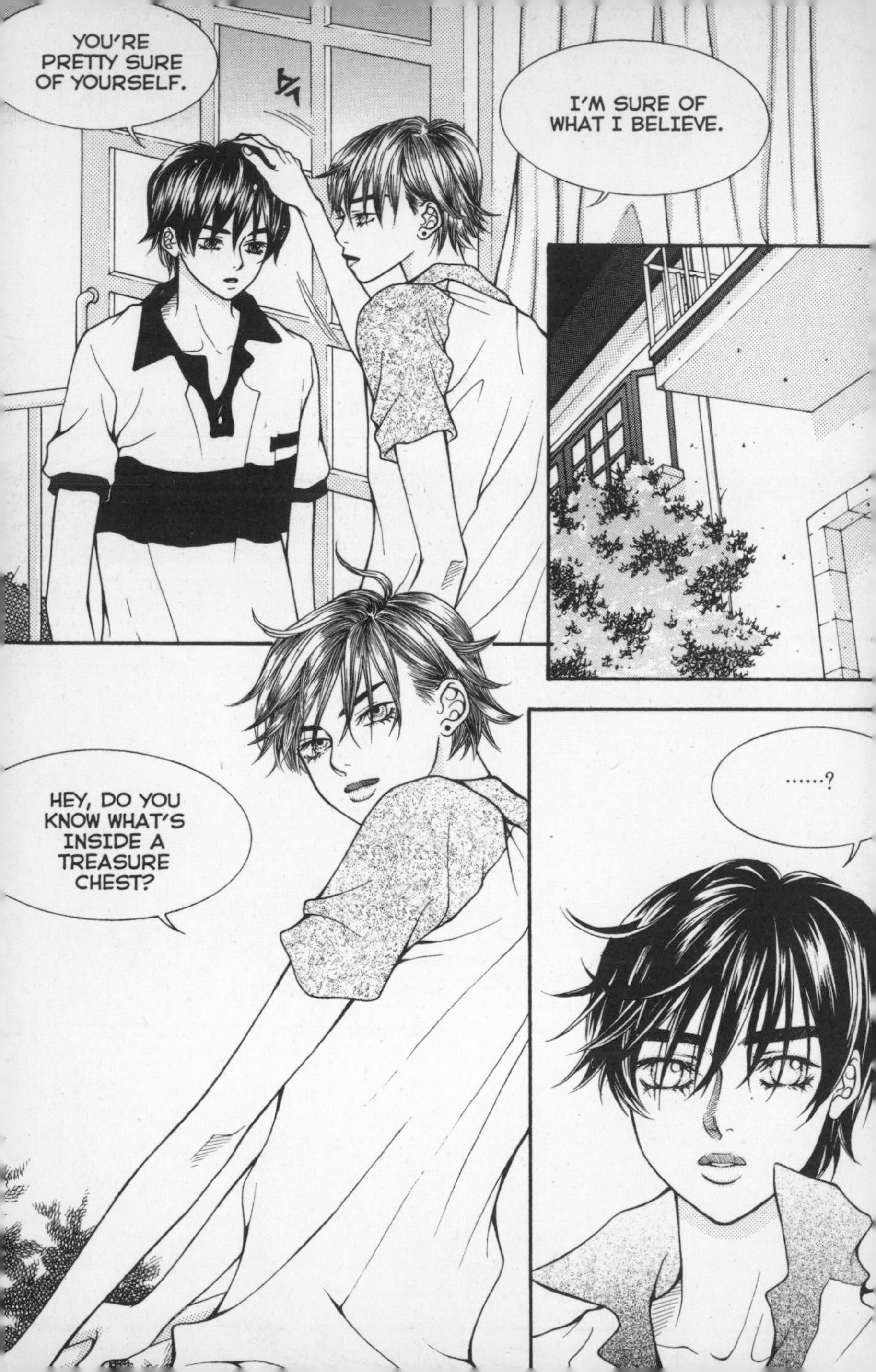
YOU'RE PRETTY SURE OF YOURSELF.
I'M SURE OF WHAT I BELIEVE.
HEY, DO YOU KNOW WHAT'S INSIDE A TREASURE CHEST?
......?

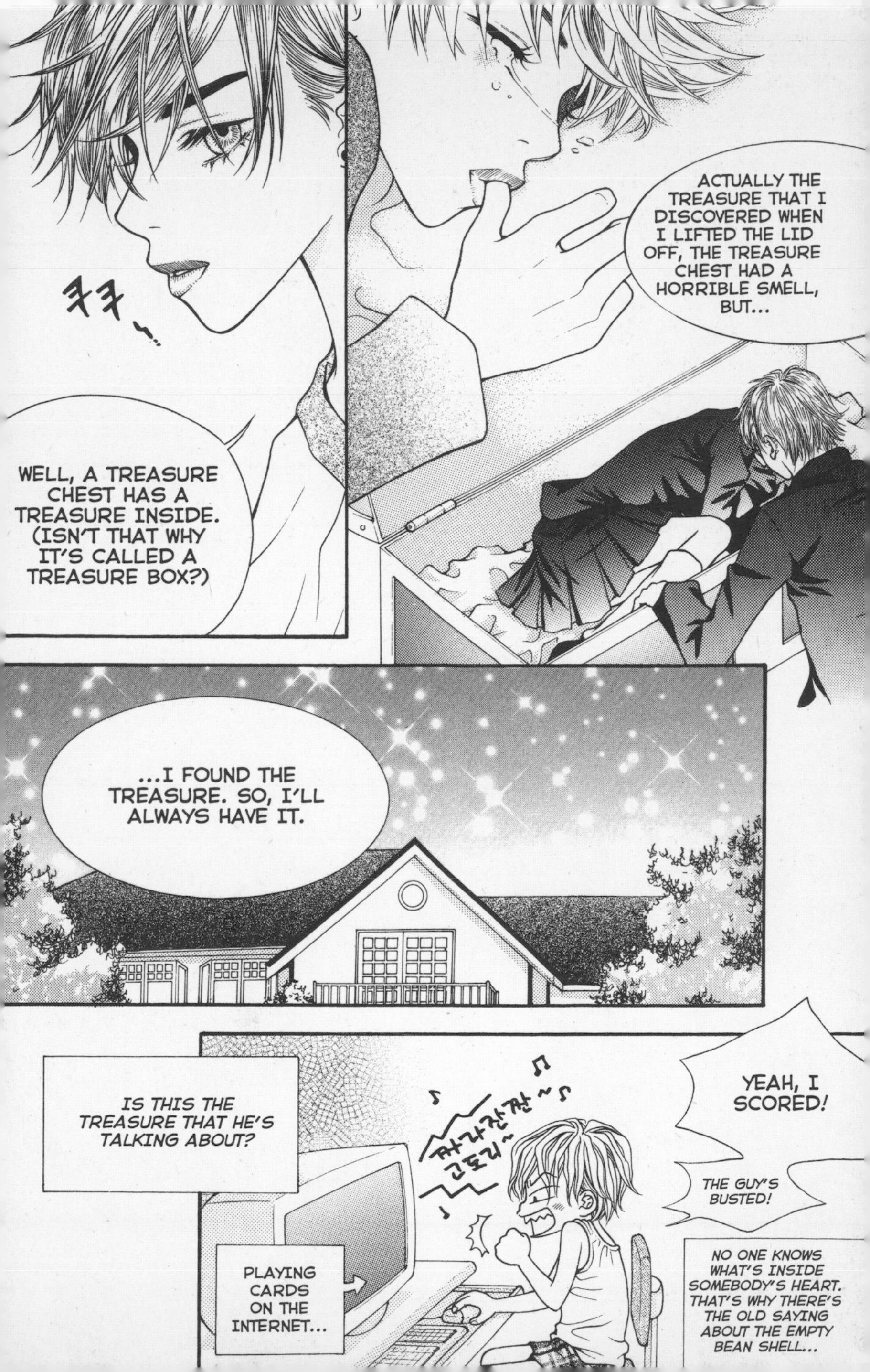
ㅋㅋ~...
WELL, A TREASURE CHEST HAS A TREASURE INSIDE. (ISN'T THAT WHY IT'S CALLED A TREASURE BOX?)
ACTUALLY THE TREASURE THAT I DISCOVERED WHEN I LIFTED THE LID OFF, THE TREASURE CHEST HAD A HORRIBLE SMELL, BUT...
...I FOUND THE TREASURE. SO, I'LL ALWAYS HAVE IT.
IS THIS THE TREASURE THAT HE'S TALKING ABOUT?
YEAH, I SCORED!
THE GUY'S BUSTED!
PLAYING CARDS ON THE INTERNET...
NO ONE KNOWS WHAT'S INSIDE SOMEBODY'S HEART. THAT'S WHY THERE'S THE OLD SAYING ABOUT THE EMPTY BEAN SHELL...

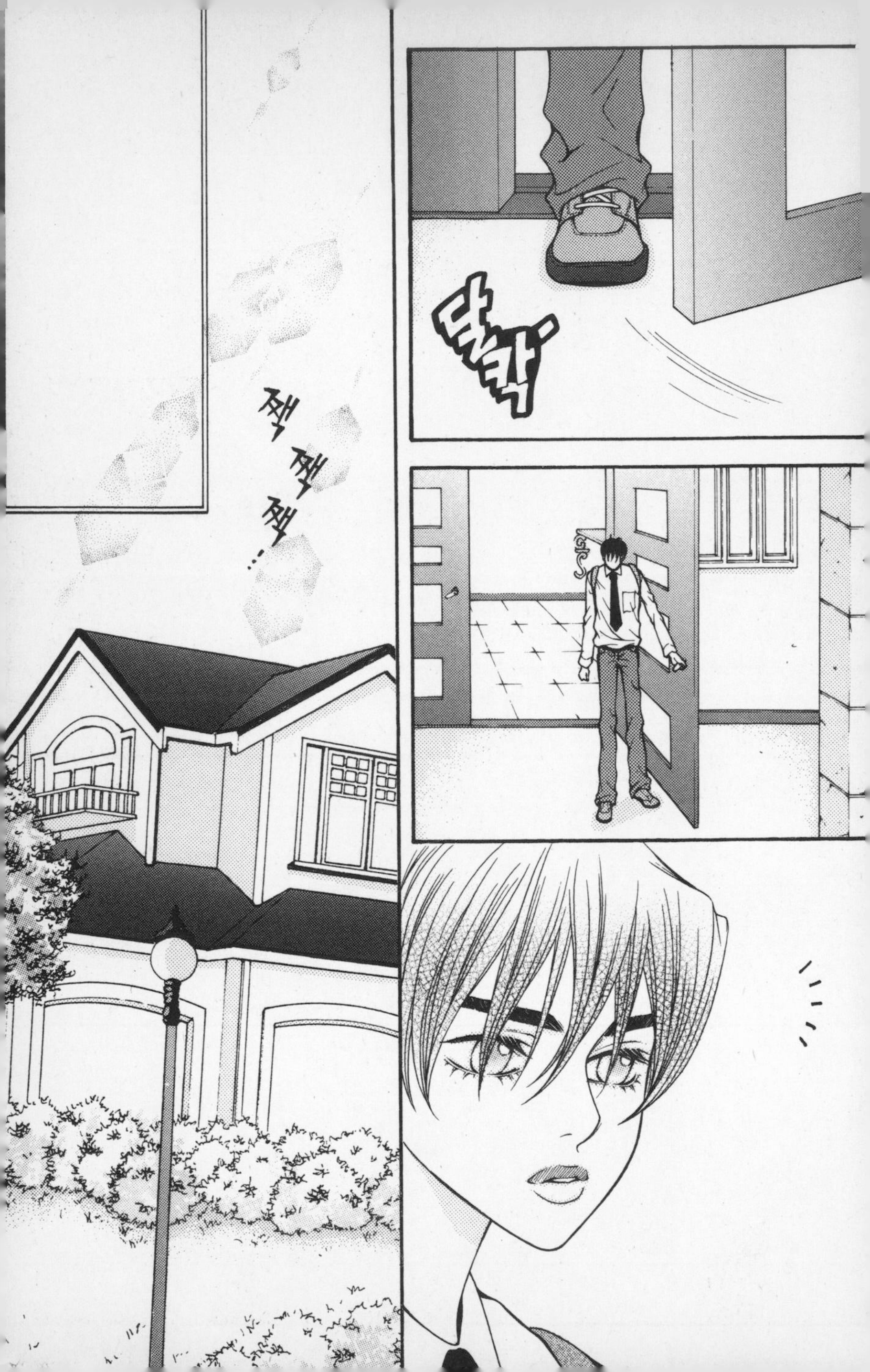
짹 짹 짹…
달칵

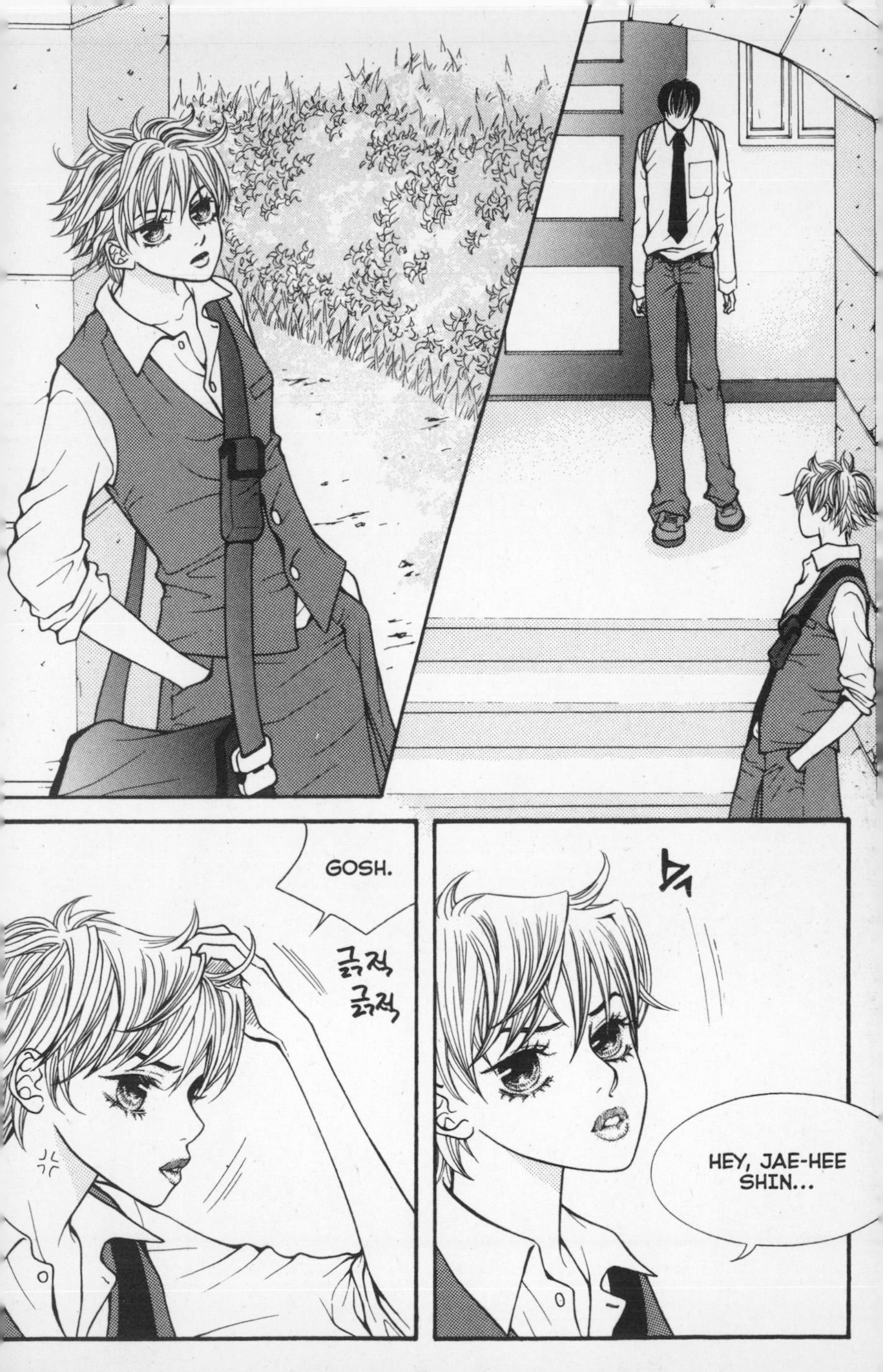
GOSH.
긁적
긁적
HEY, JAE-HEE SHIN...

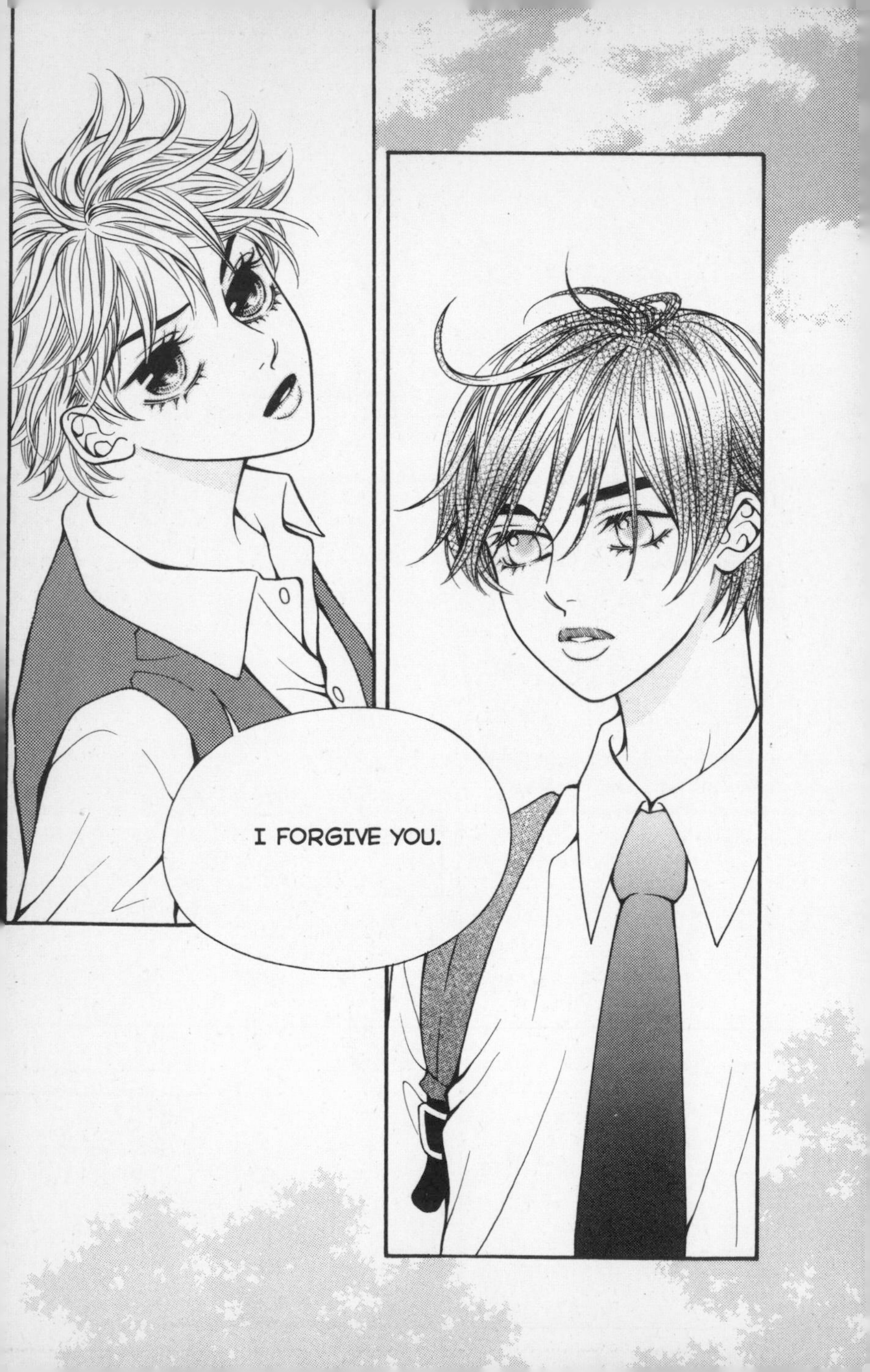
I FORGIVE YOU.

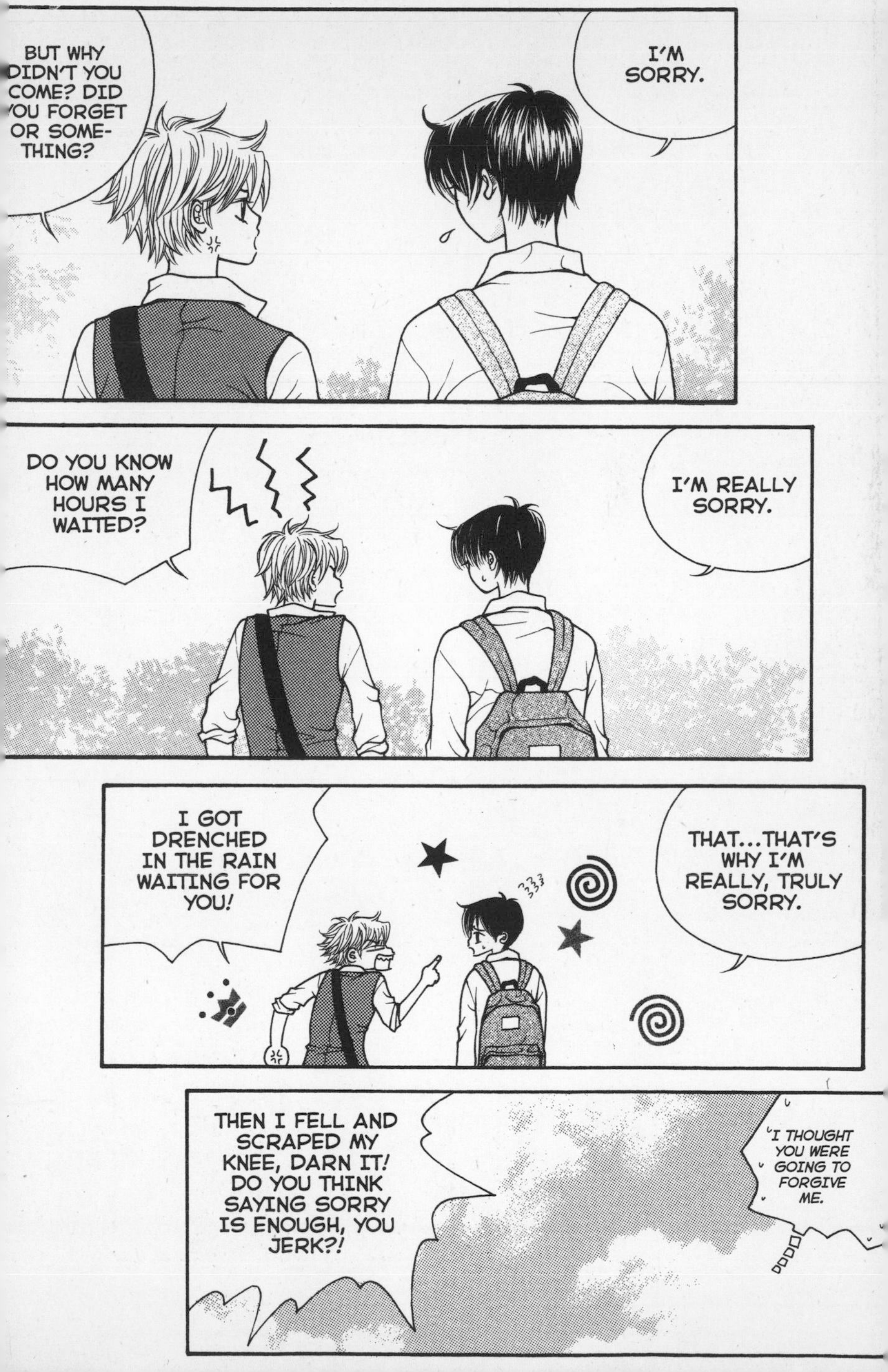
BUT WHY DIDN'T YOU COME? DID YOU FORGET OR SOME-THING?
I'M SORRY.
DO YOU KNOW HOW MANY HOURS I WAITED?
I'M REALLY SORRY.
I GOT DRENCHED IN THE RAIN WAITING FOR YOU!
THAT...THAT'S WHY I'M REALLY, TRULY SORRY.
THEN I FELL AND SCRAPED MY KNEE, DARN IT! DO YOU THINK SAYING SORRY IS ENOUGH, YOU JERK?!
I THOUGHT YOU WERE GOING TO FORGIVE ME.

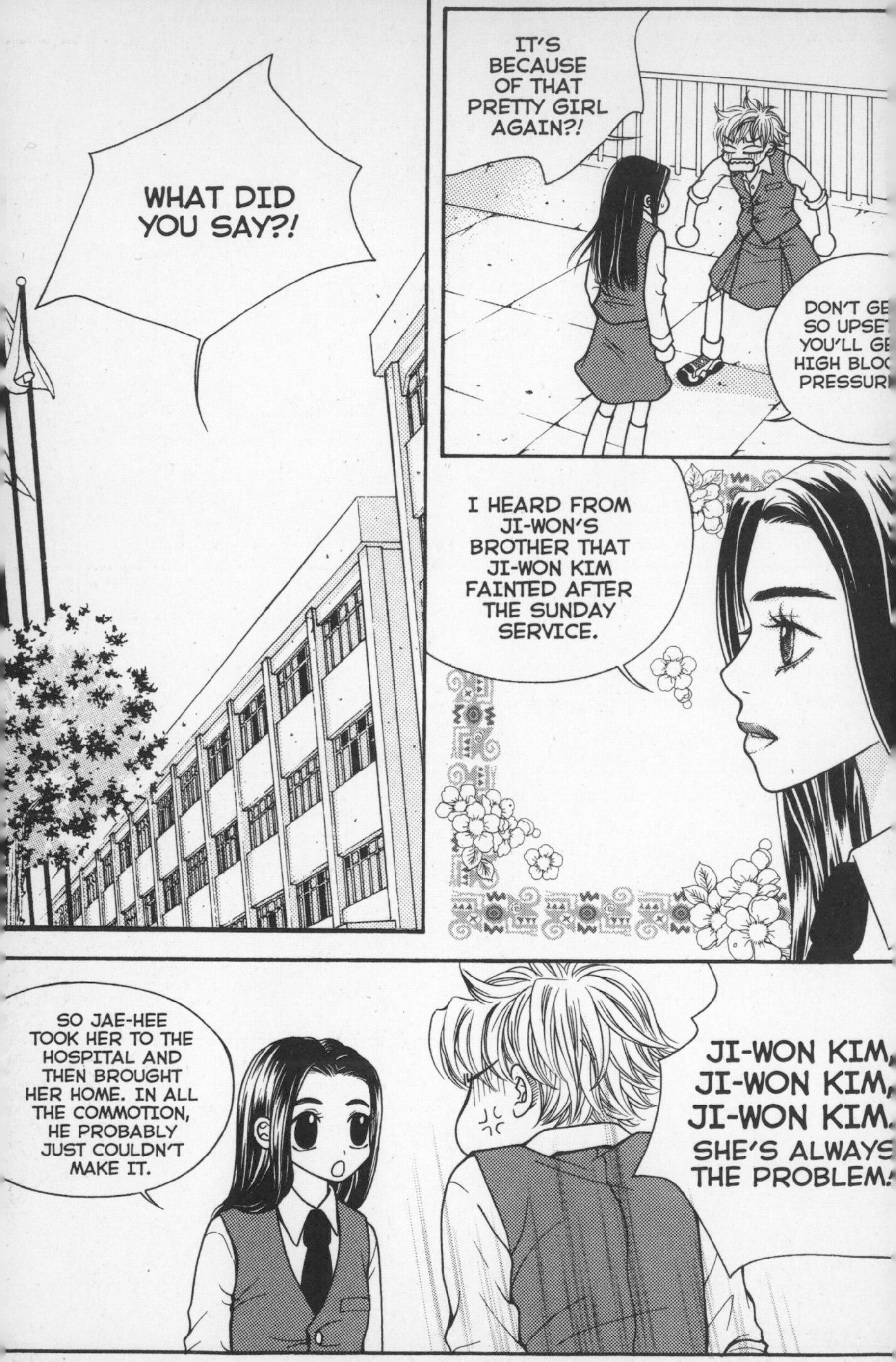
WHAT DID YOU SAY?!
IT'S BECAUSE OF THAT PRETTY GIRL AGAIN?!
DON'T GE
SO UPSET
YOU'LL GE
HIGH BLOC
PRESSUR
I HEARD FROM JI-WON'S BROTHER THAT JI-WON KIM FAINTED AFTER THE SUNDAY SERVICE.
SO JAE-HEE TOOK HER TO THE HOSPITAL AND THEN BROUGHT HER HOME. IN ALL THE COMMOTION, HE PROBABLY JUST COULDN'T MAKE IT.
JI-WON KIM, JI-WON KIM, JI-WON KIM. SHE'S ALWAYS THE PROBLEM!

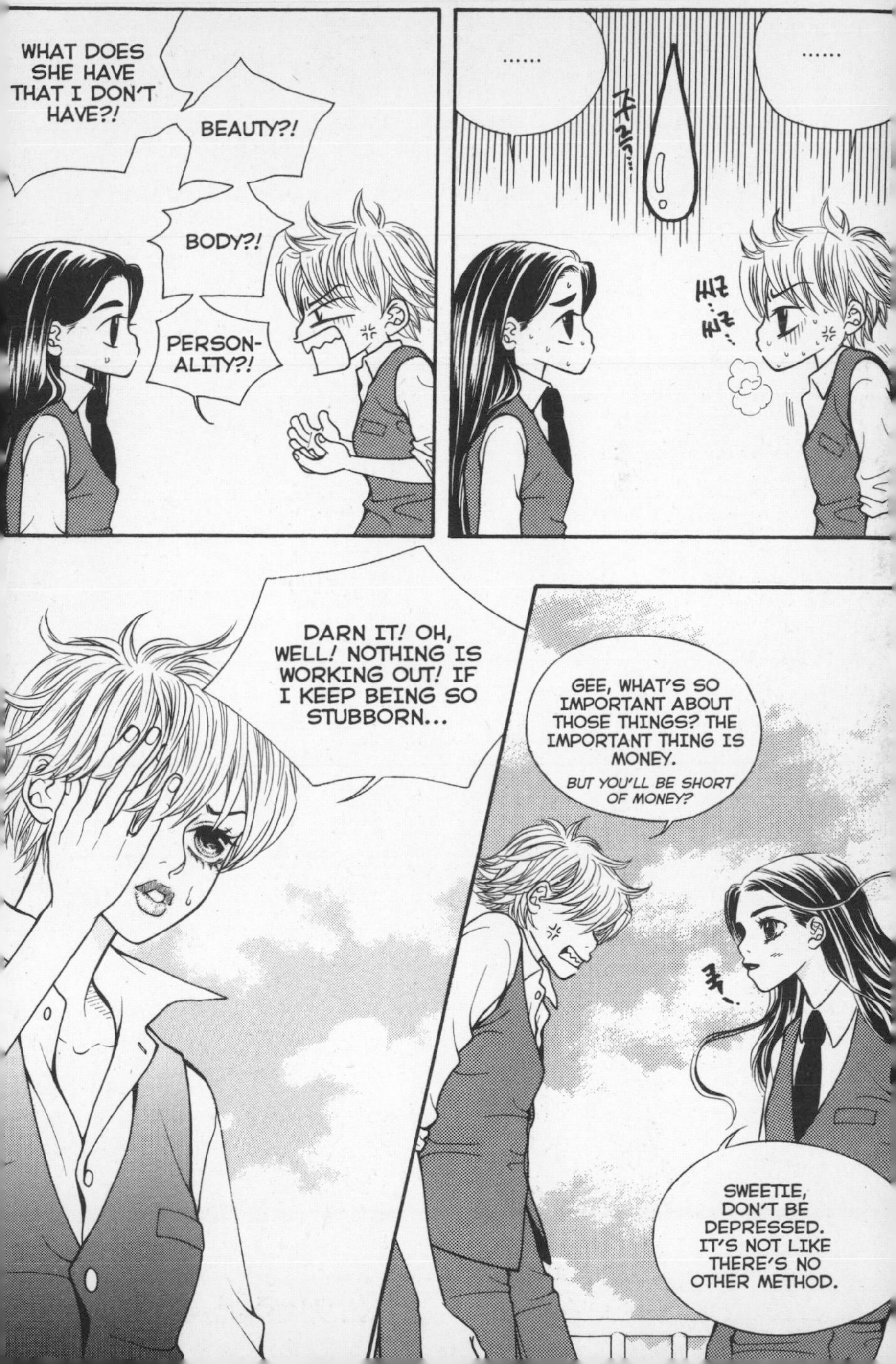
WHAT DOES SHE HAVE THAT I DON'T HAVE?!
BEAUTY?!
BODY?!
PERSON-ALITY?!
......
......
DARN IT! OH, WELL! NOTHING IS WORKING OUT! IF I KEEP BEING SO STUBBORN...
GEE, WHAT'S SO IMPORTANT ABOUT THOSE THINGS? THE IMPORTANT THING IS MONEY.
BUT YOU'LL BE SHORT OF MONEY?
SWEETIE, DON'T BE DEPRESSED. IT'S NOT LIKE THERE'S NO OTHER METHOD.

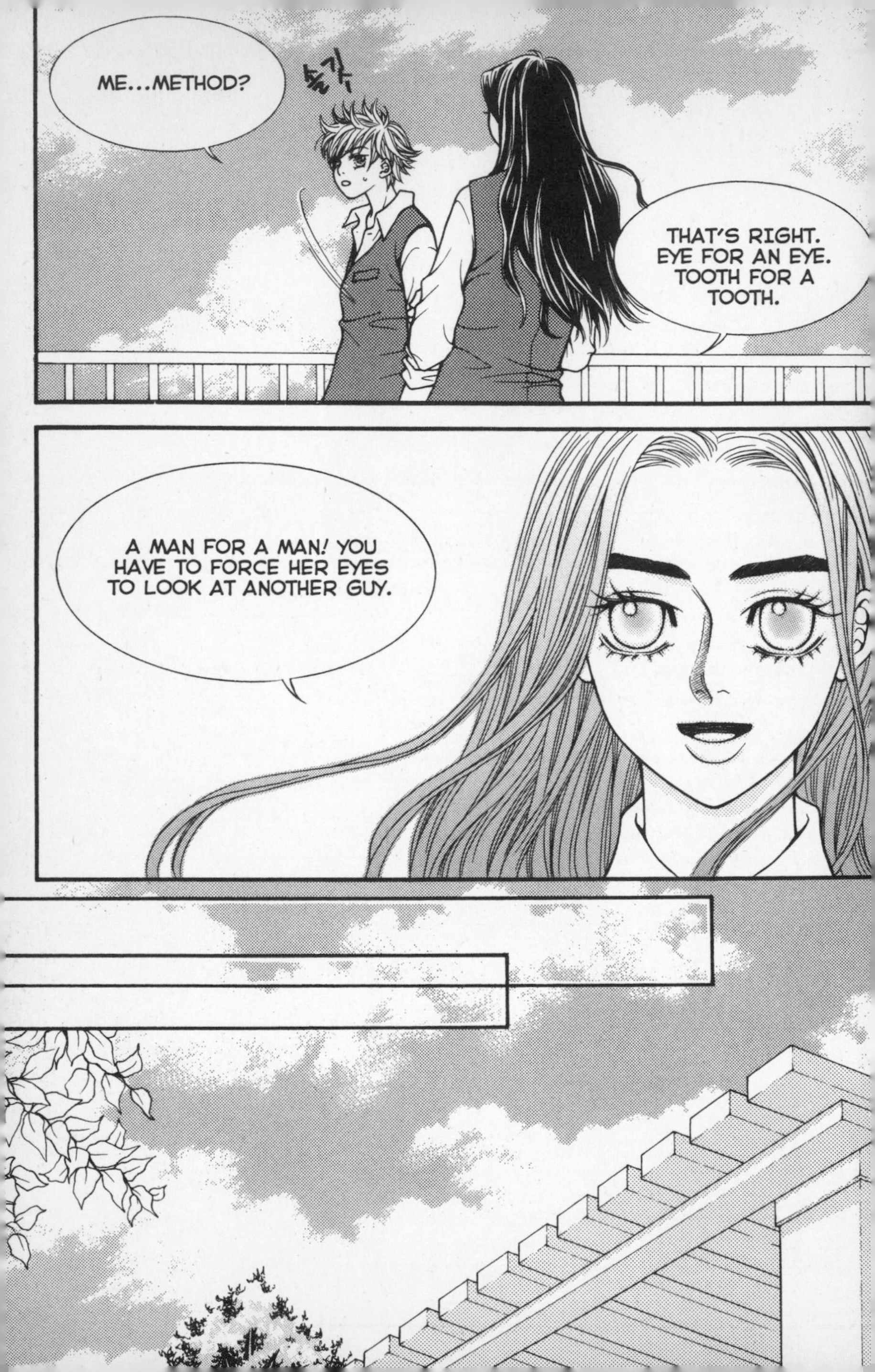
ME...METHOD?
솔깃
THAT'S RIGHT. EYE FOR AN EYE. TOOTH FOR A TOOTH.
A MAN FOR A MAN! YOU HAVE TO FORCE HER EYES TO LOOK AT ANOTHER GUY.

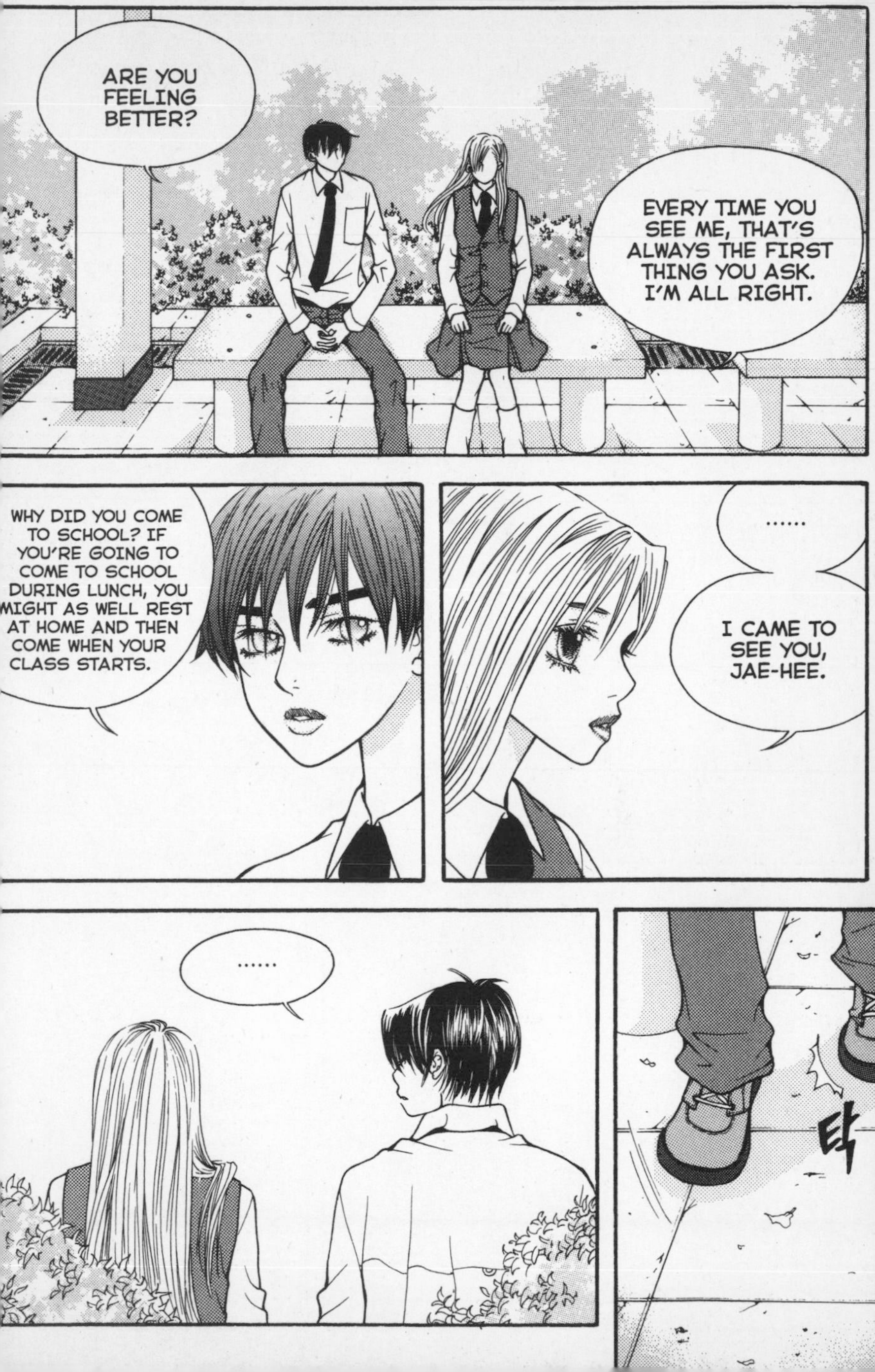
ARE YOU FEELING BETTER?
EVERY TIME YOU SEE ME, THAT'S ALWAYS THE FIRST THING YOU ASK. I'M ALL RIGHT.
WHY DID YOU COME TO SCHOOL? IF YOU'RE GOING TO COME TO SCHOOL DURING LUNCH, YOU MIGHT AS WELL REST AT HOME AND THEN COME WHEN YOUR CLASS STARTS.
......
I CAME TO SEE YOU, JAE-HEE.
......
탁

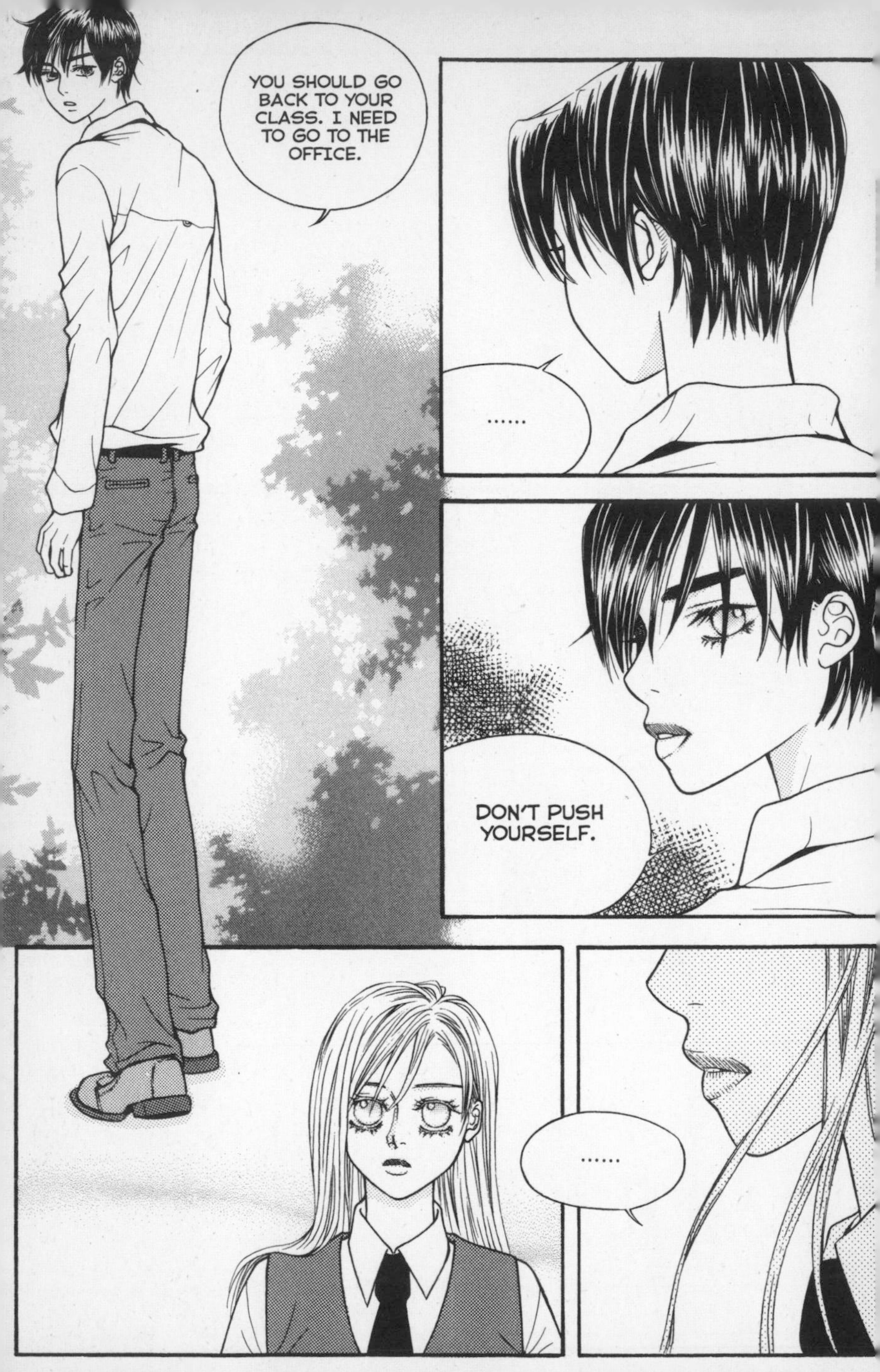
YOU SHOULD GO BACK TO YOUR CLASS. I NEED TO GO TO THE OFFICE.
......
DON'T PUSH YOURSELF.
......

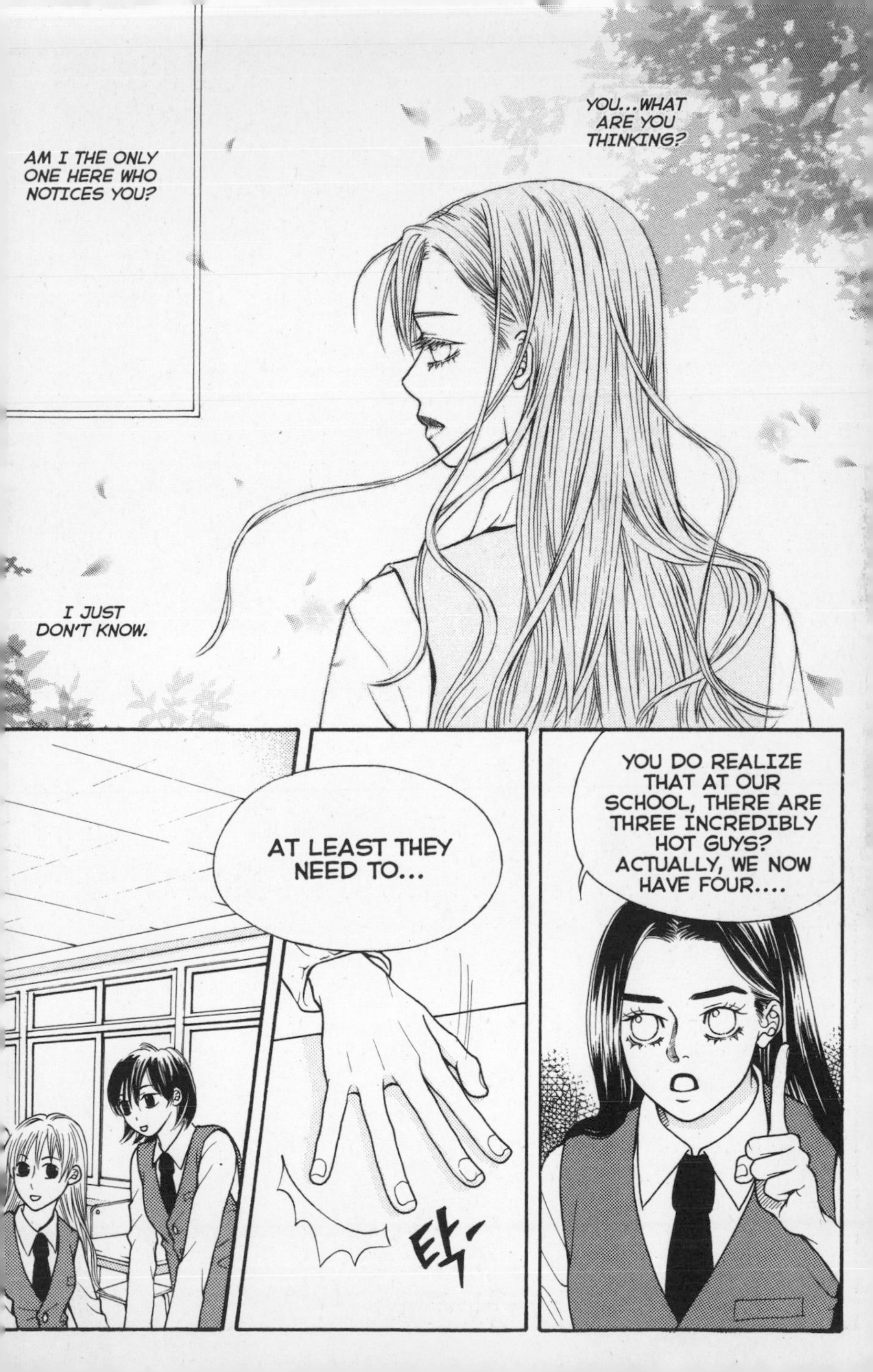
YOU...WHAT ARE YOU THINKING?
AM I THE ONLY ONE HERE WHO NOTICES YOU?
I JUST DON'T KNOW.
AT LEAST THEY NEED TO...
YOU DO REALIZE THAT AT OUR SCHOOL, THERE ARE THREE INCREDIBLY HOT GUYS? ACTUALLY, WE NOW HAVE FOUR....

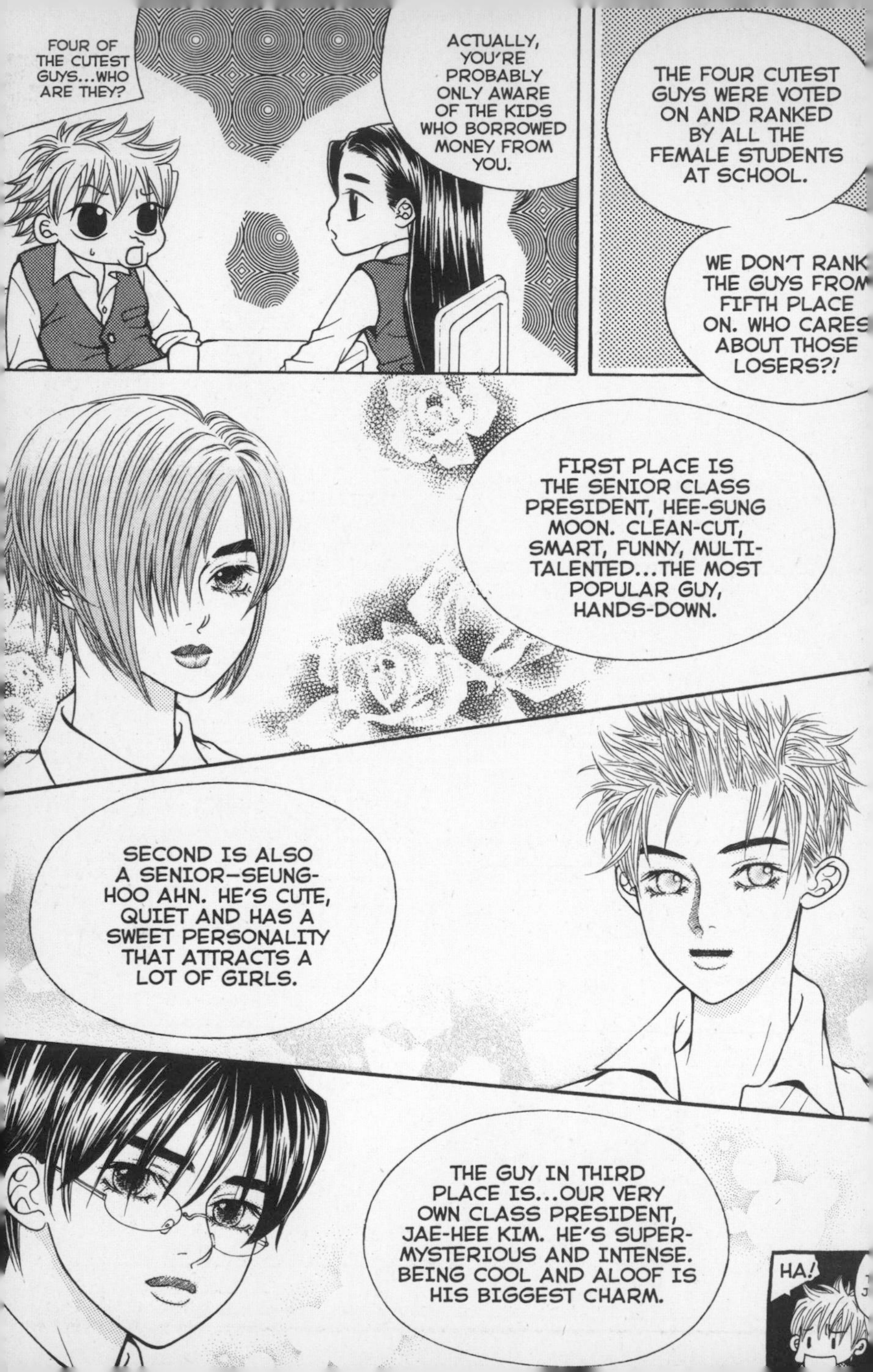
FOUR OF THE CUTEST GUYS...WHO ARE THEY?
ACTUALLY, YOU'RE PROBABLY ONLY AWARE OF THE KIDS WHO BORROWED MONEY FROM YOU.
THE FOUR CUTEST GUYS WERE VOTED ON AND RANKED BY ALL THE FEMALE STUDENTS AT SCHOOL.
WE DON'T RANK THE GUYS FROM FIFTH PLACE ON. WHO CARES ABOUT THOSE LOSERS?!
FIRST PLACE IS THE SENIOR CLASS PRESIDENT, HEE-SUNG MOON. CLEAN-CUT, SMART, FUNNY, MULTI-TALENTED...THE MOST POPULAR GUY, HANDS-DOWN.
SECOND IS ALSO A SENIOR—SEUNG-HOO AHN. HE'S CUTE, QUIET AND HAS A SWEET PERSONALITY THAT ATTRACTS A LOT OF GIRLS.
THE GUY IN THIRD PLACE IS...OUR VERY OWN CLASS PRESIDENT, JAE-HEE KIM. HE'S SUPER-MYSTERIOUS AND INTENSE. BEING COOL AND ALOOF IS HIS BIGGEST CHARM.
HA!

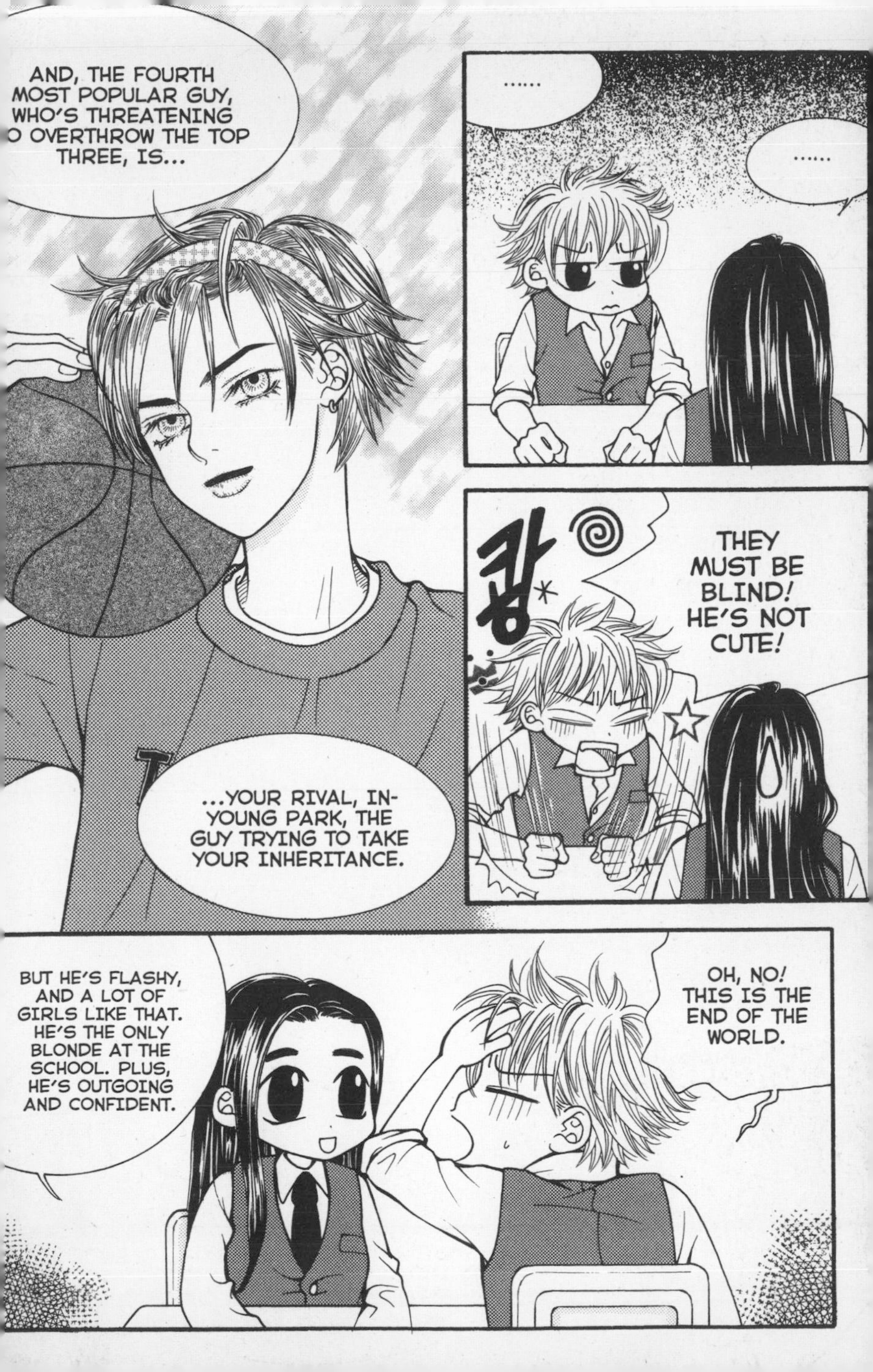
AND, THE FOURTH MOST POPULAR GUY, WHO'S THREATENING O OVERTHROW THE TOP THREE, IS...
...YOUR RIVAL, IN-YOUNG PARK, THE GUY TRYING TO TAKE YOUR INHERITANCE.
......
......
THEY MUST BE BLIND! HE'S NOT CUTE!
BUT HE'S FLASHY, AND A LOT OF GIRLS LIKE THAT. HE'S THE ONLY BLONDE AT THE SCHOOL. PLUS, HE'S OUTGOING AND CONFIDENT.
OH, NO! THIS IS THE END OF THE WORLD.

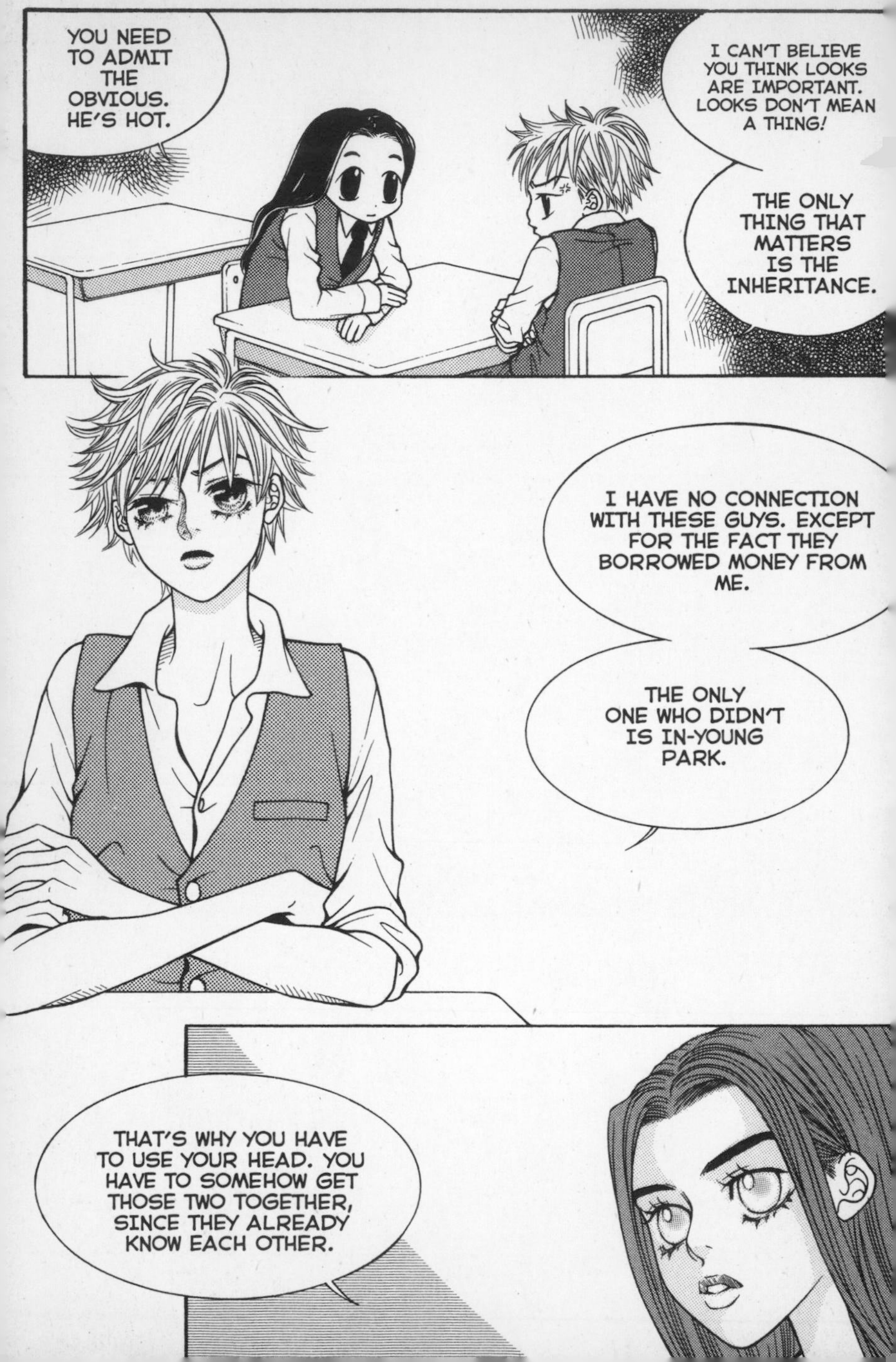
YOU NEED TO ADMIT THE OBVIOUS. HE'S HOT.
I CAN'T BELIEVE YOU THINK LOOKS ARE IMPORTANT. LOOKS DON'T MEAN A THING!
THE ONLY THING THAT MATTERS IS THE INHERITANCE.
I HAVE NO CONNECTION WITH THESE GUYS. EXCEPT FOR THE FACT THEY BORROWED MONEY FROM ME.
THE ONLY ONE WHO DIDN'T IS IN-YOUNG PARK.
THAT'S WHY YOU HAVE TO USE YOUR HEAD. YOU HAVE TO SOMEHOW GET THOSE TWO TOGETHER, SINCE THEY ALREADY KNOW EACH OTHER.

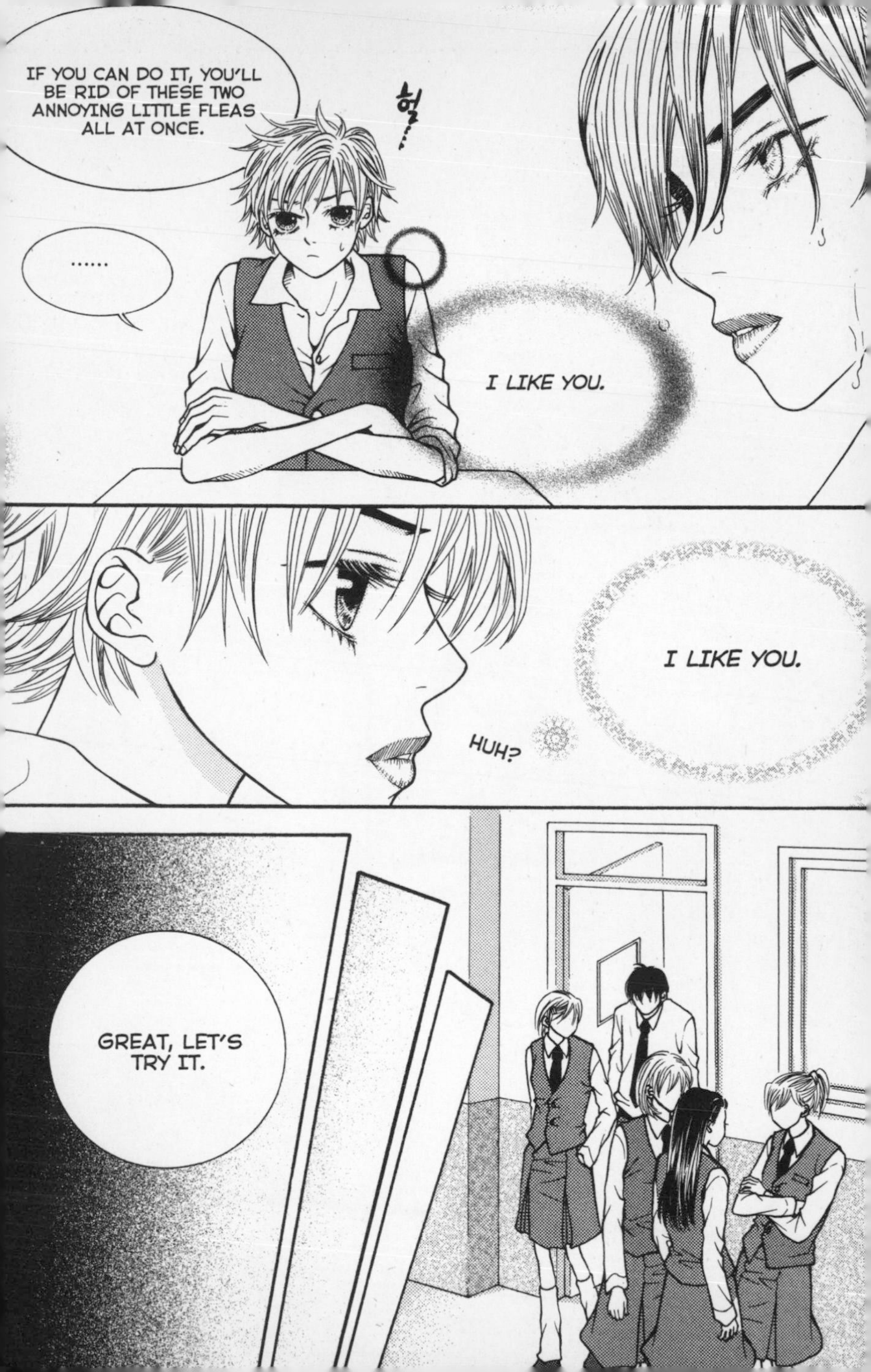
IF YOU CAN DO IT, YOU'LL BE RID OF THESE TWO ANNOYING LITTLE FLEAS ALL AT ONCE.
......
헐...
I LIKE YOU.
I LIKE YOU.
HUH?
GREAT, LET'S TRY IT.

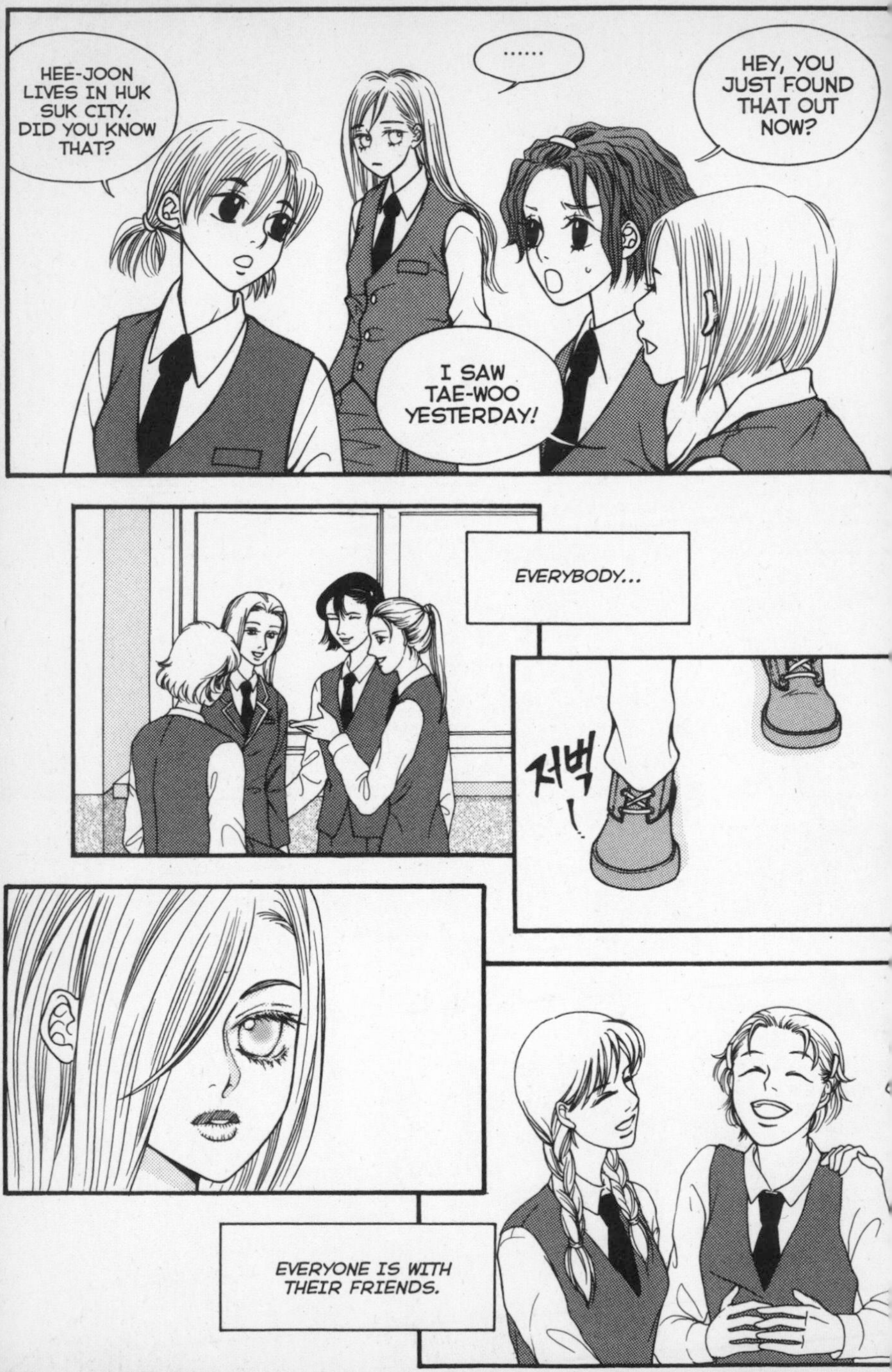
HEE-JOON LIVES IN HUK SUK CITY. DID YOU KNOW THAT?
......
HEY, YOU JUST FOUND THAT OUT NOW?
I SAW TAE-WOO YESTERDAY!
EVERYBODY...
저벅
EVERYONE IS WITH THEIR FRIENDS.

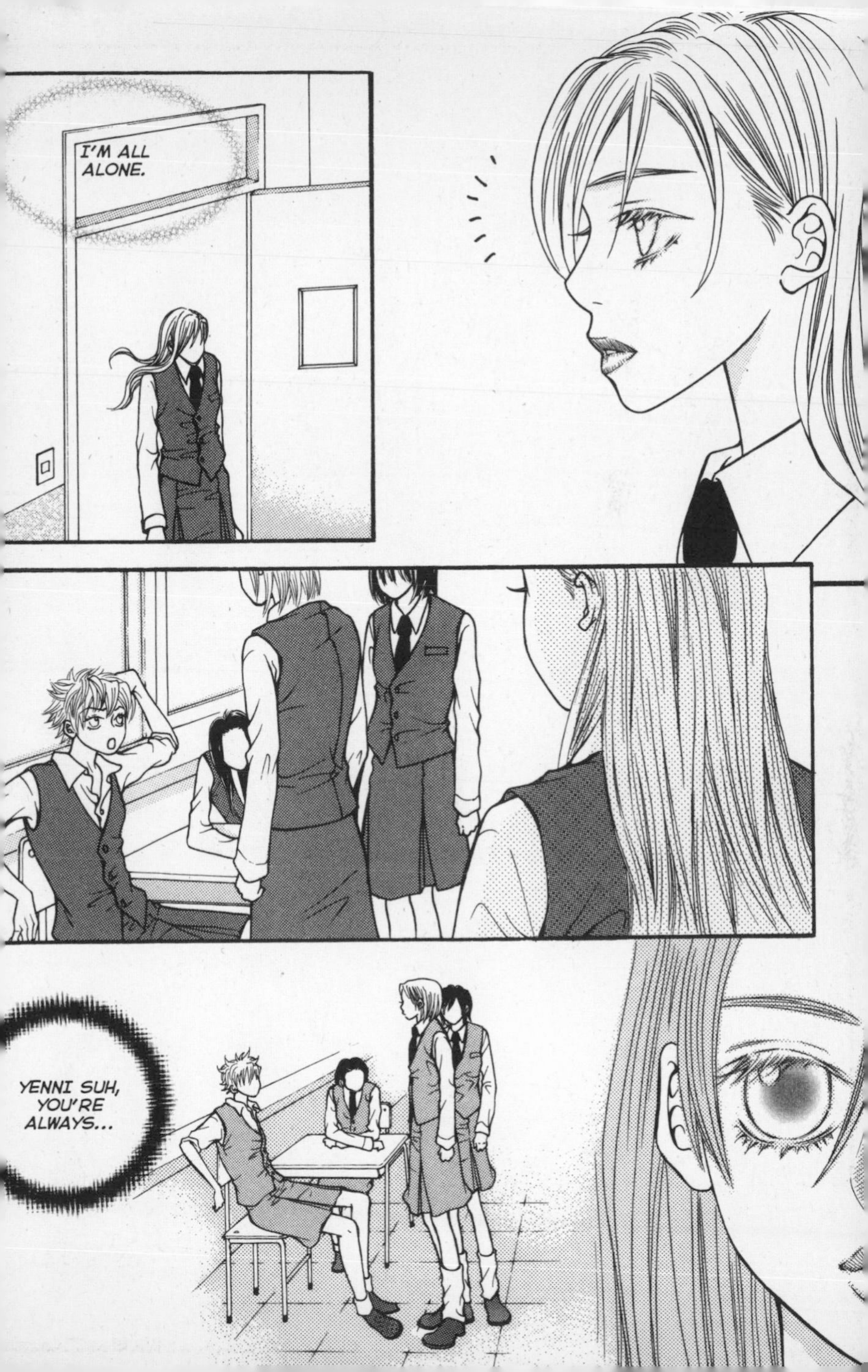
I'M ALL ALONE.
YENNI SUH, YOU'RE ALWAYS...

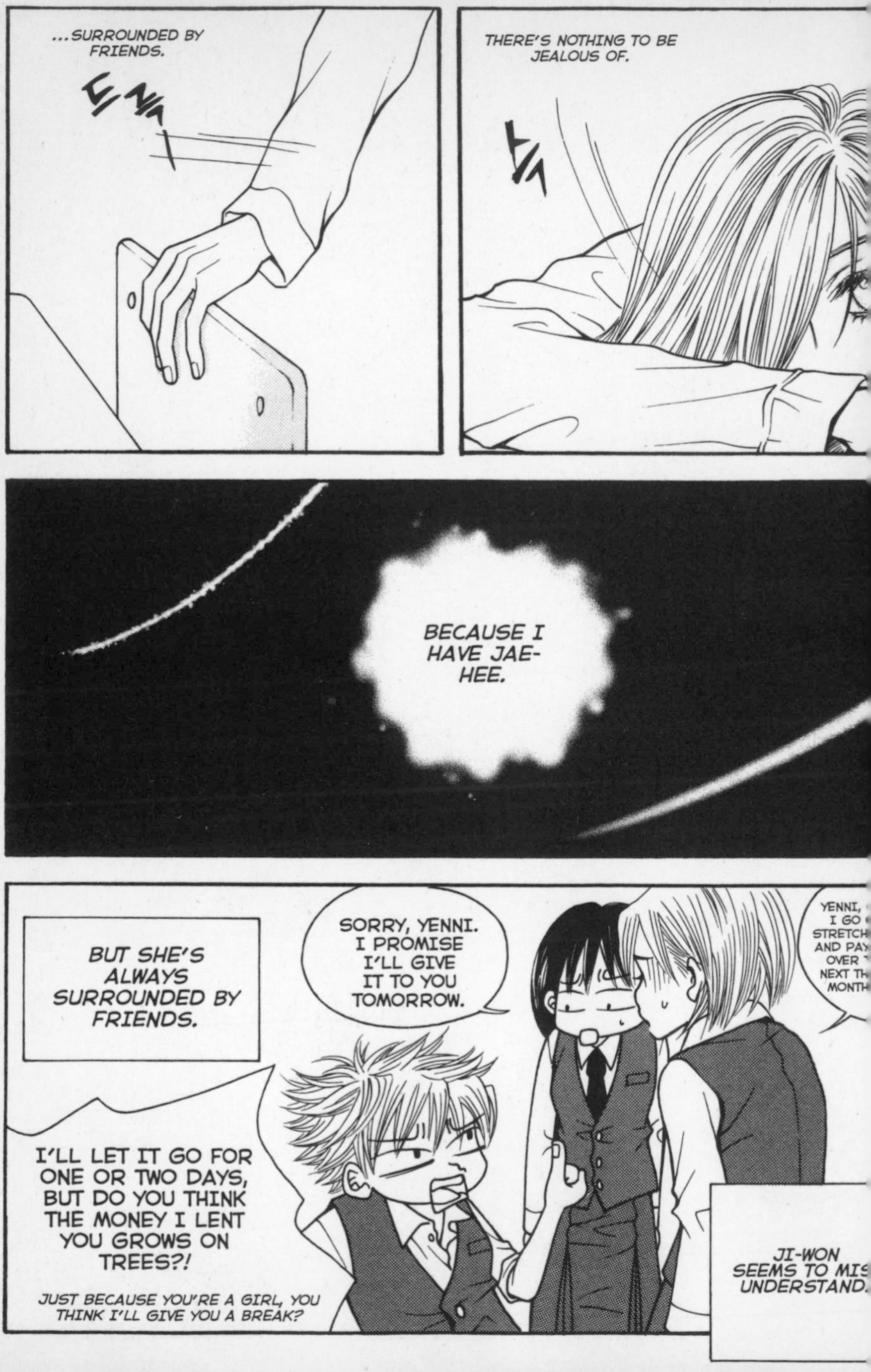
...SURROUNDED BY FRIENDS.
THERE'S NOTHING TO BE JEALOUS OF.
BECAUSE I HAVE JAE-HEE.
BUT SHE'S ALWAYS SURROUNDED BY FRIENDS.
SORRY, YENNI. I PROMISE I'LL GIVE IT TO YOU TOMORROW.
I'LL LET IT GO FOR ONE OR TWO DAYS, BUT DO YOU THINK THE MONEY I LENT YOU GROWS ON TREES?!
JUST BECAUSE YOU'RE A GIRL, YOU THINK I'LL GIVE YOU A BREAK?
JI-WON SEEMS TO MIS UNDERSTAND.

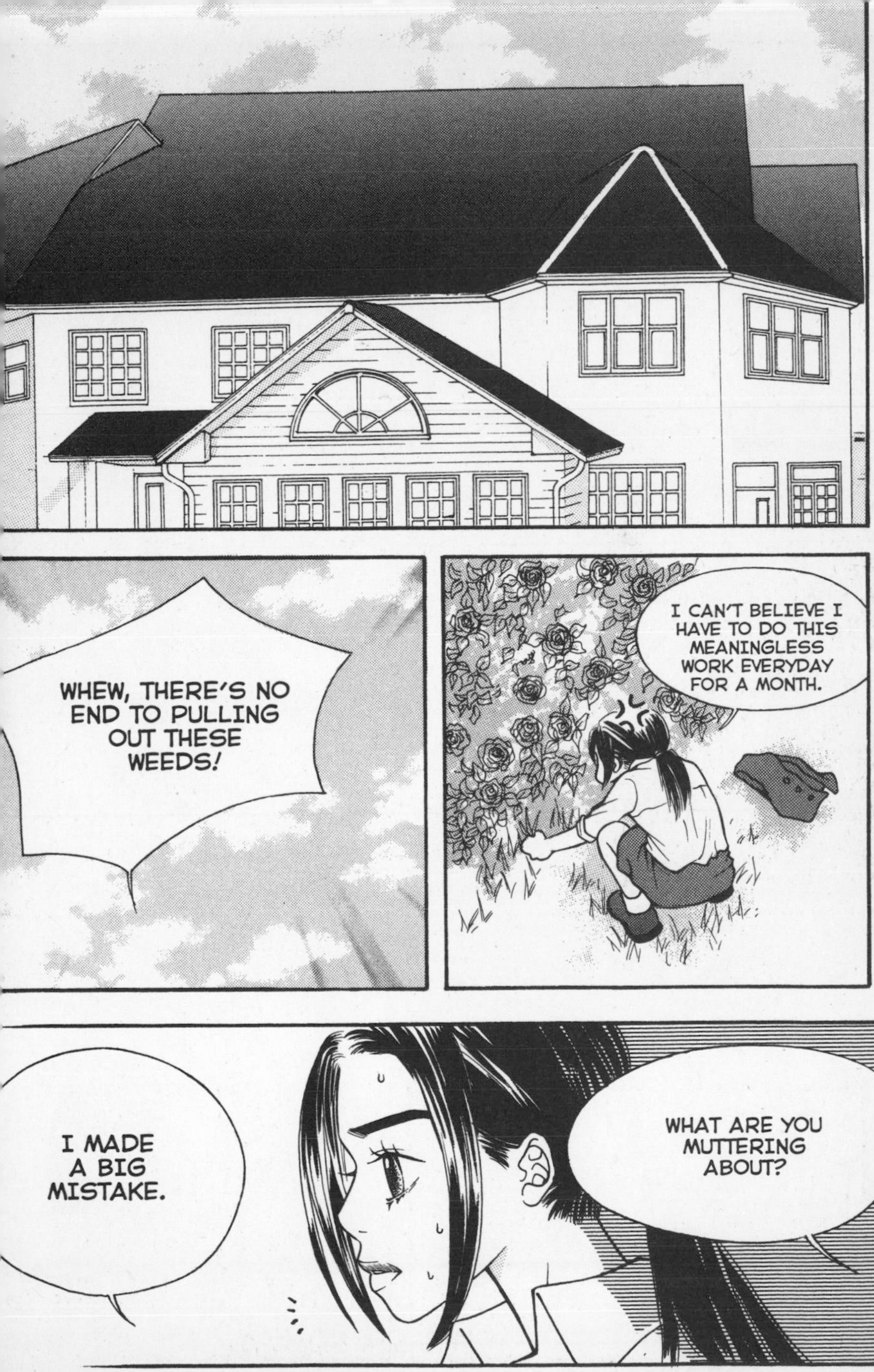
WHEW, THERE'S NO END TO PULLING OUT THESE WEEDS!
I CAN'T BELIEVE I HAVE TO DO THIS MEANINGLESS WORK EVERYDAY FOR A MONTH.
I MADE A BIG MISTAKE.
WHAT ARE YOU MUTTERING ABOUT?

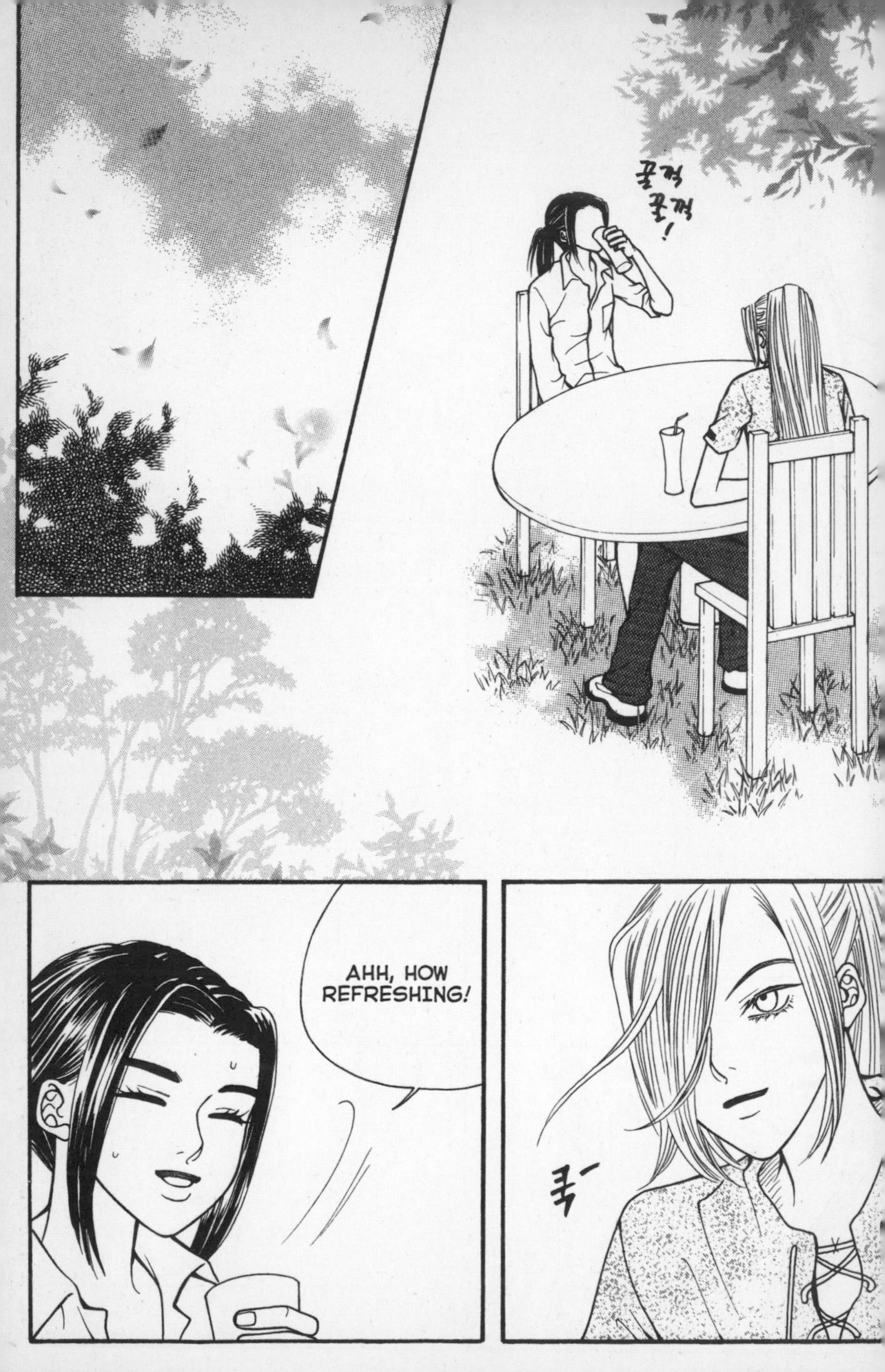
꿀꺽
꿀꺽!
AHH, HOW REFRESHING!
쿡-

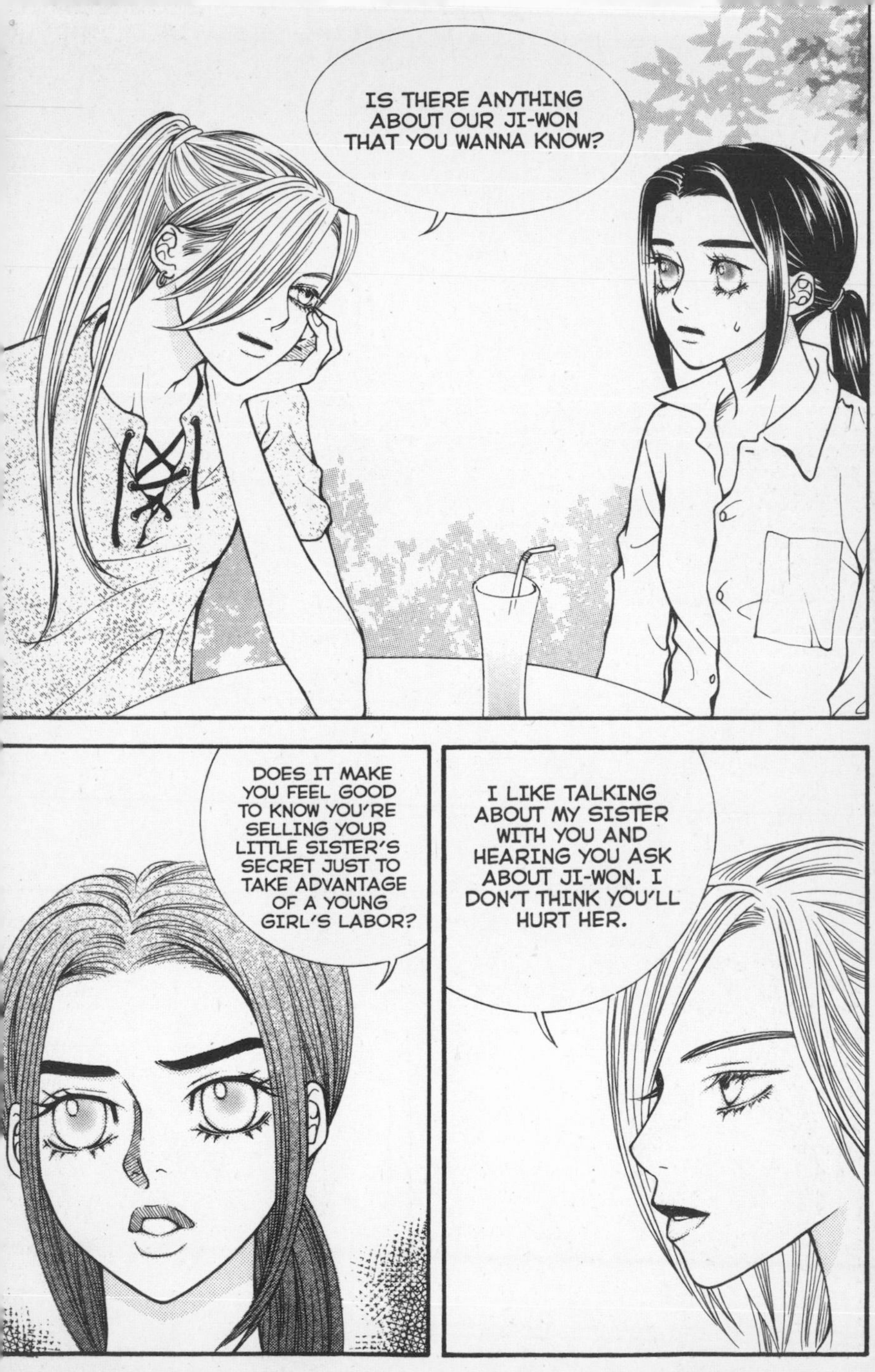
IS THERE ANYTHING ABOUT OUR JI-WON THAT YOU WANNA KNOW?
DOES IT MAKE YOU FEEL GOOD TO KNOW YOU'RE SELLING YOUR LITTLE SISTER'S SECRET JUST TO TAKE ADVANTAGE OF A YOUNG GIRL'S LABOR?
I LIKE TALKING ABOUT MY SISTER WITH YOU AND HEARING YOU ASK ABOUT JI-WON. I DON'T THINK YOU'LL HURT HER.

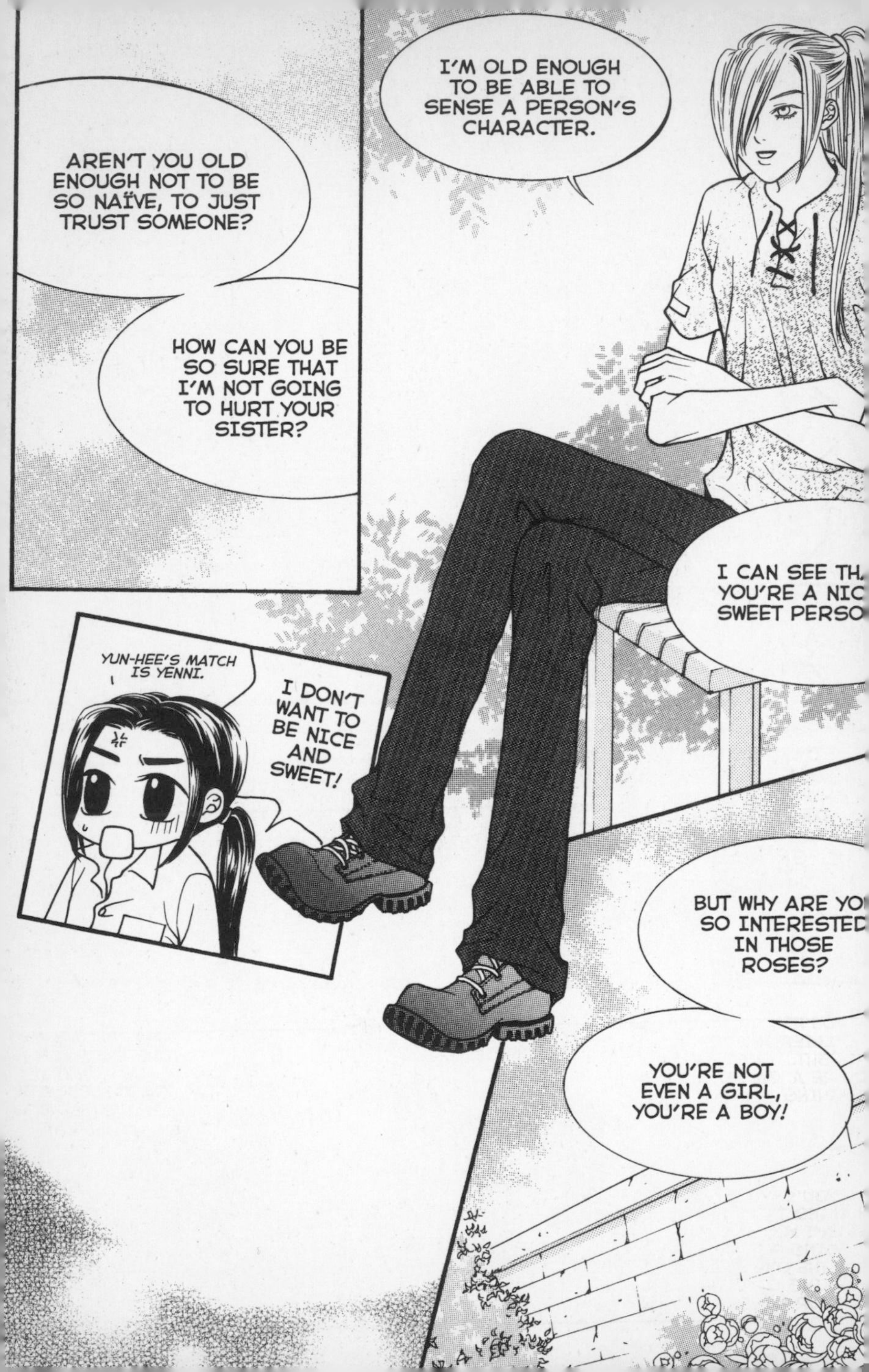
AREN'T YOU OLD ENOUGH NOT TO BE SO NAÏVE, TO JUST TRUST SOMEONE?
HOW CAN YOU BE SO SURE THAT I'M NOT GOING TO HURT YOUR SISTER?
I'M OLD ENOUGH TO BE ABLE TO SENSE A PERSON'S CHARACTER.
I CAN SEE TH YOU'RE A NIC SWEET PERSO
YUN-HEE'S MATCH IS YENNI.
I DON'T WANT TO BE NICE AND SWEET!
BUT WHY ARE YO SO INTERESTED IN THOSE ROSES?
YOU'RE NOT EVEN A GIRL, YOU'RE A BOY!

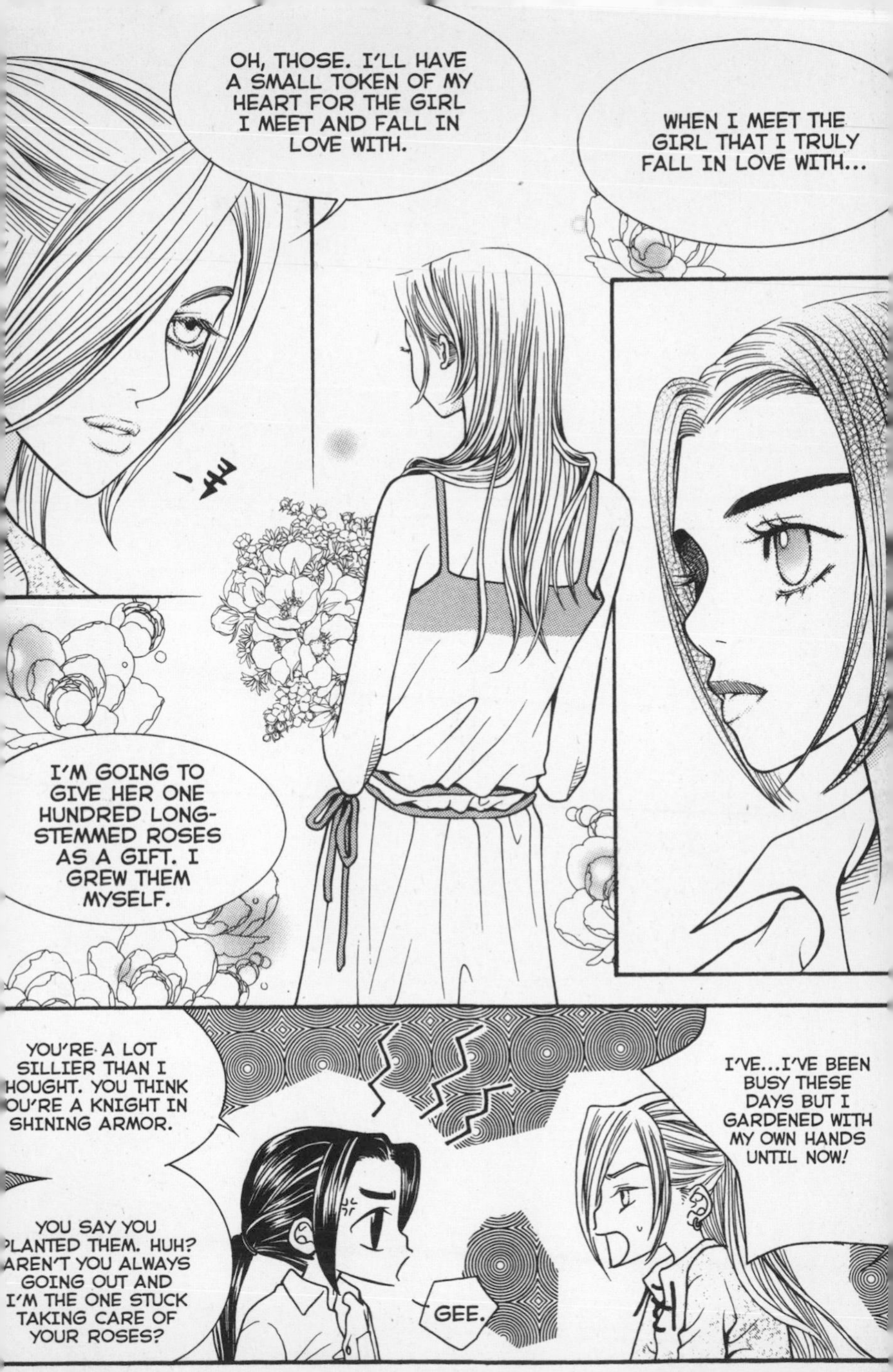
OH, THOSE. I'LL HAVE A SMALL TOKEN OF MY HEART FOR THE GIRL I MEET AND FALL IN LOVE WITH.
WHEN I MEET THE GIRL THAT I TRULY FALL IN LOVE WITH...
I'M GOING TO GIVE HER ONE HUNDRED LONG-STEMMED ROSES AS A GIFT. I GREW THEM MYSELF.
YOU'RE A LOT SILLIER THAN I HOUGHT. YOU THINK OU'RE A KNIGHT IN SHINING ARMOR.
YOU SAY YOU PLANTED THEM. HUH? AREN'T YOU ALWAYS GOING OUT AND I'M THE ONE STUCK TAKING CARE OF YOUR ROSES?
GEE.
I'VE...I'VE BEEN BUSY THESE DAYS BUT I GARDENED WITH MY OWN HANDS UNTIL NOW!

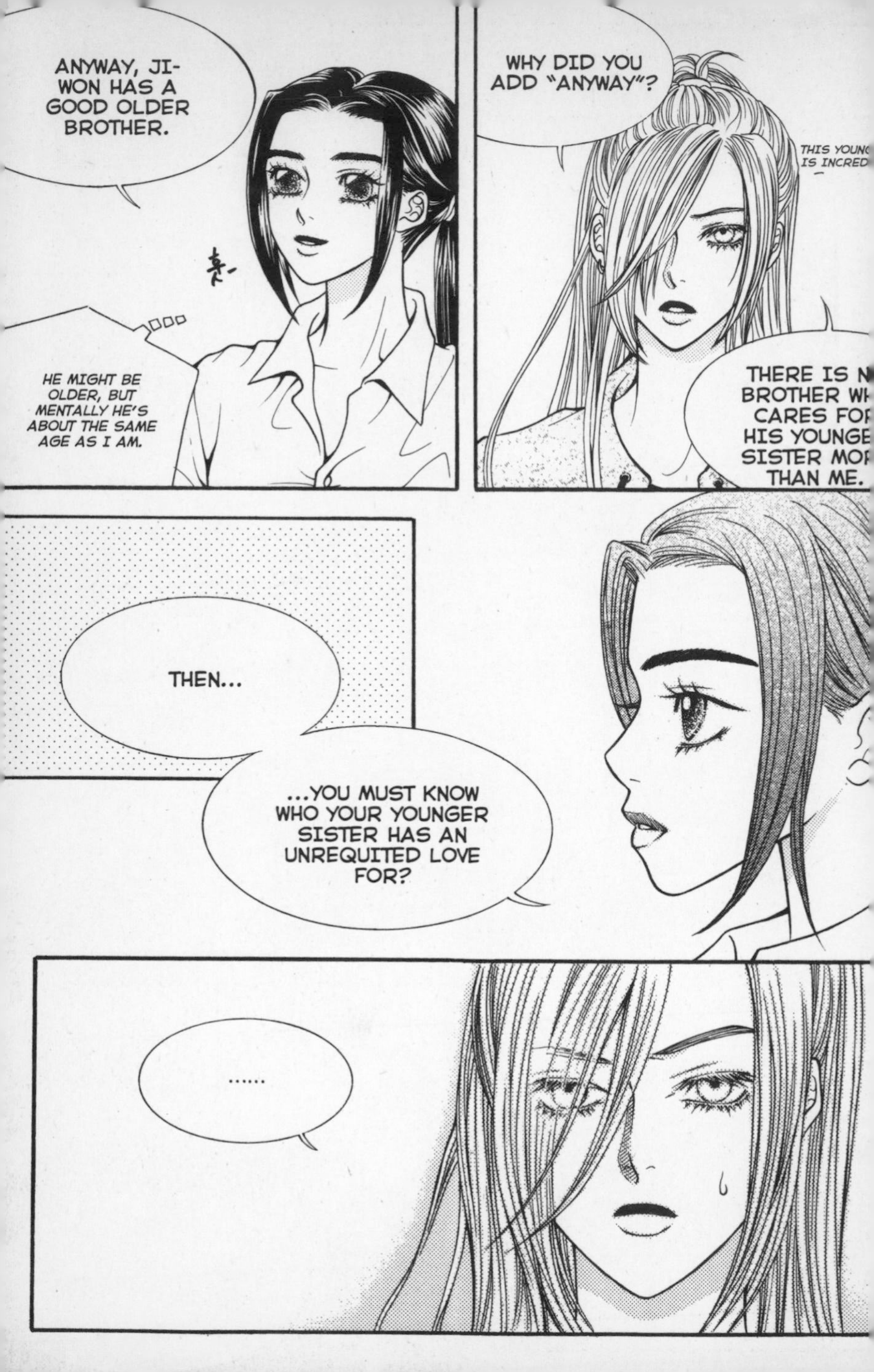
ANYWAY, JI-WON HAS A GOOD OLDER BROTHER.
HE MIGHT BE OLDER, BUT MENTALLY HE'S ABOUT THE SAME AGE AS I AM.
WHY DID YOU ADD "ANYWAY"?
THIS YOUN IS INCRED
THERE IS N BROTHER WH CARES FO HIS YOUNGE SISTER MO THAN ME.
THEN...
...YOU MUST KNOW WHO YOUR YOUNGER SISTER HAS AN UNREQUITED LOVE FOR?
......

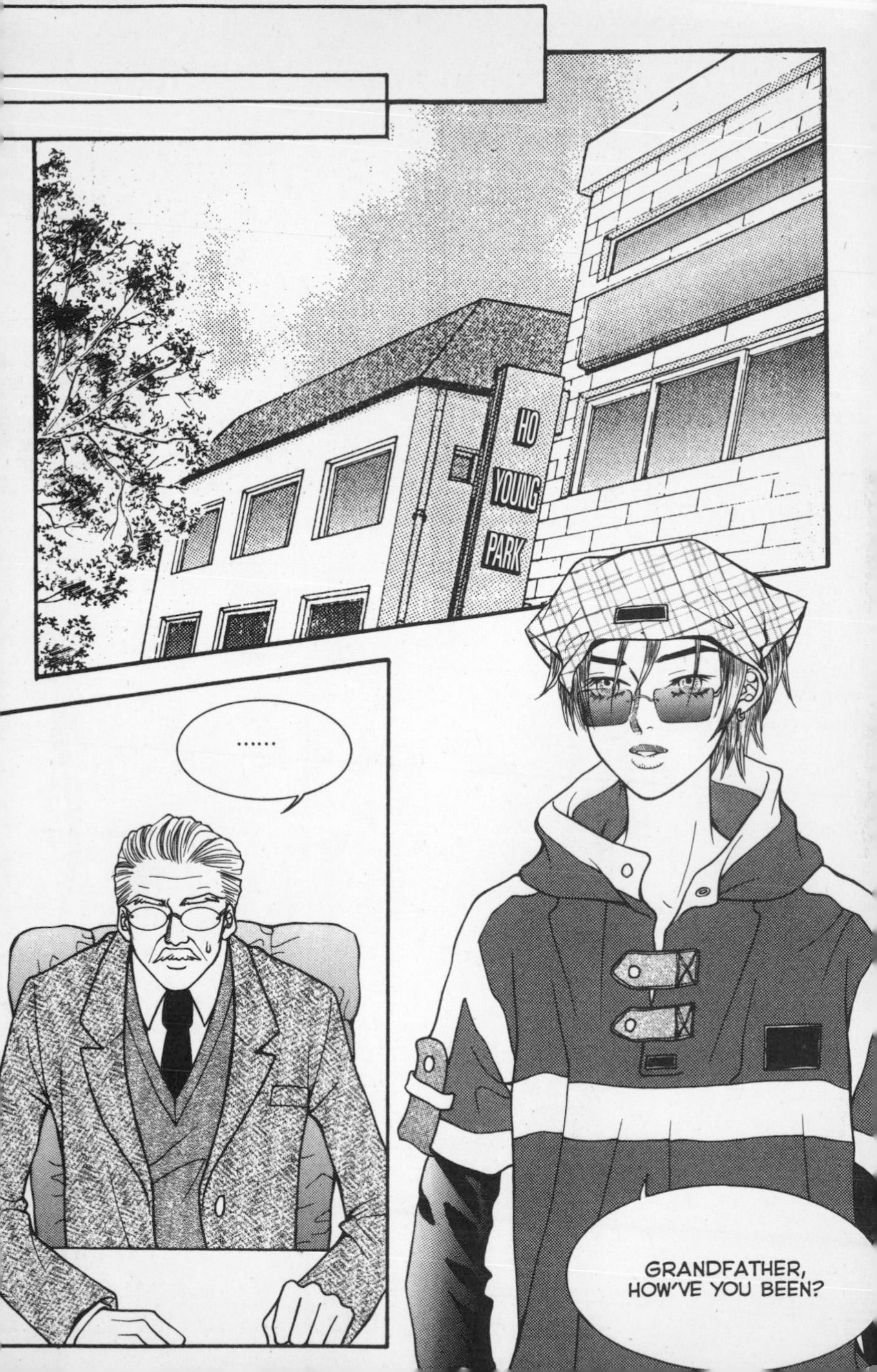
HO YOUNG PARK
......
GRANDFATHER, HOW'VE YOU BEEN?

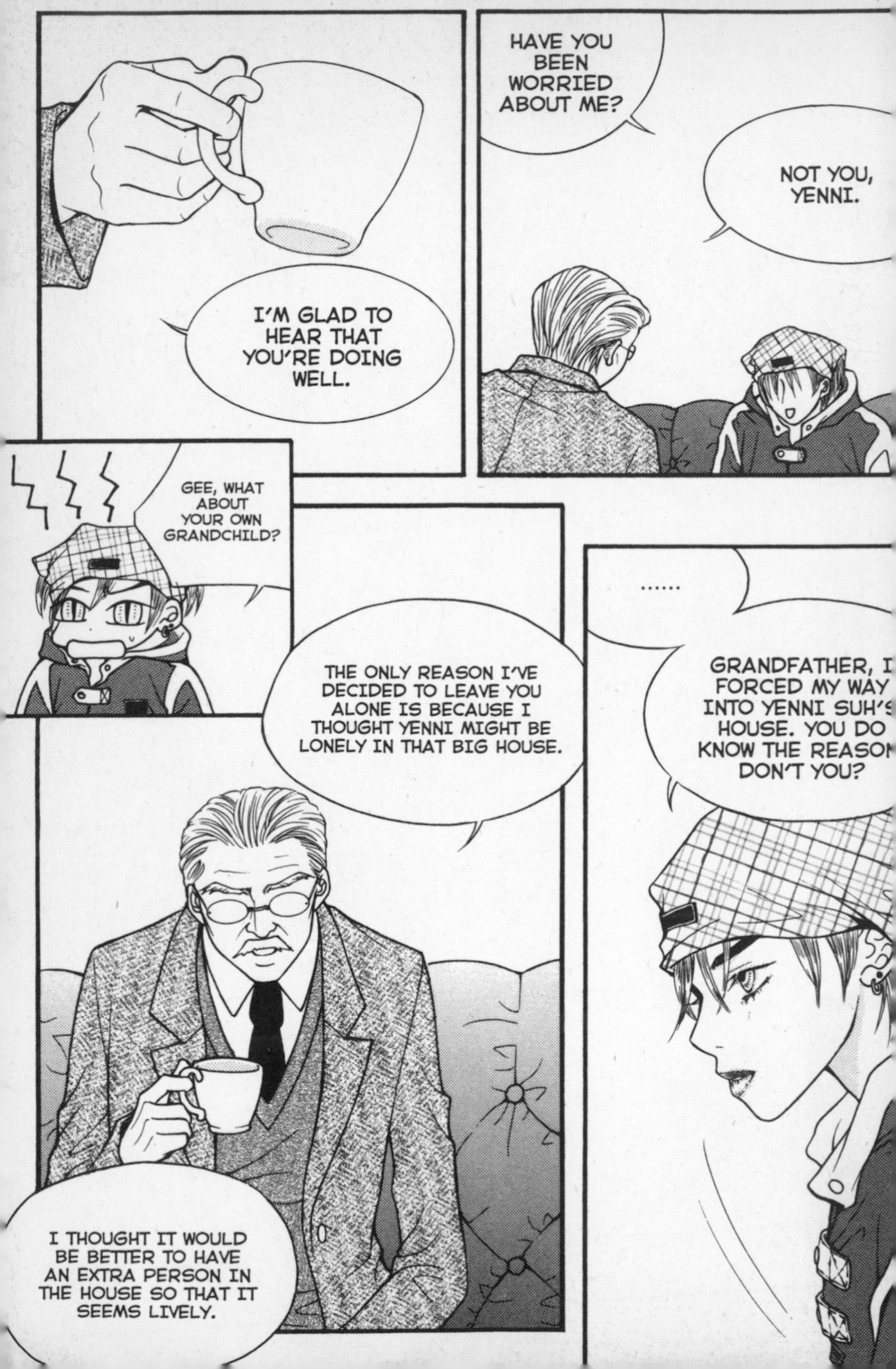
I'M GLAD TO HEAR THAT YOU'RE DOING WELL.
HAVE YOU BEEN WORRIED ABOUT ME?
NOT YOU, YENNI.
GEE, WHAT ABOUT YOUR OWN GRANDCHILD?
THE ONLY REASON I'VE DECIDED TO LEAVE YOU ALONE IS BECAUSE I THOUGHT YENNI MIGHT BE LONELY IN THAT BIG HOUSE.
I THOUGHT IT WOULD BE BETTER TO HAVE AN EXTRA PERSON IN THE HOUSE SO THAT IT SEEMS LIVELY.
......
GRANDFATHER, I FORCED MY WAY INTO YENNI SUH'S HOUSE. YOU DO KNOW THE REASON DON'T YOU?

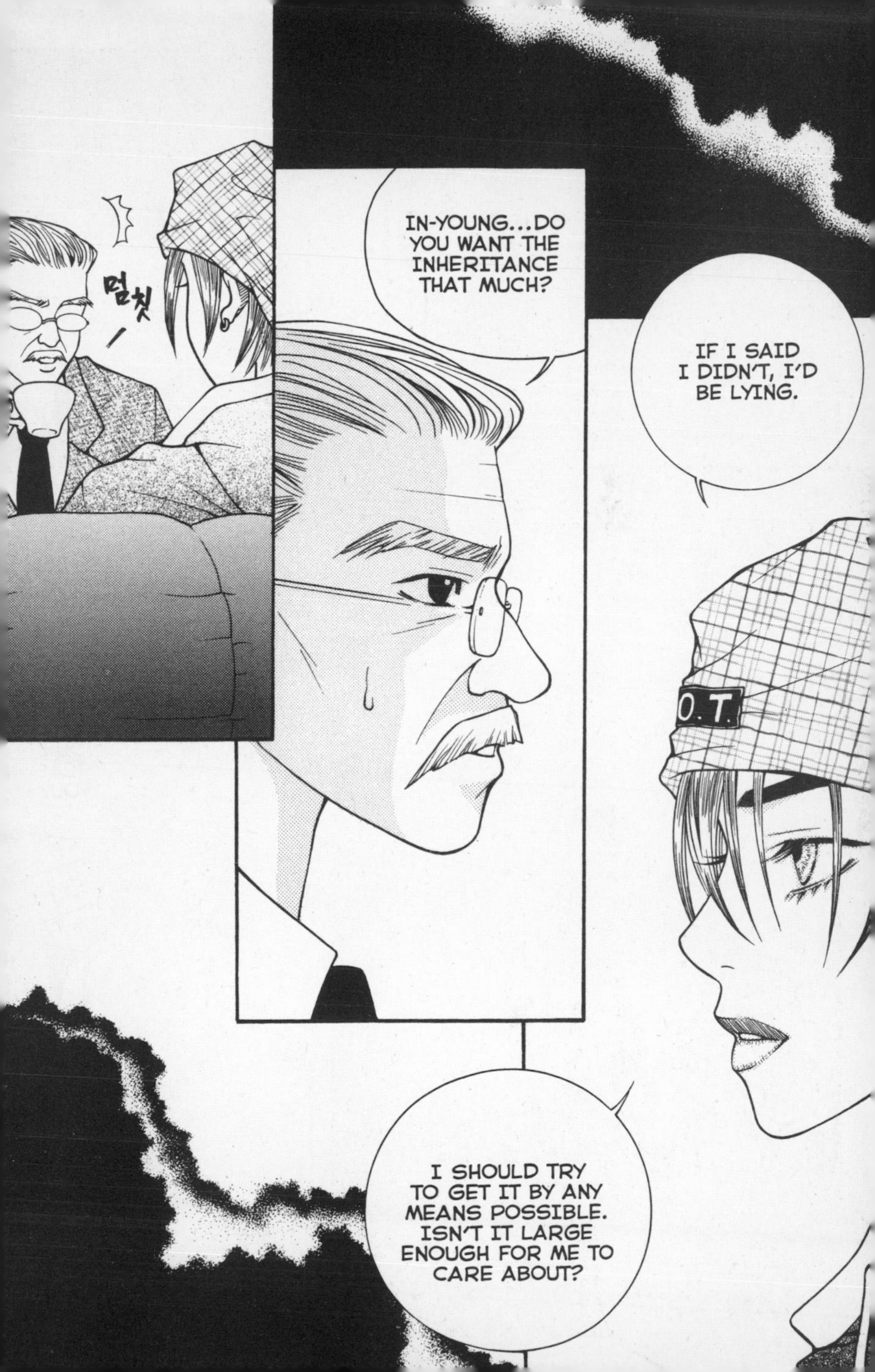

멈칫
IN-YOUNG...DO YOU WANT THE INHERITANCE THAT MUCH?
IF I SAID I DIDN'T, I'D BE LYING.
I SHOULD TRY TO GET IT BY ANY MEANS POSSIBLE. ISN'T IT LARGE ENOUGH FOR ME TO CARE ABOUT?

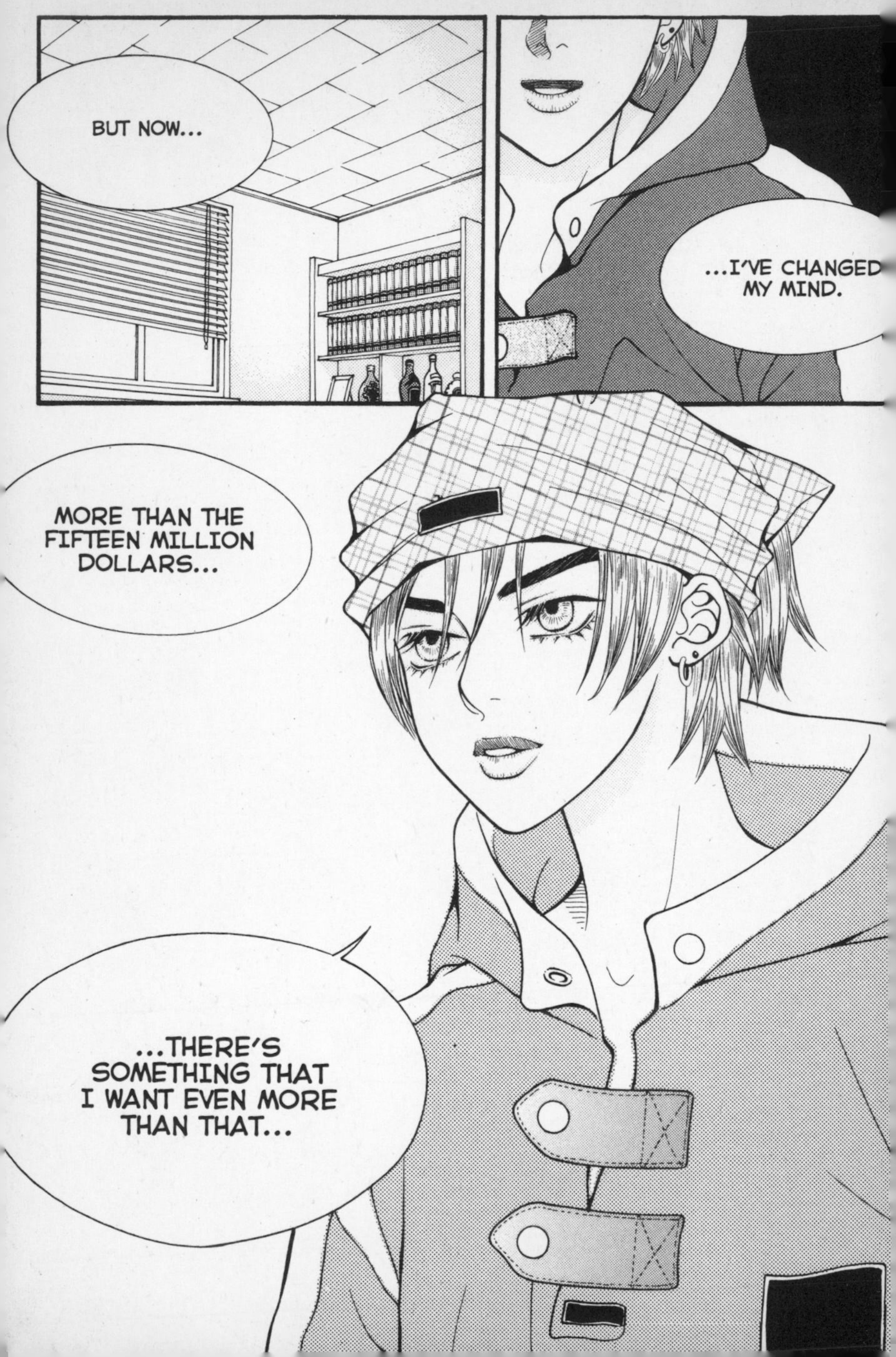
BUT NOW...
...I'VE CHANGED MY MIND.
MORE THAN THE FIFTEEN MILLION DOLLARS...
...THERE'S SOMETHING THAT I WANT EVEN MORE THAN THAT...

SPECIAL BONUS: "I'LL DO WHATEVER I WANT!"

HA HA...HELLO EVERYONE. AT LAST, LOVE OR MONEY 3 CAME OUT TO AN ANTICIPATING AUDIENCE... TIME FLIES BY...(WHAT AM I SAYING?) THESE DAYS I DON'T KNOW HOW I SPEND MY TIME... AH...I WISH I COULD GO BACK TO THE TIME WHEN I WOULD PASSIONATELY YELL OUT 'H.O.T'... (I EVEN MISS THOSE TIMES WHEN MY MOM WOULD YELL OUT 'YOU CRAZY X' WHENEVER I DID THAT) OH, BY THE WAY...DID YOU ENJOY VOLUME THREE? IS IT TOO TRIVIAL...? CHUCKLE. ANYWAY... TO THOSE WHO SENT LETTERS AND ENCOURAGED ME...TO THOSE NICE READERS WHO SENT ME PICTURES OF H.O.T.... TO THOSE WHO SENT E-MAIL... I REALLY LOVE YOU AND THANK YOU. THANKS ALSO TO SAE-JUNG WHO IS IN CHARGE AND THE LOVELY ASSISTANT YOUNG-BOK...AND TO H.O.T.... YOU ARE FOREVER #1...

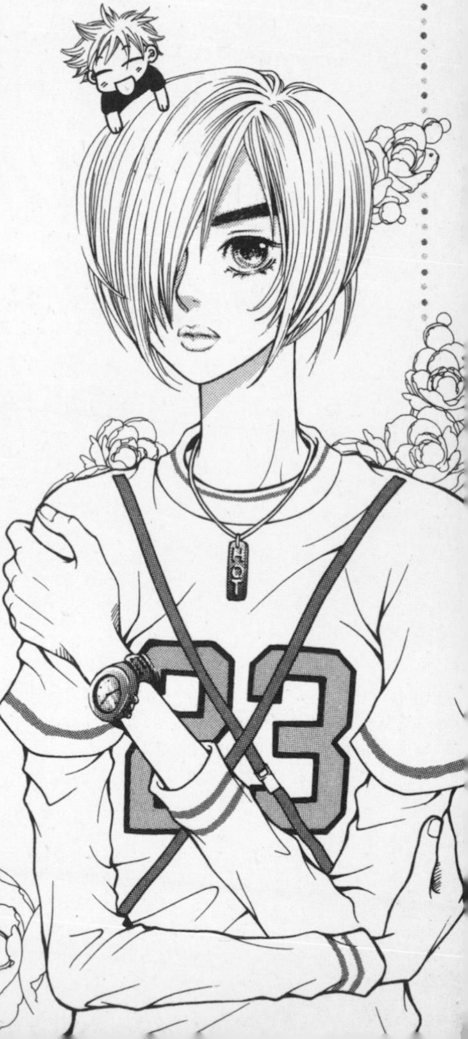

H.O.T
23

IN CASE YOU HAVEN'T GUESSED...

THE WRITER'S FAVORITE GROUP IS H.O.T.

IN THE NEXT

LOVE OR MONEY

VOLUME 4

THE LIVES OF YENNI, JAE-HEE, JI-WON, AND IN-YOUNG BECOME MAJORLY INTERTWINED. IN-YOUNG, WHO WAS ORIGINALLY AFTER YENNI SOLELY FOR HER MONEY, HAS NOW FALLEN FOR HER BEING, NOT HER BANK ACCOUNT. BUT FAMILY SECRETS ARE SOON REVEALED THAT THREATEN TO PUSH THEM APART PERMANENTLY. CAN HE WIN YENNI'S HEART, DESPITE THE ODDS AGAINST THEM? NOT IF JAE-HEE CAN HELP IT! EVEN THOUGH HE'S STILL TRAUMATIZED OVER YENNI'S BAD BEHAVIOR IN THE PAST, JAE-HEE CAN'T DENY THE FEELINGS HE HAS FOR HER. BUT JI-WON IS DOING EVERYTHING SHE CAN TO TAKE JAE-HEE'S MIND OFF YENNI. FORGET LOVE TRIANGLES-- THIS IS MORE LIKE LOVE OCTAGONS. WHO WILL END UP WITH WHO? IT'S ANYBODY'S GUESS...

TOKYOPOP SHOP

A Diva Torn from Chaos
A Savior Doomed to Love

Volume 2
Lumination

Ai continues to search for her place in our world on the streets of Tokyo. Using her talent to support herself, Ai signs a contract with a top record label and begins her rise to stardom. But fame is unpredictable—as her talent blooms, all eyes are on Ai. When scandal surfaces, will she burn out in the spotlight of celebrity?

T
TEEN
AGE 13+

Preview the manga at:
www.**TOKYOPOP**.com/princessai

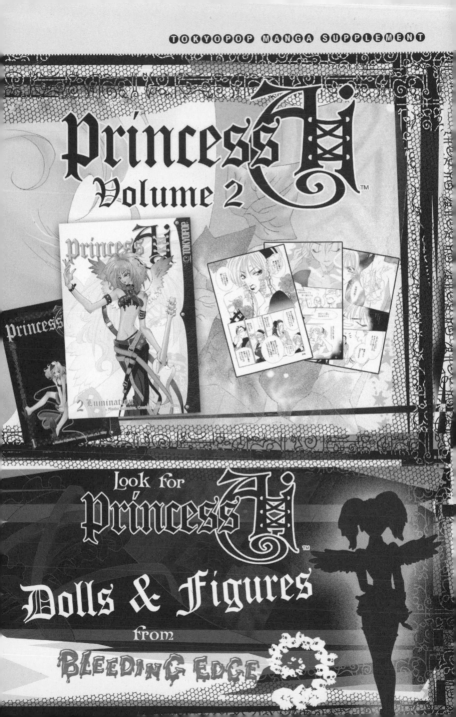

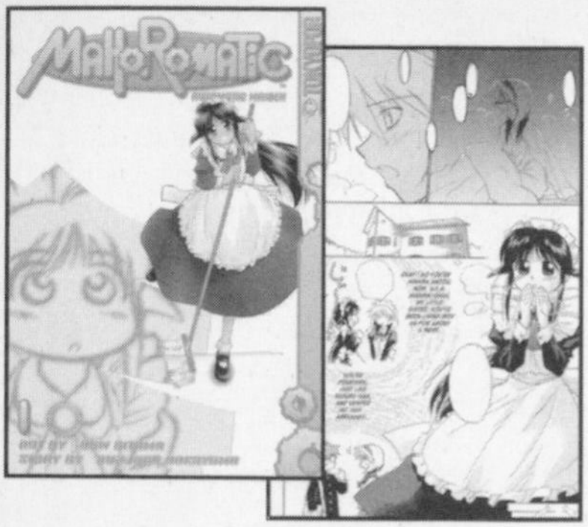
MAHOROMATIC

BY BUNJURO NAKAYAMA AND BOW DITAMA

MAHOROMATIC: AUTOMATIC MAIDEN

Mahoro is a sweet, cute, female battle android who decides to go from mopping up alien invaders to mopping up after Suguru Misato, a teenaged orphan boy... and hilarity most definitely ensues. This series has great art and a slick story that easily switches from truly funny to downright heartwarming...but always with a large shadow looming over it. You see, only Mahoro knows that her days are quite literally numbered, and the end of each chapter lets you know exactly how much—or how little—time she has left!

~Rob Tokar, Sr. Editor

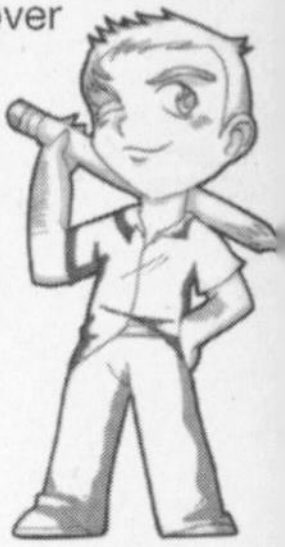

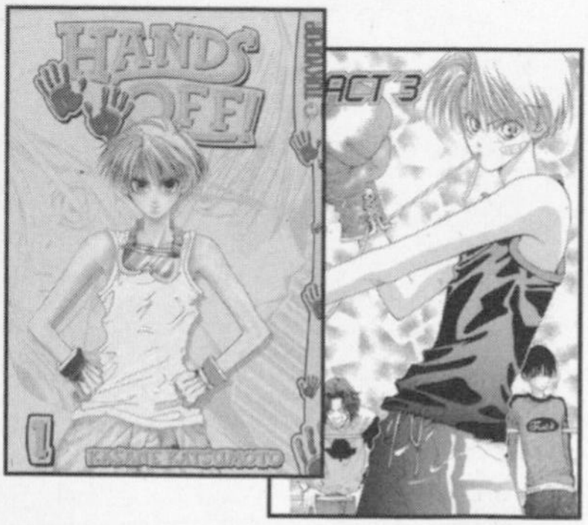
HANDS OFF!
ACT 3

BY KASANE KATSUMOTO

HANDS OFF!

Cute boys with ESP who share a special bond... If you think this is familiar (e.g. *Legal Drug*), well, you're wrong. *Hands Off!* totally stands alone as a unique and thoroughly enjoyable series. Kotarou and Tatsuki's (platonic!) relationship is complex, fascinating and heart-wrenching. Throw in Yuuto, the playboy who can read auras, and you've got a fantastic setup for drama and comedy, with incredible themes of friendship running throughout. Don't be put off by Kotarou's danger-magnet status, either. The episodic stuff gradually changes, and the full arc of the characters' development is well worth waiting for.

~Lillian Diaz-Przybyl, Jr. Editor

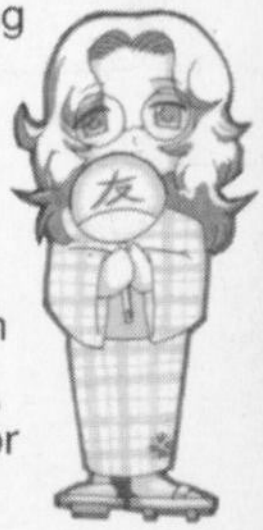

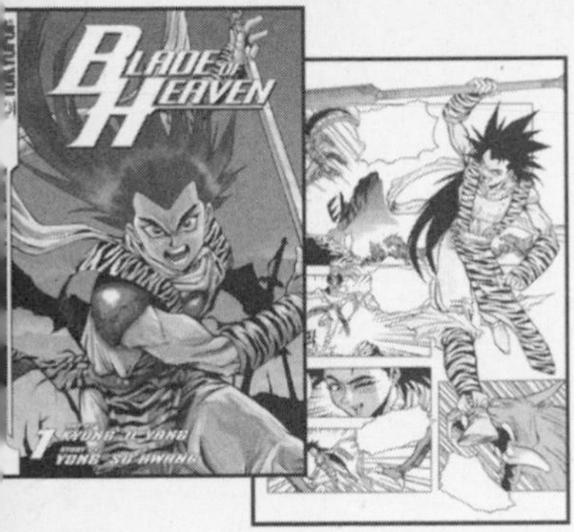
Blade of Heaven

BY YONG-SU HWANG AND KYUNG-IL YANG

BLADE OF HEAVEN

Wildly popular in its homeland of Korea, *Blade of Heaven* enjoys the rare distinction of not only being a hit in its own country, but in Japan and several other countries, as well. On the surface, Yong-Su Hwang and Kyung-Il Yang's fantasy-adventure may look like yet another "Heaven vs. Demons" sword opera, but the story of the mischievous Soma, a pawn caught in a struggle of mythic proportions, is filled with so much humor, pathos, imagination—and yes, action, that it's easy to see why *Blade of Heaven* has been so popular worldwide.

~Bryce P. Coleman, Editor

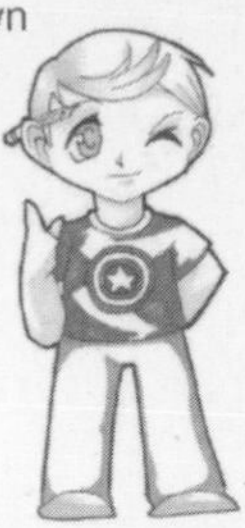

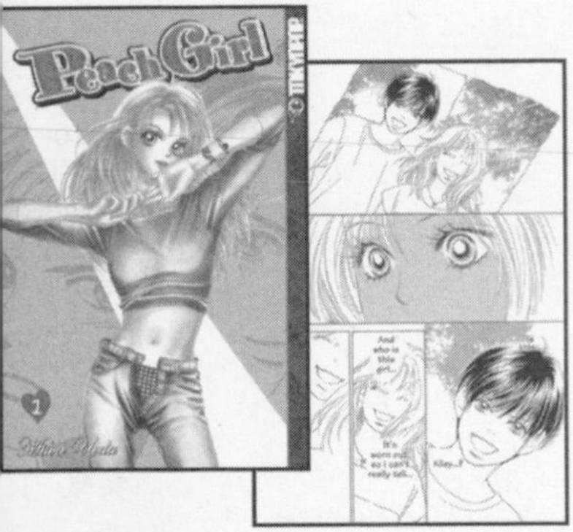
Peach Girl

BY MIWA UEDA

PEACH GIRL

Am I the only person who thinks that *Peach Girl* is just like *The O.C.*? Just imagine Ryan as Toji, Seth as Kiley, Marissa as Momo and Summer as Sae. (The similarities are almost spooky!) Plus, Seth is way into comics and manga—and I'm sure he'd love *Peach Girl*. It has everything that my favorite TV show has and then some—drama, intrigue, romance and lots of will-they-or-won't-they suspense. I love it! *Peach Girl* rules, seriously. If you haven't read it, do so. Now.

~Julie Taylor, Sr. Editor

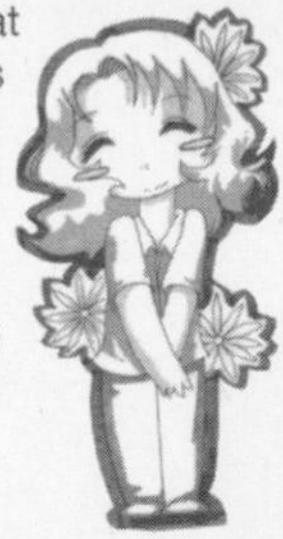

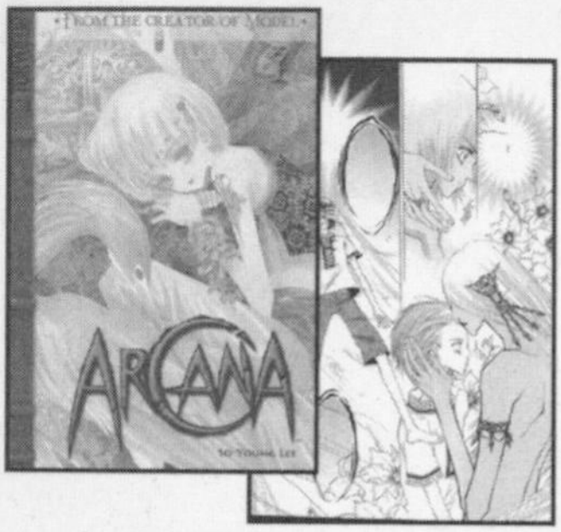
ARCANA
SO-YOUNG LEE

ARCANA

BY SO-YOUNG LEE

Inez is a young orphan girl with the ability to communicate with living creatures of all kinds. She is the chosen one, and a great destiny awaits her! Inez must bring back the guardian dragon to protect her country's fragile peace from the onslaught of a destructive demon race.

From the creator of TOKYOPOP's *Model* comes an epic fantasy quest filled with wizards, dragons, deception and adventure beyond your wildest imagination.

T
TEEN
AGE 13+

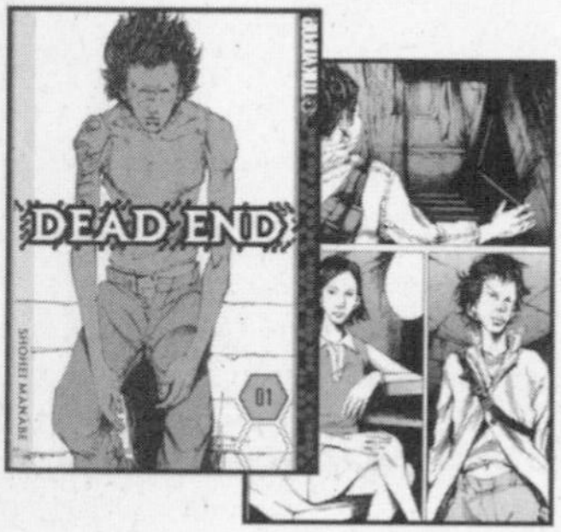
DEAD END
01
SHOHEI MANABE
TOKYOPOP

DEAD END

BY SHOHEI MANABE

When Shirou's memory is suddenly erased and his friends are brutally murdered, he is forced to piece together clues to solve a shocking and spectacular puzzle. As we follow Shirou's journey, paranoia assumes an air of calm rationality and the line between tormenter and prey is often blurred.

OT
OLDER TEEN
AGE 16+

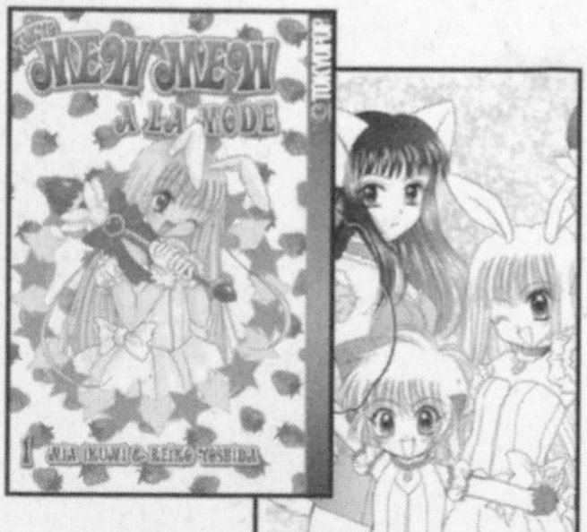
MEW MEW
A LA MODE
TOKYOPOP

TOKYO MEW MEW A LA MODE

BY MIA IKUMI AND REIKO TOSHIDA

The cats are back, and a new Mew emerges—the first Mew Mew with *two* sets of animal genes. Half cat, half rabbit, Berry joins the Mew Mew team just in time: a new gang is about to appear, and its leader loves wild game like rabbit—well done and served for dinner!

The highly anticipated sequel to *Tokyo Mew Mew* (*Mew Mew Power* as seen on TV)!

Y
YOUTH
AGE 10+

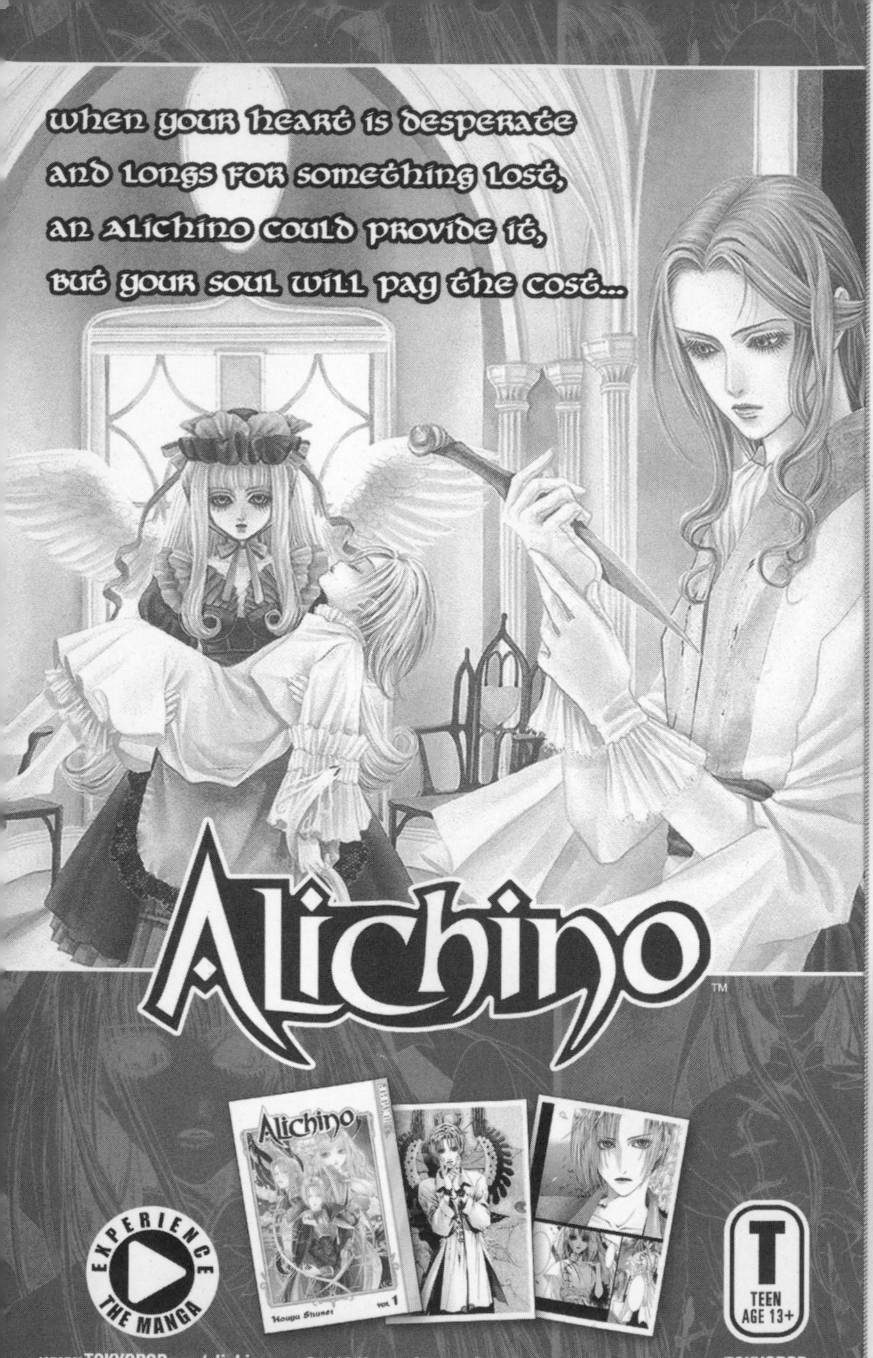
when your heart is desperate
and longs for something lost,
an alichino could provide it,
but your soul will pay the cost...
Alichino™
Alichino
Kouyu Shurei
vol. 1
EXPERIENCE THE MANGA
T
TEEN
AGE 13+
www.TOKYOPOP.com/alichino
©1998 Kouyu Shurei. ©2005 TOKYOPOP Inc.
www.TOKYOPOP.com